Choosing
a Better Life?

Edited by
John Goering and Judith D. Feins

Other Urban Institute Press Titles by John Goering
*Mortgage Lending, Racial Discrimination,
and Federal Policy*

Edited by
John M. Goering and John Wienk

Choosing a Better Life?

Evaluating the Moving
to Opportunity
Social Experiment

THE URBAN INSTITUTE PRESS
Washington, D.C.

THE URBAN INSTITUTE PRESS
2100 M Street, N.W.
Washington, D.C. 20037

Library of Congress Cataloging in Publication Data

Choosing a better life? : evaluating the Moving to Opportunity social experiment / edited by John Goering and Judith D. Feins.
    p. cm.
Includes bibliographical references.
    ISBN 0-87766-713-6 (alk. paper)
    1. Discrimination in housing—Prevention—Government policy—United States—Case studies. 2. Residential mobility—Government policy—United States—Case studies. 3. Housing policy—United States—Case studies. I. Goering, John M. II. Feins, Judith D., 1947–
    HD7288.76.U5C48 2003
    363.5'5'0973—dc21

                                                        2003007938

Printed in the United States of America

THE URBAN INSTITUTE is a nonprofit, nonpartisan policy research and educational organization established in Washington, D.C., in 1968. Its staff investigates the social, economic, and governance problems confronting the nation and evaluates the public and private means to alleviate them. The Institute disseminates its research findings through publications, its Web site, the media, seminars, and forums.

Through work that ranges from broad conceptual studies to administrative and technical assistance, Institute researchers contribute to the stock of knowledge available to guide decisionmaking in the public interest.

Conclusions or opinions expressed in Institute publications are those of the authors and do not necessarily reflect the views of officers or trustees of the Institute, advisory groups, or any organizations that provide financial support to the Institute.

This book is dedicated to
Lydia Fabillon who untimely passed away on
February 5, 2002.
She was a beloved daughter, sister, aunt, friend, and teacher.

Contents

Preface

The Moving to Opportunity (MTO) demonstration comprises two intertwined projects. For participating families, MTO was a HUD-funded rental assistance program that offered them a chance to move out of public housing projects located in deeply impoverished neighborhoods in five cities—Baltimore, Boston, Chicago, Los Angeles, and New York. Beginning in 1994, roughly 4,600 families volunteered to join MTO and became part of this housing mobility experiment. MTO is also the largest social experiment investigating the behavioral consequences for very low-income public housing residents of moving to a low-poverty neighborhood.

MTO's distinctiveness as a research project derives from its experimental design. It is the first randomized social experiment to examine whether, and with what effects, public housing families may be relocated into new, better-off neighborhoods. It enables researchers to compare the living conditions, choices, and personal outcomes of families randomly assigned to three different neighborhood environments: family public housing projects in poor neighborhoods, regular Section 8 program locations, and low-poverty communities.

The central question for the volume—as for the demonstration—is to what extent and under what conditions will moving out of a poor neighborhood and into a new, better-off area result in improvements in the lives of public housing families? Would families that elected to move become more socially and economically self-sufficient compared with families that did not make such moves? MTO's major contribution to both social science and to policy is that it permits a precise, relatively unbiased answer to the question of how much neighborhood matters.

This collection represents the first major presentation of the design, implementation, and early results for all five of MTO's cities. The contributors make use of a variety of research methods and data sources, including household and baseline surveys, census information, administrative or agency data, field observation, and qualitative interviews.

Although a number of articles have been published discussing results from individual cities, this collection is the first major summary and distillation of several years of research on the MTO experiment. It has been roughly a decade since MTO was authorized and this collection reflects research that has been conducted, analyzed, and distilled for this volume over a number of years. The research in this volume also partly reflects the synergy of ideas among the research teams.

Some contributors, such as the team that worked with the Baltimore site, began with a basic set of questions about the quality of schools in low-poverty communities (the results reported in chapter 5). They soon, however, significantly expanded their investigations to include multiple domains of life. In this case, their chapter 6 provides a summary of several separate investigations of developmental changes affecting children, teenagers, and adults in the Baltimore area. They report significant experimental effects on reading and math scores, welfare participation, and criminal behavior, but no effect on parents' wages or employment. Much of this research was done making use of nonintrusive methods, including the analysis of state and federal agency records. Other contributors, intrigued by the research of their peers, in turn sought out administrative data to learn whether comparable impacts could be detected for "their" families in other MTO locations. The research reported on the Los Angeles site, for example, reflects some of this evolution of interest.

We have divided this collection into three parts. The first part focuses on the legislative and political foundations of the demonstration and offers a summary of the results garnered from evidence and data across all five MTO locations. Chapter 1, by John Goering, Judith Feins, and Todd Richardson, offers a description of what MTO was designed to accomplish, followed by a synthesis of the important findings that have emerged to date. There is evidence presented about both the implementation of the demonstration as well as an overview of the effects of MTO on participating families. The research in this collection provides a relatively clear, although provisional, answer that neighborhood matters. Important, statistically significant changes have occurred in the lives of families that joined MTO.

Chapter 2, by John Goering, discusses historical and policy influences on MTO, including the Gautreaux demonstration in Chicago. At the time MTO was established it was uncertain whether HUD's main housing assistance program, the Section 8 voucher program, could be efficiently redesigned and implemented to assist poor, largely minority families to successfully relocate to private rental housing in neighborhoods potentially unaccustomed to such families. Early community opposition that occurred in the suburbs of Baltimore is also described in this chapter in order to help appreciate the constraints on HUD's implementation of economic deconcentration initiatives.

In chapter 3, Mark Shroder addresses the question of whether the volunteers for MTO who moved to new homes are similar to or different from other public housing families. He examines how and why successful movers in MTO differ from those who were unable to relocate. We learn that a number of household characteristics as well as program features (including housing mobility counseling) are associated with a higher probability of finding and leasing-up a new rental unit. Chapter 4, by Judith Feins, examines differences between the randomly assigned groups by the characteristics of the communities to which MTO families moved. We learn that, as intended, economic and racial mixing occurred in the aftermath of families joining the demonstration. But we also learn that there was less racial mixing than occurred in the Gautreaux program, and some evidence from data gathered in 2000 that families may be relocating to less diverse communities.

Part 2 of the book presents the core impact analyses of the effects of MTO upon the lives of children, teenagers, and adults. There are in-depth case studies of outcomes involving children and adults for the five MTO sites. Each chapter, which presents evidence on impacts roughly two to four years after families moved out of their low-income public housing developments, reflects the work of interdisciplinary teams of social scientists.

Each of the research teams initially designed relatively unique projects that addressed the early outcomes experienced by MTO families. Following their initial studies, a number of researchers felt that it was important to conduct additional inquiries. As we mentioned, Jens Ludwig and Helen Ladd began with an examination of the quality of the schools attended by children in Baltimore, as reported in chapter 5. They then proceeded to ask a range of additional questions about whether MTO had impacts on the educational experiences of individual children who participated in MTO, levels of juvenile crime, the wages and welfare status of families, and other issues. These additional studies, conducted from 1996 through 2002 with Helen Ladd, Greg Duncan, and other colleagues, are summarized in chapter 6.

Chapter 7 is on Boston and is by Lawrence Katz, Jeffrey Kling, and Jeffrey Liebman. In Boston we learn for the first time of important health effects on parents and children, including a decline in illnesses such as asthma, as a result of MTO.[1]

Chapter 8 is by Tama Leventhal and Jeanne Brooks-Gunn and focuses on New York. It addresses critically important child and adult development issues using survey data on a large sample of New York families as the children and parents encountered their new communities. In this case, the methodological and analytic skills of child psychology reveal important evidence of changes in mental and physical health for both adults and children, including important evidence on the probable impact of neighborhood setting upon methods of parenting.

In chapter 9, Maria Hanratty, Sarah McLanahan, and Becky Pettit analyze the impact on early child and adult outcomes for families in Los Angeles. They include an assessment of labor market outcomes finding, as in Boston and Baltimore, that no detectable experimental effects have yet appeared. Finally, in chapter 10, Emily Rosenbaum, Laura Harris, and Nancy Denton examine a range of outcomes related to early child and adult outcomes for families that moved in Chicago.

Part 3 of the book presents summary observations, caveats, recommendations for future research, and policy speculations and worries about what lessons from MTO may be applicable to affordable housing policy in the United States. Chapter 11 by Ingrid Gould Ellen and Margery Austin Turner, as well as chapter 13 by George Galster, provide a sense of the demonstration's accomplishments but also of the potential risks associated with poverty deconcentration.

Chapter 12, by Sandra Newman, Joseph Harkness, and Wei-Jun Yeung, makes use of research that links the Panel Study of Income Dynamics (PSID) to data on housing assistance. This data set represented, in our minds, the best possible nonexperimental surrogate for

MTO and therefore an ideal place to learn whether effects comparable to those we expected to find in MTO might appear in the larger assisted housing population, as reflected in their unique panel data. That is, is there any evidence that the effects experienced by MTO families might also occur within the broader public housing– and project-based population? This chapter reveals that some neighborhood-based educational effects did occur for children, suggesting that neighborhood can affect opportunities within a wider public housing population, although their measures of neighborhood impact and housing assistance were necessarily limited compared with MTO experimental data.

The book concludes, in chapter 14, with suggestions concerning needed research and policy issues. The most central suggestion is that the as yet incomplete MTO research framework be finished to finally provide policymakers, legislators, and researchers their first opportunity to understand and compare the human and social consequences of different housing programs in diverse metropolitan communities. MTO will provide the ability—for the first time—to understand the benefits, the monetary and social costs, and the extent to which greater opportunities exist for children and adults after they leave behind the fear and risks of conventional public housing in concentrated poverty areas.

NOTES

The bulk of the chapters in this collection are substantially revised versions of papers initially presented at a conference on MTO research results sponsored by HUD, with some financial support from the Fannie Mae Foundation. It was held in Washington, D.C., in November 1997. Most of the contributors to this collection were selected in an open, peer-reviewed grant competition for research on the first phase of MTO families' experiences. Between the initial conference and the papers presented in this collection, time was needed for most authors to obtain more complete samples of MTO families at their sites. In one site, this required delaying survey data collection until 1999 when all families were enrolled and address files were finally available.

1. Katz, Larry, Jeffrey Kling, and Jeffrey Liebman. 2001. "Moving to Opportunity in Boston: Early Results of a Randomized Mobility Experiment." *Quarterly Journal of Economics* (May) 607–54. The chapter presented in this collection is less technical and contains a few substantive additions. Table 2 presents differences in mobility for subgroups, depending upon their baseline characteristics. Table 6 presents treatment effects for specific behavior problems instead of an overall index. Table 10 reports the results from the survey question about welfare and employment (whereas the article only reported administrative results).

Acknowledgments

The editors' debts to contributors and colleagues can never be adequately repaid.

First, we must thank the many MTO families that met and talked with us, beginning in the fall of 1994. In focus group meetings that stretched from the East Coast to the West Coast and spanned several years, they helped us to begin to appreciate the early challenges and impacts of moving away from public housing and—perhaps—to opportunity. Executives and staff members of the public housing authorities and nonprofit organizations involved with MTO were indispensable to making the demonstration run effectively and humanely.

Credit for the initial support of MTO goes to HUD Secretary Jack Kemp in the George H. Bush administration and to HUD Secretary Henry Cisneros in the Clinton administration. Both secretaries supported and approved the funding necessary for this demonstration, including its research components. Over the last several administrations, a number of assistant secretaries for the Office of Policy Development and Research at HUD have offered their own support. Our considerable thanks are due to John Weicher, Michael Stegman, Xavier de Souza Briggs, Susan Wachter, and Acting Assistant Secretary Lawrence Thompson.

It was Margery Austin Turner, deputy assistant secretary for research at HUD in the Clinton administration, who was most responsible for bringing MTO from congressional mandate to full implementation. Her ideas and energy were indispensable. We also thank Alexander Polikoff, the lead attorney in the Gautreaux case and the key progenitor of MTO, for his dedication to keeping MTO focused on poor families in segregated public housing.

We also owe a number of social scientists particular thanks. One long-standing intellectual influence is Anthony Downs whose book, *Opening up the Suburbs*, offered intellectual and policy support roughly 30 years ago for the ideas embodied in MTO. James Rosenbaum's more recent and ongoing research on the Gautreaux program has served as a constant source of ideas and methodological challenges. Greg Duncan has been a consistently thoughtful colleague since the first stages of the design of MTO. He and Jeanne Brooks-Gunn were among the first social science supporters of this project and have remained consistent sources of intellectual help.

Throughout the development of this collection, a number of social scientists offered useful advice, support, and criticism. At a fall 1997 conference in Washington, pertinent comments were offered by Martha Tienda, Christopher Jencks, Judith Gueron, Jennifer Hochschild, Xavier de Souza Briggs, and George Galster. More recently, Jens Ludwig, George Galster, Jeffrey Kling, Rob Sampson, Robert Kaestner, Reynolds Farley, Sanders Korenman, Mark Shroder, Lance Freeman, and Kevin Neary have provided timely, encouraging, and insightful comments on the text. Eric Wanner and Suzanne Nichols, of the Russell Sage Foundation, facilitated the provision of most helpful comments on an earlier draft of this collection.

Participants at a number of academic conferences and workshops have provided useful thoughts and suggested important clarifications. John Goering would particularly like to thank the organizers of the European Housing Conference in Gaavle, Sweden, for hosting a useful discussion about the merits of MTO. He would also like to thank the faculty and graduate students at the New School University and at Columbia University Teachers College for their comments.

The editors need also to thank the contributors to this volume, whose patience, ideas, and commitment to MTO research have been indispensable in learning whether and to what degree federal housing programs can benefit the lives of low-income families.

John Goering
Judith D. Feins

PART I
Introduction, Overview, and Foundations

1

What Have We Learned about Housing Mobility and Poverty Deconcentration?

John Goering
Judith D. Feins
Todd M. Richardson

Research over the last decade has demonstrated that poverty in the United States has become increasingly concentrated within inner-city neighborhoods and that such concentrations have a high probability of damaging the health, education, well-being, and future opportunities of residents. The harmful effects of such "underclass," high-poverty areas appear especially severe for children whose behavior, choices, and prospects appear uniquely susceptible to neighborhood characteristics, including limited resources, peer group influences, school quality, and violent crime.

The Moving to Opportunity for Fair Housing (MTO) demonstration, a large, federally funded housing experiment, was designed to learn whether improved neighborhood opportunities can significantly affect the lives of low-income public housing residents. The core question built into the design of the program was, do neighborhoods have clearly measurable, independent effects on families' lives and opportunities? MTO, through random assignment, is learning whether offering families the chance to move out of public housing into tenant-based assistance within a lower-poverty neighborhood noticeably improves the lives of public housing residents. MTO is thus a housing mobility opportunity for participating families as well as a rigorously designed social science experiment. This chapter first summarizes the design and implementation of the demonstration and then provides a cross-site overview of the key research outcomes from the earliest research conducted on MTO families.

Research Background

While there have long been social science arguments about the harmful effects of living in concentrated-poverty neighborhoods (Wilson 1987), it is only relatively recently that there has been convincing evidence about the degree to which neighborhood environments exert influences on the behavior and life chances of adults and children (Brooks-Gunn et al. 1997; Sampson, Morenoff, and Gannon-Rowley 2002). The fundamental obstacle to providing such evidence has been the potential for systematic bias to distort findings. The problem of selection bias has been recognized by social scientists for over a decade as a crucial limitation on most research seeking to determine whether and to what degree neighborhood affects lives (Case and Katz 1991; Crane 1991; Ellen and Turner 1997; Lehman and Smeeding 1997, 262; Manski 1993; Mayer and Jencks 1989). Well over a decade ago Jencks and Mayer (1990, 119) cautioned:

> The most fundamental problem confronting anyone who wants to estimate neighborhood's effects on children is distinguishing between neighborhood effects and family effects. This means that children who grow up in rich neighborhoods would differ to some extent from children who grow up in poor neighborhoods even if neighborhoods had no effect whatever.

Since people typically select their neighborhoods to match their needs and resources, researchers restricted to cross-sectional, nonexperimental evidence must try to separate the impact of personal factors affecting choice of neighborhood from effects of the neighborhood. But it is difficult—if not impossible—to measure all these socioeconomic, personal, and local characteristics well enough to distinguish their effects. More often, the answers being sought are hidden in unmeasured factors and unexplained variation. One of the first systematic attempts at a quasi-experimental answer to the question of whether neighborhood matters to the lives of poor public housing families emerged in the late 1980s from research on the Gautreaux program in Chicago.

Before MTO There Was Gautreaux

The first research suggesting that housing mobility, or deconcentration, may have important social and educational benefits stemmed from a court-ordered racial desegregation program in Chicago. Under the name of tenant activist Dorothy Gautreaux, applicants and residents of Chicago public housing brought a class-action housing segregation lawsuit against the U.S. Department of Housing and Urban Development (HUD) and the Chicago Housing Authority (CHA) in 1966 (Davis 1993; Rubinowitz and Rosenbaum 2000). After years of litigation, which went all the way to the Supreme Court, federal courts ordered HUD and the local CHA to remedy the extreme racial segregation fostered by these agencies among public housing applicants and residents. Starting in the late 1970s, these agencies had to provide a housing mobility option throughout the Chicago region for about 7,100 black families.

The Gautreaux program took shape as a result of the court's ruling. "Gautreaux families," as they became known, were given assistance in moving out of racially isolated areas through the tenant-based Section 8 program. Families chosen for the Gautreaux program received Section 8 certificates that required them to move to either predominantly white or racially mixed neighborhoods. The families also received assistance from housing counselors to make these moves. Roughly three-quarters of all the families were required to move to mostly white (usually suburban) areas, while about one-quarter were allowed to move to more racially mixed city neighborhoods. A housing subsidy would only be offered if the family was willing to make these moves. While the eligibility criteria for participation and the housing counseling offered participants varied over time, families were always required to move to a nonsegregated neighborhood until the completion of the program in 1998 (Rubinowitz and Rosenbaum 2000).

Beginning in the late 1980s, research on the Gautreaux program suggested that the children of families moving to less-segregated suburban locations saw measurable improvements in their lives. Changes were reported for small samples of children who had been living in less-segregated neighborhoods for seven to ten years. Children moving to these suburban areas were less likely to drop out of school and were more likely to take college-track classes than their peers in a comparison group who had moved to a city neighborhood. The city neighborhoods were both poorer and more racially segregated than the suburban locations. After graduating from high school, the suburban Gautreaux children were also more likely than their city peers to attend a four-year college or to become employed full time (Rubinowitz and Rosenbaum 2000).

MTO's Purpose

The encouraging Gautreaux results, as well as increasing concern about the racial and economic isolation experienced by many public housing families (Hirsch 1983; Newman and Schnare 1997), led Congress to initiate a demonstration program aimed at offering better neighborhood opportunities to public housing residents living in distressed inner-city areas. Dimond (2000) outlines the antipoverty argument for MTO:

> Isolating poor persons in inner-city ghettos and barrios does not help them connect to the rising demand for more workers throughout the local regional labor markets. . . . Thus federal, state, and local governments act irresponsibly and waste taxpayer dollars whenever they limit housing and job-training subsidies to particular projects or places—public or private—rather than putting such subsidies directly in the hands of poor families so they can choose for themselves where best to live and learn in order to find new and better jobs (259).

In 1992, policymakers proposed offering public housing residents the chance to move to private rental housing in more affluent communities using housing vouchers. The demonstration policymakers envisioned would test whether HUD's main tenant-based housing program, the Section 8 rental assistance program, could be effectively used to assist poor, largely minority families in successfully relocating to private rental housing in working-class or middle-class neighborhoods (chapter 2 provides detail on the legislative and political origins of MTO). MTO used vouchers to help families move out of inner-city public housing developments in five cities across the country—Baltimore, Boston, Chicago, Los Angeles, and New York.

The MTO demonstration was authorized by the Housing and Community Development Act of 1992 to "assist very low income families with children who reside in public housing or housing receiving project-based assistance under Section 8 of the Housing and Community Development Act of 1937 to move out of areas with high concentrations of persons living in poverty to areas with low concentrations of such persons" (Section 152 of the Housing and Community Development Act of 1992). *High concentrations of poverty* were defined as census tracts where 40 percent or more of the residents were poor in 1990. *Low-poverty areas* were defined as census tracts where less than 10 percent of the population was poor in 1990. The 40 percent threshold follows a social science standard for defining deeply poor ("underclass") neighborhoods

(Brooks-Gunn et al. 1997; Jargowsky 1997). The 10 percent threshold corresponds to the median tract-level poverty rate across the United States in 1990.

Congress appropriated $20 million in Section 8 rental assistance for fiscal year 1992 and another $50 million for fiscal year 1993 to finance MTO. Congress also stipulated that HUD should conduct evaluations of the demonstration to determine its short- and long-term effects. To explore such impacts, HUD established a social experiment, which included a random assignment process that assigned volunteering families to different treatment groups by a computerized lottery.

From September 1994 through July 1998, public and assisted housing families that volunteered and were deemed eligible were randomly assigned to one of three groups:

1. The MTO treatment (or experimental) group, which received Section 8 certificates or vouchers useable only in areas where 10 percent or less of residents lived below the poverty level. Families in this group also received counseling assistance from a local non-profit organization in finding private rental units.
2. A Section 8 comparison group, which received regular Section 8 certificates or vouchers with no special geographic restrictions or counseling.
3. An in-place control group, which continued to receive its current project-based assistance.

The Section 8 comparison group was established to allow program designers to measure changes in location and in family outcomes resulting from the regular Section 8 program and to compare such changes with those seen in the treatment group. The in-place control group was created to measure the behavioral outcomes for children and adults who continued living in public housing developments. While MTO was targeted to a specific population (very low income families with children living in public or assisted housing in concentrated-poverty areas), its participants share many characteristics with families with dire housing needs, families excluded from the economic mainstream, and families living in poverty (HUD 2001). As we describe in chapter 2, Congress canceled a second round of funding for MTO before the program began tenant recruitment because of community opposition in one of the five sites.

MTO's Design

Methodological Shortcomings of Prior Research

As we noted earlier, issues of design and selection bias limited the utility of the Gautreaux research findings. First, Gautreaux was a racial deseg-regation program while MTO was explicitly aimed at economic decon-centration. Under the latter, families could select some neighborhoods ineligible under Gautreaux. Second, families in Gautreaux were not for-mally randomly assigned to neighborhoods but rather the program screened some participants for suitability to particular neighborhoods or communities. For example, in the program's early years, program managers and counselors identified families likely to succeed in the sub-urbs and matched them with suburban landlords and communities. Other families, judged less suitable for suburban relocation, were not placed by the program or were placed in city neighborhoods.

Third, because administrators maintained only limited information on the families that joined Gautreaux but did not move, researchers could not locate them to learn how differences in families' demographic or per-sonal characteristics affected success in moving. Fourth, evidence of the Gautreaux program's positive mobility effects is often based on small, nonrepresentative samples of enrolled families. Because of limited follow-up data, researchers studied only the families they could find many years later (Popkin, Buron, et al. 2000).

This collective set of concerns needed solutions. MTO's necessary solution to selectivity bias was to randomly assign families to a commu-nity. Removing the choice of neighborhood detaches the individual's per-sonal characteristics and preferences from the neighborhoods' potential impacts (Brooks-Gunn et al. 1997). Jencks and Mayer (1990) describe this effect:

> From a scientific perspective, the best way to estimate neighborhood effects would be to conduct controlled experiments in which we assigned families randomly to different neighborhoods, persuaded each family to remain in its assigned neigh-borhood for a protracted period, and then measured each neighborhood's effects on the children involved (119).

In addition, MTO administrators kept careful track of the locations of all families that volunteered for the demonstration and not solely those who moved. Until MTO, nothing like this type of controlled experiment had been designed and implemented to rigorously test for the effects of neigh-borhood upon the lives of low-income families.

MTO's Experimental Design

MTO used a carefully designed and implemented random-assignment process to ensure that nothing about individual or family characteristics would influence the group assignment. Assignment of families to one of the three groups was carried out using uniform procedures that were carefully monitored across the five sites. Despite some limitations in design and research follow-up, the MTO experiment reveals much about whether poor families with children willing to make substantial changes in residential location to improve their neighborhood conditions benefit.

First-Stage Research Methods

The experimental design of MTO has already permitted analyses of impacts in a variety of domains (including child educational achievement, adult employment and earnings, youth risk-taking, and the physical and mental health of family members). It also permits multiple-method or tiered assessments of cross-cutting questions that have helped verify and enhance our understanding of neighborhood impacts on families, adults, and children.

MTO has been designed as a social experiment that includes several phases of research. The first phase, conducted by teams of social scientists operating in individual MTO sites, constitutes the bulk of the evidence presented in this chapter. The latter stages of research, which are mentioned in more detail in chapter 14, will provide standardized cross-site impact evaluations of MTO over the next decade. The initial, HUD-sponsored studies on MTO presented in this volume cover varied topics carried out by researchers from a range of disciplines. Each research team used differing analytical and methodological strategies, with their research limited to one of the five MTO sites.

Central to the analyses is the ability, through MTO, to provide an estimate of the effectiveness of the *offer* of the experimental treatment in improving the lives of public housing residents *as a group*. The intent-to-treat (ITT) estimates reported in this volume recognize that some members of the target group did not use the Section 8 subsidy. The measured ITT effects include the outcomes not only for those who moved but also for those who were randomly assigned to receive the treatment but did not relocate.

We begin with a discussion of what we learned as a result of implementing MTO in the five cities. We follow this with a presentation and overview of the key research results reported by our research collaborators. At the end of this chapter, we describe the limitations of the research conducted to date. In chapter 14, we detail our thoughts about needed additional research that emerges as a result of this first step in understanding the impacts of MTO upon the lives of participants.

MTO Implementation: Characteristics and Limitations

Five local public housing authorities, selected by HUD in 1994, participated in running the MTO demonstration. The selected sites were Baltimore, Boston, Chicago, Los Angeles, and New York. In its application, each Public Housing Authority (PHA) had identified the public housing and Section 8 project-based developments in high-poverty census tracts from which it would recruit families with children under 18. Each also named a partner nonprofit agency to counsel the families assigned to the MTO treatment group.

The participating public housing authorities and nonprofit agencies were required to follow a general set of uniform rules and procedures for managing most key aspects of the demonstration, particularly its research requirements. The core administrative responsibilities for implementing MTO consisted of

- outreach to landlords and families;
- enrollment of families and creation of waiting lists;
- determination of the family's eligibility;
- random assignment; and
- counseling assistance for treatment group families.

The public housing authorities and counseling agencies also helped implement MTO's design, including data collection on the participants and the program. The counseling agencies, based on their own experience and on the availability of local funding to supplement HUD's grants, varied the form and amount of counseling assistance offered to clients (Feins, McInnis, and Popkin 1997).

The public housing authorities began MTO operations by informing all eligible residents of the targeted public and assisted housing projects in high-poverty census tracts about what MTO offered and how to apply. In most instances, administrators met with groups of tenants to explain the program and answer questions. Each site established waiting lists of applicants and invited small groups of them (working down from the top of the lists) to orientation sessions. At these sessions, the applicants found out they would be assigned by lottery to one of three groups; that they had a chance of being offered Section 8 by joining; and that, if chosen by lottery for the treatment group, they would also be provided training, counseling, and housing search assistance in moving to a low-poverty area in the city or suburbs. Families also learned that they were required to remain in the low-poverty area only for the length of their first one-year lease; after that they would be permitted to move to any area under regular Section 8 rules.

The applicants also learned about the screening criteria established by the public housing authority, which included the requirement that all tenants be up to date on their rent payments and that no family member have a criminal record. Families that enrolled agreed in writing to cooperate with the information gathering and research needed for the demonstration, and they filled out a lengthy baseline survey. Random assignment occurred only after eligibility checks, screening, and initial data collection were completed.

Implementation Questions and Results

WOULD FAMILIES VOLUNTEER FOR MTO?

When MTO was planned, no one knew whether a sufficient number of families would be motivated or willing to risk volunteering for MTO. Section 8 rental assistance was considered a somewhat less secure form of housing subsidy, because Congress has to renew commitments each year, while public housing leases seemed more permanent (Popkin, Gwiasda, et al. 2000). Also, some social scientists argued that poor families might be unable or unwilling to leave their neighborhoods because these areas provided them with essential institutional and social supports (Ross, Reynolds, and Geis 2000; Thompson 1999). Families from such poor, minority-concentrated areas might also be urged to remain behind to devote their energies to improving those areas (Calmore 1999; Wilkinson 2000).

In MTO, among the families eligible to apply, about one-quarter chose to do so; roughly 5,300 families volunteered in the five cities. These families were then screened for the following eligibility criteria: (1) the family included a child under 18; (2) they were tenants in good standing (up to date on rental payments); (3) all family members were on the current lease; and (4) no member had a criminal background or history, as required (with some variation) by the local Section 8 program rules.

In total, across the five sites, 4,608 families were found eligible and randomly assigned. With approximately 285 vouchers for HUD to allocate per site, there was a sufficient number of families for the demonstration.

WHY DID FAMILIES JOIN MTO?

Fear of crime and the experience of criminal victimization were primary factors in families' decisions to participate in the MTO demonstration. When applicants were asked during their baseline interviews why they wanted to move away from the public housing developments in which they lived, more than half (54.8 percent) identified the fear of crime, gangs, and drugs as the principal motivation. More than three-quarters of those who applied for MTO reported getting away from drugs and gangs as their first or second most important reason for wanting to move. More than half (57.3 percent) said that they wanted a better house or apartment, and more than a third (39.3 percent) wanted to find a better school for their children. Employment was identified as a motivation for moving by only a small proportion of applicants.

WHO JOINED MTO?

Were MTO volunteers typical residents of their developments or were they different from the other residents that did not apply? Some analysts thought it likely that MTO would attract the most motivated and resourceful families, or "the very people who might otherwise take an active role in improving these communities" (Thompson 1999, 126).

The eligibility criteria established by both HUD and the local public housing authorities, as noted earlier, partly determined who participated. For example, families with no children were not eligible for the demonstration. But residents also made decisions about whether they were interested in trying MTO. Thus, both self-selection and screening played a role in shaping the population of families joining the demonstration.

Comparing the program families with residents of the same public housing developments that did not volunteer for MTO shows that the groups' demographic and socioeconomic characteristics differed significantly (table 1.1). Compared with public housing families who did not join, MTO households were

Table 1.1. *Characteristics of MTO and Non-MTO Families from the Same Public Housing Developments: Baltimore, Boston, Los Angeles, and New York*

	MTO households (N = 2,414)	Non-MTO households (N = 6,813)
Black non-Hispanic (percent)	54	51
Hispanic (percent)	39	45
Female head (percent)	93	78
Mean age, head (years)	35	41
Median age, head (years)	33	39
Standard deviation	9	13
Mean no. of children under 18	2.5	2.3
Median no. of children under 18	2	2
Standard deviation	1.4	1.4
Mean household size	3.7	3.7
Median household size	3	3
Standard deviation	1.5	1.6
Percent receiving AFDC	75	51
Percent employed	22	30
Mean income	$9,365	$10,769
Median income	$8,252	$8,645
Standard deviation	$4,810	$7,465

Source: HUD (1999), p. 32.

Notes: All differences between groups, except household size, are significant at the 0.05 level. The data are from the June 1998 MTO data files and from HUD's Multifamily Tenant Characteristics System database for the same public housing developments as of July 1996. Non-MTO families include only families with minor-age children. Data provided by the Chicago Housing Authority were not complete enough and were therefore omitted. In addition, data were unavailable for families from Section 8 projects, so that the non-MTO household information applies only to families living in public housing developments targeted for MTO enrollment. Some data fields had errors. For example, the incomes for families from public housing were truncated by deleting households whose annual income exceeded $50,000, and the head of household age was limited to ages 17 to 90.

- headed by younger adults (average age of 35 versus 41);
- more often headed by females (93 versus 78 percent);
- less likely to be Hispanic (39 versus 45 percent) and slightly more likely to be African American (54 versus 51 percent);
- slightly poorer (with median income of $8,200 versus $8,600);
- less likely to have heads who were employed (22 percent versus 30 percent); and
- more likely to receive welfare payments.

In addition, baseline survey data reveal that the heads of families who volunteered for MTO typically reported *weak* social ties with their neighbors rather than close and supportive relationships. These differences suggest that—even with public housing authorities screening out families with criminal records and poor rent histories—the families volunteering for MTO were typically younger and poorer; they also had lower levels of labor force attachment and higher dependence on welfare than their neighbors. This evidence suggests that the eligibility and screening criteria, in combination with self-selection, did not result in a bias toward those families with greater resources. Rather, MTO may have served a more needy population than the residents of public housing in general. It is nonetheless clear that volunteers for MTO were not fully representative of the average tenants within their own authorities and projects.

How Many Families Leased-Up?
MTO's experimental design permits the analysis of outcomes for the entire randomly assigned population receiving the different *offers* of assistance. However, the hypothesized impacts of MTO depend not just on families being offered Section 8 assistance, but also on their success in using the certificates or vouchers to achieve residential mobility. In other words, success depended on families' ability to move out of project-based housing in concentrated-poverty neighborhoods and into other environments.

All the possible impacts of life in better neighborhoods depended on some share of families' success in "leasing up," or finding a new unit that met all program requirements. Each family had to find an available rental unit that met members' needs, adhered to Section 8 requirements (i.e., passed housing inspection and rented for an amount within the local fair market rent), and had a landlord willing to participate in Section 8 and to accept the family as tenants.

Prior research demonstrates that not all Section 8 certificate and voucher holders are able to use their housing assistance. It also reveals that successful lease-up is influenced by applicant characteristics, market features, and market conditions (Finkel and Buron 2001; U.S. HUD 2000). Lease-up success rates also vary over time and among cities. Table 1.2 shows the lease-up rates for the regular Section 8 programs in the five MTO sites, which in some cases were only serving homeless families or other emergency cases. These rates ranged from 65 to 90 percent. In contrast, the lease-up rate for the MTO comparison group, which received regular Section 8 assistance, averaged 60 percent.

Table 1.2. *Expected and Actual Lease-Up Rates in the MTO Demonstration* (percent)

MTO site	Expected lease-up rate	Actual lease-up rate: Section 8 comparison group	Actual lease-up rate: MTO experimental group
Baltimore	90	72.3	57.9
Boston	90	47.6	46.4
Chicago	70	65.8	33.8
Los Angeles	85	75.4	61.2
New York City	65	49.1	44.9

Sources: HUD (1996), p. 7; HUD (1999), p. 17.

In all five sites, the lease-up rates for families in the demonstration's Section 8 comparison group were lower than those for the non-MTO Section 8 programs. However, the differences varied, with Boston and Baltimore showing the largest gaps (42.4 percent and 17.7 percent, respectively). In Chicago, the gap was less than 5 percent. The lease-up rate for MTO treatment group families across the five cities, at 48 percent, was even lower. It ranged from a high of more than 61 percent in Los Angeles to a low of only 34 percent in Chicago.

These lower lease-up rates may have reflected the fact that families in MTO were already securely housed through project-based housing subsidies. Thus they were less needy than emergency applicants and had lower housing costs than other low-income renters not receiving subsidies. Therefore, the incentive to lease-up through MTO was likely lower than that of the typical Section 8 applicant. Lower lease-up rates may also reflect other factors associated with how landlords and communities react to applicants, including the possibility or fear of discrimination. They may also reflect our current inability to shape housing mobility counseling to fit the needs of individual applicants and landlords.

COULD MTO FAMILIES SUCCESSFULLY MOVE TO LOW-POVERTY AREAS?
In addition to the challenge of leasing-up, the families in the MTO treatment group and their counseling agencies faced uncertainty regarding the availability of apartments meeting rent requirements and landlord willingness to accept the families in low-poverty areas. Potential barriers included stereotypes about public housing residents, preconceptions about Section 8, and concerns about potential differences in behavior or

lifestyle between current residents and families leasing-up. A substantial number of landlords, however, was willing to accept Section 8 vouchers, often for the first time, and to rent to former public housing residents. Despite community opposition to the MTO program in one part of Baltimore County, all Section 8 allocations were finally used (more detail on this issue is offered in chapter 2).

As the demonstration required, treatment group families chose neighborhoods located throughout the city and suburbs of each metropolitan area where 10 percent or less of the population lived in poverty. Only a small proportion (12 percent) of Section 8 comparison group families initially chose similar locations. Most remained in areas closer to their original public housing sites.

WHICH FAMILIES LEASED-UP THROUGH MTO?

For all five sites, successful lease-up was positively associated with families' dissatisfaction with their original neighborhoods and their degree of confidence (at baseline) about finding a new unit (Shroder chapter). Current enrollment in adult education of some type was also associated with a greater chance of finding a new unit to rent. The level of housing counseling received by the treatment families also helped predict lease-up. Owning a car or holding a valid driver's license also made it easier to move, especially for families that had to move farther away to find low-poverty neighborhoods. On the other hand, larger families and Hispanic families found it harder to find a new home. Thus, those who moved through MTO appear to be different in some ways from those who were offered Section 8 rental assistance but failed to lease-up.

WOULD NEIGHBORHOODS ACCEPT OR REJECT MTO FAMILIES?

In recent research, some Section 8 families have reported that the experience of discrimination—or fear of encountering discrimination—limited their housing search (Turner, Popkin, and Cunningham 2000). So far, however, there is no evidence that MTO families experienced substantial direct racial hostility or community opposition to their moves. In Chicago, Rosenbaum, Harris, and Denton (in this collection) indicate that some families reported some initial unfriendliness in their new communities. But the authors conclude that "there is little evidence in our data of hostile reactions for either group of families [treatment group or Section 8 comparison]," since "these events could in some sense be considered routine friction." Other researchers (Hanratty, McLanahan, and Pettit chapter) also reported some evidence of tension between Hispanics and blacks in Los Angeles upon the initial moving-in period, but they found no evidence that the tension persisted. A recently completed qualitative survey of 58 adult MTO participants in all five sites reported little evidence of discrimination, with a number of respondents speaking very positively about living in more diverse communities (Popkin, Harris, and Cunningham 2002). However, in Boston, residents used a racial epithet against a black teenager moving with an MTO family. Preliminarily, then, there is no evidence of substantial neighborhood or community opposition to the arrival of MTO families, although research on this issue is incomplete.

WOULD MTO FAMILIES REMAIN IN LOW-POVERTY AREAS?

Did the families who moved out of public housing to low-poverty areas remain there, or did they move back into more familiar, higher-poverty communities after the one-year requirement was fulfilled? The answer to this question matters because the potential benefits of moves to communities of opportunity may take some years to accrue. Research suggests that positive effects on child development, educational outcomes, and adult prospects (compared with continued life in public housing in deeply poor areas) might develop in a five- to ten-year time frame, *but only if* the families remain in distinctly different neighborhoods (Leventhal and Brooks-Gunn 2001).

Analysis of a 1997 survey of all the MTO families that joined the program from 1994 through 1996 shows where they were living and the characteristics of those areas (table 1.3). The results show that movers in the treatment group tended to live in lower-poverty areas in 1997. Indeed, more than a third (34.5 percent) of the MTO treatment group—but just 10.6 percent of the comparison group and less than 3 percent of the in-place group—were living in low-poverty neighborhoods. Roughly 45 percent of the treatment group was living in high-poverty areas (largely the nonmovers who had remained in their initial public housing developments), compared with 38 percent of the Section 8 comparison group and 74 percent of the controls. The Section 8 comparison group had the lowest share of families still in concentrated-poverty areas largely because of that group's relatively high lease-up rates.

The second panel of table 1.3 focuses on the *movers* in the treatment and comparison groups. It shows that almost 75 percent of the treatment group families that had moved were still living in a low-poverty community in 1997. Roughly 2 percent (13 families out of 860) had moved back to a high-poverty area. Another 123 families, or 23 percent of all the treat-

Table 1.3. *Poverty and Racial Characteristics of Locations in Late 1997* (percent)

	MTO treatment group	Section 8 comparison group	In-place control group	All groups combined
Proportion of all families living in:				
Low-poverty areas (< 10%)	34.5	10.6	2.8	18.1
Areas 10–19% poor	7.9	18.0	6.1	9.8
Areas 20–39% poor	12.5	33.7	16.9	19.3
High-poverty areas (40%+)	45.2	37.7	74.2	52.8
Proportion of MTO movers living in:				
Low-poverty areas (< 10%)	74.7	14.5	NA	46.7
Areas 10–19% poor	13.6	27.4	NA	20.0
Areas 20–39% poor	9.3	45.4	NA	26.1
High-poverty areas (40%+)	2.4	12.6	NA	7.2

Sources: Public housing authority and counseling agency tracking logs, 1997 canvass, other tracking sources.

Notes: The sample is the MTO population randomly assigned through December 31, 1996, with a completed 1997 canvass and with useable origin and current addresses. Coverage is as follows: MTO treatment group 90.1 percent; Section 8 comparison group 90 percent; in-place control group 90.5 percent. Data are weighted to minimize overall variance and to adjust for differences in random assignment ratios between sites and over time. Percentages may not add to 100 because of rounding.

NA = not applicable

ment group movers, had relocated into mid-poverty areas (with poverty rates between 10 and 39 percent). In the Section 8 comparison group, 12.6 percent (58 families out of 816) had either initially moved to, or subsequently returned to, a high-poverty area. More than 70 percent were living in communities with poverty rates of between 10 and 40 percent. These 1997 data suggest that the movers remained in new areas long enough for the hypothesized benefits of better neighborhoods to begin accruing. The chapter by Feins shows some evidence of moves in later years (by 2000) to higher concentrations of poverty by some families; the aggregate effects of these moves and relocations are in need of further study.

MTO Research Findings to Date

Research results on MTO to date derive from two sources. The first is analyses of data from the five MTO sites, including baseline survey and tracking data (tables 1.1, 1.2, and 1.3). The second set of results comes from research conducted by teams of social scientists. These teams used a number of different methods and data sources including HUD administrative data, baseline surveys, follow-up surveys of families, qualitative interviews, and administrative data on juvenile crime, labor market outcomes, and school performance.

A number of statistically significant experimental results have been found in the early research undertaken with MTO families. Tables 1.4, 1.5, and 1.6 present evidence of statistically significant differences between the treatment group and the control groups. These tables provide an overview of research findings on neighborhoods (table 1.4), outcomes for children (table 1.5), and outcomes for adults (table 1.6).

Again, the focus here is on only the ITT effects, which are measured by looking at the difference between the average outcome for the entire MTO treatment group or the entire Section 8 comparison group and the outcome for the control group. For example, the average poverty rate for census tracts occupied by members of the treatment group was 32.3 percent in 1997. The ITT effect is the difference between that rate and the control group's average poverty rate (48.1 percent); thus, the ITT effect is 15.8 percent. The treatment-on-treated (TOT) effect—that is, the estimated effect on those persons who successfully leased-up under MTO—is generally higher, as it is measured only for those participants who actually took up the treatments (moved with Section 8). The analysis below focuses on intent-to-treat effects. (Notably, whenever intent-to-treat effects were statistically significant, the corresponding treatment-on-treated effects proved significant.)

Neighborhood and School Characteristics

Table 1.4 reports differences in the neighborhood and school characteristics of the neighborhoods in which MTO participants live. Three characteristics distinguish MTO neighborhoods.

MTO FAMILIES LIVE IN MORE ECONOMICALLY AND RACIALLY MIXED COMMUNITIES

The 1997 survey of families at all five MTO sites enables us to examine whether residential locations differed significantly among the randomly assigned groups. After their initial moves and one-year leases, treatment group families were no longer constrained to live in low-poverty areas. Nonetheless, one to three years after random assignment, treatment group families lived in significantly more affluent and more racially mixed

Table 1.4. *Early Evidence of MTO Impacts—Differences in Neighborhood and School Characteristics by Treatment Group*

Type of impact	MTO site(s)	Population	MTO treatment group	Section 8 comparison group	In-place control group
Differences in neighborhood after 1–3 years	All sites	All households in MTO as of 12/31/1996			
Poverty percentage of current location			32.3**	33.4**	48.1
Median income of current location			$24,075**	$21,246**	$13,920
Percent black population of current location			38.2**	40.3	48.6
Differences in total crime rate per 100,000 population in census tract	Los Angeles	Households in MTO as of 12/18/1996	6137.25**	5984.21**	8018.40
Differences in average test scores for schools attended by MTO children in 1997	Boston	Households in MTO as of 5/1996			
School's percentile, reading test score			15.9**	10.9	8.3
School's percentile, math test score			16.0**	12.6	9.9

Differences in resources and characteristics scores for schools attended by MTO children after random assignment and initial relocation	Baltimore	School-age children of all households in MTO			
Percent children receiving free lunch			66.82**	80.82*	84.82
5th grade raw reading test pass rate			11.84**	7.84**	5.84
5th grade raw math test pass rate			18.40**	15.40**	12.40
Differences in perceived safety of current neighborhood	Baltimore	Adults in MTO as of 9/4/1997			
Percent reporting neighborhood has problems with drugs and crime			27.8**	60.8	NA
Differences in perceived safety of current neighborhood	Los Angeles	Adults in MTO as of 12/18/1996			
Percent reporting very safe neighborhood			27.5*	6.7	10.1

Sources: Feins (2000), exhibit 9 (differences in neighborhood); Hanratty, McLanahan, and Pettit (2001), table 6 (differences in total crime); Katz, Kling, and Liebman (2001), table IV (differences in average test scores); Ludwig, Ladd and Duncan (2001) table 9, (differences in resources); Norris and Bembry (2001), table 16 (differences in perceived safety . . . problems with drugs); Hanratty, McLanahan, and Pettit (2001), table 7 (perceived safety . . . very safe neighborhood).

Note: Differences reported are based on intent-to-treat comparisons (full group) rather than adjusted treatment-on-treatec results.

NA = not applicable

*Statistically significant difference from in-place control group (intent-to-treat effect) at $p < 0.10$ level.

**Statistically significant difference from in-place control group (intent-to-treat effect) at $p < 0.05$ level.

Table 1.5. *Early Outcomes for MTO Children*

Type of impact	MTO site(s)	Population	MTO treatment group	Section 8 comparison group	In-place control group
Differences in child behavior	Boston	Children age 6 to 15 in households in MTO as of May 1996			
Percent of seven behavior problems, boys			23.6**	21.3**	32.6
Percent of seven behavior problems, girls			17.0	14.3	19.3
Percent with at least one close friend in neighborhood, boys			73.8	72.8	74.7
Percent with at least one close friend in neighborhood, girls			67.7**	63.3**	82.3
Differences in child health	Boston	Children age 6 to 15 in households in MTO as of May 1996			
Percent with any asthma attacks requiring medical attention in past six months			4.7*	9.4	9.8
Percent with any accident or injury requiring medical attention in past six months			4.6*	6.8	10.5

Differences in number of arrests per 100 juveniles age 11–16	Baltimore	Children age 11 to 16 of all MTO households			
Arrests for violent crimes			1.4**	1.6*	3.0
Differences in school test scores	Baltimore	Children age 5 to 12 of all MTO households			
Elementary school CTBS percentile reading scores			32.47**	31.52**	25.13
Elementary school CTBS percentile math scores			36.25**	30.25	28.77

Sources: Katz, Kling, and Liebman (2001), table VI (child behavior and child health); Ludwig, Duncan, and Hirschfield (2001), table 3 (number of arrests); Ludwig, Ladd, and Duncan (2001), table 6 (school test scores).

Notes: Differences reported are based on intent-to-treat comparisons (full group) rather than adjusted treatment-on-treated results, which would include only movers.

*Statistically significant difference from in-place control group (intent-to-treat effect) at $p < .10$ level.

**Statistically significant difference from in-place control group (intent-to-treat effect) at $p < .05$ level.

Table 1.6. *Early Evidence of MTO Impacts—Outcomes for MTO Adults*

Type of impact	MTO site(s)	Population	MTO treatment group	Section 8 comparison group	In-place control group
Health effects					
Differences in depressive behaviors	New York	All mothers in MTO through Dec. 31, 1998			
Percent unhappy, sad, or depressed			33.0**	46.2	50.6
Differences in adult health	Boston	Adults in MTO as of May 1996			
Percent reporting overall health is good or better			69.3**	74.0**	57.8
Welfare and labor market effects					
Differences in welfare and labor market effects for household heads	All Sites	Adults in MTO surveyed via 1997 long form canvass[a]			
Average percent on welfare			58	58	57
Average percent employed			35	34	37
Average number of weekly hours worked			33.3	31.5	33.9

	Baltimore — Adults of all MTO households	Los Angeles — Adults in MTO as of Dec. 18, 1996	Boston — Adults in MTO as of May 1996
Differences in rate of welfare receipt			
Average percent of household heads on welfare during 13 quarters after random assignment	38**	41	44
Differences in weekly hours worked	33.1*	37.2*	26.8
Differences in adult economic outcomes			
Percent adults receiving public assistance 7 to 9 quarters after random assignment	49.9	46.0	49.5
Percent adults with employment earnings 7 to 9 quarters after random assignment	44.4	46.3	43.4

Sources: Leventhal and Brooks-Gunn (2001), table 6 (differences in depressive behavior); Katz, Kling, and Liebman (2001), table IX (differences in adult health); Goering, Feins, and Richardson (forthcoming) (differences in welfare and labor market); Ludwig, Duncan, and Pinkston (2000) (differences in rate of welfare receipt); Hanratty, McLanahan, and Pettit (2001), table 8 (differences in weekly hours worked); Katz, Kling, and Liebman (2001), table VII (differences in adult economic outcomes).

Note: Differences reported are based on intent-to-treat comparisons (full group) rather than adjusted treatment-on-treated results.

a. The long form was administered to households participating in MTO under the original random assignment ratio;

*Statistically significant difference from in-place control group (intent-to-treat effect) at $p < .10$ level.

**Statistically significant difference from in-place control group (intent-to-treat effect) at $p < .05$ level.

communities than either the Section 8 comparison group or the in-place control group families.

Late in 1997, the average poverty rate of residential locations for both the MTO treatment group families and the Section 8 comparison group families was significantly lower (by 15–16 percentage points) than the poverty rates of areas where in-place control group families lived. Moreover, median incomes in the treatment group families' neighborhoods were 73 percent higher than median incomes in the control group neighborhoods. Moreover, median incomes were 53 percent higher in Section 8–only group locations compared with the controls.

Area racial composition also differed significantly. In 1997, in each of the five metropolitan areas, the MTO treatment group families lived in less-segregated neighborhoods than either the Section 8 comparison group families or families that remained in place. Using the percentage black population as an indicator, there is a statistically significant 10 percentage point reduction in black population in the treatment group families' locations compared with the locations of control group families. But there was no significant difference for Section 8–only families (see chapter 4).

MTO FAMILIES IN LOS ANGELES LIVED IN AREAS WITH LOWER CRIME RATES

In one site—Los Angeles—MTO families lived in areas with significantly less crime. Measured at the census tract level (total crimes per 100,000 population), MTO treatment group families and Section 8 comparison group families lived in areas with significantly fewer crimes (23 percent and 25 percent fewer crimes, respectively). The fact that regular Section 8 families benefited from moves from high-poverty projects is an important finding that supports other early outcomes. In Chicago, feelings of safety among treatment group movers were of critical importance in subsequent adjustments.

SCHOOLS ATTENDED BY MTO CHILDREN IN BOSTON AND BALTIMORE WERE BETTER

Research teams in both Boston and Baltimore were able to demonstrate that schoolwide reading and math scores or pass rates were significantly better in treatment group children's schools, relative to the schools attended by children of in-place control group families. In Baltimore, these indicators were also significantly better for the schools of children from Section 8–only families.

Families' Views of Their Neighborhoods

The early MTO research has also demonstrated significant improvements in families' views of their neighborhoods. These views contrast with the higher levels of fear and dissatisfaction expressed by MTO applicants at baseline. As noted earlier, many families enrolled in MTO because of their fear of the crime conditions in public housing or Section 8 project-based developments. Most of the MTO research teams reported that freedom from this fear is among the earliest, clearest outcomes of the demonstration.

As shown in table 1.4, significantly fewer Baltimore families in the treatment group reported neighborhood problems with drugs and crime, compared with reports from the Section 8 comparison group. A significantly higher proportion of MTO treatment group members in Los Angeles reported very safe neighborhoods at follow-up, compared with those in the control group. The difference between the Section 8 comparison group and the in-place control group, however, was not significant. In Chicago, MTO mothers were asked about the risks and opportunities their current locations offered to teenagers. Those in the MTO treatment group reported significantly reduced risks compared with their old locations, while those in the Section 8 comparison group reported lower levels of improvement.

Outcomes for Children

Drawing on early evidence of MTO impacts on individuals in the demonstration, table 1.5 reports findings about children's behavior, health, and educational achievement, as well as results on youth involvement in violent crime.

The Boston research team found significantly fewer behavioral problems among boys in both the MTO treatment and the regular Section 8 groups, compared with boys from the in-place group. A significantly higher proportion of girls in both treatment groups reported at least one close friend in the neighborhood. Treatment group children were also less likely to be injured or to experience an asthma attack. In fact, among children with asthma in Boston, the number of attacks requiring medical attention over the prior six-month period fell significantly.

SOME EDUCATIONAL IMPROVEMENTS ARE EVIDENT

As noted earlier, MTO children appear to be attending better schools (table 1.4). In addition, Ludwig, Ladd, and Duncan (2001), while acknowledging some data limitations, report direct evidence of MTO's positive effect on individual children's school performance in Baltimore. By matching standardized reading and math scores (obtained from schools) for a sample of Baltimore children to identifying information for the MTO subjects, they found statistically significant improvements for the treatment group. However, early MTO research did not include direct educational testing of children in MTO families.

JUVENILE CRIME HAS DECLINED

In a Baltimore study, using outcome measures from juvenile arrest records taken from administrative (police and court) data, researchers found that providing families with the opportunity to move to lower-poverty neighborhoods reduced arrests for violent criminal behavior by teenagers in those families. They showed that, starting 1.0 to 1.5 years after random assignment, arrests of male juveniles in the treatment group for violent crime declined relative to those in the control group, but the difference for boys from the Section 8–only group was not statistically significant. Reductions in robbery accounted for about half this decline. The research also found higher rates of property crime arrests relative to the control group but this result was not statistically significant once researchers controlled for differences in preprogram characteristics.

Outcomes for Adults in MTO Families

MTO researchers have uncovered some significant early effects on the well-being of participating adults (table 1.6).

ADULTS IN NEW YORK AND BOSTON EXPERIENCED
IMPROVED PHYSICAL AND MENTAL HEALTH

In New York, parents in the MTO treatment group reported significantly better health and emotional well-being than parents in the control group. Section 8 comparison group parents enjoyed more modest improvements. Treatment group mothers were much less likely to report being depressed or feeling tense. Treatment group parents also provided more structure for their children and used less restrictive parenting behavior. Researchers measured these effects using standard batteries of interview questions, developed and tested in previous child and family research. Improvements in adult health were also found in Boston. In that city, adults in both the treatment and regular Section 8 groups were more likely to report that their overall health was good or better after moving. They also reported reduced stress.

CHANGES IN WAGES AND WELFARE STATUS

At the time of MTO's design, proponents expected that moves from high-poverty communities to low-poverty communities would have gradual, positive effects on adult employment. MTO designers based this expectation on evidence that a complicated set of factors improves the work situations and wages of inner-city, minority families. Job discrimination in new communities, poor access by public or private means of transportation, and limited human capital (skills) could all hinder a poor person's success in obtaining a better-paying job (O'Regan and Quigley 1999). Simply relocating families to a community whose residents are employed at good jobs will not necessarily—or quickly— translate into increased human capital for newcomers. In addition, the Gautreaux research, the building block for MTO, did not suggest that poor public housing families could be easily or quickly absorbed into local labor markets, particularly given the declining number of well-paid jobs available to persons with limited education and skills during the 1980s (Duncan and Rodgers 1991). Thus, wage changes would not likely appear in the short run.

When MTO was authorized, there was little expectation for major reform of welfare laws. However, following the end of AFDC and the inception of the TANF program, the number of families on welfare nationwide has dropped by roughly half, at least partially as a result of the enactment of new welfare statutes (Kaushal and Kaestner 2000; Schoeni and Blank 2000; Weaver 2000). In the early 1990s, only 44 percent of single mothers nationwide were employed while by 1999 this proportion had increased to 65 percent. In addition, research on the wage growth of low-income workers suggests that only modest changes can be expected. Low-wage workers typically earn wage increases of only 4 to 6 percent for a year of full-time employment and these increases are lessened for both black men and women (Gladden and Taber 2000, 189).

MTO researchers in three sites have examined the link between moves, wages, and welfare usage (table 1.6). Researchers in Baltimore used state unemployment insurance records to learn whether MTO families there had experienced any detectable change in welfare status or earnings. Their data covered the period from 1985 though the first quarter of 1999, or an average of 3.8 years of postprogram information on the MTO families. The authors found that the number of treatment group families on welfare during the postprogram period was 6 percentage points lower than for the in-place control group. In addition, the Section 8 comparison group's rate of welfare receipt was 5 percentage points lower than that of the in-place control group in the first program year. This margin dissipated in subsequent years, while the gap between the treatment and control groups grew to nearly 10 percentage points by the third year. That is, assignment to the treatment group reduced welfare receipt relative to the control groups, but assignment to the Section 8 group had little effect beyond the first year.

Surprisingly, these researchers did not find any significant change in either employment or earnings—even though in interviews the treatment group reported having better job and training opportunities in their new neighborhoods (Ludwig, Duncan, and Pinkston 1999). The authors conclude that "these differences in welfare-to-work transitions are . . . not reflected in quarterly earnings data from the state UI (Unemployment Insurance) system, because many of the jobs and earnings changes are not captured by the UI data" (Ludwig, Duncan, and Pinkston 1999, 29).

In Boston, the receipt of public assistance by MTO families dropped by half, and employment for all groups increased by more than one-half. Employment rates for the full MTO population increased from 27 percent at the time of baseline interview to 43 percent one to three years later. However, the MTO treatment had no significant effect on the employment or earnings of household heads (as revealed in Massachusetts' administrative earnings data on household heads) or welfare receipt in the three years after random assignment up through December 1998. In Los Angeles, participating families on average also experienced declines in their use of welfare assistance and increases in employment and wages. Maria Hanratty and her colleagues, however, find no experimental difference in these outcomes.

Multisite data from the 1997 MTO canvass also permit a test of whether MTO had any short-term impacts on employment, public assistance, hours worked, and weekly wages for heads of households. Those data show that, an average of 2.4 years after random assignment, substantially more heads of household across the sites were employed and many fewer were receiving public assistance. Employment rates for MTO heads of household rose 14 percentage points in that period, while public assistance rates fell 16 percentage points. Despite (or perhaps because of) these changes in employment and welfare rates, however, we found no significant difference between experimental effect on employment rates, hours worked per week, or use of public assistance at the time of the 1997 canvass (table 1.6).

MTO Research Limitations

The MTO design and research have a number of limitations. First, as described earlier, the families that volunteered to join MTO differed somewhat from the families in the same public housing developments that chose not to join and therefore there are issues of the generalizability of findings to the larger universe of public housing. Screening requirements may have discouraged some families from applying. The requirements also eliminated a number of other families.

In addition, design-wise MTO enrollment occurred during a period when central-city crime rates were high, particularly in the years 1994–95. Drive-by shootings, gang wars, and drug-related violence were common in the neighborhoods where MTO families were living. This phenomenon likely may have made some people more interested in joining the demonstration.

MTO's mid-decade timing had another drawback: the census data used to identify high-poverty areas (from which to recruit families) and low-poverty areas (to which experimental group families could move) were outdated. Housing counselors in MTO sites frequently raised questions about the suitability of certain census tracts that technically met the low-poverty definition. Use of the poverty rate as the sole criterion for identifying opportunity areas also has limitations and may have been particularly misleading at mid-decade.

Other aspects of the demonstration's implementation also limit the ability to generalize from MTO results. In MTO, the treatment received by families assigned to the experimental group included both a location-restricted housing voucher and some degree of counseling to assist in lease-up. The services provided by the nonprofit counseling organizations to the treatment group families varied in breadth, depth, and intensity across the sites (Feins et al. 1997), a factor that might lead to some differences in program impacts. For example, differences in counseling affected lease-up rates (chapter 3 by Shroder). They may have also affected how well families in the treatment group adapted to their new neighborhoods and how long they remained in low-poverty areas. In three sites, a single nonprofit provided counseling throughout the demonstration period. The effects of any distinctive practices at the three agencies could easily be mixed with the effects of site-specific housing markets and other characteristics.

Another limitation of the research evidence presented in this collection concerns the lack of comparability of outcomes across sites. Because each initial MTO research study used a unique design, results typically reflect outcomes for only one MTO site, and sample sizes are small. Thus, researchers might arrive at different conclusions if the tests of MTO outcomes could be conducted on larger, multisite samples.

Finally, while the research teams have collected considerable evidence about what changes have occurred as a result of participation in MTO, little is known about *why* and *how* these changes took place. That is, little information is known about the neighborhood processes related to reported outcomes.

Summary Observations

While we provide our final observations and recommendations in chapter 14, the MTO research results appear to support a few concluding observations. First, MTO has shown that, at least on a small scale, it is possible to reverse the historical practice of concentrating poor minority households in poor minority neighborhoods. Second, preliminary research on MTO families has demonstrated that beneficial, statistically significant changes have occurred in families' lives within two to four years of their participation in MTO. These effects appear most noticeably for children.

In the area of education, MTO children in Baltimore experienced notable gains in academic achievement, as measured by standardized test scores, compared with children in the control group. If future research corroborates these results, the demonstration will have achieved major educational benefits for younger children much earlier than anticipated. Qualitative research conducted in 2001, however, suggests that a small number of parents in that sample did not move their children to new schools but kept them in the schools serving their original high-poverty neighborhoods (Popkin, Harris, and Cunningham 2002). The extent to which families moved to low-poverty communities but did not take advantage of local resources and institutions represents a crucial issue for the next stage in MTO.

Third, results appeared in the lives of families earlier than we had anticipated, based upon Gautreaux research. Lastly, on some measures both the treatment group as well as regular Section 8 comparison group families experienced benefits. However, it is unclear whether such effects will atrophy or last for the regular Section 8 group. In one case, in Baltimore, the benefits experienced by the comparison group dissipated over time, raising some doubt about the robustness of changes in the lives of family members.

The MTO demonstration, then, not only provides a clearer understanding of how residential mobility programs can be effective, but it also provides a preliminary social science foundation for a new phase of research on neighborhood effects upon the poor. MTO's ability to measure and document the conditions under which changes occur in poor people's lives as a result of a change in neighborhood is among HUD's most significant social science and policy legacies. MTO research also constitutes a vital part of research investigations into the question of how and why neighborhoods matter in the lives of adults and children (Sampson, Morenoff, and Gannon-Rowley 2002).

There are then a number of important research and policy issues (see chapter 14) that need to be addressed by future research aimed at clearer appreciation of the consequences of life in high-poverty public housing developments compared to life in less concentrated Section 8 comparison and treatment group neighborhoods. Such research can also help establish a clearer set of conditions under which a programmatic extension of the MTO program might be developed. Knowing in which communities and neighborhoods, and for which types of families, such a program may work best will greatly aid in offering alternatives to life within high-rise, high-poverty communities.

REFERENCES

Brooks-Gunn, Jeanne, Greg Duncan, Tama Leventhal, and J. Lawrence Aber. 1997. "Lessons Learned and Future Directions for Research on the Neighborhoods in which Children Live." In *Neighborhood Poverty. Volume 1: Contexts and Consequences for Children,* edited by Jeanne Brooks-Gunn, Greg Duncan, and J. Lawrence Aber (279–98). New York: Russell Sage Foundation.

Calmore, John. 1999. "Viable Integration Must Reject the Ideology of 'Assimilationism'. " *Poverty & Race* 8(6): 7–8.

Case, Anne, and Lawrence Katz. 1991. "The Company You Keep: The Effects of Family and Neighborhood on Disadvantaged Youth." Working paper 3705. Boston: National Bureau of Economic Research.

Crane, Jonathan. 1991. "The Epidemic Theory of Ghettos and Neighborhood Effects on Dropping Out and Teenage Childbearing." *American Journal of Sociology* 96(5): 1226–59.

Dimond, Paul. 2000. "Empowering Families to Vote with Their Feet." In *Reflections on Regionalism,* edited by Bruce Katz (249–71). Washington, D.C.: Brookings Institution.

Duncan, Greg, and Willard Rodgers. 1991. "Has Children's Poverty Become More Persistent." *American Sociological Review* 56 (August): 538–50.

Ellen, Ingrid Gould, and Margery Turner. 1997. "Does Neighborhood Matter? Assessing Recent Evidence." *Housing Policy Debate* 8(4): 833–66.

Feins, Judith D. 2000. "Moving to Opportunity: First Cross-Site Analysis of Locational Impacts." Unpublished paper. Cambridge, Mass.: Abt Associates Inc.

Feins, Judith D., Debra McInnis, and Susan J. Popkin. 1997. "Counseling in the Moving to Opportunity for Fair Housing Demonstration Program." Cambridge, Mass.: Abt Associates Inc.

Finkel, Meryl and Larry Buron. 2001. *Study on Section 8 Voucher Success Rates: Quantitative Study of Success Rates in Metropolitan Areas.* Volume 1. Office of Policy Development and Research, HUD.

Gladden, Tricia, and Christopher Taber. 2000. "Wage Progression among Less Skilled Workers." In *Finding Jobs: Work and Welfare Reform,* edited by David Card and Rebecca Blank (160–92). New York: Russell Sage Foundation.

Goering, John, Judith Feins, and Todd Richardson. 2003. "A Cross-Site Analysis of Initial Moving to Opportunity Demonstration Results." *Journal of Housing Research* 13(1): 1–30.

Hanratty, Maria, Sarah McLanahan, and Becky Petit. 2001. "The Impact of the Los Angeles Moving to Opportunity Program on Residential Mobility, Neighborhood Characteristics, and Early Child and Parental Outcomes." Office of Policy Development and Research, HUD.

Hirsch, Arnold. 1983. *Making the Second Ghetto: Race and Housing in Chicago, 1940–1960.* New York: Cambridge University Press.

HUD (U.S. Department of Housing and Urban Development). 1996. "Moving to Opportunity for Fair Housing Demonstration: Program Operations Manual." Office of Policy Development and Research. Washington, D.C.: HUD.

———. 1999. "Moving to Opportunity for Fair Housing Demonstration: Current Status and Initial Findings." Office of Policy Development and Research. Washington, D.C.: HUD.

———. 2000. "Section 8 Tenant-Based Housing Assistance: A Look Back after 30 Years." March. HUD.

———. 2001. "A Report on Worst-Case Housing Needs in 1999." January. Office of Policy Development and Research, HUD.

Jargowsky, Paul. 1997. *Poverty and Place: Ghettos, Barrios, and the American City.* New York: Russell Sage Foundation.

Jencks, Christopher, and Susan Mayer. 1990. "The Social Consequences of Growing Up in a Poor Neighborhood." In *Inner-City Poverty in the United States,* edited by Laurence Lynn and Michael McGeary (111–86). Washington, D.C.: National Academy Press.

Katz, Larry, Jeffrey Kling, and Jeffrey Liebman. 2001. "Moving to Opportunity in Boston: Early Results of a Randomized Mobility Experiment." *Quarterly Journal of Economics* 116(2): 607–54.

Kaushal, Neeraj, and Robert Kaestner. 2000. "From Welfare to Work: Has Welfare Reform Worked?" Unpublished paper. New York: National Bureau of Economic Research.

Lehman, Jeffrey, and Timothy Smeeding. 1997. "Neighborhood Effects and Federal Policy." In *Neighborhood Poverty. Volume 1: Context and Consequences for Children*, edited by Jeanne Brooks-Gunn, Greg Duncan, and J. Lawrence Aber (251–78). New York: Russell Sage Foundation.

Leventhal, Tama, and Jeanne Brooks-Gunn. 2001. "Changing Neighborhoods and Child Well-Being: Understanding How Children May Be Affected in the Coming Century." In *Children at the Millennium: Where Have We Come From? Where Are We Going?*, edited by Timothy J. Owens and Sandra L. Hofferth (263–301). New York: Elsevier Science.

Ludwig, Jens, Greg Duncan, and Paul Hirschfield. 2001. "Urban Poverty and Juvenile Crime: Evidence from a Randomized Housing-Mobility Experiment." *Quarterly Journal of Economics* 116(2): 655–80.

Ludwig, Jens, Greg Duncan, and Joshua Pinkston. 2000. "Neighborhood Effects on Economic Self-Sufficiency: Evidence from a Randomized Housing-Mobility Experiment." Northwestern University/University of Chicago Joint Center for Poverty Research Working Paper Number 159.

Ludwig, Jens, Helen Ladd, and Greg Duncan. 2001. "Urban Poverty and Educational Outcomes." (January). In *Brookings-Wharton Papers on Urban Affairs: 2001*, edited by William Gale and Janet Rothenberg Pack (147–201). Washington, D.C.: Brookings Institution.

Manski, Charles. 1993. "Identification of Endogenous Social Effects: The Reflection Problem." *Review of Economic Studies* 60(3): 531–42.

Mayer, Susan, and Christopher Jencks. 1989. "Growing Up in Poor Neighborhoods: How Much Does It Matter?" *Science* 243 (March 17): 41–45.

Newman, Sandra, and Ann Schnare. 1997. ". . . And a Suitable Living Environment: The Failure of Housing Programs to Deliver on Neighborhood Quality." *Housing Policy Debate* 8(4): 703–41.

Norris, Donald, and James Bembry. 2001. "Moving to Opportunity in Baltimore: Neighborhood Choices and Neighborhood Satisfaction." Unpublished paper, University of Maryland, Baltimore.

O'Regan, Katherine, and John Quigley. 1999. "Accessibility and Economic Opportunity." In *Essays in Transportation Economics and Policy*, edited by Jose Gomez-Ibanez, William Tye, and Clifford Winston (437–66). Washington, D.C.: Brookings Institution.

Popkin, Susan, Laura Harris, and Mary Cunningham. 2002. "Families in Transition: A Qualitative Analysis of the MTO Experience." Office of Policy Development and Research, Washington, D.C.: HUD.

Popkin, Susan, Larry Buron, Diane Levy, and Mary Cunningham. 2000. "The Gautreaux Legacy: What Might Mixed-Income and Dispersal Strategies Mean for the Poorest Public Housing Tenants?" *Housing Policy Debate* 11(4): 911–42.

Popkin, Susan, Victoria Gwiasda, Lynn Olson, Dennie Rosenbaum, and Larry Buron. 2000. *The Hidden War: Crime and the Tragedy of Public Housing in Chicago*. New Brunswick, New Jersey: Rutgers.

Ross, Catherine, John Reynolds, and Karlyn Geis. 2000. "The Contingent Meaning of Neighborhood Stability for Residents' Psychological Well-Being." *American Sociological Review* 65(4): 581–97.

Rubinowitz, Leonard, and James Rosenbaum. 2000. *Crossing the Class and Color Lines: From Public Housing to White Suburbia.* Chicago: University of Chicago Press.

Sampson, Robert, Jeffrey Morenoff, and Thomas Gannon-Rowley. 2002. "Assessing 'Neighborhood Effects:' Social Processes and New Directions in Research." *Annual Review of Sociology* 28: 443–78.

Schoeni, Robert and Rebecca Blank. 2000. "What Has Welfare Reform Accomplished? Impacts on Welfare Participation, Employment, Income, Poverty, and Family Structure." NBER Working Paper 7627. Cambridge, Mass.: National Bureau of Economic Research.

Thompson, Phillip. 1999. "Public Housing in New York City." In *Housing and Community Development in New York City,* edited by Michael H. Schill (119–42). Albany: State University of New York.

Turner, Margery, Susan Popkin, and Mary Cunningham. 2000. *Section 8 Mobility and Neighborhood Health: Emerging Issues and Policy Challenges.* Washington, D.C.: The Urban Institute.

Weaver, R. Kent. 2000. *Ending Welfare As We Know It.* Washington, D.C.: Brookings Institution Press.

Wilkinson, Doris. 2000. "Integration Dilemmas in a Racist Culture." In *Race and Ethnicity in the United States: Issues and Debates,* edited by Stephen Steinberg (154–60). Malden, Mass.: Blackwell.

Wilson, William Julius. 1987. *The Truly Disadvantaged: The Inner City, The Underclass, and Public Policy.* Chicago: University of Chicago Press.

2

Political Origins
and Opposition

John Goering

The Moving to Opportunity demonstration has its roots in three broad policy and political movements. The first is the long history of efforts by the federal government to reduce the concentration of poor families within inner cities, including within inner-city public housing complexes. The second, overlapping source is the court system's attempts to desegregate public housing. The third source is the recent evidence from randomized social experiments testing the limits of housing policy innovation.

Each of these root sources, or policy foundations, was influential in shaping the broad political and policy parameters for the MTO demonstration. Beyond these broader influences, key actors in Congress, in the private sector, and among the public determined the programmatic content and implementation of the demonstration. The most important decision was Congress' allocation in 1993 of $70 million for roughly 1,400 housing vouchers and the delivery of housing counseling to help families move. An additional $150 million, planned for 1994, was cancelled because of strong community opposition at one of the sites. This chapter reviews the sources of MTO and describes the events that determined its final form and size.

MTO's Antipoverty Roots: Reducing Ghetto Poverty

The political and policy origins of most of America's major urban programs can be traced back to the Great Depression, a period of economic crisis that led the government to establish social security, Federal Housing Administration home insurance, and public housing projects (Skocpol 1992). For various reasons, public housing for families, begun as a temporary refuge for the working poor, soon became a permanent home for many poor, mainly minority households (Goering, Kamely, and Richardson 1995; Hirsch 1983; Massey and Denton 1993). Public housing also became part of inner-city "underclass" life (Hartman 1963).

For decades, policymakers intermittently attempted to reduce this racial and class isolation. For example, in 1968 The Kerner Commission articulated a core dyad that persists as a fulcrum for policies. Do nothing, the Commission argued, and the country would quickly become "two societies; one, largely Negro [sic] and poor, located in the central cities; the other, predominantly white and affluent, located in the suburbs and in outlying areas" (U.S. National Advisory Commission 1968, 22). The alternative to such racial and social isolation, the commission recommended, was to fund both "ghetto enrichment" and "policies that would encourage black families to move out of central city areas" (U.S. National Advisory Commission 1968, 22). Enacting policies that achieve these goals, however, has proved remarkably elusive. For example, in the 1970s, then–HUD Secretary George Romney initiated efforts to generate a small number of integrated, scattered-site housing projects throughout the United States; however, opposition from the Nixon administration derailed those efforts (Bonastia 2000; Lemann 1991).

During the Carter administration, a number of task forces were established within HUD, apparently to create mobility opportunities. A Gautreaux task force, followed by an Assisted Housing Mobility task force, had the goals of promoting mobility and deconcentration (Vernarelli 1986). The administration's broader efforts to promote region-wide mobility away from inner cities took the form of a Regional Housing Mobility Program directed by HUD's then–assistant secretary, Robert Embry. The Regional Mobility program, initiated in a small number of communities, soon encountered its own set of obstacles—resistance from within the minority community. Advocates for the minority poor believed that the government intended to forcibly displace the poor so that inner cities could be more efficiently rebuilt and gentrified to house the white middle class (Calmore 1979; De Bernardo 1979). Relations between HUD and community advocates became so contentious that Assistant Secretary Embry reported receiving death threats.[1]

The controversy at first stopped the program from expanding, though it continued to operate using previous funding commitments. The Reagan administration, which took office in 1981, promptly terminated the program, calling it an inappropriate form of "social engineering" (Goering 1986). The initiative left no research or public data imprint that could serve as a vehicle for understanding the program's constituents, whether it had worked, and whether participating families had experienced any significant benefits.

For nearly the next 20 years, policymakers at HUD and in Congress opposed research and demonstrations concerning either racial or economic deconcentration, and policymakers moved slowly to redress a number of pending claims of illegal segregation (Edsall and Edsall 1992; Hays 1995; Vernarelli 1986).

Remedying Illegal Racial Segregation

The second of MTO's three policy roots came by order of the federal courts. The racial and poverty impacts of public housing programs had become so egregious by the 1960s that many tenants had filed lawsuits charging violations of civil rights laws. Plaintiffs in various cities alleged that the federal government and local public housing agencies (PHAs) illegally segregated minority, mostly black public housing residents, denying them the choice of living in integrated housing. Federal courts almost uniformly agreed that HUD and PHAs illegally denied minority poor families the choice to live in less-segregated, better-off communities. The courts typically ordered a remedy designed to reduce the racial segregation found in public housing, such as a housing voucher program (Bonastia 2000; Briggs, Darden, and Aidala 1999; Vale 2000). Beginning with the Section 8 program in 1974, plaintiffs included Section 8 tenant-based housing as a critical ingredient in many remedial orders.

Such lawsuits often could do little to achieve the goal of reducing racial segregation within the stock of public housing units (Goering 1986; Polikoff 2002; Popkin, Buron, et al. 2000). The resulting housing voucher programs did, however, offer project tenants the chance to move out of their segregated communities.

Among the housing segregation lawsuits begun against HUD was a 1966 case brought by Chicago public housing resident Dorothy Gautreaux

(Davis 1993; Rubinowitz and Rosenbaum 2000). Starting in the late 1970s, HUD targeted annual allocations of Section 8 tenant-based assistance to the Gautreaux program.

The Gautreaux program was designed to offer black applicants for (or residents of) segregated projects the opportunity to move out of racially isolated areas through the Section 8 program. Families chosen for the program received Section 8 rental certificates that required them to move either to predominantly white or racially mixed neighborhoods. Families would not receive any housing subsidy unless they were willing to make these moves.

The second component of the Gautreaux program relief required HUD to hire a local nonprofit agency to offer moving advice and counseling to families. Participating families were provided varying levels of support and counseling by the nonprofit Chicago Leadership Council for Metropolitan Open Communities. The eligibility criteria and forms of counseling offered by the Leadership Council varied somewhat over the roughly 20 years of the Gautreaux program, but the requirement that families move to a nonsegregated neighborhood, and the availability of counseling, remained constant until the program's end in 1998 (Rubinowitz and Rosenbaum 2000).

In the late 1980s, research on the impact of the court-ordered Gautreaux program provided evidence that these moves resulted in positive social and educational effects for the families that had moved (Davis 1993). Rubinowitz and Rosenbaum (2000) provided evidence that showed children moving into racially integrated communities and exposed to less-segregated neighborhoods over a period of seven to ten years saw improvements in educational performance. These children were less likely to drop out of school and more likely to take college-track classes than were their Gautreaux peers who had moved to poorer, relatively segregated parts of Chicago. The Gautreaux researchers also identified changes in adult movers' job situations. Adults who moved to the suburbs had higher employment rates than adults moving to city areas, although the wages they earned and the number of hours they worked did not differ significantly from the city dwellers (Popkin, Gwiasda, et al. 2000).

The Gautreaux research suggested that moving from poor, racially isolated areas in inner-city Chicago to integrated suburban communities had fostered major improvements in the lives of the poor. The policy message thus seemed clear: moving out of public housing projects into more suburban communities could change lives.

Social Experiments at HUD: The Idea of Random Assignment

The third and last policy root for MTO is the practice of using randomized social experiments to understand and evaluate the effects of policy innovations (Galster 1996; Shroder 2000). In the history of federal housing policy, few major experimental demonstrations have been aimed at understanding the impacts of federally subsidized rental assistance on the deconcentration of public housing poverty. In the early 1970s, the Experimental Housing Allowance Program (EHAP) helped establish the programmatic and research basis for the Section 8 tenant assistance program (Galster 1996; Hays 1995; Winnick 1995). Two decades would pass before Congress agreed to initiate a second experiment—the Moving to Opportunity demonstration. MTO became HUD's first major social experiment aimed at understanding the method for managing and examining the behavioral impacts of the deconcentration of public housing families in multiple metropolitan housing markets.

Key Design Decisions

Creating MTO as a social experiment was the central research design decision affecting the utility of its research and policy conclusions. Such a design, as discussed in chapter 1, was necessitated by the personal selection bias inherent in the design of most prior research, including the Gautreaux research. If policymakers could not distinguish the effects of a demonstration from the personal motivations and enthusiasms of demonstration participants, they could never be certain that their efforts had been effective. MTO's random-assignment procedure eliminates this source of bias.

There were other major decisions, choices, and policies that affected the shape, size, and reach of MTO. This series of decisions determined the final form of the demonstration; one that ended somewhat differently than it had begun.

In early 1989, Alexander Polikoff, the lead counsel for the Gautreaux litigation, sent a string of letters to officials at HUD, including then-Secretary Jack Kemp, encouraging them to expand Gautreaux-like opportunities to other cities. Gautreaux not only worked, he argued, but was also cost-effective. "Apart from the Section 8 certificates," he wrote Secretary Kemp, "administration of the program involved a one-time per family cost of $1,500. Compared to the societal costs of the alternatives for these families (remaining in distressed neighborhoods), this may be one of the biggest bargains around," Polikoff argued.

After some staff-level opposition to the idea of expanding Gautreaux,[2] HUD policy officials, in the spring of 1990, agreed to be briefed on the results of the research (which came out of Northwestern University) and on the operation of the Chicago Gautreaux housing mobility program. Then–HUD Secretary Jack Kemp also demonstrated willingness to address the issue of racial segregation. The briefing, held in June 1990, helped persuade a core set of senior career staff that a new Gautreaux-like proposal had merit.

During the first stage of discussions with HUD, Polikoff proposed that HUD support a request for counseling assistance tied to an allocation of vouchers. The argument he made was that "absent the services provided by a Gautreaux-type agency, too many inner-city families living in poverty do not actually have mobility prospects in middle-class suburban communities that seem to them distant and foreign" (unpublished letters to HUD). At this stage, there was no conversation about restricting the use of Section 8 to a small subset of better-off neighborhoods. In fact, the legislative draft prepared for Congress in 1991 only requested authorization for a three-year demonstration testing whether counseling alone improved voucher deconcentration effectiveness.

The draft legislation outlined a demonstration that offered roughly five local housing authorities additional Section 8 assistance with a counseling component. Under Polikoff's original plan, counseling would have been covered by local, rather than HUD, funds. Ultimately, HUD provided partial funding for the counseling agencies, requiring the agencies to contribute matching resources.

MTO offered public housing families with children living in one of the demonstration's high-poverty areas the choice to move away. Neither the applicant's race nor the race of the destination neighborhoods factored into eligibility. Thus, the next major design decision was to replace the race-conscious objectives of Gautreaux with poverty and income criteria.

Soon after Polikoff's initial letters, key members of Kemp's staff agreed that the demonstration would focus on "providing assisted families the choice of moving from economically depressed neighborhoods to areas of high job potential."[3] Polikoff agreed with the decision to "delink" the program design from the issue of race. But both HUD staff and Polikoff understood that the labeling of any new mobility demonstration as an economic—rather than a racial—deconcentration effort was largely political choice. The cities and areas targeted for MTO would be almost exclusively black and Hispanic, though the racial composition of the receiving communities was unclear at the early design stages. MTO would be enacted as an economic desegregation initiative (Downs 1973; Roisman 2001).

The next major design choice for MTO was its size and scale. Polikoff, in his 1991 draft proposals, intended for MTO to assist at least 5,000 families. He specified three years of funding with an annual allocation of 1,700 rental assistance vouchers to be distributed among five localities. The number of vouchers issued, however, was significantly lower.

MTO's first wave of funding, which merged funding from fiscal years 1992 and 1993 into one lump sum of roughly $70 million, was meant to assist an estimated 1,350 families. Because of controversy surrounding the demonstration and changes in the political landscape, Congress cancelled the second wave of support—an additional $150 million—tentatively scheduled for fiscal year 1994.

MTO's authorization included a requirement for the comprehensive evaluation of its effects and costs, as the Senate staff wanted a clear record of lessons learned. Polikoff and the HUD staff understood the need for both an annual report as well as periodic evaluations. In fact, HUD staff established the requirement of random assignment for the demonstration and inserted it into the Request for Proposals that HUD issued to eligible local public housing authorities.

A growing, increasingly important experimental research literature in social policy interventions made random-assignment one of the most critical decisions affecting the design of MTO (Crane 1998).[4] Designers established a series of data-collection and random-assignment techniques. HUD's plan included funding for technical assistance, provided by Abt Associates, to ensure that the program used standardized procedures across all the five selected cities. Abt provided random-assignment software and monitored its use to ensure that MTO administrators properly allocated tenants to the required three experimental subgroups. The final legislation for MTO required both annual reports and a final evaluation because these requirements would help establish effective practices as well as confirm Gautreaux's findings that "the 'payoff' from the program was potentially quite high: educated kids and working parents rather than grist for the prison and welfare mills."[5]

The final design of MTO required families in the treatment group to move into low-poverty areas. The idea for adding the destination requirement emerged after the Clinton administration arrived in 1993. Mark

Shroder, policy analyst and researcher at HUD, years later commented on the timing of this decision: "We would never have asked [Bush administration officials] to approve that design [requirement]. If Bush Senior had won in 1992, we would probably have implemented a test of the effectiveness of counseling in moving voucher holders voluntarily to areas of low poverty; the experimental group would have had vouchers plus counseling but no limits on where they could go, the control group would have simply had vouchers."[6] One of MTO's key experimental conditions—restrictions on the areas that families using MTO vouchers could move to—came about relatively late in the design process, after political opportunities had changed.

MTO planners initially thought of including one control group; while that group would receive regular Section 8 assistance, it would not have to select a low-poverty neighborhood and would not receive any special counseling. Control participants would be treated the same as other Section 8-assisted families.

In a meeting convened by HUD with outside academic and policy experts in early 1994, participant Paul Leonard, then a senior policy analyst with the Center for Budget and Policy Priorities in Washington, D.C., made a persuasive argument that HUD needed traditional public housing residents of project-based complexes as a second comparison group. The second, in-place control group would include families that had volunteered but were not awarded Section 8 assistance. These families would continue living in their conventional public housing projects.

This proposal permitted a comparison of MTO's behavioral and social outcomes for families living in HUD's two major forms of assisted housing: project-based developments and routine Section 8 treatment group families. HUD readily agreed to this recommendation, and it was incorporated into the demonstration's final design requirements.

MTO's design, therefore, reflected a combination of legislative and funding choices as well a number of design decisions recommended by policy experts and researchers. The MTO demonstration became a poverty-focused, rather than a race-focused, project. While initially conceived as a three-year effort to assist 5,000 families, it became a one-year demonstration that assisted roughly 285 families per city. Significantly, MTO included an experimental design and a long-term evaluation plan that would test whether the program would produce substantial personal and public sector welfare benefits (HUD 2000).

It would take a year of implementation work after HUD submitted its Request for Proposals before agencies were selected and trained, research forms were perfected, and families were told about the opportunity. Beginning in fall 1994, the first families signed up for the new demonstration. Before MTO enrollment could begin in the Baltimore area, however, the project encountered community opposition that led to the termination of MTO's final year of funding support.

Trouble in Essex: The Political Predicament of Poverty Deconcentration

The first signs of trouble came in the early spring of 1994. A government employee who lived in the eastern section of Baltimore County asked to come to HUD to make a copy of the MTO application that had been submitted by the Housing Authority of Baltimore City. Talking with him the day he came, his anxieties were clear to me: He said he feared for the quality of his own neighborhood and was concerned that his young daughters might date a black person from one of the MTO families. He was also angry that the MTO demonstration appeared to be a "secret." It seemed no one in the county had been informed about the demonstration, and he and his neighbors were worried. His visit to HUD was an effort to learn whether Baltimore County had been targeted as home for people from the city's public housing projects.

It is essential to understand that his fears were shaped by the substantial political and social gulf that separates the city from Baltimore County. The city lies within the horseshoe-shaped county, and many county residents had fled the city because its racial and economic makeup had changed, in their minds, for the worse.

Baltimore City was the second smallest city selected for MTO (after Boston). As one of the poorest and oldest cities selected, it had the longest tradition of providing public housing (Hirsch 2000; McDougall 1993). One commentator described the city's housing environment this way: "[Large groups of] low-income blacks were moved into public housing units, straining the system with extreme social problems . . . Failing buildings and inadequate city services went hand in hand with ineffective schools, alcoholism, traffic in drugs, unwanted pregnancies, and a high rate of juvenile delinquency" (McDougall 1993, 56).

By the late 1970s, Baltimore had become, according to the same commentator, two cities: "a black inner city and a white outer city and suburban area; the latter growing, the former decaying. While many parts of the outer suburban economy flourished, the inner-city economy was in a depression, and blacks suffered the most" (McDougall, 1993, 61). By 1990, Baltimore City housed more than 150,000 of the area's poorest families (nearly 22 percent of the total poor for the whole metropolitan area).

By 1998, Baltimore's population had also shrunk to 646,000 people, down from more than 900,000 in 1970. Yet Baltimore County had grown from 1.15 million in 1970 to 1.80 million in 1998. This divergence in the demographic profile and political interests of residents in the city versus the suburbs helped set the stage for MTO's troubles. As in many metropolitan areas, the inner city and suburbs were fairly racially and economically distinct. "The division of Baltimore and its metropolitan area into a prosperous white and a declining black community has exacerbated racial tension . . . whether the reason for the division has been class or race" (McDougall 1993, 106).

The outer parts of Baltimore County, particularly the eastern areas of Essex and Dundalk, had begun to experience their own troubles (Orfield 1997). Topping this list was the decline in the number of industrial jobs, as steel and aviation plants moved away. Many of the residents of the eastern section of the county were working-class families whose members had worked in the steel and shipping factories along the county's waterfront (Newman 1995, 83–4). But these once-prosperous blue-collar areas had now begun to deteriorate. "Once home to large contingents of employees from Bethlehem Steel, Martin Aircraft, Western Electric, and other industrial endeavors, the area steadily declined as employers left or downsized and neighborhoods where former workers lived became depressed" (Galster, Metzger, and Waite 1999, 3–25). Unemployment in the Essex area, for example, was double the rate for the rest of the county in 1990. Moreover, the minority population in the county grew 60 percent between 1980 and 1990, while the minority population in the Essex area increased more than 90 percent (Lucas 1997).

By 1994, when HUD announced the MTO award to Baltimore, many residents were experiencing hard economic times, and Baltimore County had a relatively large proportion of poor residents. Yet, despite the need for more affordable housing, the county had resisted applying for any federal funds that required building low-income public housing. While county officials rejected the idea of building public housing projects, they welcomed the development of privately owned, subsidized Section 8 rental housing. In fact, many of these developments had been placed in the same, weakened areas of the county that were potentially part of the MTO demonstration (Galster, Tatian, and Smith 1999; Lucas 1997; McDougall 1993).

Soon after HUD's official announcement of the MTO agreement with the Housing Authority of Baltimore City in March 1994, a small number of county residents formed the Eastern Political Association (EPA), a new group that opposed MTO. The members' opposition was partly based on media coverage that linked the impending demolition of some of Baltimore's worst public housing with MTO's arrival. Their stance also reflected the growing sense of economic vulnerability within their communities.

EPA sponsored a number of community meetings with the purpose of distributing information discrediting MTO. Central to the group's opposition was the belief that moving public housing residents into the county would not stop with the small numbers of MTO families. EPA's members firmly believed that virtually all the city's public housing complexes were going to be demolished under the HOPE VI program and that the residents of the projects would be moved into their neighborhoods (Carson and Gilbert 1994; Galster et al. 1999).[7]

Residents were not just concerned about the potential number of poor families. The residents of Essex feared what hundreds of other communities have feared: poor families of color moving into their neighborhoods, bringing the pathologies of the city. "HEAR US SHOUT," were the opening words on an anti-MTO poster, which continued by warning, "People living in drug- and crime-infested Lafayette homes and Murphy homes could be moving to Essex. The Moving to Opportunity program could affect our neighborhoods, our schools, and the number of families receiving county social services. But this is not a racial issue. It is a matter of safety and quality education for Essex residents"[8] The announcement of MTO triggered anxieties and fears among local residents alarmed by the overall decline of their neighborhoods (Galster et al. 1999, 881).

County residents became convinced, through the efforts of groups such as EPA, that, as one commentator put it, "their economically depressed neighborhoods have been targeted to become new ghettos by well-paid, uncaring federal bureaucrats who live in wealthy suburbs far away" (Carson 1994). One of the leaders of this movement, Jerry Hersl, explained his feelings: "People here moved from Baltimore City, and they worked for that move. Now somebody could move in down the street, not have a job, get a 100-percent rent subsidy, send their kids to the same school I'm sending my kids to. And that's not fair" (Montgomery 1994). Concerns about fairness and vulnerability, linked to all-too-familiar code words about race, characterized MTO's beginning in Baltimore.

HUD and Baltimore City housing officials attempted to address the rumors and ill feeling by participating in a community meeting on June 21, 1994, at the Chesapeake High School in Baltimore County. Their objective was to offer information to counter the rumors and misstatements that had been circulating about MTO. They brought maps to show that the poverty levels of large portions of the eastern section of the county were too high to qualify the areas' residents for MTO. However, a few minutes after the presentation had begun, the meeting "turned into a noisy, racially tinged free-for-all" (Carson and Gilbert 1994). Nothing that the HUD official or the other speakers could say helped stem participants' anger and fears.

After that meeting, despite statements by federal and some local officials, county political leaders convinced local residents that unwanted neighborhood racial change was soon going to be forced on them. In September 1994, the EPA sent out a flyer saying, "The (MTO) program has every indication of being the start of a much larger federal housing program, which could include moving as many as 18,000 families. Our government has cloaked this program in secrecy and has denied community input. Without a doubt, MTO will have a negative impact on crime, education, taxes and quality of life in our communities" (flyer available from author).

Because fall 1994 was an election year, numerous public forums allowed critics to fuel community opposition to MTO. Almost all politicians campaigning at the federal, state, or local levels in Baltimore County area expressed negative opinions about MTO. For example, a candidate for the Maryland House of Delegates was quoted by a Baltimore County newspaper as saying, "MTO is a Democratic project, and Republicans believe it is a total waste of taxpayers' money" (Edkins 1996: 25). Another state Democratic delegate was quoted as saying that, while he didn't "have anything against the poor," many people in public housing were "undisciplined, unskilled, take dope, and have to be taught how not to steal" (*The Essex Avenue News* 1994, 2a). Yet another Democratic candidate for the House of Delegates stated, "I pledge to lead community efforts against any infringement of nuisance laws, health standards, or housing standards that may have been brought about by MTO. I also pledge to provide leadership in lobbying landlords in our community not to participate in MTO" (*The Essex Avenue News* 1994, 2a; see also Edkins 1996). The Republican candidate for governor, Delegate Ellen Sauerbrey, stated that she too opposed the program as "social engineering" and that "once you start messing around with people's property values, you're asking for trouble."[9]

U.S. Senator Barbara Mikulski from Maryland had long been a staunch supporter of federal housing programs and was a key supporter of the HOPE VI program. Her key staff member on housing and HUD issues, Kevin Kelly, quickly learned about the opposition from the angry citizens of Baltimore County and from local congressmen. They argued that their suburbs were already struggling with local unemployment and that no jobs or real opportunities were available for MTO families.

While anti-MTO resentments resembled opposition to other programs, such as attempts to promote school integration through busing, no one at HUD, Kelly felt, seemed able to deal with the problem. He concluded that HUD, the local PHA, and the nonprofit organization managing MTO had "totally botched" MTO implementation in Baltimore.[10] As a direct result of this turmoil, key HUD staff were "pretty much told to kill MTO altogether."[11]

A compromise, however, was reached: HUD agreed not to launch the second stage of MTO with funding that had already been appropriated. On September 3, 1994, a Senate-House joint conference committee on appropriations ended the approximately $150 million provision that would have financed the second year of funding for MTO (Mariano 1994). Senator Mikulski, commenting at the time, noted, "The program has been bungled by the city administration and by the group that was supposed to administer it . . . There has not been enough consultation with the community out there. That has exacerbated discontent to the point that it would be only a hollow opportunity for the poor people in the program" (Brandt 1994). Thus, the trouble in Essex directly translated into a setback for the administration's efforts to promote more regional mobility within the Section 8 program, although key HUD officials, most notably Secretary Cisneros, managed to keep one full year of MTO funding alive.[12]

Press commentaries on the decision to terminate MTO proliferated for an additional couple of weeks. One writer observed, "No one wants the poor around, particularly the black poor . . . In the grim shadows of the post-civil rights era, the black poor have become our modern lepers. It's easy to understand those people in Dundalk and Essex: There is a lot of crime committed by poor blacks" (Olesker 1994). But the author, acknowledging the complexity of this message, singled out the local politician for his role. "Instead of reasons [he] plucks fears. He brings stereotyping back into season. And his timing couldn't be more calculating" (Olesker 1994, B1). By spring 1995, *The New York Times* published MTO's obituary under the headline "Housing Voucher Test in Maryland Is Scuttled by a Political Firestorm" (De Witt 1995). MTO appeared to have died.

Was Community Opposition Unavoidable?

An assessment of the role for MTO in future housing policy and program options requires some assessment of the sources of responsibility for the outburst of community opposition to MTO. Planners and policymakers could probably have been more proactive and less naïve about the likely intensity and potential impacts of suburban opposition. More proactive coalition building to enlist suburban support for such efforts might have also helped. If federal and local officials had explained the purposes and limits of MTO earlier in the implementation process, they may have staved off some opposition.

Given the long history of so-called NIMBY ("not in my backyard") opposition to most of HUD's prior attempts to deconcentrate poverty, attempts to anticipate opposition may well have been a waste of time (Downs 1973). Many residents of Baltimore City and the surrounding counties probably did not receive adequate information about the distinctions between both MTO and HOPE VI. But the handful of families involved in MTO at the time (fewer than 150) suggested that such a tiny project needed less, rather than more, bureaucratic and political involvement.

Local residents had indeed been panicked into believing some of the worst class and racial stereotypes. As in many communities, community tolerance or calls for social justice did not emerge to offset such politically manipulated fears (*NBC Dateline* 2000). There is also some evidence from the Baltimore area that residents' fears about the negative effects of subsidized housing had some foundation.

According to research by Galster, Tatian, and Smith (1999), after certain thresholds of Section 8 concentration, neighborhood property values can decrease. These effects appeared in what they term "vulnerable" neighborhoods, where housing values were low to moderate. The effect occurred independent of race. If researchers confirm this finding in other sites—using data specifically on vouchers and low-poverty communities—the results may help clarify the conditions under which measurable thresholds or concentrations of assisted families make a community less able to accommodate additional subsidized housing (Guhathakurta and Mushkatel 2002).

The story of MTO exclusion is not neat and simple. To many white residents, MTO was an act of governmental unfairness. Seen by the minority poor, MTO and other assistance programs were but modest down payments toward correcting the racial bias they had experienced; experiences invisible to many of their fellow white Baltimore residents (Feagin and Sikes 1994). HUD planners and administrators had no tools with which to redress such deep tensions and misunderstandings.

MTO Continued Despite Opposition

Hostilities in Baltimore County cooled by late 1994, with virtually no public meetings or protests following the November election. This cooling occurred in part because Congress reacted to the opposition and appeared to "cancel MTO." The MTO demonstration, however, did not end.

The MTO demonstration and its research activities continued despite the reduced size of the program; between 1994 and 1998, all allocated vouchers had been used.[13] MTO moved ahead in Baltimore, where the intended number of families received counseling and moved. None of the other MTO sites experienced any comparable community or political opposition. The program was neither a "debacle" nor effectively "eviscerated" as Galster et al. (2003) suggests. HUD in fact managed to add a modest number of additional families from two of the participating PHAs that allocated some of their turnover vouchers for use in the demonstration. Altogether, MTO served more than 1,600 families.[14]

Conclusion

MTO's uniqueness as both a HUD deconcentration initiative and a major experimental research program makes it a critical tool in addressing a host of policy, political, and research questions. MTO builds on prior efforts to address the twin ills of poverty and racial isolation; it is also one of the few research tools enabling policymakers to robustly answer the question of whether and how neighborhoods matter to the lives of poor adults and children. The demonstration, created in roughly sequential steps, was shaped by differing policy, political, and research interests. Its final form is the result of political circumstance, leadership, and serendipitously timed research.

As noted in the concluding chapter, it is critical that future research on MTO address whether MTO families that moved to better-off neighborhoods have been productive, well-adjusted neighbors. To what extent has the stability of the neighborhoods been measurably affected—either positively or negatively—by the presence of a small number of MTO movers? Can we discern points at which the social problems of such neighborhoods may "tip" because of the entrance of low-income movers? What are the conditions under which such changes occur, and do they occur uniformly across all cities and neighborhoods? Were any of the worst fears of the Essex community confirmed? If negative effects did occur, have positive achievements among children and parents sufficiently countered them?

It may well turn out that programs such as MTO are ill-suited for cities with the socioeconomic and political dynamics of Baltimore during the late 1990s. Any programmatic extension of MTO, though, could offer opportunities to hundreds of additional low-income and public housing families in communities whose social and institutional fabric is not so badly frayed or racist. If the next stage of MTO research corroborates the results summarized in this collection, then the economic and social benefits could offset some part of the most countervailing risks, and may establish a new framework for public discourse about metropolitan economic integration.

NOTES

1. Interview with Robert Embry on August 23, 2000.
2. A staff member wrote "[W]e have found that the existing opportunities for mobility amongst very low-income families is sufficient." Letter of James Hamernick, acting deputy assistant secretary for multifamily housing programs, to Alexander Polikoff; April 18, 1989.
3. One of Secretary Kemp's key assistants, Mary Brunette, decided to add "for Fair Housing" as part of MTO's formal title. This addition did not alter the income-based demonstration requirements. Communication from Jill Khadduri, March 27, 2002.

4. Interviews with former Director of Policy Development in HUD's Office of Policy Development and Research (PD&R) Jill Khadduri, August 23, 2000, and March 27, 2002. Dr. Mark Shroder, at HUD's PD&R, was the person most responsible for establishing the experimental, long-term panel design for MTO; interview with Shroder on August 25, 2000. In October 1990, staff wrote a memo to John Weicher, then–assistant secretary of PD&R, to propose the fiscal year 1991 demonstration "to Improve Access to Metropolitan Wide Housing and Employment Opportunities." By October 1991, the idea for a Gautreaux-like replication (then called MODEM or the moving to opportunities demo) was in place and the thresholds of 40 percent and 10 percent of the poverty level were established.

5. At the initial drafting stages, MTO was also focused on helping income-eligible families on PHA waiting lists. This focus was narrowed in the final statute to include only current occupants and residents of either conventional public housing developments or Section 8 project-based housing located in areas that were deeply poor. MTO would have as one of its indirect benefits the option to help relocate a small number of families out of public housing developments, at a time when Congress was concurrently planning to demolish many inner-city projects under the HOPE VI program (HUD 1996).

6. Communication from Mark Shroder, at HUD, March 12, 2002.

7. To appreciate MTO's design and implementation it is necessary to know that MTO was not "the only game in town" for public housing families in 1994. One of the parallel programs that directly, if inadvertently, affected MTO was an initiative demolishing many of the worst public housing projects in larger cities; projects from which some MTO families would move. The new program was HOPE VI, and its goal was to enable relocating Section 8 families to return to their old communities after the buildings had been fully refurbished. With congressional backing, HUD was provided funding for HOPE VI with the objective of demolishing the most troubled urban public housing projects and replacing them with rebuilt mixed-income communities. The initial goal was to tear down roughly 100,000 units (HUD 1996; Popkin, Buron, et al. 2000). In several of the areas selected for MTO, eligible families knew that they had the choice to stay and wait for better housing or to relocate. Some families told us they preferred to remain and see what would result. MTO, then, was clearly not designed to be the "silver bullet" for ghetto poverty or the only policy choice available to public housing residents (Brown and Richman 1997; Dimond 2000; Downs 1994; Goetz 2000; Kingsley, Johnson, and Pettit 2001; Salama 1999; Weisberg 2000).

8. Flyers quoted were distributed by an Essex landlord at community meetings held in Essex and Dundalk, Maryland in June 1994. See Edkins 1996; copies are available from the author.

9. Other newspaper accounts appeared in the *Dundalk Eagle* and *The Baltimore Sun*.

10. Telephone interview with Kevin Kelly, October 2, 2000.

11. Communication from former HUD Deputy Assistant Secretary Margery Austin Turner, September 1, 2000.

12. Former HUD Chief of Staff Bruce Katz commented that HUD Secretary Henry Cisneros had "almost single-handedly" introduced metropolitan thinking back into HUD and had been the intellectual driving force behind using Section 8 on a regional scale. MTO had been among his first major priorities for supplemental funding when he

arrived at HUD in 1993. Interview with Bruce Katz on September 1, 2000; personal communication from Margery Austin Turner, September 1, 2000.

13. In the Baltimore area, the Community Assistance Network (CAN) provided counseling to families about the potential risks of moving into the contested parts of Baltimore County. As a result, only one mother made a move to those sections of eastern Baltimore County, where resistance had been the most determined. CAN also provided local elected officials with weekly briefings about any planned or actual moves into their community. Their regular reports helped to greatly reduce officials' anxiety, and the issue quickly receded from community concern. Interview with former CAN Executive Director Robert Gaydjs, October 16, 2000.

14. In September 2000, roughly six years after MTO encountered community opposition in Baltimore, a similar problem emerged. A judicially mandated requirement to provide housing to poor, inner-city public housing residents within nonpoor parts of the city engendered heated concern from the neighborhoods where the poor had been slated to move. Shields (2000a) reports "Homeowners in Northeast Baltimore are fighting city plans to move public housing families into their neighborhoods as part of a court settlement" (Shields 2000a, 1). As with MTO, the arguments against the movement of such families into these neighborhoods were about unfairness. "There are a lot of people out there who have worked hard to buy their homes," the neighbors again protested (Shields 2000a, 6b; 2000b). The analogy with MTO was explicit: "In 1994, the city unveiled a program called Moving to Opportunity that called for more than 1,000 [sic] poor city families to be given subsidized housing in the suburbs. About 250 families took advantage of the program before Congress killed the funding after fears that cities would dump their poor in the suburbs" (Shields 2000a, 6b).

REFERENCES

Bonastia, Chris. 2000. "Why Did Affirmative Action in Housing Fail during the Nixon Era? Exploring 'Institutional Homes' of Social Policies." *Social Problems* 47(November): 523–42.

Brandt, Ed. 1994. "Relocation Program Won't Grow: New Money Halted in Housing Plan for Inner City Families." *The Baltimore Sun.* September 10, p. B1.

Briggs, Xavier de Souza, Joe Darden, and Angela Aidala. 1999. "In the Wake of Desegregation: Early Impacts of Public Housing on Neighborhoods in Yonkers, New York." *APA Journal* 65 (winter): 27–49.

Brown, Prudence, and Harold Richman. 1997. "Neighborhood Effects and State and Local Policy." In *Neighborhood Poverty Volume 2: Policy Implications in Studying Neighborhoods*, edited by Jeanne Brooks-Gunn, Greg Duncan, and J. Aber. (164–81). New York: Russell Sage Foundation.

Calmore, John. 1979. "Fair Housing vs. Fair Housing: The Conflict between Providing Low-Income Housing in Impacted Areas and Providing Increased Housing Opportunities through Spatial Deconcentration." *Housing Law Bulletin* 9 (November/December): 1–12.

Carson, Larry. 1994. "Housing Controversy Replay." *The Baltimore Sun,* August 7, p. E1.

Carson, Larry, and Pat Gilbert. 1994. "Plan to Relocate Families from Inner City Fuels Fears." *The Baltimore Sun.* July 31, p. B1.

Crane, Jonathan, ed. 1998. *Social Programs That Work.* New York: Russell Sage Foundation.

Davis, Mary. 1993. "The Gautreaux Assisted Housing Program." In *Housing Markets and Residential Mobility,* edited by G. Thomas Kingsley and Margery Austin Turner (243–53). Washington, D.C.: Urban Institute Press.

De Bernardo, Henry. 1979. "Analysis of HUD's Regional Housing Mobility Program." Unpublished Report. Philadelphia, August 31.

De Witt, Karen. 1995. "Housing Voucher Test in Maryland Is Scuttled by a Political Firestorm." *The New York Times.* March 28, p. B10.

Dimond, Paul. 2000. "Empowering Families to Vote with Their Feet." In *Reflections on Regionalism,* edited by Bruce Katz. Washington, D.C.: Brookings Institution.

Downs, Anthony. 1973. *Opening up the Suburbs.* New Haven: Yale.

———. 1994. *New Visions for Metropolitan America.* Washington, D.C.: Brookings Institution.

Edkins, Laura. 1996. "The Controversy over Moving to Opportunity for Fair Housing." (January). M.A. Thesis submitted the Department of Sociology, George Washington University, Washington, D.C.

Edsall, Thomas, and Mary Edsall. 1992. *Chain Reaction: The Impact of Race, Rights, and Taxes on American Politics.* New York: W. W. Norton.

Essex Avenue News. 1994. "Community Skeptical of Moving to Opportunity, Asks for Facts." June 23, pp. 1a–2a.

Feagin, Joe, and Melvin Sikes. 1994. *Living with Racism: The Black Middle-Class Experience.* Boston: Beacon Press.

———, ed. 1996. *Reality and Research: Social Science and U.S. Urban Policy Since 1960.* Washington, D.C.: Urban Institute Press.

Galster, George, Kurt Metzger, and Ruth Waite. 1999. "Neighborhood Opportunity Structures of Immigrant Populations, 1980 and 1990." *Housing Policy Debate* 10(2): 395–442.

Galster, George, Peter Tatian, and Robin Smith. 1999. "The Impact of Neighbors Who Use Section 8 Certificates on Property Values." *Housing Policy Debate* 10(4): 879–917.

Galster, George, Peter Tatian, Anna Santiago, Kathryn Pettit, and Robin Smith. 2003. *Why NOT in My Back Yard? Neighborhood Impacts of Assisted Housing.* New Brunswick, N.J.: CUPR Press, Rutgers University.

Goering, John, ed. 1986. *Housing Desegregation and Federal Policy.* Chapel Hill: University of North Carolina.

Goering, John, Ali Kamely, and Todd Richardson. 1995. "The Location and Racial Composition of Public Housing in the United States." HUD-1519-PDR (March). Washington, D.C.: HUD.

Goetz, Edward. 2000. "The Politics of Poverty Deconcentration and Housing Demolition." *Journal of Urban Affairs* 22(2): 157–73.

Guhathakurta, Subhrajit, and Alvin Mushkatel. 2002. "Race, Ethnicity, and Household Characteristics of Section 8 Clients and Their Impact on Adjacent Housing Quality." *Urban Affairs Review* 37 (March): 521–42.

Hartman, Chester. 1963. "The Limitations of Public Housing: Relocation Choices in a Working Class Community." *Journal of the American Institute of Planners* 29 (November): 283–96.

Hays, R. Allen. 1995. *The Federal Government and Urban Housing*. Albany: State University of New York Press.

Hirsch, Arnold. 1983. *Making the Second Ghetto: Race and Housing in Chicago, 1940–1960*. New York: Cambridge University Press.

———. 2000. "Searching for a 'Sound Negro Policy': A Racial Agenda for the Housing Acts of 1949 and 1954." *Housing Policy Debate* 11(2): 393–441.

HUD. See U.S. HUD.

Kingsley, G. Thomas, Jennifer Johnson, and Kathryn Pettit. 2001. "HOPE VI and Section 8: Spatial Patterns in Relocation." Washington, D.C.: The Urban Institute.

Lemann, Nicholas. 1991. *The Promised Land: The Great Black Migration and How It Changed America*. New York: Alfred A. Knopf.

Lucas, Wendy. 1997. "Perry Hall, Baltimore, Maryland Housing and Neighborhood Study: Putting FHA Housing on the Map." HUD, Washington, D.C. Unpublished report.

Mariano, Ann. 1994. "Hill Panel Halts Plan to Move Poor Families." *The Washington Post*. September 3, p. E1.

Massey, Douglas S., and Nancy A. Denton. 1993. *American Apartheid: Segregation and the Making of the Underclass*. Cambridge, Mass.: Harvard University Press.

McDougall, Harold. 1993. *Black Baltimore: A New Theory of Community*. Philadelphia: Temple University Press.

Montgomery, Lori. 1994. "U.S. Plan to Spread Out the Poor Creates a Storm." *Detroit Free Press*. July 14, p. 1A.

NBC Dateline. 2000. "Breaking Away: Out of Public Housing." Maria Shriver. August 11, transcript, part three, "New Neighbors."

Newman, Sandra. 1995. "Poverty Concentration as a Policy Strategy." Occasional Paper no. 17 (February). Baltimore: Institute for Policy Studies, The Johns Hopkins University.

Olesker, Michael. 1994. "Playing on Fears: DePazzo Exploits Stereotype of Poor." *The Baltimore Sun*. September 6, p. B1.

Orfield, Myron. 1997. *Metropolitics: A Regional Agenda for Community and Stability*. Washington, D.C.: Brookings Institution.

Polikoff, Alexander. 2002. "Cabrini-Green to Willow Creek." Unpublished chapter 4 in *Waiting for Gautreaux: Biography of a Lawsuit*. Unpublished draft manuscript, available from author.

Popkin, Susan, Larry Buron, Diane Levy, and Mary Cunningham. 2000. "The Gautreaux Legacy: What Might Mixed-Income and Dispersal Strategies Mean for the Poorest Public Housing Tenants?" *Housing Policy Debate* 11(4): 911–42.

Popkin, Susan, Victoria Gwiasda, Lynn Olson, Dennie Rosenbaum, and Larry Buron. 2000. *The Hidden War: Crime and the Tragedy of Public Housing in Chicago*. New Brunswick, New Jersey: Rutgers.

Roisman, Florence. 2001. "Opening the Suburbs to Racial Integration: Lessons for the 21st Century." *Western New England Law Review* 173: 173–221.

Rubinowitz, Leonard, and James Rosenbaum. 2000. *Crossing the Class and Color Lines: From Public Housing to White Suburbia*. Chicago: University of Chicago Press.

Salama, Jerry. 1999. "The Redevelopment of Distressed Public Housing: Early Results from Hope VI Projects in Atlanta, Chicago, and San Antonio." *Housing Policy Debate* 10(1): 95–142.

Shields, Gerald. 2000a. "City's Plan on Housing Attacked: ACLU Lawsuit Result to Put Poor Residents into Neighborhoods." *The Baltimore Sun.* September 21, p. 1.

———. 2000b. "Neighbors Air Fears over Plan for Poor." *The Baltimore Sun.* September 25, p. 1.

Shroder, Mark. 2000. "Social Experiments in Housing." *Cityscape* 5(1): 237–59.

Skocpol, Theda. 1992. *Protecting Soldiers and Mothers: The Political Origins of Social Policy in the United States.* Cambridge, Mass.: Harvard University Press.

U.S. HUD. 1996. "An Historical and Baseline Assessment of Hope VI: Cross-Site Report." (August). HUD-1620-PDR. Washington, D.C.: Office of Policy Development and Research.

———. 2000. "Section 8 Tenant-Based Housing Assistance: A Look Back after 30 Years." March. Washington, D.C.: HUD.

U.S. National Advisory Commission on Civil Disorders (Kerner Commission): Report. 1968. New York: Dutton.

Vale, Lawrence. 2000. *From the Puritans to the Projects: Public Housing and Public Neighbors.* Cambridge: Harvard University.

Vernarelli, Michael. 1986. "Where Should HUD Locate Existing Housing: The Evolution of Fair Housing Policy." In *Housing Desegregation and Federal Policy,* edited by John Goering (214–34). Chapel Hill: University of North Carolina.

Weisberg, Jacob. 2000. "For the Sake of Argument." *The New York Times Magazine.* (November 5).

Winnick, Louis. 1995. "The Triumph of Housing Allowance Programs: How a Fundamental Policy Conflict was Resolved." *Cityscape* 1 (September): 95–121.

3

Locational Constraint, Housing Counseling, and Successful Lease-Up

Mark Shroder

Federal policy tools that could affect the concentration of poverty in metropolitan areas have been much advocated, seldom implemented, and never analyzed. This chapter estimates the impact of locational constraint and intensity of counseling services on low-income families' participation in federal housing voucher programs using data from the Moving to Opportunity experiment.

Today, tenant-based housing assistance helps more families than either public housing or project-based private housing assistance. By April 2001, the Department of Housing and Urban Development (HUD) had funded more than 1.8 million voucher units under contracts with public housing authorities (HUD 2001, L7).

Vouchers have grown in popularity for several reasons. They offer the assisted household locational choice. Typically, voucher programs cost substantially less than project-based alternatives (HUD Office of Policy Development and Research 2000b; Shroder and Reiger 2000). Vouchers allow continued assistance to tenants of projects where project-based subsidies are no longer tenable (e.g., because buildings are crime-ridden or impossible to rehabilitate at a reasonable cost, owners refuse to renew their subsidy agreements, or owners have allowed the building to deteriorate below minimum standards). Finally, vouchers do not artificially concentrate poverty. Voucher families generally reside in neighborhoods with lower concentrations of poverty than residents of public or private project-based assisted housing (HUD Office of Policy Development and Research 2000a; Khadduri, Shroder, and Steffen 1999; Newman and Schnare 1998).

But critics assert that voucher programs do not work in certain markets and for certain households (Dreier and Atlas 1995; Maney and Crowley 1999; U.S. Senate Subcommittee 2000). For a low-income family, having access to a voucher does not necessarily mean the family can use it. To benefit, the family must enter into a lease with a private owner in accordance with program rules. These rules prohibit subsidizing units in substandard condition or units with above-market rents, criteria determined by a local public housing authority. As a result, lease-up can involve a significant search effort. Some searches do not succeed. Raising lease-up rates would help the federal government better address the severe housing problems of low-income families.

Policymakers have been particularly interested in improving lease-up rates in low-poverty areas. Voucher tenants' success in these areas would reduce the risk of saturating high-poverty neighborhoods with voucher subsidies—a cycle that could simply recreate the deepening poverty observed in many housing projects.

A local voucher program's ability to deconcentrate poverty—rather than to simply relocate a sample of families with limited resources from one neighborhood to another—has become one measure of success. In 2000, HUD increased the Fair Market Rent schedule—which significantly influences a family's potential housing subsidy—in metropolitan areas where many voucher holders live in the same neighborhoods. The greater subsidy should provide these families wider neighborhood choice. Voucher programs have also received greater funding support for housing counseling in major metropolitan markets where voucher users tend to cluster in the same neighborhoods. When families living in the most distressed public and private project-based assistance participate in voucher programs, administrators devote funds to counseling to ensure families are fully informed about housing units available in the broader metropolitan area.

Despite some calls to restrict voucher moves, national deconcentration policy has operated through influence rather than prohibition. Policymakers have not adopted locational constraints that might, for example, restrict voucher holders' ability to move to high-poverty areas, nor have they allowed local agencies to institute them. Even if locational constraints were intended to raise the voucher family's long-run well-being, policymakers fear that such constraints could reduce lease-up by making the program less adaptable to the family's desires.

The local political motivation for locational constraint, moreover, might not be to advance the family's best interests. For example, a local voucher program might use the restrictions to keep families from moving into neighborhoods that perceive a threat from slum landlords and ill-behaving poor people. Again, such constraints might affect whether certain families lease units anywhere. To date, the federal government has not sanctioned such constraints, despite arguments from influential policy-makers (Jackson 1999).

Limited information about the larger metropolitan housing market and certain short-term barriers, such as lack of transportation to search for suitable units, likely contributes to the high concentration of the poor in central cities. Housing counseling programs informing voucher participants and helping them overcome short-term move barriers are one way to address this information gap.

The MTO demonstration featured both a locational constraint and a counseling component. These features allow us to test whether a locational constraint reduces the usability of vouchers and whether counseling can offset the constraint. Because families were randomly assigned to the different treatment groups, any correlation between membership in a treatment group and household characteristics, whether observed or unobserved, was also random and should not bias the correlation of treatment with outcome in a large sample. Moreover, the extensive data collection as families entered the MTO program allows us to control directly for many household characteristics.

A simple economic model captures much of the variation in participants' lease-up rates. Families that lease-up differ systematically from those that do not. In particular, they have many important differences in measures of aspiration and attitude.

Several substantive policy findings emerge. The MTO locational constraint, even with effective counseling, reduced the probability of lease-up by roughly 14 percentage points. The intensity of housing counseling markedly raised the lease-up rate, but not by enough to offset the effect of the locational constraint.

Previous Research

The lessons from studies of participation, or "take-up," in other means-tested programs, such as welfare, food stamps, and unemployment insurance, are not easy to apply to Section 8 lease-ups. As in these programs, a voucher applicant qualifies on the basis of need. He or she will face some opportunity cost in making the application and may incur some "stigma" cost (Moffitt 1983). The other benefit programs, however, do not contain a secondary step analogous to the voucher lease-up step. Before receiving the voucher, an approved recipient must find an acceptable unit owned by someone willing to accept the family and the subsidy.

Take-up in employment and training programs has a long, not very theoretical, but useful literature. For example, Burstein, Roberts, and Wood (1999) find that individuals with the fewest work limitations, best health, highest mental status, fewest transportation problems, and best attitude toward work are the most likely to participate in a return-to-work program for workers with disabilities, presumably because they anticipate the most benefit from a rehabilitation program and the least cost from attempting it.

The only significant quantitative study of voucher lease-up in the past decade was by Kennedy and Finkel (1994). Kennedy and Finkel found an overall success rate of 80 percent, much higher than MTO's rate of 54 percent. The differences between the data used in their study and this chapter are worth noting:

- Kennedy and Finkel looked at 33 large housing authorities constituting a representative sample of all metropolitan areas; this chapter looks at just the five large metropolitan areas served by MTO.
- A family in the earlier study could use its voucher to subsidize the rent in the unit occupied before program entry, as long as that unit met minimum housing standards; this option was not available in MTO.
- Baseline data were less rich in the Kennedy and Finkel study, especially in measures of attitude and aspiration.
- Unlike the voucher programs studied in Kennedy and Finkel, MTO limited eligibility to families with children.
- MTO families were all previously assisted in high-poverty housing projects, while the families in the earlier study had no previous assistance.
- The sample in the Kennedy and Finkel study was not subject to locational constraints on voucher use, and respondents received little housing counseling or search assistance.

Kennedy and Finkel's findings for 32 of their 33 housing authorities (New York was treated separately) are summarized in table 3.1.

Table 3.1. *Summary of Kennedy/Finkel Findings*
Success by moving of 1,050 households (the national sample, excluding New York City)

Variable	Effect
Minority	+ (weak)
Elderly	−
Disability	−
Working	− (weak)
Not a couple, no children	− (weak)
Doubled up in another's home	+
Homeless	+
Prefers to stay in current unit	−
Pre-program gross rent/maximum potential rent subsidy	+ (weak)
Income less than $100/month	+
Number of bedrooms required under occupancy rules (This effect was captured in several variables, with all signs significantly negative.)	−
FMR/income	+
Access to car	+
Want better housing (as opposed to lower rent)	+

Source: Kennedy and Finkel (1994), D27.

In general, the probability findings are intuitive. Factors that would raise the net benefit of the subsidy tend to raise the lease-up probability, while factors that can make search more difficult tend to lower it. Only one finding requires much elaboration. Research in the 1980s showed that the effect of minority status on lease-up depends on metropolitan area. Representatives of the majority group in the local Section 8 submarket lease-up more often than minorities in that submarket. For example, a Hispanic household is more likely to succeed in San Antonio, where Hispanic voucher tenants outnumber non-Hispanics, than in Detroit, where they do not. Similarly, a black household is more likely to succeed in Birmingham than in Seattle. Therefore, the national average minority effect is not very meaningful.

According to Kennedy and Finkel's results, search intensity matters: 18 percent of families who failed to lease-up never actually visited a unit other than the one they lived in. The average number of units visited by families who leased a new unit was 9; the average number visited by those who failed to lease but saw at least one other unit was 12.

A Simple Economic Model of Lease-Up

A family that moves from its former dwelling must first search for another place to stay. The analysis assumes that failure to lease-up means that the family stopped searching, because even a family with a very low probability of landlord acceptance would find some unit at which it would be accepted with probability approaching one if it applied for a number of units approaching infinity; the housing markets in the five metropolitan areas, although not infinite, are very large. Infinite search, however, would be irrational. Search is a forward-looking act, and the model assumes that engagement in search depends on a calculation that the expected net benefits exceed the costs.

Let V_o be the value of living in the current dwelling, and let V_A be the expected (pre-inspection) value of living in the next unit that the head of household will examine. The net benefit of change of abode is $V_A - V_o$, which may be thought of either as a dollar value or a subjective quantity. The probability that the household would actually be able to occupy the next unit that the head will examine, if the head chose to apply for it, is P. The expected net benefit of search is then $P^*(V_A - V_o)$. Against that quantity the household head must consider the cost of looking for, examining, and applying for one more unit, C, which costs may be out-of-pocket, psychic, or both, but in any case are measured in the same units as the net benefit. The head will search (continue searching) only if

$$(1) \qquad P^*(V_A - V_o) - C > O.$$

A more complex economic model would incorporate the effects of learning, which could change the subjective probability of acceptance, the net benefit of moving, and the costs of search. Similarly, a more complex model would consider whether a family stopped searching once it found a minimally acceptable new unit or continued searching in an effort to find a better one. This higher level of complexity would not be supported by the data available, nor is it required by this particular research.

This model, using logit analysis, incorporates variables related to the probability of acceptance, the net benefit of moving, and the cost of search. Implementation of the model depends on the success of survey research in eliciting attitudinal information that has behavioral content. The research team collected an unusually rich set of variables at baseline to allow subsequent analysis to control for nonexperimental sources of variation in outcomes. Many such variables involve expectations, attitude, and aspiration on the part of the household. Table 3.2 summarizes the variables proposed and the hypothesized direction of effect on lease-up.

Indicators of the Probability of Being Able to Occupy the New Unit

The concern here is whether the owner of the unit is likely to agree to lease to the family holding a housing voucher. The following factors could be expected to affect the owner's decisionmaking process:

- *Metropolitan area vacancy rate.* The overall tightness of the rental housing market, might affect a low-income family's ability to rent easily.
- *Size of household.* The stock available for rent to large families is small, and the market that serves them is disproportionately tight.
- *Composition of household.* Owners do not want troublesome tenants. Unfortunately, teens and young adults are more likely to cause trouble.
- *Ethnicity.* Past research indicates lower probability of successful lease-up among groups that are not in the racial/ethnic majority of the local Section 8 population. Householders belonging to the dominant local voucher population will find owners more accepting than will nonmembers. The implication for MTO is that Hispanics in the demonstration will have a lower probability than blacks of being accepted by landlords.
- *Elicited confidence in finding a unit.* People who say they are "very sure" that they can find an acceptable unit should have a higher subjective probability of acceptance than those who do not.

Indicators of the Net Benefit of Changing Unit

The families in MTO differed from one another in the benefit they could expect from moving.

- *Ties to current neighborhood.* If the head has many friends near his or her current apartment, or goes to church nearby, moving will mean a greater loss than otherwise.
- *Discomfort with whites.* The participants in MTO are nearly all black and Hispanic, living in heavily minority neighborhoods. Those who

Table 3.2. *Variable Definitions and Descriptive Statistics*

	Predicted effect	Mean	Std. dev.	Min.	Max.	Comment
Outcome: Leased-Up		0.54	0.5	0	1	
Probability indicators						
Metro area vacancy rate	+	6.75	1.57	4	9.7	From Census Bureau; calendar year of random assignment
Size of household	−	3.67	1.47	1	11	
Number of school-age children	+	1.62	1.24	0	7	
Number of preschool children	+	0.88	0.93	0	6	
Hispanic head	−	0.27	0.44	0	1	Missing coded as 0
Uncertainty about finding an apartment (1 = very sure, 5 = very unsure)	−	1.94	1.05	1	5	Missing coded as 3
Net benefit indicators						
Uncertainty about liking a new neighborhood (same scale as above)	−	1.8	1.01	1	5	Missing coded as 3
Usual church is within 15 minutes of origin project	−	0.3	0.46	0	1	Missing coded as 0
Has many friends in neighborhood	−	0.11	0.32	0	1	Missing coded as 0
Comfort with children in nearly all-white school (−1 = bad, very bad; 0 = good, not sure; 1 = very good)	+	0.063	0.47	−1	1	Missing coded as 0
Housing condition (1 = excellent or good, 2 = fair, 3 = poor)	+	1.99	0.73	1	3	Missing coded as 2

	Predicted sign	Mean	SD	Min	Max	Notes
Dissatisfaction with neighborhood (2 = very dissat., 1 = dissat., 0 = other answer)	+	1.18	0.86	0	2	Missing coded as 0
Feel very good about moving	+	0.82	0.38	0	1	
Preferred distance from origin (0 = same neighborhood, 1 = same city, 2 = area suburbs, 3 = out of metro area)	+	1.52	0.88	0	3	
Head attended school last week	+	0.0991	0.3	0	1	Missing coded as 0
Previously applied (Boston only)	+	0.11	0.31	0	1	
Cost indicators						
Hourly wage	−	1.83	3.46	0	30	Top-coded; missing set at 0
Weekly hours of work	−	7.82	14.55	0	60	Top-coded; missing set at 0
SSI/SSDI/SS Survivor benefits	−	0.21	0.41	0	1	Missing set at 0
Car or license (0 = no car or license, 1 = license only, 2 = owns car that runs)	+	0.53	0.77	0	2	Missing set at 0
Years in metro area	+	23.89	11.73	0	76	
MTO treatment group	−	.571	.495	0	1	
Intensity of counseling services	+	17.08	16.57	0	41	Set at 0 for all comp group members
Statistical controls						
Baltimore		.144		0	1	
Boston		.207		0	1	
Chicago		.214		0	1	
Los Angeles		.192		0	1	
N		3,048	(1,740 MTO, 1,308 control)			

Source: MTO database, author's tabulations.

are uncomfortable with sending their children to largely white schools would gain less benefit from moving, at least in the experimental treatment, where many of the eligible neighborhoods are largely white.

- *Satisfaction with current unit and current neighborhood.* Those who are more satisfied with their current housing and current neighborhood will have less reason to move.
- *Comfort with change.* Those who are confident that they will enjoy living somewhere they have never lived before will see more value in moving, as will those who "feel good" about the idea of moving.
- *Preferred location.* Those who would prefer to live elsewhere in the city, out in the suburbs, or out of the metropolitan area altogether will have more reason to move than those who want to stay in the same neighborhood.
- *In school.* People get an education to change their lives, so a participant in the demonstration who is currently going to school should be more ready for other life changes than one who is not.
- *Previously applied for Section 8 (in Boston).* Even a person who expected to benefit from moving with assistance might not have applied for a voucher before the demonstration, because waiting lists in large central cities are usually either closed most of the year or quite long. Applying for subsidy in four of the sites was something of an exercise in futility, with Boston being the exception. Each of the 64 housing authorities in the Boston area maintains its own waiting list. Because waiting lists are more accessible, a previous application at the Boston site should be a reliable indicator that the participant thought that moving would have net benefits.

The difference in rents between the prospective and current unit is *not* an element of this model. Participants in the demonstration could expect to pay 30 percent of adjusted income whether they moved or stayed, except that families with vouchers choosing to lease units that cost more than the local payment standard can make up the difference out of their own pockets. Thus, the option to pay more for preferred housing is inherent in the search decision.

Indicators of the Cost of Search

In addition to out-of-pocket search costs, the value of time spent searching for units, the physical strain of looking for a unit, and the emotional drain of looking for a unit or having an application turned down differed among participants.

- *Hourly wage.* Economic theory holds that those who have higher wages have higher hourly costs for all nonwork activities, including housing search.
- *Hours of work per week.* The head of household has a time constraint and work cuts into the time available for search.
- *Receipt of disability income.* If the household receives Supplemental Security Income, Social Security Disability Income, or survivors benefits, the head or some other member is more likely to have a disability, making search more difficult.
- *Possession of car or license.* Ownership of a car that runs should reduce the costs of search. Failing that, holding a valid driver's license should also reduce search costs if the head can occasionally borrow somebody else's car.
- *Years in the metro area.* The longer the head has lived in the metropolitan area, the easier the search process should be.
- *Experimental treatment.* Participants assigned to the MTO treatment could only use the assistance in low-poverty neighborhoods, which were both physically and socially distant from their point of origin.
- *Intensity of counseling services.* Feins, McInnis, and Popkin (1997) rated the service intensity of the nonprofit organizations on a 45-point scale that recognized the range of content, the resource commitment, and the degree of staff intervention on behalf of clients. Program character varied by site, because of differences in market conditions, external funding, and the philosophies of the nonprofits. More intense housing services might include preparing clients to practice presenting themselves to owners and managers, helping with housing information sources, helping with neighborhood selection, helping with budgeting for rent and utilities, showing potential neighborhoods and units to clients, finding possible units for clients, and contacting landlords or managers for clients. More intense social services might include vocational training and education referral, help with child care, parenting and budget counseling, advocacy with the welfare system, free furniture, help with utility hookups, security deposits, or movers. More intense follow-up services involved adjustment to the new neighborhood, such as transportation and child care issues, landlord-tenant relations, problems with the new school

system, the new welfare office, or the housing subsidy payment. These ratings varied from 9 (Leadership Council, Chicago) to 41 (Beyond Shelter and On Your Feet, Los Angeles). Higher intensity of services should have reduced the cost of search.

Data and Results

This chapter analyzes the outcomes for 3,048 families for whom lease-up was an option: the 1,740 eligible participants in the experimental MTO group or the 1,308 eligible participants in the Section 8 comparison group for whom sufficient data were available.

Our model leads us to expect that a locational constraint on voucher use would reduce the lease-up rate, but that counseling services would raise that rate. The experimental intervention itself combines the locational restriction and the availability of counseling services. The net effect is an empirical question. We begin by presenting the rate of lease-up in the MTO and Section 8 comparison groups by site, using both unadjusted and cohort-adjusted means from the experiment.

Table 3.3 gives two tests of the proposition that the lease-up rates differ for experimental and control groups, by site. In the upper panel, the raw average lease-up rate is the outcome variable. In Baltimore, Chicago, and Los Angeles, the intervention significantly reduced the lease-up rate. In Boston and New York, the effect on lease-up was insignificant.

The difficulty with using the raw outcome for this purpose is that the investigators changed the intake probabilities into the assignment groups over time: twice in Baltimore; thrice in Boston, Chicago, and Los Angeles; and four times in New York. Cohort membership might nonrandomly influence the outcome for two general reasons: the housing market might have changed and the origin project might be different. Market effects would be felt by both groups; the raw data seem to show a falling lease-up rate for both groups in Baltimore and Boston, and a rising rate for both groups in New York. Origin project is important because outreach for the experiment was conducted sequentially to targeted projects and cohort membership is therefore associated with project residency. The particular project in which the family lives, in turn, might be associated with household characteristics.

Accordingly, the lower panel of table 3.3 presents the same test on the mean of the cohort-weighted outcome. Let P_s be the fraction of the com-

Table 3.3. *Effects of the Intervention on Lease-Up*

Raw Outcome

	Baltimore	Boston	Chicago	Los Angeles	New York
MTO mean lease-up rate (N)	0.58 (250)	0.46 (363)	0.34 (452)	0.64 (307)	0.48 (368)
Comparison group mean lease-up rate (N)	0.72 (188)	0.48 (269)	0.67 (199)	0.76 (278)	0.50 (374)
t-statistic	−3.04	−0.51	−7.97	−3.12	−0.52
p-value	0.003	0.61	0.000	0.002	0.60

Note: Small differences between the first two rows and the equivalent tables in Goering et al. (1999, 14–17) reflect the deletion of observations with many missing explanatory variables, for consistency with the logit results presented in table 3.4.

Cohort-Weighted Outcome

	Baltimore	Boston	Chicago	Los Angeles	New York
MTO mean lease-up rate	.54	.44	.35	.64	.49
Comparison group mean lease-up rate	.77	.51	.67	.78	.48
t-statistic	−4.10	−1.52	−7.57	−3.23	0.15
p-value	.000	.13	.000	.001	.88

Source: MTO database, author's computation.

bined sample at a site (both experimentals and controls) that are cohort members—that is, they were all randomly assigned during the period when a particular assignment ratio was in place. Let P_i be the fraction of the treatment group at the site who are cohort members. The cohort-weighted outcome is the product of the raw outcome (lease-up = 1, not leased = 0) and P_S/P_i.

We again find that the experimental treatment significantly reduced lease-up in Baltimore, Chicago, and Los Angeles, but not in New York. In Boston, we now see a reduction in lease-up that is of marginal significance.

In the absence of statistical evidence, we might suspect that the inner-city housing market contributes significantly to these impacts. Baltimore, Chicago, and Los Angeles all had loose inner-city rental markets during the period of the demonstration, while those in Boston and New York were relatively tight. However, household characteristics and the character of the counseling effort may also differ across sites. We can directly examine the effects of market conditions, counseling effort, and household characteristics and attitudes using multivariate logit.

Table 3.4 presents the results of that analysis in two initial panels: (1) families assigned to the MTO experimental treatment and (2) families assigned to the standard Section 8 comparison group.

Model performance is reasonably good. In the experimental group, where 48 percent leased-up, the logit correctly predicts 65 percent of outcomes. In the Section 8 comparison group, 61 percent leased-up, and the logit correctly predicts 70 percent of outcomes.

Probability of acceptance indicators all have the expected signs. Metro area vacancy rate and size of household are highly significant in both groups. Hispanic headship significantly reduces the success rate in the treatment group. The head's own subjective probability of successful search is significantly predictive of success in the control group. Holding size of household constant, replacing an adult family member with a preschool child would significantly raise the probability of lease-up in the control group.

Net benefit indicators also perform predictably. The level of dissatisfaction with the origin neighborhood is strongly associated with lease-up in both groups, as is having had a previous application in Boston. Ties to church and friends strongly discourage lease-up by the controls. The level of comfort with having one's children in a nearly all-white school was a better predictor of success among experimental families (who would have faced the issue more often) than among the controls.

A significant difference between the groups is the effect of the preferred distance from the origin neighborhood. Lease-up under MTO required a move out of the neighborhood, while lease-up in the comparison group did not; thus, treatment group members who preferred to live in the suburbs or beyond had an advantage, while similarly ambitious members of the comparison group were disadvantaged in lease-up.

Heads who were uncertain that they would like living in a completely new area were notably less successful in the MTO group. Dissatisfaction with housing condition was significantly associated with successful lease-up in the control group. Directly elicited assessment of subjective benefit to moving (feeling "very good" about it) is also associated with lease-up in the control group. Contemporaneous enrollment in adult

Table 3.4. *Logistic Regression: Dependent Variable = 1 If Family Leases-Up*

	Experimental group		Section 8 group	
	Coefficient	Std error	Coefficient	Std error
Probability of acceptance indicators				
Metro area vacancy rate	0.247***	0.073	0.533***	0.103
Size of household	−0.258***	0.082	−0.245***	0.091
Number of school-age children	0.108	0.081	0.148	0.101
Number of preschool children	0.084	0.095	0.423***	0.109
Hispanic head	−0.387***	0.143	−0.214	0.160
Uncertainty about finding an apartment	−0.056	0.058	−0.153**	0.071
Net benefit indicators				
Uncertainty about liking a new neighborhood	−0.194***	0.062	−0.121	0.077
Belongs to a church within 15 minutes of origin project	−0.045	0.117	−0.438***	0.136
Has many friends in neighborhood	−0.066	0.162	−0.405**	0.203
Comfort with children in nearly all-white school	0.243**	0.113	0.120	0.137
Housing condition	0.091	0.074	0.209**	0.092
Dissatisfaction with neighborhood	0.176***	0.066	0.184**	0.080
Feel very good about moving	0.140	0.145	0.465***	0.175
Preferred distance from origin	0.181***	0.061	−0.153**	0.074
Head attended school last week	0.407**	0.180	0.219	0.221
Previously applied (Boston only)	0.657***	0.224	0.607**	0.273
Cost indicators				
Hourly wage	0.013	0.026	−0.015	0.028
Weekly hours of work	−0.008	0.006	0.001	0.007
SSI/SSDI/SS Survivor benefits	−0.322**	0.132	−0.304*	0.160
Car or license	0.161**	0.075	0.082	0.091
Years in metro area	−0.011**	0.005	−0.013**	0.006
Intensity of counseling services	0.030**	0.012		
Controls				
Baltimore	−0.504*	0.265	−0.282	0.301
Boston	−0.162	0.236	−0.227	0.245
Chicago	−0.818**	0.350	−0.749**	0.357
Los Angeles	−0.429	0.296	0.040	0.316
Constant	−1.629**	0.646	−2.268***	0.675
N	1,740		1,340	
Reference group	New York MTO		New York comp	

Source: MTO database, author's computation.

* = Significant at $p < 0.10$; ** = significant at $p < 0.05$; *** = significant at $p < 0.01$.

education is significantly associated with lease-up in the treatment group.

The *cost* indicators have more mixed results. Receipt of disability benefits and possession of a car, or at least a license, both have the expected signs and are significant in one or both groups. The intensity of counseling services is strongly associated with lease-up in the MTO group. Wage and hours per week, however, are completely insignificant. Number of years in the metro area is highly significant, but with the wrong sign. This result suggests that a more complex "psychological" model than the one estimated here may be in order.

Table 3.5 compares the impact of the locational constraint, the intensity of counseling services, and the influence of unmeasured site-specific factors on success for the two groups. As shown in table 3.4, the model has reasonable predictive power. Of the 3,048 participants, 53.8 percent leased-up under the demonstration, while the model correctly predicts the outcome in 64.7 percent of outcomes.

In general, locational constraint overwhelms counseling intensity. The coefficient on intensity of counseling services indicates that counseling would have to be raised 52 points above the mean to neutralize the effects of assignment to the treatment group. The intensity variable has a maximum theoretical value of 45 points.

Simulation using the coefficients in table 3.5 indicates that a household with mean characteristics would have had a 62.3 percent probability of leasing-up in the control regime, with counseling services set at zero, but a 48.8 percent probability in the experimental regime, with counseling intensity set at 29.9, the experimental mean.

It does not follow that counseling intensity has little value. Suppose a family with mean characteristics was assigned to the experimental treatment. The same simulation predicts that if the treatment came with a service intensity one standard deviation above the mean, the family would have a 54.9 percent lease-up probability; with service intensity one standard deviation below the mean, the probability declines to 42.7 percent. The simulated probability of lease-up for a control family with mean characteristics but no counseling is 62.3 percent; the coefficient in table 3.5 implies that with counseling intensity equal to the treatment group mean this probability would rise to 77.8 percent. While this latter application is speculative, the evidence from this analysis is not that the counseling was ineffective but that the locational constraint was more powerful.

Table 3.5. *Logistic Regression: Dependent Variable = 1 If Family Leases-Up*

	Combined sample	
	Coefficient	Std error
Probability of acceptance indicators		
Metro area vacancy rate	.305***	.057
Size of household	−.250***	.060
Number of school-age children	.127ⁿ	.067
Number of preschool children	.228***	.070
Hispanic head	−.270***	−.105
Uncertainty about finding an apartment	−.082*	.044
Net benefit indicators		
Uncertainty about liking a new neighborhood	−.167***	.047
Belongs to a church within 15 minutes of origin project	−.227***	.087
Has many friends in neighborhood	−.201	.124
Comfort with children in nearly all-white school	.189**	.086
Housing condition	.121**	.056
Dissatisfaction with neighborhood	.176***	.050
Feel very good about moving	.268**	.110
Preferred distance from origin	.042	.364
Head attended school last week	.346**	.137
Previously applied (Boston only)	.606***	.171
Cost indicators		
Hourly wage	.006	.019
Weekly hours of work	−.004	.004
SSI/SSDI/SS Survivor benefits	−.283***	.100
Car or license	.135**	.057
Years in metro area	−.011***	.004
Assigned to MTO	−1.302***	.251
Intensity of counseling services	.025***	.008
Controls		
Baltimore	−.260	.193
Boston	−.178	.161
Chicago	−.707***	.228
Los Angeles	−.069	.206
Constant	−.756*	.052
N	3,048	
Reference group	New York comp	

Source: MTO database, author's computation.

* = Significant at $p < 0.10$; ** = significant at $p < 0.05$; *** = significant at $p < 0.01$.

Unmeasured site-specific influences exhibit a statistically significant relationship with lease-up in table 3.5 at just one site, Chicago. HUD publicly questioned the overall management capacity of the voucher program in Chicago and obliged the public housing authority to contract out its administration in December 1995, at which point 208 of the 651 Chicago families in the demonstration had already been randomly assigned. Participants entering the demonstration before December 1995 had an overall lease-up rate of 40 percent; those entering from that date forward leased up at a 46 percent rate. The contractor asserts that it has had to overcome the persistent belief among landlords that the program would not pay subsidies on time, an alleged failing of the prior regime.

More broadly, Chicago high-rise public housing projects have one of the worst reputations for violent crime in the United States (Kotlowitz 1991; Lemann 1991). This reputation might have affected landlords' willingness to enter into leases with families coming from those projects to a greater extent than in other sites.

Discussion of Findings

Vouchers have become the leading form of housing subsidy, but the allocation of assistance accomplishes nothing for families that do not use them. For various reasons, policymakers have considered constraining the locations in which vouchers might be used. But they have hesitated to implement such constraints, partly out of concern for the effect on lease-up. They have funded counseling efforts to improve lease-up, especially outside of low-income neighborhoods, but no rigorous evidence on their effectiveness is available.

The MTO experiment provides ample data to analyze the reasons for eligible families' failure to lease-up. A simple economic model of search appears to capture a substantial fraction of the variation in lease-up rates among families enrolled in the demonstration. Two factors—the likelihood of owner acceptance and the net benefit of the move—appear particularly important in determining lease-up. Some indicators of search cost also predict voucher moves.

These findings have significant policy implications. First, locational constraints significantly reduce lease-up. According to the simulation analysis, lease-up for the average MTO experimental household was 14 percentage points lower than for the Section 8 comparison household, even with intense housing counseling services. Thus, any policy decision to constrain vouchers will likely lower the take-up rate, whether the decision is to keep voucher holders out of poor neighborhoods (to protect the children from bad influences), out of working-class neighborhoods (to protect the neighborhood from tipping into poverty), or out of middle-class neighborhoods (to protect the residents from exposure to the risks associated with or perceived from poor families). Even where the motivation is to enhance the welfare of the assisted family, policymakers should be cautious about raising additional participation hurdles for very low-income families. The promising early results of the MTO demonstration have come at some cost to nonmover families that, if given the chance, would likely have leased-up in higher-poverty neighborhoods.

Much of the "failure" to lease-up reflects lack of search motivation. For some households, locational constraints will further reduce this motivation. We can apply this lesson outside of the voucher program.

Project-based assistance is the extreme locational constraint—assistance can be used for one unit only. Thus, if the assisted projects are not very widely distributed across neighborhoods (which they seldom are), project-based assistance will have a high (unmeasured) failure rate. When project-based subsidies are concentrated in a few areas, many poor families will not apply for help. In rural areas and some urban sites, standard-quality subsidized housing may remain empty, while one family after another on the local waiting list refuses to occupy the units. The absence of the white non-Hispanic poor in big-city housing projects targeted by MTO is an eloquent silence.

The second most important policy finding is that the intensity of housing counseling services matters. Housing counseling in the demonstration was not cheap—costs averaged \$3,077 per lease-up (Goering et al. 1999). But the analysis suggests that a slight rise in service intensity (from one standard deviation below the mean to one standard deviation above it) would raise the lease-up rate 12 percentage points in the experimental group.

Third, the positive effects of having either an automobile and/or a license and the negative effects of having a disability (incorporated in the model using a proxy) suggest that more targeted counseling services could boost lease-up rates. At a relatively low cost, counseling services could transport potential voucher holders to look for housing, and they could make special arrangements for persons with disabilities. The strong tie between being in school and higher lease-up rates suggests that targeted voucher distribution may also improve success rates. For example, public housing agencies could give families headed by an adult enrolled in an educational program priority.

Finally, Chicago's lower rate deserves comment. A typical Chicago participant was significantly less likely to lease-up than his or her counterpart in New York, despite that city's famously tight housing market. Two factors could explain the "Chicago effect." First, lack of administrative capacity in the Chicago voucher program, since resolved by contracting out certain tasks, could have hurt participation. Second, the violent reputation of Chicago public housing neighborhoods may have made some landlords unwilling to accept vouchers, though demolition and relocation may be improving that reputation. Both administrative problems and public housing violence festered for years, as the federal government deferred to local pressures.

Two fruitful directions for further research should be noted. First, the model employed is fairly simple. Economists who wished to go beyond the findings here could incorporate feedback and learning, landlord acceptance functions, and public housing authority review processes.

Models measuring psychological factors, such as satisfaction, uncertainty, and discomfort, could also complement this research. Such measures often have more predictive power at the individual level than such standard economic indicators as the hourly wage. While not typically collected in surveys, individual preference data might hold additional clues to lease-up success. For example, the counterintuitive effect of "years in the metro area"—which would seem likely to raise the lease-up rate (by reducing the cost of search) but appears to do the opposite—might mean that some mechanism outside the ordinary boundaries of economics plays a role in moving decisions. Katz, Kling, and Liebman (2001) report a counterintuitive (to economists) gender asymmetry in Boston: "Behavior problems among boys are positively related to take-up, problems among girls are negatively related to take-up."

Second, researchers could further explore implications for broader samples of families. Lease-up relates to the expected benefit of search. All else equal, the families that expected the greatest benefit from moving were the most likely to move. It is reasonable to assume that families expecting no net benefit did not apply for the demonstration vouchers. Accordingly, the demonstration's impact on ultimate outcomes (e.g., education, employment, earnings, arrests, health, and economic dependency) applies to a narrower population than all eligible families. Indeed, the demonstration will ultimately result in measures of the benefit of better neighborhoods to the subgroup of low-income families that think they will be better off. Thus, the impact will be concentrated not only among families that think they will benefit, but also among families that find landlords who consider them acceptable risks.

NOTES

The author gratefully acknowledges the receipt of data from Todd Richardson and Judith Feins and the comments of Todd Richardson, Larry Orr, Steven Kennedy, John Goering, Jeff Kling, Jeff Lubell, and two anonymous referees.

REFERENCES

Burstein, Nancy R., Cheryl A. Roberts, and Michelle L. Wood. 1999. "Recruiting SSA's Disability Beneficiaries for Return-to-Work: Results of the Project NetWork Demonstration: Final Report." http://www.ssa.gov/policy/policyareas/evaluation/project_network/ABTpartrelp.pdf. (Accessed September 26, 2002.)

Dreier, Peter, and John Atlas. 1995. "Housing Policy's Moment of Truth." *The American Prospect* 6(22).

Feins, Judith D., Debra McInnis, and Susan J. Popkin. 1997. "Counseling in the Moving to Opportunity Demonstration Program." http://www.wws.princeton.edu:80/~kling/mto/quick.html. (Accessed September 26, 2002.)

Goering, John, Joan Kraft, Judith Feins, Debra McInnis, Mary Joel Holin, and Huda Elhassan. 1999. "Moving to Opportunity for Fair Housing Demonstration Program: Current Status and Initial Findings." Washington, D.C.: U.S. Department of Housing and Urban Development, Office of Policy Development and Research.

HUD. See U.S. Department of Housing and Urban Development.

Jackson, Jesse L. Jr. 1999. "South Suburbs Suffer Section 8 Saturation." *Chicago Sun-Times,* December 26.

Katz, Lawrence F., Jeffrey R. Kling, and Jeffrey B. Liebman. 2001. "Moving to Opportunity in Boston: Early Results of a Randomized Mobility Experiment." *Quarterly Journal of Economics* 116(2): 607–54.

Kennedy, Stephen D., and Meryl Finkel. 1994. "Section 8 Rental Voucher and Rental Certificate Utilization Study: Final Report." Washington, D.C.: HUD Office of Policy Development and Research.

Khadduri, Jill, Mark Shroder, and Barry Steffen. 1999. "Can Housing Assistance Support Welfare Reform?" Paper presented to the fall research conference of the Association for Public Policy Analysis and Management, Washington. D.C., Nov. 4–6.

Kotlowitz, Alex. 1991. *There Are No Children Here: The Story of Two Boys Growing Up in the Other America.* New York: Doubleday.

Lemann, Nicholas. 1991. *The Promised Land: The Great Black Migration and How It Changed America.* New York: Alfred A. Knopf.

Maney, Brian, and Sheila Crowley. 1999. "Scarcity and Success: Perspectives on Assisted Housing." Washington, D.C.: National Low Income Housing Coalition.

Moffitt, Robert. 1983. "An Economic Model of Welfare Stigma." *American Economic Review* 73(5): 1023–35.

Newman, Sandra J., and Ann B. Schnare. 1998. ". . . And a Suitable Living Environment: The Failure of Housing Programs to Deliver on Neighborhood Quality." *Housing Policy Debate* 8(4): 703–41.

Shroder, Mark, and Arthur Reiger. 2000. "Vouchers versus Production Revisited." *Journal of Housing Research* 11(1): 91–107.

U.S. Department of Housing and Urban Development. 2001. "Congressional Justifications for 2002 Estimates." Part 1. Washington, D.C.: HUD.

U.S. Department of Housing and Urban Development, Office of Policy Development and Research. 2000a. "Economic Cost Analysis of Different Forms of Assisted Housing." Issue Brief No. 2. Washington, D.C.: HUD.

———. 2000b. "Voucher Recipients Enjoy Much Greater Choice about Where to Live Than Residents of Public Housing and Are Less Likely to be Concentrated in Distressed Neighborhoods." Issue Brief No. 1. Washington, D.C.: HUD.

U.S. Senate Subcommittee on VA, HUD, and Independent Agencies of the Committee on Appropriations. 2000. "Empty Promises: Subcommittee Staff report on HUD's Failing Grade on the Utilization of Section 8 Vouchers." Washington, D.C.: U.S. Government Printing Office.

4

A Cross-Site Analysis of MTO's Locational Impacts

Judith D. Feins

This chapter examines where participating families lived in 1997, one to three years after they joined the Moving to Opportunity program, and whether the locations among the three randomly assigned groups differed significantly. The results draw on the follow-up survey of participating families conducted between August and December 1997. The sample for the survey—known as the 1997 Moving to Opportunity canvass—comprised families who joined the program in any of the five sites through the end of 1996. Overall, the canvass effort reached 94 percent of the 2,883 families that enrolled during that time and almost 65 percent of the 4,608 families participating in the Moving to Opportunity program overall.[1] (See appendix A for additional tabulations, including updated findings using data from a second canvass conducted in 2000.) The analysis finds that, one to three years after program entry, families assigned to the MTO experimental and Section 8 comparison groups (the two groups whose members were able to move with Section 8 subsidies through this program) live in less-poor and less-segregated neighborhoods than the in-place control group. These effects are substantial for movers, and they are significantly greater for the experimental than for the comparison group. Thus, the combination of geographical restrictions and counseling for the experimental group had a clear treatment effect, beyond the effects of receiving a Section 8 subsidy. Enduring locational differences between the groups are important, because the hypothesized benefits of moving to better neighborhoods may well depend on staying in such neighborhoods for a sustained period. Future research will examine that question.

Data Sources

Early research on the MTO demonstration primarily used data from the enrollment period, when families entered the demonstration, received their random assignment, received a Section 8 certificate or voucher (unless assigned to the control group), and succeeded or failed to move to private-market housing. Some researchers conducted local (single site) updates on families' locations and conditions. But until the 1997 canvass, no one collected systematic follow-up data across all sites. For many families that joined MTO between 1994 and 1996, the survey was the first direct contact about the program since their initial moves.[2]

The analysis also draws on applicant data collected at program entry, particularly the extensive Participant Baseline Survey. That survey, administered before random assignment, contains information on various topics, including why families joined MTO, their expectations about moving, individuals' views of current living conditions, and how they see their current ties to neighbors. The baseline also provides a snapshot of family composition and socioeconomic factors. A standard HUD form completed for Section 8 eligibility processing provided additional preassignment data.

Families in the MTO experimental and Section 8 comparison groups were tracked through their housing searches, using information on family milestones recorded by the local public housing authorities and nonprofit counseling organizations. These milestone logs also provided data for the families that did not move and the families in the control group.

Description of the Sample

The research sample consists of 2,601 families that completed 1997 canvasses and have useable beginning and current addresses. The sample represents just over 90 percent of the families enrolled in MTO through the end of 1996 and is distributed fairly evenly across sites and across the assignment groups.[3]

Like the MTO program population as a whole, the racial composition of the sample is largely African American, particularly at the Baltimore and Chicago sites (table 4.1). The other three sites enrolled substantial numbers of Hispanic families (appendix table 4.A1). Only the Boston program enrolled a significant number of non-Hispanic white families.[4] Women head most MTO households. In Los Angeles, however, a small portion of households are two-parent families headed by males. For all participating families, the median number of children is two to three.

The MTO program families have average incomes of about $9,000. Half to three-quarters depend on welfare as their primary income source. Most heads of household (two-thirds to three-quarters) are not employed. And one-third to one-half the household heads are not high school graduates, although some surveyed participants were attending school.

Data on participating families' background conditions and experiences offer insights on why they joined the housing mobility program (table 4.2). At every site, at least three-quarters of respondents said getting away from drugs and gangs was the first or second most important reason for wanting to move. A high proportion of families also expressed dissatisfaction with their public housing neighborhoods. Respondents reported high rates of victimization on a range of crimes.[5]

Not all families selected to participate were able to move through the program, known in program terms as "leasing-up" (figure 4.1).[6] Just under half the families assigned to the MTO experimental group moved under the program. Around two-thirds of the families assigned to the Section 8 comparison group participated. Thus, this chapter reports results for a sample of 905 program movers out of a population of 2,601 families. Lease-up rates for the sample, which contained early demonstration cohorts, differ slightly from the lease-up rates for the MTO sample overall. For the program, lease-up rates were 47 percent for the MTO experimental group and 60 percent for families assigned to the Section 8 comparison group.[7]

Where Were Families Living in 1997?

Preprogram Locations

The MTO demonstration recruited families from public or assisted housing in the poorest census tracts of five central cities—Baltimore,

Table 4.1. *Demographic and Socioeconomic Characteristics of MTO Families by Random Assignment Group* (percent distributions—weighted data)

	Experimental group	Section 8 group	Control group	All groups
Race of head of household (%)				
African-American	68.5	67.1	68.6	68.3
White	6.9	8.8	7.5	7.6
American Indian	0.7	0.3	1.0	0.7
Asian/Pacific Islander	2.1	2.6	1.4	2.0
Other	21.8	21.1	21.5	21.4
Ethnicity of head of household (%)				
Hispanic	30.6	31.7	31.3	31.1
Non-Hispanic	69.4	68.3	68.7	68.9
Sex of head of household (%)				
Male	8.1	9.1	8.4	8.4
Female	91.9	90.9	91.6	91.6
Marital status of head of household (%)				
Never married	60.7	62.8	63.3	62.1
Married	11.1	11.5	9.7	10.7
Widowed	10.3	9.0	10.4	10.0
Divorced	17.9	16.7	16.6	17.2
Median number of children	2	2	2	2
Average total household income	$9,082	$9,097	$9,069	$9,082
Percent with AFDC as primary income source	59.6	60.9	62.4	60.8
Head of household currently in school? (%)				
Yes	13.3	17.3	14.7	14.8
No	86.7	82.7	85.3	85.2

Table 4.1. *Continued*

	Experimental group	Section 8 group	Control group	All groups
Head of household a graduate? (%)				
High school	44.3	42.6	39.1	42.2
GED	16.5	19.7	20.8	18.7
Neither	39.2	37.7	40.0	39.1
Head of household currently working? (%)				
Full-time	16.5	17.0	16.1	16.5
Part-time	10.7	9.7	9.7	10.1
Not working	72.8	73.4	74.2	73.4
Number of cases	1,086	664	851	2,601
Missing cases	18–150	7–65	9–94	34–309

Source: MTO participant baseline survey.

Notes: Percentages may not add to 100 because of rounding. Data are weighted to minimize overall variance while adjusting for differences in random assignment ratios between groups and over time. The head of household is the respondent to the baseline survey. Household income is determined following the rules for Section 8 eligibility. Sample is MTO population randomly assigned through December 1996 with completed 1997 canvass and useable origin and current addresses. Coverage as follows: MTO treatment group 90.1 percent, Section 8 comparison group 90.0 percent, in-place control group 90.5 percent.

Boston, Chicago, Los Angeles, and New York. According to census data,[8] these five areas had bleak economic prospects in 1990:

- More than half the population (on average) was living in poverty;
- Nearly three-quarters of all families were headed by a single female parent;
- More than 30 percent of all residents were high school dropouts;
- Both men and women had high unemployment and low labor force participation rates; and
- More than 40 percent of the families had no employed member.

Moves through the MTO Demonstration

As previously noted, of the 2,601 families in the study sample, 905 were able to move through MTO, using their Section 8 certificates and vouchers.

Table 4.2. *Background Conditions and Experiences of MTO Families by Random Assignment Group*
(percent distributions—weighted data)

	Experimental group	Section 8 group	Control group	All groups
Moved more than 3 times in 5 years?				
Yes	8.6	9.9	11.3	9.8
No	91.5	90.1	88.7	90.2
Ever lived outside the [city] area?				
Yes	28.8	27.9	27.2	28.1
No	71.2	72.1	72.8	71.9
Most important reason for wanting to move?				
Get away from drugs, gangs	56.5	48.1	52.5	53.1
Get a bigger/better apartment	22.9	26.8	24.6	24.4
Better schools for my children	14.0	18.4	15.6	15.6
Get a job	1.4	0.9	1.5	1.3
Be near my job	0.3	0.5	0.4	0.4
Be near my family	0.8	1.2	1.1	1.0
Have better transportation	0.1	0.4	0.2	0.2
Other reasons	4.0	3.7	4.1	4.0
Second most important reason for wanting to move?				
Get away from drugs, gangs	27.5	31.2	30.3	29.3
Get a bigger/better apartment	27.7	27.2	27.4	27.5
Better schools for my children	30.5	30.6	29.5	30.2
Get a job	4.9	4.0	4.5	4.6
Be near my job	0.6	0.8	0.7	0.7
Be near my family	2.8	1.9	2.5	2.5
Have better transportation	1.0	0.2	1.1	0.8
Other reasons	5.1	4.1	4.1	4.5
Where want to move?				
Elsewhere in my neighborhood	5.8	7.1	7.2	6.6
Different neighborhood in city	56.7	59.8	57.4	57.7
Different neighborhood in suburbs	18.9	16.8	16.8	17.7
Different city outside the area	15.9	15.1	16.1	15.8
Other	2.6	1.2	2.4	2.2

Table 4.2. *Continued*

	Experimental group	Section 8 group	Control group	All groups
Condition of current house or apartment?				
Excellent	5.2	4.1	5.2	4.9
Good	24.2	20.3	23.3	22.9
Fair	47.7	50.3	46.0	47.8
Poor	23.0	25.3	25.5	24.4
Satisfaction with current neighborhood?				
Very/somewhat satisfied	13.5	13.7	12.6	13.3
In the middle	18.3	21.2	19.7	19.5
Very/somewhat dissatisfied	68.2	65.1	67.7	67.3
Experienced this in the past 6 months?				
Purse/wallet/jewelry snatched	23.8	23.9	23.6	23.8
Threatened with knife or gun	20.9	25.5	24.4	23.1
Beaten or assaulted	21.9	23.1	23.5	22.7
Stabbed or shot	10.1	9.5	12.0	10.6
Break-in (attempted or actual)	24.7	27.8	25.3	25.7
Number of cases	1,086	664	851	2,601
Missing cases	35–53	22–36	20–40	85–122

Source: MTO participant baseline survey.

Notes: Percentages may not add to 100 because of rounding. Data are weighted to minimize over-all variance while adjusting for differences in random assignment ratios between groups and over time. The head of household is the respondent to the baseline survey. Household income is determined following the rules for Section 8 eligibility. Sample is MTO population randomly assigned through December 1996 with completed 1997 canvass and useable origin and current addresses. Coverage as follows: MTO treatment group 90.1 percent, Section 8 comparison group 90.0 percent, in-place control group 90.5 percent.

These families had been assigned to either the MTO experimental group or the Section 8 comparison group. (Those in the in-place control group could not move through MTO.) Other chapters in this volume describe the locations chosen by the treatment group families and compare them with the locations selected by the regular Section 8 group (who were not restricted to moving to low-poverty areas and who did not receive counseling services).

Figure 4.1. *MTO Movers: Lease-Up Rates by Group*

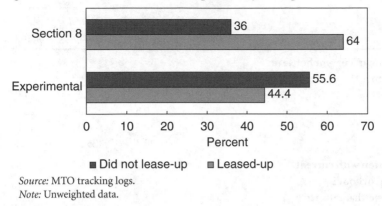

Source: MTO tracking logs.
Note: Unweighted data.

Other Moves by Sample Families

By the second half of 1997, a substantial number of families had either moved for the first time or moved again (table 4.3). Of the nearly 500 families in the experimental group who made program moves, over 100 moved again on their own.[9] For the 605 families that did not lease-up during the MTO demonstration, nearly 200 subsequently moved. Overall, more than a quarter of the experimental group (27.6 percent) made subsequent moves.

As noted before, a greater proportion of the families assigned to the Section 8 comparison group made program moves. But they show a fairly similar proportion of subsequent moves. Analysis of the Section 8 comparison group shows that

- Of the one-third of this group (237 families) that did not move through MTO, some 70 families did move by late 1997.
- In addition, a quarter of the families that had made program moves moved again.
- Overall, about 27 percent made subsequent moves by the time of the 1997 canvass.

Finally, more than a third of the families in the control group—which was not eligible to make MTO moves—had moved on their own by mid-1997. This high mobility rate may reflect families' choices, or it may reflect the recent efforts in the public housing program to demolish or

Table 4.3. *Program Mobility and Subsequent Mobility among MTO Families*

	Experimental group	Section 8 group	Control group	All groups
1. Total families[a]				
Number (Percent)	1,089 (100)	658 (100)	850 (100)	2,596 (100)
2. Families making MTO program moves				
Number (Percent)	484 (44.4)	421 (64.0)	NA	905 (34.9)
3. MTO mover families making second moves[b]				
Number (Percent)	117 (10.7)	106 (16.1)	NA	223 (8.6)
4. Families not making MTO program moves				
Number (Percent)	605 (55.6)	237 (36.0)	NA	842 (32.4)
5. MTO nonmover families making own moves[c]				
Number (Percent)	183 (16.8)	70 (10.6)	290 (34.1)	543 (20.9)
6. All subsequent (nonprogram) moves				
Number (Percent)	300 (27.6)	176 (26.8)	290 (34.1)	766 (29.5)
7. Families still at origin address				
Number (Percent)	422 (28.0)	167 (25.4)	560 (65.9)	1,148 (44.2)

Sources: MTO tracking logs, 1997 canvass, and other tracking sources.

Notes: Percentages may not add to 100 because of rounding. Data are weighted to minimize overall variance while adjusting for differences in random assignment ratios between sites and over time. "Own moves" are defined as known moves apart from the initial move made with a Section 8 certificate or voucher issued through the MTO demonstration. Sample is MTO population randomly assigned through December 1996 with completed 1997 canvass and useable origin and current addresses. Coverage as follows: MTO treatment group 90.1 percent, Section 8 comparison group 90 percent, in-place control group 90.5 percent.

NA = not applicable

a. Rows 2, 5, and 7 add up to Row 1.

b. Row 3 is a subset of Row 2.

c. Row 5 is a subset of Row 4.

redevelop the severely distressed stock. Because the site public housing authorities recruited MTO families from some extremely troubled developments, the in-place group and those who did not lease-up in the other groups are far more likely to move (or to be moved by the housing authority) than public housing residents in the past.

As a combined result of the MTO program moves and subsequent moves, only 44 percent of the sample families were at their origin addresses late in 1997. Some 26 percent of the families were still at MTO move addresses (representing 682 of the original 905 MTO movers), and 30 percent of the families were at another location.

Characteristics of 1997 Locations

All the families in the MTO demonstration lived in central cities at the time they joined. By late 1997, however, 10 percent lived in the suburban parts of their metropolitan areas, and 2 percent lived in places outside their metropolitan areas. These proportions differed markedly by group: 10 percent of the Section 8 comparison group and 3 percent of the in-place control group lived in suburban areas, compared with 15 percent of the experimental group families.

Table 4.4 shows how the families' locations differed by poverty and race in late 1997. Taking the randomly assigned groups as a whole (movers and nonmovers together), more than 33 percent of the MTO experimental group families lived in low-poverty areas, compared with 11 percent of Section 8 comparison group families and 3 percent of control group families (first panel).

Looking specifically at movers, the differences are even greater (second panel). Nearly three-quarters of the MTO experimental group families were living in low-poverty areas in late 1997, and almost 90 percent were in areas where fewer than 20 percent of residents were poor. By contrast, just 15 percent of the comparison group families lived in the lowest-poverty areas, and only 42 percent lived in areas with less than 20 percent poverty population.

The bottom two panels of table 4.4 show the household distribution by the size of the black population in the census tract. Although MTO moves were determined by poverty and not by race, the demonstration built on the desegregative efforts of Gautreaux and other court-ordered remedies for discrimination. A natural question, then, is whether MTO encouraged

Table 4.4. *Poverty and Racial Characteristics of Locations in Late 1997* (percent distributions—weighted data)

	Experimental group	Section 8 group	Control group	All groups
Percent of all families living in:				
low-poverty areas (< 10%)	34.5	10.6	2.8	18.1
areas 10–19% poor	7.9	18.0	6.1	9.8
areas 20–39% poor	12.5	33.7	16.9	19.3
high-poverty areas (40%+)	45.2	37.7	74.2	52.8
Percent of MTO movers living in:				
low-poverty areas (< 10%)	74.7	14.5	NA	46.7
areas 10–19% poor	13.6	27.4	NA	20.0
areas 20–39% poor	9.3	45.4	NA	26.1
high-poverty areas (40%+)	2.4	12.6	NA	7.2
Percent of all families living in:				
areas < 10% black	25.4	18.0	14.2	19.9
areas 10–39.9% black	18.9	24.1	17.7	19.8
areas 40–69.9% black	13.8	19.0	16.5	16.0
areas 70+% black	41.9	39.0	51.6	44.3
Percent of MTO movers living in:				
areas < 10% black	41.5	20.4	NA	31.7
areas 10–39.9% black	20.7	23.7	NA	22.1
areas 40–69.9% black	10.9	20.3	NA	15.3
areas 70+% black	27.0	35.6	NA	31.0

Sources: PHA and NPO tracking logs, 1997 canvass, other tracking sources.

Notes: Percentages may not add to 100 because of rounding. Data are weighted to minimize overall variance while adjusting for differences in random assignment ratios between sites and over time. The sample is the MTO population randomly assigned through December 1996 with completed 1997 canvass and with useable origin and current addresses. Coverage is as follows: MTO treatment group, 90.1 percent; Section 8 comparison group, 90 percent; and in-place control group 90.5 percent.

NA = not applicable

movers to also leave segregated areas. As the table shows, in late 1997 some 44 percent of all MTO families—including 42 percent of the experimental group, 39 percent of the Section 8 comparison group, and 52 percent of the control group—lived in areas where more than 70 percent of the population was black. By contrast, only a quarter of MTO experimental group movers and a third of Section 8 comparison group movers lived in mostly black areas. About 40 percent of experimental group movers and about 20 percent of comparison group movers lived in areas with a very small black population share (under 10 percent).

Appendix table 4.A4 updates table 4.4 using data from a subsequent MTO canvass in 2000 and from other tracking sources through the first part of 2001. It also covers the entire MTO program population, not just the early cohorts canvassed in late 1997. It shows the same basic patterns found for 1997, though the proportions living in each type of area changed in some instances. Comparing the patterns in terms of neighborhood poverty, the proportion of MTO experimental group movers in low-poverty areas is lower (66.6 percent versus 74.7 percent), although about a third of the experimental group as a whole is still living in low-poverty locations. A parallel but smaller reduction is observed for Section 8 comparison group movers. Comparing the patterns in terms of neighborhood racial composition, table 4.A4 shows a greater proportion of experimental group movers to be living in areas of more than 40 percent black population (45.4 percent versus 37.9 percent), while this proportion is slightly reduced for the comparison group movers (53.7 percent versus 55.9 percent). These figures are affected by both the difference in sample and the passage of time; it will fall to future analysis to determine the contributions of various factors.

Description of 1997 Locations

A more detailed look at locational characteristics suggests that the MTO experimental group families fared better on a number of indicators. Table 4.5 summarizes indicators associated with concentrated poverty (percent of persons in poverty, percent of households receiving public assistance income, percent of female-headed families with children, percent of high school dropouts, unemployment rate, male and female labor force participation rates, and percent of families with no workers) and other indicators associated with opportunity (percent of persons with incomes twice the poverty level, percent of households with wage

Table 4.5. *Mean Characteristics of MTO Families' Origin and Late 1997 Locations, by Group* (1990 Census, weighted tract-level data)

Tract Characteristic	Origin locations All groups	Locations in late 1997 Experimental group	Section 8 group	Control group	All groups
Concentrated poverty indicators					
Percent persons in poverty	55.5	32.2	33.1	47.9	37.6
Percent of households receiving public assistance income	44.1	26.2	27.1	38.6	30.5
Percent female-headed families with own children	73.1	49.7	52.0	66.6	55.8
Percent high school dropouts	31.5	23.7	25.0	29.6	26.0
Unemployment rate in 1990	25.8	16.5	15.9	22.5	18.3
Labor force participation					
Males	54.5	65.4	65.0	57.7	62.8
Females	38.3	50.7	49.8	42.3	47.7
Percent families with no workers in 1989	40.9	25.4	25.0	35.6	28.6
Opportunity indicators					
Percent of people with incomes twice the poverty level	24.1	49.5	45.1	30.6	42.2
Percent of households with wage or salary income	52.5	67.1	66.9	57.2	63.8
Percent of people with education beyond high school					
Some college	10.2	14.9	14.1	11.6	13.6
College graduate	9.9	17.7	15.4	11.4	15.0
Percent 16–19-year-olds in school	67.1	71.5	69.8	68.0	69.9
Percent owner-occupied housing	7.9	30.1	26.6	13.9	23.9

(continued)

Table 4.5. *Mean Characteristics of MTO Families' Origin and Late 1997 Locations, by Group (1990 Census, weighted tract-level data) (Continued)*

Tract Characteristic	Origin locations	Locations in late 1997			
	All groups	Experimental group	Section 8 group	Control group	All groups
Other indicators					
Median family income[a]	$11,279	$21,632	$20,426	$14,142	$16,670
Racial composition					
Percent white	17.4	33.2	27.8	20.9	27.8
Percent black	64.7	51.7	53.2	61.7	55.3
Percent Hispanic origin	25.1	19.0	23.2	23.4	21.5
Percent English not first language	29.6	25.0	29.0	28.3	27.1
Median house value[a,b]	$32,500	$79,800	$65,500	$55,000	$66,800
Median gross rent[a]	$237	$427	$426	$258	$333
Number of cases	2,601	1,085	664	851	2,600
Number of different tracts	102	460	361	252	796
Missing cases	0	0–3	0	0–5	0–5

Sources: 1997 MTO canvass, 1990 U.S. Census.

Notes: Percentages may not add to 100 because of rounding. Data are weighted to minimize overall variance while adjusting for differences in random assignment ratios between groups and over time. Sample is MTO population randomly assigned through December 1996 with completed 1997 canvass and useable origin and current addresses. Coverage as follows: MTO treatment group 90.1 percent, Section 8 comparison group 90.0 percent, in-place control group 90.5 percent.

a. Median of the distribution of tract-level medians.

b. In New York, more than half the origin tracts had no owner-occupied units.

or salary income, percent of people with some college or college gradu-ate, and percent of population in owner-occupied housing). It also reports other general indicators. The first column shows the character-istics of *origin locations* for the sample as a whole. The remaining columns report indicators for current (late 1997) census tracts.[10] The data reveal several interesting patterns:

- According to the concentrated poverty indicators, the origin loca-tions, on average, were somewhat more distressed than the current locations of the sample as a whole.
- According to these same indicators, the in-place control group fam-ilies were living in notably more distressed locations in 1997 com-pared with the other groups.
- In most cases, the indicators of concentrated poverty were more favorable for MTO family locations than for the regular Section 8 group areas. The differences, however, were small.
- According to opportunity indicators, the origin neighborhoods were occupied by people with more limited educations, employ-ment, incomes, and assets.
- According to the opportunity indicators, the average tract charac-teristics were more favorable for the MTO treatment group than for the Section 8 comparison group. Moreover, the opportunity indicators for both the MTO and comparison groups were more favorable than for the in-place control group.
- The median family income of the tracts occupied by treatment group families in late 1997 was 50 percent higher than the median income for the tracts occupied by in-place control group families. Median house values and median rents were also higher for treat-ment group families.
- However, even though the average values of the indicators of opportunity differed in the expected ways, the pair-wise differences were not significant, owing to the substantial variance around the mean for each indicator.

Appendix table 4.A5 updates the information in table 4.5. It shows the average characteristics of the origin addresses for the entire MTO pop-ulation; it then shows the mean characteristics of residential locations in 2001. Although the sample is substantially larger and the data more recent than those analyzed in this chapter, the patterns of difference in locational characteristics are similar to the 1997 results. As with the differences observed between table 4.4 and 4.A4, the underlying patterns will need to be examined in future research.[11]

Determinants of 1997 Location

We now examine the factors that affected the locations where MTO families lived late in 1997. What do these factors tell us about the impact of the MTO treatment (the combination of counseling and location restriction to a low-poverty destination) on residential location, after one to three years?

Objective of the Analysis

This analysis sheds light on the durability of locational effects in the MTO demonstration. Specifically, analysts are interested in the benefits poor families might realize by living in neighborhoods with fewer poor people, more middle-income and working people, better educational opportunities, and so on. These hypothesized effects depend on a period of "exposure" of MTO family members to the characteristics of the new area.[12] The analysis here examines whether the MTO treatment has influenced the overall patterns of residential choices one to four years after program participation—that is, whether the treatment effect has endured over that period for this part of the program population.

As noted earlier, substantial numbers of families from all three groups have made independent moves, some taking place after the initial program moves and others made by families who were assigned to the in-place control group or were unable to use the certificates or vouchers offered through the MTO demonstration. Program participation might well affect subsequent moves by families who leased-up through MTO, but the program should not affect the locational outcomes of moves by nonparticipants.[13]

Analytic Approach

A multivariate analysis was performed to examine more closely the effect of program and family characteristics on the nature of the families' locations in late 1997. The analysis uses three different dependent variables: the percent of persons in poverty in the current census tract;

the median income of families in the current census tract; and the percent black population of the current census tract. The first dependent variable (percent poverty population) was selected because of its direct relationship to the MTO program rules regarding eligible locations for movers in the MTO experimental group. The second dependent variable (tract median income) was selected as an indicator of the positive attributes of opportunity locations. The third dependent variable (percent black population) was selected because of MTO's potential for fostering racially desegregative moves.

Four sets of independent variables were tested for their relationships to these current location characteristics.

- The first set represents the demonstration's *experimental design* in the form of dummy variables for assignment to the MTO experimental or Section 8 comparison group. (The in-place control group is the omitted category.) A variable measuring the time since random assignment was also tested.
- The second set consists of *family characteristics,* including race, ethnicity, and number of children born to the head. Dummy variables were created for small families (one child) and large families (more than three children).
- The third set of independent variables consists of the head's *background characteristics and experiences,* measured at the time of program entry. Factors tested in this set include whether the head was a college graduate, whether the head was in school, whether the head was working full- or part-time, presence of public assistance income, presence of work income, total household income, previous high mobility, dissatisfaction with current neighborhood, and preference for a suburban move.
- The fourth set of independent variables consists of dummy variables for four of the five demonstration sites, with New York City as the excluded category. These dummies represent a combination of *market and program features* of the different sites.

In general, the results of multivariate regression analysis using the dependent and independent variables described were consistent with hypotheses about how participation in MTO would affect locational outcomes. The signs were as expected, the overall models and many individual coefficients were highly statistically significant, and significant treatment effects were detected.

The research design for MTO, with its three-way group assignments, was developed with the knowledge that a substantial proportion of the treatment group (and perhaps also of the regular Section 8 group) would not end up actually receiving Section 8 assistance through MTO, because not everyone assigned to the groups that were offered the opportunity to move through Section 8 would actually succeed in doing so. As shown in figure 4.1, the proportions of *participants* in these groups—the percentage of all assigned who did lease-up and move—were 44 percent and 64 percent, respectively.

In a multivariate analysis with experimental data, the coefficients for the experimental group dummies represent the effect of the treatment on all those assigned to the treatment. With three-way random assignment, the coefficients for the experimental group dummies represent the effects of MTO and regular Section 8 on all families assigned to those two groups, relative to the control group of families who continue to receive project-based housing assistance. Thus, the coefficients apply to both movers and stayers, and the mixes of movers and stayers in each group affect their magnitude.

However, from these coefficients it is possible to derive estimates of the effects of MTO and regular Section 8 on those who actually receive assistance: that is, on the movers in these two groups. Again, the estimates are relative to similar members of the control group of families that continue to receive project-based housing assistance. The derivation of these estimates for movers uses the "no-show" adjustment, which is made on the assumption that the program has no effect on those who do not receive any assistance.[14]

Both the full-group (unadjusted) coefficients and the mover-only (adjusted) coefficients can be tested for their differences relative to the omitted group (the in-place controls) and also for their differences relative to each other. Table 4.6 summarizes the tests for significant differences (experimental effects) in selected multivariate models. (The full model results, shown in table 4.7, are presented later.)

The models analyze the determinants of current location for MTO families, using three characteristics of current location as dependent variables: poverty percentage, median income, and percent black population. As shown in tables 4.4 and 4.5, the mean values of these characteristics differed markedly among the groups.

Table 4.6 shows the coefficient for the MTO experimental group (top panel), the Section 8 comparison group (second panel), and the

Table 4.6. *Summary of Tests for Program Effects on the Late-1997 Location of MTO Families*

	Dependent variable of model		
Group assignment variables	Poverty percentage of 1997 location	Median income of 1997 location	Percent black population of 1997 location
Intercept	48.1**	$13,920**	48.6**
Experimental group			
All assigned (coefficient)	−15.8**	$10,155**	−10.4**
All assigned (std. error)	.92	566.86	1.29
All assigned (confidence interval)	[−17.6, −14.0]	[$9044, $11,266]	[−12.9, −7.9]
Movers only			
Coefficient	−35.5**	$22,828**	−23.4**
Std. error	2.08	$1,281	2.89
Confidence interval	[−40.9 −30.1]	[$19,523, $26,133]	[−29.1, −17.7]
Section 8 group			
All assigned (coefficient)	−14.7**	$7,326**	−8.3**
All assigned (std. error)	1.05	$642.88	1.46
All assigned (confidence interval)	[−16.8, −12.6]	[$6,066, $8,586]	[−11.2, −5.4]
Movers only			
Coefficient	−23.0**	$11,451**	−13.0**
Std. error	1.63	$1,004.79	2.28
Confidence interval	[−27.2, −18.7]	[$8,858, $14,043]	[−17.43, −8.48]
Significance of treatment effects			
Experimental group vs. control group			
All assigned	**	**	**
Movers only	**	**	**
Section 8 group vs. control group			
All assigned	**	**	**
Movers only	**	**	**

(continued)

Table 4.6. *Summary of Tests for Program Effects on the Late-1997 Location of MTO Families (Continued)*

	Dependent variable of model		
Group assignment variables	Poverty percentage of 1997 location	Median income of 1997 location	Percent black population of 1997 location
Experimental vs. Section 8 group			
All assigned	—	*	—
Movers only	**	**	**
Number of observations	2,598	2,598	2,598

Sources: MTO participant baseline survey, PHA and nonprofit counseling organization tracking logs, 1997 canvass, other tracking sources.

Notes: Data are weighted to minimize overall variance while adjusting for differences in random assignment ratios between groups and over time. Sample is MTO population randomly assigned through December 1996 with completed 1997 canvass and useable origin and current addresses. Coverage as follows: MTO treatment group 90.1 percent, Section 8 comparison group 90 percent, in-place control group 90.5 percent. Three cases are missing.

* = significant at $p \leq .05$; ** = significant at $p \leq .01$. Confidence intervals at $p \leq .05$.

differences in effects between these two groups. In each panel, the estimated coefficients and their standard errors for the full group are shown first; the coefficients and their standard errors for movers only (using the "no-show" adjustment) are shown next.[15] Finally, the table reports confidence intervals around the estimated and adjusted coefficients.

Findings on Program Effects

The findings on MTO program effects on current (late 1997) location can be summarized as follows:

- Each of the estimated coefficients for the MTO experimental and Section 8 comparison groups as a whole is significantly different from zero ($p < .01$) for all three dependent variables. Thus, in all three cases, there are significant effects for these two groups as a whole relative to the in-place controls.
- For all three dependent variables, there are significant treatment effects for the MTO experimental group movers compared with the Section 8 comparison group movers (i.e., after both are adjusted for "no-shows"). This finding means that the treatment received by the

MTO experimental group movers did result in different locational outcomes relative to the regular Section 8 group.

- One dependent variable, the tract median family income, also has a significant treatment effect for the entire MTO experimental group as a whole, compared with the entire Section 8 comparison group. This result indicates that the effect of the counseling and location targeting on movers' tract median income was strong enough to create a statistically significant effect across the entire assigned group.

In short, these findings mean that the two treatments each have separate effects on location as of late 1997, an average of two years subsequent to participation, and that these effects differ between the two treatments. For the whole MTO experimental and Section 8 comparison groups, the effects amount to a 15–16 point difference in the poverty percentage and an 8–10 point difference in the percent black population. The reduction in the poverty percentage for MTO experimental group *movers* is 35 points (relative to the poverty percentages of in-place control group neighborhoods), significantly greater than the reduction of 23 points for the Section 8 comparison group *movers*. Most striking are the differentials relative to median income of the census tract: more than $10,000 for the MTO experimental group as a whole and nearly $23,000 for the movers in that group, compared with about $7,300 for the entire Section 8 comparison group and under $12,000 for that group's movers.

Findings on Other Determinants of Location

Table 4.7 reports on the broader set of factors—apart from program effects—influencing 1997 location for the MTO families in this sample. The first column shows the coefficients for the factors affecting the poverty rate of the census tract in which each family was living. Being an MTO experimental group mover reduced the poverty rate by 35 points, compared with 23 points for the Section 8 comparison group mover, and (as shown in table 4.6) the difference between these effects was statistically significant ($p < .01$). Other factors associated with lower poverty rates were the head of household having just one child, the head being in school, and living in the Boston area. Living in the Chicago area, by contrast, was associated with higher poverty rates, all else equal.

The middle column of table 4.7 shows the coefficients for the factors affecting the median income of the families' late-1997 Census tract locations. While the poverty rate was the indicator used to target (and limit)

Table 4.7. *Factors Affecting Characteristics of Late-1997 Locations*

	Dependent variable of model		
Independent variables	*Poverty percentage of 1997 location*	*Median income of 1997 location*	*Percent black population of 1997 location*
Intercept	48.10**	$13,920**	48.59**
Group assignment			
Experimental group			
All assigned	−15.79**	$10,155**	−10.40**
Movers only	−35.50**	$22,828**	−23.38**
Section 8 group			
All assigned	−14.68**	$7,326**	−8.29**
Movers only	−22.95**	$11,451**	−12.96**
Family characteristics			
One child	−2.15*		
Black			17.05**
Background conditions and experiences			
Head in school	−3.46*	$2,540**	
Head working full- or part-time		$1,316*	
Head prefers suburban move		$2,393**	
Site/market			
Baltimore			13.31**
Boston	−7.38**	$4,192**	−12.19**
Chicago	14.32**	−$4,939**	31.52**
Los Angeles			−21.01**
R²	0.2078	0.1683	0.4089
Adjusted R²	0.2059	0.1661	0.4073
Number of observations	2,598	2,598	2,598

Sources: MTO participant baseline survey, PHA and nonprofit counseling organization tracking logs, 1997 canvass, and other tracking sources.

Notes: Data are weighted to minimize overall variance while adjusting for differences in random assignment ratios between groups and over time. Sample is MTO population randomly assigned through December 1996 with completed 1997 canvass and useable origin and current addresses. Coverage as follows: MTO treatment group 90.1 percent, Section 8 comparison group 90 percent, in-place control group 90.5 percent. Three cases are missing.

* = significant at $p \le .05$; ** = significant at $p \le .01$.

moves by experimental group families, median income may be a better indicator of the overall economic well-being of local residents. Being assigned to the MTO experimental group raised the tract median income by more than $10,000, compared with more than $7,000 for the Section 8 comparison group; the statistically significant difference ($p < .05$) between these figures indicates that the program effects on tract median income were strong enough to produce differences not just for movers but for the entire assigned groups. And being an experimental group mover raised the median income almost $23,000, while being a regular Section 8 mover raised it by only half that amount. This difference was also statistically significant ($p < .01$). Other baseline characteristics associated with higher-income locations were the head of household being in school, working full- or part-time, and expressing a preference for suburban locations. Again, living in Boston was associated with larger income differences between the current neighborhoods of treatment group members and controls, while living in Chicago was associated with smaller income differences.

The third model shown in table 4.7 examines the factors affecting the racial composition (percent black population) of the tracts occupied by sample families late in 1997. The level of the intercept in this equation (last column of the exhibit) indicates that the in-place control group families were living in tracts with nearly 50 percent black population (setting all other variables in the model to zero). The coefficient for all families assigned to the MTO experimental group indicates a reduction of 10 percentage points in this figure, and the reduction is more than 23 percentage points for movers. Section 8 comparison group movers were located in tracts with an average share of black population about 13 points lower than the in-place control group families. The race of the participating family also influenced the choice of location, with black families living in locations averaging a 17 percentage point larger black population than other families. Finally, all four site dummies showed significant effects on tract racial composition: living in Baltimore or Chicago was associated with a higher racial differential between the treatment groups and the controls, while living in Boston or Los Angeles was associated with a lower racial differential.

Enduring Effects on Location

This chapter has examined the locational outcomes of the MTO demonstration in late 1997, one to three years after program participation by the

2,601 families in the sample. It examined the characteristics of the areas where the families were living at that time to determine whether treatment effects (the combined result of the offer of Section 8 assistance and the geographic restrictions and counseling for the MTO experimental group) have endured over that period.

The findings reveal two types of significant treatment effects. First, families assigned to the MTO experimental and Section 8 comparison groups (the two groups whose members were able to move with Section 8 subsidies) lived in less-poor and less-segregated neighborhoods than the in-place control group. Second, not only are these effects much larger for movers, they are also significantly greater for MTO experimental group movers than for Section 8 comparison group movers. Thus, the geographic restrictions and counseling for the MTO experimental group have a clear treatment effect, beyond the effects of receiving Section 8 assistance.

MTO's locational effects are important because of the hypothesized impacts better neighborhoods have on the lives of the adults and children who move there. Future research on locational effects among the entire MTO population after more time has passed will shed further light on these effects.

NOTES

This research was supported in part by a Daniel McGillis Development and Dissemination grant from Abt Associates. The author wishes to thank Carissa Climaco for her invaluable assistance to the project.

1. The canvass sample, consisting of 2,883 families, accounts for 62.5 percent of the full MTO population. In all, 4,608 families joined MTO and were randomly assigned in the demonstration. The remainder of the families joined in 1997 and 1998; enrollment for MTO was completed in July 1998. Appendix table 4.A1 compares this sample with the full program population.

2. Some families may have been interviewed by local researchers, but not all local research included nonmovers or families assigned to the in-place control group. For the latter, this may well have been the first direct contact since they were informed of their random assignment and told they would not receive Section 8 assistance through MTO.

3. Appendix tables 4.A2 and 4.A3 show the characteristics of this sample by site.

4. Exploration of the responses on the MTO baseline race and ethnicity questions (which mirror those in the census) shows two different patterns. Respondents identifying themselves as African American and answering the ethnicity question were by and large not of Hispanic origin; further, a substantial number of African-American respondents skipped the ethnicity question. And those of Hispanic origin generally considered themselves neither white nor African American (except for some Los Angeles respon-

dents that categorized themselves as white). Hispanics instead often used the "Other" category in answering the race question.

5. The victimization rates reported in the Participant Baseline Survey were about four times higher than those reported in a 1994 national survey of residents of public housing family developments. Other MTO researchers have noted that the victimization reports in the baseline survey may have been exaggerated because applicants thought this might help them be accepted for the program. See Katz, Kling, and Liebman (this volume) citing Zelon et al. (1994).

6. Those assigned to the in-place control group were not offered or given Section 8 tenant-based subsidies with which to make such moves.

7. The differences are a result of the timing of site start-up, the pace of enrollment, and local housing market conditions; all these factors affected the proportion of families enrolled by the end of 1996 and the lease-up rates of those coming into the program later.

8. As expected, the origin neighborhoods looked the same for all three of the randomly assigned groups.

9. At this time, the proportion of experimental group or comparison group families moving again with Section 8 is not known.

10. Notice, too, that the families in the MTO and regular Section 8 groups are dispersed across a larger number of different census tracts than the in-place families.

11. A full analysis of residential locations for the MTO population will be conducted as part of the interim evaluation research, for which data were collected in 2002. That study will also take advantage of data from the 2000 Census to update the characteristics of the locations.

12. There is no decisive literature on the length of exposure needed, however.

13. It is interesting to speculate about whether families assigned to the MTO experimental group, who received counseling but did not succeed in leasing-up, might still have been affected by the treatment. If they should later have the opportunity to get a Section 8 voucher, one wonders if their locational choices would be affected by MTO. However, in reality, the residents of public and Section 8 project-based housing are not likely to receive another Section 8 offer. And if such an offer materialized in the context of demolition or redevelopment of public housing, additional services are usually designed to help families relocate quickly, with far less focus than in MTO on the quality of the destination neighborhoods.

14. This procedure is described in Bloom (1984). To see how the estimate of effect on recipients is derived, first note that the average effect on all those assigned to a given treatment, Eo, is the weighted average of the effects on those who receive the treatment, Er, and those who do not receive it, Enr, where the weights are the proportions of recipients, p, and nonrecipients, $(1 - p)$:

$$Eo = pEr + (1 - p)Enr.$$

Under the assumption that the treatment has zero effect on nonrecipients:

$$Eo = pEr,$$

solving for the effect on recipients:

$$Er = Eo/p.$$

15. The adjustment applies to both panels.

REFERENCES

Bloom, Howard S. 1984. "Accounting for No-Shows in Experimental Evaluation Designs." *Evaluation Review* 8: 225–46.
Zelon, Harvey, et al. 1994. *Survey of Public Housing Residents: Crime and Crime Prevention in Public Housing.* Research Triangle Park, N.C.: Research Triangle Institute.

APPENDIX 4A

Supplementary Tables on MTO's Locational Impacts

Table 4.A1. *Comparison of 1997 Canvass Sample with Full MTO Population on Demographic and Socioeconomic Characteristics* (percent distributions—weighted data)

	1997 Canvass sample all groups[a]	Full MTO population all groups[b]
Race of head of household (%)		
African-American	68.3	64.4
White	7.6	8.3
American Indian	0.7	0.6
Asian/Pacific Islander	2.0	2.0
Other	21.4	24.8
Ethnicity of head of household (%)		
Hispanic	31.1	30.3
Non-Hispanic	68.9	69.7
Sex of head of household (%)		
Male	8.4	8.8
Female	91.6	91.2

Table 4.A1. *Continued*

	1997 Canvass sample all groups[a]	*Full MTO population all groups*[b]
Head of household's marital status (%)		
Never married	62.1	61.9
Married	10.7	11.5
Widowed	10.0	9.3
Divorced	17.2	17.3
Median number of children	2	3
Average total household income	$9,082	$9,310
Percent with AFDC as primary income source	60.8	59.1
Head of household currently in school? (%)		
Yes	14.8	16.2
No	85.2	83.8
Head of household a graduate? (%)		
High school	42.2	40.7
GED	18.7	18.6
Neither	39.1	40.7
Head of household currently working? (%)		
Full-time	16.5	16.5
Part-time	10.1	11.4
Not working	73.4	72.1
Number of cases	2,601	4,608
Missing cases	34–309	68–335

Source: MTO participant baseline survey.

Notes: Percentages may not add to 100 because of rounding. Data are weighted to minimize overall variance while adjusting for differences in random assignment ratios between groups and over time. The head of household is the respondent to the baseline survey. Household income is determined following the rules for Section 8 eligibility. Differences in race, marital status, and family size are related to the later entry (1997–98) of Los Angeles families into the MTO population.

a. MTO population randomly assigned through December 1996 with completed 1997 canvass and useable origin and current addresses. Coverage as follows: MTO treatment group 90.1 percent, Section 8 comparison group 90.0 percent, in-place control group 90.5 percent.

b. Full MTO program population (all cases ever randomly assigned).

Table 4.A2. *Demographic and Socioeconomic Characteristics of MTO Families by Site* (percentage distribution—weighted data)

	Baltimore	Boston	Chicago	Los Angeles	New York	All sites
Race of head of household (%)						
African-American	97.8	40.1	98.3	51.5	53.5	68.3
White	0.0	15.2	0.2	19.6	3.7	7.6
American Indian	0.3	1.3	0.2	0.4	1.1	0.7
Asian/Pacific Islander	0.0	5.6	0.0	2.9	1.0	2.0
Other	1.9	37.8	1.3	25.6	40.7	21.4
Ethnicity of head of household (%)						
Hispanic	1.7	44.3	0.7	46.4	48.5	31.1
Non-Hispanic	98.4	55.7	99.3	53.6	51.5	68.9
Sex of head of household (%)						
Male	2.3	8.9	5.1	21.0	7.5	8.4
Female	97.7	91.1	94.9	79.0	92.5	91.6
Head of household's marital status (%)						
Never married	74.2	57.5	67.9	55.1	55.1	62.1
Married	3.4	11.8	6.7	22.8	11.2	10.7
Widowed	8.8	12.4	8.6	6.7	12.1	10.0
Divorced	13.6	18.3	16.9	15.4	21.7	17.2

Median number of children	2	2	3	3	2	2
Average total household income	$6,905	$10,443	$8,200	$9,341	$10,456	$9,082
Percent with AFDC as primary income source	62.9	53.6	56.2	75.1	60.7	60.8
Head of household currently in school? (%)						
Yes	16.6	18.0	10.9	12.8	13.2	14.8
No	83.4	82.0	89.1	87.2	86.8	85.2
Head of household a graduate? (%)						
High school	43.6	43.9	47.8	35.0	38.8	42.2
GED	14.1	23.6	18.4	8.7	18.7	18.7
Neither	42.4	32.5	33.8	56.3	35.3	39.1
Head of household currently working? (%)						
Full-time	14.1	20.1	15.9	17.0	14.4	16.5
Part-time	10.0	12.2	7.8	10.5	9.1	10.1
Not working	75.9	67.9	76.4	72.5	76.5	73.4
Number of cases	564	661	471	416	489	2,601
Missing cases	0–58	4–66	1–46	1–46	12–25	34–309

Source: MTO participant baseline survey.

Notes: Percentages may not add to 100 because of rounding. Data are weighted to minimize overall variance while adjusting for differences in random assignment ratios between sites and over time. The head of household is the respondent to the baseline survey. Household income is determined following the rules for Section 8 eligibility. The sample is MTO population randomly assigned through December 1996 with completed 1997 canvass and useable origin and current addresses. Coverage as follows: Baltimore 88.1 percent; Boston 91.2 percent; Chicago 88.4 percent; Los Angeles 80.6 percent; New York 87.0 percent; whole sample 90.2 percent.

Table 4.A3. *Background Conditions and Experiences of MTO Families by Site* (percent distributions—weighted data)

	Baltimore	Boston	Chicago	Los Angeles	New York	All sites
Moved more than 3 times in 5 years?						
Yes	12.0	11.1	10.6	8.2	5.8	9.8
No	88.0	89.0	89.4	91.8	94.2	90.2
Ever lived outside the [city] area?						
Yes	20.1	31.5	20.6	48.1	23.8	28.1
No	79.0	68.5	79.4	51.9	76.2	71.9
Most important reason for wanting to move?						
Get away from drugs, gangs	54.1	56.2	50.9	60.2	43.8	53.1
Get a bigger/better apartment	27.0	27.2	20.5	10.7	32.2	24.4
Better schools for my children	12.2	8.5	22.7	24.1	16.2	15.6
Get a job	1.2	0.9	2.5	1.4	0.9	1.3
Be near my job	0.5	0.6	0.2	0.4	0.0	0.4
Be near my family	0.4	1.5	0.7	0.6	1.5	1.0
Have better transportation	0.0	0.5	0.3	0.4	0.0	0.2
Other reasons	4.6	4.6	2.2	2.2	5.4	4.0
Second most important reason for wanting to move?						
Get away from drugs, gangs	27.7	28.5	27.7	29.7	33.6	29.3
Get a bigger/better apartment	28.8	34.8	23.2	21.1	24.6	27.5
Better schools for my children	30.8	21.7	34.0	38.1	31.2	30.2
Get a job	5.4	1.3	9.9	5.4	2.6	4.6
Be near my job	0.7	0.8	0.4	1.1	0.6	0.7
Be near my family	1.9	4.5	0.9	1.4	2.6	2.5
Have better transportation	0.4	2.1	0.4	0.7	0.2	0.8
Other reasons	4.4	6.4	3.6	2.6	4.6	4.5

Where want to move?

Elsewhere in my neighborhood	4.7	12.2	3.1	4.8	6.0	6.6
Different neighborhood in city	64.6	51.4	71.2	48.0	53.1	57.7
Different neighborhood in suburbs	23.3	15.8	18.1	13.1	17.0	17.7
Different city outside the area	5.9	18.5	6.0	32.0	20.1	15.8
Other	1.6	2.1	1.5	2.1	3.8	2.2
Condition of current house or apartment?						
Excellent	6.8	4.7	5.3	5.4	2.1	4.9
Good	27.4	21.9	25.7	17.2	22.0	22.9
Fair	38.3	47.9	46.7	58.3	51.5	47.8
Poor	27.5	25.5	22.3	19.1	25.3	24.4
Satisfaction with current neighborhood?						
Very/somewhat satisfied	10.2	19.9	12.3	15.1	7.2	13.3
In the middle	10.3	26.2	18.6	25.3	17.1	19.5
Very/somewhat dissatisfied	79.5	53.9	69.1	59.7	75.7	67.3
Experienced this in the past six months?						
Purse/wallet/jewelry snatched	24.2	13.0	24.4	30.9	31.9	23.8
Threatened with knife or gun	26.0	13.3	23.7	31.1	26.5	23.1
Beaten or assaulted	24.6	15.1	27.9	25.8	23.8	22.7
Stabbed or shot	11.6	8.0	11.0	13.3	10.4	10.6
Break-in (attempted or actual)	25.7	17.6	25.5	48.1	19.0	25.7
Number of cases	564	661	471	416	489	2,601
Missing cases	3–19	4–17	16–32	33–43	19–25	78–128

Sources: MTO participant baseline survey; HUD Form 50058.

Notes: Percentages may not add to 100 because of rounding. Data are weighted to minimize overall variance while adjusting for differences in random assignment ratios between sites and over time. The head of household is the respondent to the baseline survey. Household income is determined following the rules for Section 8 eligibility. Sample is MTO population randomly assigned through December 1996 with completed 1997 canvass and useable origin and current addresses. Coverage as follows: Baltimore 88.1 percent; Boston 91.2 percent; Chicago 88.4 percent; Los Angeles 80.6 percent; New York 87.0 percent; whole sample 90.2 percent.

Table 4.A4. *Poverty and Racial Characteristics of Locations in 2001* (percent distributions—weighted data)

	Experimental group	Section 8 group	Control group	All groups
Percent of all families living in:				
low-poverty areas (< 10%)	32.3	9.1	4.4	16.9
areas 10–19% poor	10.0	18.2	9.3	12.2
areas 20–39% poor	17.9	33.8	22.1	23.8
high-poverty areas (40%+)	39.8	38.9	64.2	47.1
Percent of MTO movers living in:				
low-poverty areas (< 10%)	66.6	12.1	NA	39.6
areas 10–19% poor	13.7	26.3	NA	20.0
areas 20–39% poor	13.6	43.0	NA	28.1
high-poverty areas (40%+)	6.1	18.6	NA	12.3
Percent of all families living in:				
areas < 10% black	22.4	18.1	15.9	19.1
areas 10–39.9% black	17.0	23.7	17.8	19.2
areas 40–69.9% black	15.3	21.3	17.9	17.9
areas 70+% black	45.2	37.0	48.4	43.8
Percent of MTO movers living in:				
areas < 10% black	36.2	20.1	NA	28.3
areas 10–39.9% black	18.4	26.2	NA	22.3
areas 40–69.9% black	14.5	20.0	NA	17.2
areas 70+% black	30.9	33.7	NA	32.3

Sources: PHA and NPO tracking logs, 2000 MTO canvass, other tracking sources.

Note: Percentages may not add to 100 because of rounding. Data are weighted to minimize over-all variance while adjusting for differences in random assignment ratios between sites and over time. Sample is all families in the MTO population (randomly assigned at any time during the demonstration) with useable origin and current addresses. Coverage as follows: MTO experimental group 99.3 percent; Section 8 comparison group 98.6 percent, in-place control group 98.7 percent.

NA = not applicable

Table 4.A5. *Mean Characteristics of MTO Families' Origin and 2001 Locations, by Group* (1990 Census, weighted tract-level data)

| | Origin locations | 2001 locations | | | |
| | | | | | |
Tract characteristic	All groups	Experimental group	Section 8 group	Control group	All groups
Concentrated poverty indicators					
Percent persons in poverty	56.1	32.1	33.4	44.9	36.5
Percent of households receiving public assistance income	46.4	27.4	27.7	38.2	30.8
Percent female-headed families with own children	71.7	49.0	50.6	60.6	53.1
Percent high school dropouts	32.5	24.8	23.0	29.4	26.4
Unemployment rate in 1990	27.1	17.2	16.2	22.1	18.5
Labor force participation					
Males	54.9	65.6	65.2	60.0	63.7
Females	37.9	50.7	48.9	43.4	47.9
Percent families with no workers in 1989	42.3	25.7	25.2	34.1	28.2
Opportunity indicators					
Percent of people with incomes twice the poverty level	23.3	49.3	44.0	32.9	42.6
Percent of households with wage or salary income	51.8	67.3	67.3	59.5	64.9
Percent of people with education beyond high school					
Some college	10.1	15.2	13.9	11.9	13.8
College graduate	8.8	16.5	14.2	11.3	14.2

(*continued*)

Table 4.A5. *Mean Characteristics of MTO Families' Origin and 2001 Locations, by Group (1990 Census, weighted tract-level data)(Continued)*

Tract characteristic	Origin locations	2001 locations			
	All groups	Experimental group	Section 8 group	Control group	All groups
Percent 16–19-year-olds in school	66.6	65.6	70.0	67.3	69.9
Percent owner-occupied housing	8.3	31.4	25.6	18.5	25.7
Other indicators					
Median family income[a]	$10,933	$22,829	$20,119	$14,913	$18,477
Racial composition					
Percent white	17.4	31.0	27.7	22.6	27.4
Percent black	64.7	55.3	51.9	58.7	55.4
Percent Hispanic origin	27.8	19.0	28.2	26.4	24.0
Percent English not first language	31.4	24.5	33.4	30.8	29.0
Median house value[a,b]	$54,900	$87,500	$89,900	$71,100	$84,700
Median gross rent[a]	$238	$432	$430	$283	$399
Number of cases	4,608	1,820	1,349	1,429	4,608
Number of different tracts	187	781	696	481	1,349
Missing cases	0–29	12	15–17	19–22	46–52

Sources: 2000 MTO canvass, other tracking sources, 1997 MTO canvass, 1990 U.S. Census.

Notes: Data are weighted to minimize overall variance while adjusting for differences in random assignment ratios between groups and over time. Sample is entire MTO population (all families ever randomly assigned) with useable origin and current addresses. Coverage as follows: MTO treatment group 99 percent, Section 8 comparison group 99 percent, in-place control group 99 percent.

a. Median of the distribution of tract-level medians.

b. In New York, more than half the origin tracts had no owner-occupied units.

PART II
Research Findings
from the Five MTO Sites

5

The Effects of MTO
on Educational Opportunities
in Baltimore

Helen F. Ladd
Jens Ludwig

T his chapter uses information from the Baltimore MTO demonstration to measure the effects of residential relocation programs on
children's educational opportunities. The results are encouraging in many
ways. We find that schools attended by Section 8 comparison and experimental MTO movers had higher pass rates, more affluent student bodies,
and more resources compared with the schools attended by control group
children. Yet the changes, particularly for the experimental group, are not
as substantial as we would have predicted given the types of schools
located in Baltimore-area census tracts with large concentrations of
affordable rental housing, in large part because MTO movers relocated at
higher-than-expected rates to other parts of Baltimore City rather than
the suburbs. We also find that the differences across MTO groups in the
standardized-test pass rates for the schools that children attend may be
owing mostly to differences in the student bodies that each school serves
rather than to the effectiveness of the schools themselves. Improved "peer
groups" may thus be one of the most important changes in educational
opportunities that results from the MTO program in Baltimore. Based on
the findings reported in the next chapter, changes in peer groups may be
sufficient to improve the educational outcomes of at least the younger
children in the Baltimore MTO site.

Three Steps to Successful Relocation

Three steps are required for generating improved educational outcomes through residential relocation programs such as MTO. Since none of these steps is assured, careful empirical research is required to determine the overall effects of such programs on educational opportunities and outcomes. The brief discussion of these three steps in this section puts into perspective the empirical work reported in this chapter, which focuses on educational opportunities at the school level.

Step 1: Successful Relocation

Families in the experimental group had to successfully identify and obtain private-market housing in a census tract with a low poverty rate. In addition, the children themselves had to accompany the family to the new neighborhood.

Despite the assistance provided to members of the experimental group in Baltimore by the local nonprofit, the Community Assistance Network (CAN), not all families successfully relocated. For various reasons, including federal requirements for the Section 8 program, many landlords were reluctant to accept Section 8 tenants.[1] The combination of the standards for Section 8 payments with the requirement that a family move to a low-poverty tract reduced the set of available private apartments. Many of the experimental group families lacked automobiles, and many had networks of friends and family within their old neighborhoods. When directly faced with the trade-offs involved in relocating to a low-poverty neighborhood, some families chose not to move. Some children may have also stayed behind, living with friends or relatives, because they did not want to leave their neighborhoods.

Step 2: Improvements in Educational Opportunities

Student performance, as measured by test scores, is typically much higher in affluent suburban schools than in urban schools serving mostly poor students. This observation alone does not mean that relocation to suburban areas will improve educational opportunities. Several other considerations come into play.

First, high average student outcomes within a school need not be a good measure of how effectively the school contributes to the learning of its students. Such outcomes may instead largely reflect the socioeconomic backgrounds of the school's students. Moreover, to the extent that some schools are more effective than others in educating students from particular backgrounds, a school with high average test scores need not be a good school for a specific student. Consequently, the value that MTO children would receive from attending different schools throughout the metropolitan area may not be directly aligned with the average test scores of those schools.

However, working in the other direction is the potential for positive spillover effects from the presence of motivated, high achieving students. Thus, the characteristics of a school's population may itself be viewed as an input into the educational process to the extent that students seek to emulate their more motivated and high-achieving peers (Jencks and Mayer 1990). In addition, to the extent that high average outcomes reflect the availability of above-average resources, all students would presumably benefit from those resources.

Limitations on the residential mobility of the MTO families provide a second complication. The success of the MTO program in inducing changes in the school and neighborhood contexts of children may be limited by the fact that participating families are restricted to areas where they can find affordable housing.

Even if MTO children enrolled in schools with higher average test scores and more overall resources, their educational opportunities might not have improved. For example, some MTO children might have been placed in less-demanding classes, been assigned to classes disproportionately attended by low-income or minority students, or been put in classes with less-able teachers than the school's average classroom. Similarly, MTO children might have chosen or been relegated to peer groups within the school or neighborhood that are disproportionately composed of other low-income minority children. In this case, improvements for MTO children in the quality of schooling as measured by average school characteristics and student outcomes could overstate the improvements in their educational opportunities.

Step 3: Reaction of Families to New Neighborhoods and Schools

To benefit, relocated children must respond positively to neighborhoods and school changes. As described earlier, children must be motivated by— rather than discouraged by—better-off peers.

Similarly, MTO parents need to respond to more demanding schools and more affluent neighbors by increasing their time and material inputs into their children's education. MTO parents who became less confident in their ability to help their children with schoolwork or to participate in school activities could offset any gains.

Finally, it may be important for MTO families to remain in low-poverty neighborhoods to experience long-term gains. Some families, after initial difficulties, may return to areas near their original neighborhoods.

Data

The data in this chapter come from two main sources: survey data collected by Abt Associates (1997) at the time of application to MTO (referred to interchangeably as "pre-program," "Abt," or "baseline" data) and school-level data on student performance, mobility, and socioeconomic characteristics for every school in Maryland ("school data").[2] The following chapter describes the effects of MTO on the academic outcomes of the children who participated in the program. This chapter sets the stage for that analysis by describing the MTO program's impacts on children's schools.

Abt Baseline Surveys

Households applying to participate in MTO completed a baseline survey questionnaire designed by Abt Associates asking about household members (including adults' education and employment histories and children's completed grade level, participation in gifted or special education programs, and supervision during the day and evenings), reasons for applying to MTO, feelings about their current housing conditions, services in the current neighborhood (such as travel times to work and church), recent experiences with crime, social interactions with and assistance from neighbors, and parental involvement with children's schools. Baseline survey results are available for each family in the program.

School Data

School-level data come primarily from the Maryland Department of Education. The dataset provides information for 1,287 public schools for the 1992–93, 1993–94, and 1994–95 academic years.[3]

The dataset contains information on the socioeconomic characteristics of students (such as percent eligible for free or reduced price lunch programs[4]), the proportion of minority students, withdrawals and entries during each school year, dropout rates, the proportion of graduating students who go on to two- and four-year colleges, the percentage of students who are absent less than 5 days and more than 20 days. The analysis also uses data on student pass rates on the standardized reading and math tests that are part of the Maryland School Performance Assessment Program.[5] Finally, we have data from the Maryland Department of Education for school resources measured at the school-district (county) level.

Sample of Children's Schools

Central to the analysis is the set of schools attended by MTO children, identified through two methods:

1. *School records.* For the Baltimore County and City school districts (the residence of most MTO families), school officials were able to identify the schools attended by 370 of the 1,319 MTO children. The return rate for the City was low because student identification numbers did not correspond to Social Security Numbers, and the district had difficulty identifying children by name. The return rate was higher, but still only 50 percent, in Baltimore County, which uses Social Security Number as the student identifier. Several additional schools were identified by the Anne Arundel and Montgomery school districts.

2. *Follow-up surveys.* Follow-up surveys were the other main source of information on schools. Since we included questions about school names only on the child surveys (and not on the parent surveys), we obtained school names only for the randomly selected school-aged child from the surveyed families.[6] Some of these schools overlap with those identified from district records. Others represent schools in counties that did not respond to requests for school information.

This strategy generated school matches for 605 of the MTO children. Because the school districts sometimes identified school information for multiple children from the same family, the number of families from which our sample is drawn (396) is less than the number of children in the sample. For various reasons, this set of MTO children may not be representative of the overall school-aged population in the MTO program. However, along most dimensions, the children in our subsample are similar to the other children in the MTO program. Appendix A shows that they differ only in that they are somewhat older and tend to come from smaller families (largely because of our sampling strategy).

Predicted Moves and Opportunities

The MTO program, by facilitating the move out of public housing, changed the set of residential choices available to low-income families, though it did not guarantee educational improvements. Schooling opportunities for these families' children also changed. The magnitude and significance of the resulting changes were limited in two ways. First, participants' low incomes and Section 8 subsidies restricted them to areas with affordable rental housing. Second, MTO's experimental families had to move to census tracts with poverty rates of less than 10 percent. How do these constraints affect potential location decisions and the quality of schools that participating families can access?

Housing Market and Program Constraints

To answer this question, we identify affordable housing for MTO families as the voucher standard in each jurisdiction augmented by $100 (appropriately deflated to make the figures comparable to rents in the 1990 Census). Based on these rents, we use 1990 Census data to calculate the number of rental units affordable to MTO participants in each census tract, expressed as a share of the total number of affordable rental units in the Baltimore metropolitan area.[7,8] These calculations account for the variation in Section 8 voucher payment standards by county and housing unit size.[9] Since many landlords are reluctant to accept vouchers or certificates in lieu of cash, the estimates likely overstate the access of MTO families to the private housing market.

Estimates for the distribution of affordable rental housing throughout the Baltimore metropolitan area (defined as Baltimore City, Baltimore County, Anne Arundel County, and Howard County) show that more than half of all the rental units within the Baltimore metropolitan area that MTO families could afford are located in Baltimore City (table 5.1).

Table 5.1. *Population and Housing Market Characteristics for Baltimore* (percent)

	Baltimore City	Baltimore Area[a]	Anne Arundel County	Baltimore County	Columbia, MD	Howard County[b]
% of population in poverty	21.4	4.4	4.0	5.1	2.9	2.8
% of population black	64.5	12.7	12.0	13.6	20.4	5.6
% housing units rental	46.8	29.3	25.7	32.1	30.8	22.5
Rental vacancy rate	8.4	7.4	5.6	7.8	12.7	7.6
Units that are rental and affordable (as share of total stock of rental, affordable units in Balt. metro area)	53.9	46.1	12.1	28.0	3.7	2.4
Vacant units that are rental and affordable (as share of total stock of vacant rental, affordable units in Balt. metro area)	53.4	46.6	8.8	29.4	6.1	2.3
Units that are rental, affordable, and in low-poverty area ($< 10\%$) (as share of total stock of rental, affordable units in low-pov. areas within Balt. metro area)	22.7	77.3	23.0	41.3	7.9	5.2
Vacant units that are rental, affordable, and in low-poverty area ($< 10\%$) (as share of total stock of vacant rental, affordable units in low-pov. areas within Balt. metro area)	22.0	78.0	17.8	41.5	13.7	5.0

Source: Author's calculations from 1990 U.S. Census data.
Notes: Affordable defined using the Section 8 voucher payment standards, as described in text. Low-poverty tracts defined as those with poverty rates below 10 percent in 1990.
a. Baltimore area defined as Anne Arundel, Baltimore, and Howard counties.
b. Excludes Columbia, Maryland.

Given the transportation advantages and access to friends and family obtained by relocating within the city, together with the possibility of racial discrimination in the suburbs, this pattern suggests that families in the comparison group of the MTO program are more likely to move to other parts of the city than to move to the suburbs.

Families in the experimental group—which were required to move to census tracts with low poverty rates—are less likely to remain in the city. Almost four-fifths of all of the affordable rental units in low-poverty tracts in the Baltimore area are located outside the city. However, the exodus from the city is not likely to be dramatic given other forces such as availability of public transportation and support groups that may keep these families in the city.

School Quality in Areas Available to MTO Families

Of particular interest is how the constraints imposed both by the rental housing market and the program requirement of low-poverty census tracts affect the educational opportunities available to MTO children as measured by the resources of the schools, the challenges they face, and student outcomes.

The resources available to schools reflect various considerations—such as local property tax revenue, how state education aid is distributed among school districts, how the district distributes resources to local schools, and the amount of federal aid available through the Chapter 1 program and other programs to meet the needs of disadvantaged students.

Unfortunately, information on resources is only available at the district level (table 5.2). The city of Baltimore, with only $124,290 in property wealth per pupil, has less than half the wealth of the other Baltimore area school districts. Hence, it is significantly less able to raise revenue for local schools through property taxes. Federal and state aid, which together enable the city to spend about 90 percent of what Baltimore County schools can spend on education, helps offset the disparity. But the greater educational needs of city children likely keeps the gap in the level of educational services fairly large.

Table 5.3 describes the characteristics of students within Baltimore area public schools by four categories that are relevant for the MTO program. The categories include the 65 MTO baseline schools, attended by the children of MTO enrollees when they signed up; the 114 other public schools in Baltimore City, which represent the set available to most

Table 5.2. *Resources of Selected School Districts (1994–95 School Year)*

	Baltimore City	Baltimore County	Anne Arundel County	Howard County	State total (weighted)
Property wealth per pupil	$124,290	$269,442	$259,609	$282,594	$234,000
Spending per pupil	$5,566	$6,191	$6,144	$6,571	$6,106

Source: Maryland Department of Education.

comparison-group children; the 328 schools in the Baltimore suburbs, some of which the children in the experimental group can attend; and, for comparison, all 1,256 public schools in the state. All the averages are weighted by school enrollment, so that they refer to the school of the typical student in each category.

Some of the challenges facing city schools—whether MTO baseline or other schools—are much greater than those facing suburban schools. The city schools have many more poor children (as measured by participation in subsidized lunch programs), children who are absent more than 20 days per year, and much higher rates of student mobility, as measured by the percentage of students leaving the school in any year. By these measures, children who move out of public housing projects to other parts of the city are likely to end up in schools facing many of the same challenges confronting their old schools. Although the non–baseline city schools did face somewhat smaller challenges than the city baseline schools in terms of absenteeism and mobility, significant challenges remain in all of the city schools. In contrast, a move out of the city could, in principle, put a child in a school with a significantly more advantaged student body. Given

Table 5.3. *Student Characteristics*

	MTO baseline	City	Suburbs	Rest of state
(As a percent of all students)				
Free and reduced price lunch	66.8	70.6	17.8	30.4
Absent > 20 days	40.3	21.4	8.9	13.6
Withdrawals	25.8	20.5	10.4	12.6

Source: Maryland Department of Education.

the constraints of the housing market, however, such an outcome is not guaranteed.

Student outcomes can be measured in several ways: by high school dropout rates, the proportion of graduates continuing on to college, or student test performance. City dropout rates are typically much higher than those in the suburbs or the state as a whole. In 1994–95, about 13 percent of students in the MTO baseline schools dropped out, compared with 9.5 percent in the rest of the city schools and 2.8 percent in the suburban schools. Similarly, the percentage of high school graduates continuing on to college was much lower in the city than in the suburbs.

Test results for fifth-grade students on the Maryland School Performance Assessment Program show similar patterns (table 5.4). The rates of satisfactory performance for all fifth-graders are extremely low in the MTO baseline and city schools relative to schools in the Baltimore area and the rest of the state (although rates in those areas are fairly low as well).

Because most children in the MTO program are African American, it is instructive to look at the comparisons for black students alone (rows 3 and 4 of table 5.4).[10] The results are similar to those for all students: typ-

Table 5.4. *Student Outcomes*

Percent satisfactory	MTO baseline	City[a]	Suburbs[b]	Rest of state
All students				
5th grade reading	8.4	9.7	35.7	29.8
5th grade math	16.2	17.2	54.8	45.2
Black students				
5th grade reading	7.9	8.1	18.5	14.0
5th grade math	15.6	15.0	29.8	22.3
Value added				
(All students, medians)				
5th grade reading	−3.07	−2.84	−0.66	−0.34
5th grade math	−3.29	−5.79	0.50	−0.21

Source: Maryland Department of Education. Value-added estimates by the authors based on table C5.1.

Note: Results by jurisdiction are weighted by school enrollments.

a. Baltimore public schools excluding those schools identified as serving MTO students at the time of baseline.

b. Baltimore County, Anne Arundel County, and Howard County.

ically, test results are the weakest for the MTO baseline schools and are only slightly better for all city schools. Results for schools in the larger Baltimore area and for the whole state are significantly better.

Because high average test scores may largely reflect the socioeconomic backgrounds of a school's students rather than the effectiveness of the school itself, we may prefer to measure a school's effectiveness by its "value added." Our measure of a school's value added is the actual fifth-grade pass rate on the state reading and math tests minus the pass rates predicted for the school, based on its students' socioeconomic characteristics and third-grade pass rates (bottom of table 5.4). (See appendix B for an in-depth description of this value-added measure.)

To mitigate the influence of errors in our value-added calculations for individual schools, we report the median (rather than the mean) value-added measure for each category of school. The more negative an entry is, the less effective the category of schools. A school could emerge as ineffective for any of the following reasons: it has too few resources, it uses those resources ineffectively toward student learning, or its concentration of disadvantaged children generates negative spillover effects. By this value-added measure, schools in the city appear less effective than the schools in the suburbs or in the state as a whole.

By adding to the value-added equation dichotomous indicator variables for the affordability of the housing stock, we can examine the relative effectiveness of the public schools that are located in the census tracts that are most accessible to MTO comparison group families. (In the absence of information about school catchment areas, each school is assumed to serve students in the census tract where it is located.) The accessibility measures require a two-step process: first, we rank the schools in the Baltimore area by the percentage of the area's housing stock that is affordable and accessible under Section 8 standards; second, we divide them into quartiles, which allows for a nonlinear relationship between rental housing and school quality. Schools in the lowest quartile—that is, those with the lowest proportion of housing units affordable to MTO families—serve as our base category. A separate variable is included to indicate schools in Maryland outside the Baltimore area.

The schools that are likely to be most accessible to families with Section 8 vouchers appear to be significantly less effective in mathematics than those located in census tracts with fewer affordable rental units (table 5.5). The quartile 3 and 4 coefficients of −0.27 and −0.16 imply that student pass rates in these relatively more accessible areas are 16 and 7 percent

Table 5.5. *Selected Coefficient Estimates from Value-Added Regressions for 5th Grade Reading and Math in 1993* (quartiles defined by percentage of affordable and rental housing in tract)

	Quartile 1 (lowest)	Quartile 2	Quartile 3	Quartile 4 (highest)	Rest of Maryland
Reading	Base	−0.13*	−0.04	−0.07	0.18**
		(1.93)	(0.48)	(0.86)	(3.39)
Math	Base	−0.11	−0.27**	−0.16*	0.01
		(1.26)	(2.73)	(1.70)	(0.12)

Source: Authors' calculations of 1990 U.S. Census data and Maryland public school data.

Notes: t-statistics in parentheses. Cells contain coefficients estimated from a value-added model, which includes student socioeconomic and mobility variables, along with each school's 3rd grade pass rate in 1993.

*Difference is statistically significant at $p < 0.10$; **Difference is statistically significant at $p < 0.05$.

lower, respectively, than pass rates in the least accessible census tracts (quartile 1).

Experimental group families will be similarly constrained to apartments with rents below the Section 8 payment standards. However, the MTO requirement that such families move to low-poverty census tracts eliminates as a possibility much of the housing in the Baltimore area. Do housing market constraints then push experimental families into the least-effective schools within the area's low-poverty tracts? Are the schools they attend, in fact, better than those in areas with more poverty?

In table 5.6, we construct a separate category for all the schools located in higher-poverty census tracts (10 percent or more) in the Baltimore area and classify the remaining schools by quartiles based on the availability of affordable housing. Schools in low-poverty areas with the smallest proportions of affordable rental housing serve as the comparison group in this analysis; a separate indicator variable is included for Maryland schools outside of the Baltimore area.

Housing programs that do not require families to move to low-poverty areas may condemn the children of movers to the least-effective schools. The regression results shown in table 5.6 imply that the schools serving the low-poverty areas with the lowest proportion of affordable rental housing have pass rates that are 46 percent higher in reading and 32 percent higher in math compared with schools in the higher-poverty census tracts. Within the set of low-poverty census areas schools may be somewhat less

Table 5.6. *Selected Coefficient Estimates from Value-Added Regressions for 5th Grade Reading and Math Pass Rates in 1995* (quartiles defined by the percentage of affordable and rental housing within low-poverty census tracts)

	> 10% poverty	Quartile 1 (lowest)	Quartile 2	Quartile 3	Quartile 4 (highest)	Rest of Maryland
Reading	−0.64**	Base	−0.10	−0.11	−0.03	0.11*
	(5.20)		(1.28)	(1.45)	(0.41)	(1.89)
Math	−0.66**	Base	−0.06	−0.13	−0.21**	−0.04
	(4.88)		(0.58)	(1.33)	(2.12)	(0.60)

Source: Authors' calculations of 1990 U.S. Census data and Maryland public school data.

Notes: t-statistics in parentheses. Cells contain coefficients estimated from value-added models, which include student socioeconomic and mobility variables, as well as each school's 3rd grade pass rate in 1993.

*Difference is statistically significant at $p < 0.10$; **Difference is statistically significant at $p < 0.05$.

effective in areas with more affordable rental housing, although the results here are somewhat sensitive to how we specify the value-added model.

School and Neighborhood Outcomes

The previous section focused on how the market and program constraints implicit in the MTO demonstration may limit the potential gains in educational opportunities from residential relocation. The analysis presented here suggests that the schools that MTO movers attend are if anything of somewhat lower quality than we had predicted based on the availability of rental housing within the Baltimore area.

Program Population

The participants in the MTO program reflect the census tracts from which they moved, ones in which the average poverty rate was 67 percent in 1990. At the program's start, the tracts had four low-rise and four high-rise public housing projects. Together the projects housed 3,807 families who had an average income of $6,880. Virtually all (99.6 percent) of the families were African American (Goering, Carnevale, and Teodoro 1996). Information from the baseline surveys (table 5.7) indicates that MTO

Table 5.7. *Characteristics of Baltimore MTO Households and Children*

	Total	Experimental	Section 8	Control
Families (N)	638.0	252.0	188.0	198.0
Householder age	35.1	35.8	34.3	34.8
African American (%)	97.4	96.8	97.2	98.4
Female householder (%)	94.7	96.0	92.0	95.5
Receive AFDC at baseline (%)	80.3	79.3	81.6	80.4
Householder educ. (%)				
Has high school degree	41.7	44.1	45.8	34.8
Has G.E.D.	14.9	15.0	13.0	16.6
Number of children	2.62	2.57	2.75	2.55
HH has school-age child (%)	80.7	83.4	77.8	80.1
Child in K–6	65.0	64.7	64.4	66.0
Child in grades 7–8	23.2	27.0	18.9	22.5
Child in high school	13.9	16.6	11.7	12.6
HH engagement w/child's school (%)				
Attended meeting last 12 mos.	81.6	83.1	77.1	83.9
Attended event last 12 mos.	68.4	66.2	71.2	68.7
Volunteered last 12 mos.	47.5	50.2	50.3	41.4
HH has child who receives services for (%):				
gifted/advanced education	16.0	17.0	17.8	13.1
learning problems	21.2	19.5	25.6	19.4
behavioral/emotional problems	12.7	13.7	12.8	11.5
HH has child with physical, emotional, or mental problem[a] (%)	13.6	13.7	15.0	12.0
Has child who was suspended past 2 yrs	24.5	26.6	23.3	23.0
Has been called by school to discuss problems a child was having w/school or behavior	37.6	40.7	35.0	36.1

Source: Authors' calculations of 1990 U.S. Census data and Maryland public school data.
HH = head of household
AFDC = Aid to Families with Dependent Children
   a. Defined as a physical, emotional, or mental problem for which the child receives special medicine or equipment or that makes it hard for the child to get to school or play active games or sports.

applicants were almost exclusively African-American families, headed by a female, with very low incomes.

The average MTO household in Baltimore had 2.6 children. Four out of five families contained at least one school-age child at the time they applied. The educational experiences of the MTO children at the time of the baseline surveys varied greatly, with some doing well and others having problems. About one in five MTO families had a child who had received services for learning problems. At the same time, about one in six had a child receiving services for gifted or advanced education. The baseline surveys also showed that parents were involved in their children's schools. The majority attended a meeting or event at the child's school in the past year, and nearly half volunteered at the school. These figures are consistent with national samples of African-American and white parents (Cook and Ludwig 1997).

With random assignment of families to the three treatment groups (experimental, comparison, and control), the characteristics of MTO families should differ across groups only by chance. This expectation appears to hold up. Based on averages by group, shown in table 5.7, we use multivariate analysis of variance to test the null hypothesis that the sets of means are equal across each of the three MTO groups (see Johnson and Wichern 1992). The relevant test statistic implies families in the three groups are not different with respect to these variables.[11]

Relocation Patterns

Not surprisingly, the proportion of families that relocate through the MTO program is higher among the comparison than experimental groups (73 versus 58 percent) (table 5.8). Of the experimental group relocaters, 59 percent relocated to Baltimore City; the rest relocated primarily within Baltimore County (24 percent) and Howard County (13 percent). Although the program required experimental group relocaters to move to census tracts with 1990 poverty rates below 10 percent, that standard slipped in some cases: around 9 percent of relocaters moved to areas with poverty rates between 10 and 20 percent. In contrast, the vast majority of comparison group families who relocated moved to other parts of Baltimore City (88.5 percent). Of the comparison group relocaters, around one in seven moved to tracts with poverty rates with less than 10 percent, while more than a third moved to tracts with poverty rates of at least 30 percent.

Table 5.8. *Relocation Outcomes for Experimental and Comparison Groups*

	Experimental	Comparison
Total families randomly assigned	252	188
Percent of families who relocated through the MTO program	58	73
Destination of relocators (%)		
Baltimore City	59.0	88.5
Anne Arundel County	1.4	0.0
Baltimore County	24.0	7.7
Harford County	0.7	0.0
Howard County	13.0	3.8
Montgomery County	0.7	0.0
(*Number for whom we have relocation info*)	(*146*)	(*130*)
Percent minority in destination census tract[a]		
0–9.9	10.7	1.6
10–19.9	11.4	10.9
20–29.9	20.0	3.1
30–39.9	10.0	10.9
40–49.9	8.6	9.3
50 plus	38.6	63.6
Percent poor in destination census tract[a]		
0–9.9	90.0	15.5
10–19.9	9.3	27.1
20–29.9	0.0	19.4
30–39.9	0.0	27.1
40–49.9	0.0	8.5
50 plus	0.0	1.6

Source: Authors' calculations of 1990 U.S. Census data and Maryland public school data.

a. Calculations taken from Abt Associates (1997). Column does not add to 100 percent because one family in each group relocated outside of Baltimore PMSA, for which Abt did not calculate census tract characteristics.

School Quality for MTO Children

Estimates of the effect of randomly assigning families to particular groups within MTO, known as the "intent-to-treat" effect (Manski 1996) show that MTO successfully moved children in both the comparison and experimental group into schools with greater resources and more favorable student characteristics compared with the control group (table 5.9). Less clear is whether MTO moved children into schools that were actually more effective. (Appendix C describes the methods used to calculate these results).

Compared with children in control-group families, children in the experimental group ended up in schools with fewer poor students, as measured by the percent of students on free and reduced price lunch (18 percentage points lower than the control group) and in Chapter 1 programs (17 percentage points lower) and by the lower withdrawal rates (4 percentage points lower). These schools also had more resources, with around $34,000 more wealth per pupil and $200 more in annual expenditures per pupil (equal to 27 and 4 percent of the Baltimore City averages, respectively). Thus, these schools faced fewer challenges than schools serving children in the control group.

Not surprisingly, these schools also had higher test scores. The average fifth-grade pass rates on the Maryland standardized reading and math tests exceeded those of the control group's schools by about 6 percentage points in both subjects. These differences are sizable compared with the average Baltimore City fifth-grade pass rates of 8.4 percent for reading and 16.2 percent for math. At the eighth-grade level, similarly large differences are evident: the experimental group's schools have pass rates in reading that are 8 percentage points higher than the schools serving the control group; the difference in pass rates equals 12 percentage points.

The results differ markedly if we focus instead on each school's value-added—the residuals from the value-added regressions. For both the experimental and control groups, the value-added residuals are negative in both reading and math, suggesting that these schools underperform relative to what we would have expected given the socioeconomic characteristics of their students. In addition, the differences in the value-added residuals are not statistically significant. Apparently, being assigned to the experimental group does not substantially improve the average effectiveness of the schools the children will attend. Stated differently, the larger pass rates observed in those schools appears to reflect the higher proportion of children from economically advantaged backgrounds rather than the pure contribution of the school to students' learning.

For children in the comparison group, being randomly assigned to this group generally appears to improve schooling opportunities—though the effects are generally between one-quarter and one-half the magnitude

Table 5.9. *Effects of MTO Random Assignment on School Characteristics and Quality*

	Experimental[a]	Comparison[a]	Control[a]
School characteristics			
Percent free lunch (595)	66.82**	80.82*	84.82
Withdrawal rate (595)	6.94**	15.94	23.94
Percent special ed (604)	12.92	14.92	13.92
School enrollment (604)	697.34	717.82	731.59
School resources			
Wealth per pupil, $1,000s (596)	158.4**	135.5**	124.5
Expenditures per pupil, $s (605)	5,593**	5,451**	5,391
Instructional staff per 1,000 students (596)	57.7**	56.9**	56.6
Outcomes (raw pass rates)			
Reading—5th grade (445)	11.84**	7.84**	5.84
Reading—8th grade (99)	12.27**	6.27	4.27
Math—5th grade (442)	18.40**	15.40*	12.40
Math—8th grade (99)	20.48**	12.48	8.48
Outcomes ("value-added")[b]			
Reading—5th grade (400)	−1.34	−2.34	−2.34
Math—5th grade (430)	−4.57	−0.57	−3.57

Source: Authors' calculations from Maryland Department of Education data.

Notes: Statistical tests calculated from regression of school quality measures against MTO treatment group assignment variables, using Huber/White standard errors that are adjusted for nonindependence of observations (see appendix C). Resource variables measured at school district (county) level. All school characteristic and outcome variables measured in 1995; school resource variables are measured in 1994. To reduce standard errors for the experimental and comparison group variables, regression equations also include baseline survey covariates likely to be relevant for child's school quality.

a. Experimental and comparison values are calculated as control group school quality plus effect of assignment to experimental or comparison group, as estimated from regression equation as discussed in appendix A.

b. Value-added outcome variables are measured as difference between school's 1995 actual 5th grade pass rate and the 5th grade pass rate as predicted by 1995 student characteristics (free lunch and withdrawal rates) and school's 1993 3rd grade pass rates (see text). Negative values indicate that the school is "underperforming" relative to what we would have predicted given the socioeconomic composition of the school's student body.

*Difference between experimental or comparison group and control group is statistically significant at $p < 0.10$.

**Difference between experimental or comparison group and control group is statistically significant at $p < 0.05$.

of the effects for the experimental group. For example, assignment to the comparison group reduced the proportion of students on free and reduced-price lunch by 4 percentage points (compared with an 18 percent reduction for the experimental group); expenditures per student were $60 higher (compared with $202 for the experimental group); and average pass rates in reading were 2 percentage points higher (compared with 6 percentage points for the experimental group). When the outcome variable is our value-added measure of school effectiveness, we find that the schools serving comparison group students appear to be no more effective than schools serving children in the control group.[12]

It should be noted that the Department of Housing and Urban Development's HOPE VI program funded the demolition of several high-rise housing projects in Baltimore at the time of MTO. Because about 18 percent of Baltimore MTO families were living at baseline in projects targeted by HOPE VI, this program could complicate our analysis by generating additional residential mobility among the control group and thereby diminish the differences across MTO groups in neighborhood characteristics. But as it turns out, we obtain generally similar results when we estimate separate intent to treat effects for MTO families that reported baseline addresses in one of the buildings affected by HOPE VI.[13]

Effects on School Characteristics and Quality

Not all the families in the MTO experimental and comparison groups were able to lease-up. Meanwhile, some families in the control group, which received no relocation assistance through MTO, did relocate, with a few (less than 3 percent) moving to low-poverty areas. This relocation rate is higher than for other MTO sites, possibly because of the HOPE VI program and other factors. While some movement is typical, control-group children might not remain in their baseline schools for other reasons: some parents may have found ways to send their children to schools outside the local catchment area, others may have rotated children among relatives living in different catchment areas, or children may have been expelled from school. Thus, many MTO families did not receive the "treatment" prescribed for their random-assignment group. Consequently the analysis of the effects of being assigned to each of the different treatment groups understates the effects of relocating to a low-poverty area.

To determine the effects of relocating to a low-poverty area, we examine how the schools of the families who successfully relocated to areas of low poverty and the schools of other families differ. Because successful relocation may be nonrandom, we cannot simply compare the schools of relocaters with those of nonrelocaters. Instead, we need to use the outcome of the random-assignment process as an instrumental variable in the estimation process. (For a description of this method, see appendix C).

Which families were most likely to relocate? Compared with families in the control group, families in the experimental group were 51 percentage points more likely to relocate to a low-poverty area, while those in the comparison group were 6 percentage points more likely to do so (table 5.10). Families with more children were less likely to relocate to a low-poverty area, perhaps reflecting the difficulty of finding large enough quarters within those communities. Families with higher incomes were also less likely to relocate, which is consistent with the idea that families with relatively greater labor market success in their current neighborhoods may perceive fewer gains from relocating.[14] Householders with at least a high school degree or its equivalent were more likely to relocate to a low-poverty area, which could reflect one of two things: (1) more educated participants had greater motivation, or ability, to complete workshop counseling and to navigate the challenges of finding and leasing an apartment, or (2) more educated householders had greater motivation or ability to take advantage of improved employment or schooling opportunities in low-poverty areas.

The differences in school quality measures between families who have and have not relocated show that relocating to a low-poverty area moves MTO children to schools with more favorable characteristics (table 5.11). (Appendix C explains how results in table 5.10 allow us to adjust for nonrandom relocation.) As would be expected given the 58 percent relocation rates for families in the experimental group, the effects of relocating on school characteristics, such as socioeconomic status of the student body, resources, and average math and reading pass rates are nearly twice as large as the estimated effects associated with being randomly assigned to the experimental group. In contrast, relocating to a low-poverty area apparently did not put the children in schools that are more effective, as measured by our value-added variables.[15]

Actual versus Predicted Changes in School Quality

How do the schools that the children of MTO relocaters (both in the experimental and in the comparison group) attend compare with the schools

Table 5.10. *Effects of Random Assignment on Relocation to Low-Poverty Areas* (< 10%)

Explanatory variables.	Dependent variable: 1 if relocated to low-poverty rate, 0 otherwise	
	Full sample	Experimental and controls only
Random assignment to group:		
Experimental	0.51 (0.03)**	0.52 (0.03)**
Comparison	0.06 (0.03)**	NA
Householder has GED	0.09 (0.04)**	0.06 (0.05)
Householder has H.S. degree	0.05 (0.03)*	0.05 (0.04)
Number of children in HH	−0.02 (0.01)*	−0.02 (0.01)*
Total HH income ($1,000s)	−0.01 (0.003)**	−0.01 (0.004)**
Householder married	−0.08 (0.07)	−0.10 (0.09)
Last 12 months, adult in HH has:		
Attended meeting at school	0.04 (0.04)	−0.004 (0.05)
Attended event at school	0.02 (0.03)•	0.05 (0.04)
Volunteered at school	−0.04 (0.03)	−0.05 (0.04)
Child receives services for:		
Gifted/advanced education	−0.003 (0.05)	0.05 (0.06)
Learning problem	0.02 (0.05)	−0.01 (0.07)
Child has been suspended during last 2 years	−0.08 (0.05)*	−0.06 (0.06)
N	594	417
Adjusted R-squared	0.37	0.38

Source: Authors' calculations of Abt baseline survey of MTO Baltimore families.

Notes: Model estimated using ordinary least squares regression. Huber/White standard errors in parentheses (adjusted for nonindependence of observations).

NA = not applicable; HH = household

*Difference is statistically significant at $p < 0.10$; ** Difference is statistically significant at $p < 0.05$.

that we predicted they'd attend, based on the distribution of affordable rental housing within the Baltimore area? As shown in table 5.12,[16] schools attended by comparison and experimental group relocaters have fewer resources, more poor students, lower test scores, and are less effective than predicted.[17]

Most of the discrepancies between the actual and predicted analysis appear to be a question of neighborhood preference: MTO families were

Table 5.11. *Effects of Relocation to Low-Poverty Areas (< 10%) on School Characteristics and Quality*

	Families that relocate to low-poverty area[a]	All nonrelocaters
School characteristics		
Percent free lunch (595/418)	49.87**	82.60
Withdrawal rate (595/418)	16.78**	23.61
Percent special ed (595/418)	11.80	14.32
School enrollment (595/418)	657.35	724.22
School resources		
Wealth per pupil, $1,000s (596/419)	190.2**	129.3
Expenditures per pupil, $s (596/419)	5,754**	5,418
Instructional staff per 1,000 students (596/419)	58.5**	56.7
Outcomes (raw pass rates)		
Reading—5th grade (442/309)	16.87**	6.49
Reading—8th grade (99/72)	19.99**	5.38
Math—5th grade (442/309)	22.16**	13.22
Math—8th grade (99/72)	30.14**	10.23
Outcomes (value-added)[b]		
Reading—5th grade (400/280)	−1.56	−2.42
Math—5th grade (427/301)	−4.89	−3.14

Source: Authors' calculations from Maryland Department of Education data.

Note: To reduce standard errors for the experimental and comparison group variables, regression equations also include baseline survey covariates likely to be relevant for child's school quality.

a. School quality for families that relocate is calculated as school quality for experimental and control group families that do not relocate plus effect of relocation, as estimated from regression equations described in appendix A.

b. Value-added outcome variables are measured as the difference between school's 1995 actual 5th grade pass rate and the 5th grade pass rate as predicted by 1995 student characteristics (free lunch and withdrawal rates) and school's 1993 3rd grade pass rates (see text). Negative values indicate that the school is "underperforming" relative to what we would have predicted given the socioeconomic composition of the school's student body.

*Difference between experimental group relocators and nonrelocators is statistically significant at $p < 0.10$.

**Difference between experimental group relocators and nonrelocators is statistically significant at $p < 0.05$.

Table 5.12. *Actual Changes in School Quality for MTO Families Compared with Predictions Based on Analysis of Affordable Housing Stock in Baltimore Area*

	Experimental group relocators (< 10% pov tract)			Comparison group relocators		
	Actual	Predicted[a]	Predicted[b] (Adjust for suburban-move rate)	Actual	Predicted[a]	Predicted[b] (Adjust for suburban-move rate)
School characteristics						
Percent free/reduced lunch	56.81	26.81	44.60	80.01	46.27	71.33
Withdrawal rate	17.34	14.17	15.84	22.65	17.38	21.74
Percent special ed	12.62	14.29	14.68	15.30	16.32	17.66
School enrollment	656.09	651.42	645.92	682.99	615.68	594.01
School resources						
Wealth per pupil ($1,000s)	192.8	237.7	184.0	141.2	200.9	141.3
Expenditure per pupil ($)	5,901	6,072	5,859	5,639	5,774	5,648
Instructional staff per 1,000 students	54.4	56.2	55.0	54.0	55.4	54.3

(continued)

Table 5.12. *Actual Changes in School Quality for MTO Families Compared with Predictions Based on Analysis of Affordable Housing Stock in Baltimore Area (Continued)*

	Experimental group relocators (< 10% pov tract)			Comparison group relocators		
	Actual	Predicted [a]	Predicted [b] (Adjust for suburban-move rate)	Actual	Predicted [a]	Predicted [b] (Adjust for suburban-move rate)
Outcomes (raw pass rates)						
Reading, 5th grade	17.19	29.43	20.38	8.83	21.49	10.80
Math, 5th grade	25.58	45.01	31.66	16.53	35.09	21.00
Outcomes ("value-added")						
Reading, 5th grade	−0.42	0.02	−1.57	−1.62	−0.61	−2.38
Math, 5th grade	−1.82	−0.53	−2.35	−0.91	0.27	−0.13

Source: Authors' calculations of 1990 U.S. Census data and Maryland public school data.

a. Predicted school quality is calculated as average school quality in Baltimore metropolitan area, using the housing accessibility measures for each school's census tracts (discussed in the "Predicted Moves and Opportunities" section of this chapter) as the school's weight.

b. We first calculate the quality of the schools that experimental and comparison children would attend if their families allocated themselves across suburban neighborhoods and schools in proportion to the availability of affordable rental housing. We then perform a similar calculation for the schools that families would attend if they distributed themselves throughout Baltimore City in proportion to the availability of affordable rental housing. The adjusted predicted school quality for the experimental group is then equal to the proportion of experimental group relocators who stay within the city (59 percent) times the predicted school quality for city relocation, plus the proportion of experimental group relocators who move to the suburbs (41 percent) times the predicted school quality for suburban relocation. This last step is repeated for the comparison group, using the proportion of comparison group families who move to the suburbs versus city.

more attracted to rental units within Baltimore City than to those in the suburbs. To adjust for this preference, we recalculated the predictions, accounting for the actual split between suburban and city locations. Of the experimental group families, 59 percent chose to stay in the city. Accordingly, we predicted school characteristics assuming that 59 percent were distributed in the city (in line with the available, affordable housing stock in low-poverty areas) and assuming that the other 41 percent were distributed in a similar way in the suburbs. We used a similar approach for the comparison group families.

The results indicate that the schools actually serving children in experimental or comparison group families that relocated still have lower-than-predicted pass rates in reading and math. Yet according to the other measures of school quality (including the value-added measure), the experimental and comparison group families chose schools that were similar to the predicted measures.

Early Impacts

How has MTO changed the educational opportunities of children in Baltimore, and how might these changes translate into future educational outcomes? First, consider the comparison group families (Section 8 vouchers only). Assuming such families relocated to areas in line with the availability of affordable housing under the Section 8 guidelines, a disproportionate share would have stayed in Baltimore City, and their children would have attended schools that were fairly similar to those they had left behind.

For experimental families, the additional constraint that they move to low-poverty census tracts would make them more likely to move to the suburbs. However, this requirement might make it more difficult for them to relocate successfully. Assuming that families moved successfully, children in the experimental families should end up attending better schools, regardless of whether school quality is measured by the student body's socioeconomic status, the resources available to the school, students' average pass rates on standardized tests, or value-added measures of school effectiveness.

The neighborhoods and schools chosen by MTO families largely conform to these predictions. As expected, a smaller proportion of families in the experimental group successfully relocated than in the comparison group. And among those who did relocate, a larger share left Baltimore

City for the suburbs. Assignment to the experimental group also helped move children into schools with more resources, more affluent students, and higher pass rates on standardized reading and math tests. The surprising finding—and one that deserves further investigation—is that the value-added of the schools attended by the children in the experimental group appears no greater than that of the schools the children left behind.

Compared with the control group, a smaller share of students in the comparison group received subsidized lunches, while a larger share passed the Maryland tests. The comparison schools, however, also do not appear any more effective than the control schools by our value-added measure.

One explanation for the finding that children in the comparison group improved their schools by moving is that their families care about and were able to identify which schools in the neighborhoods they could access offered the best education. An alternative explanation is that their previous adverse experiences with crime led them to seek areas with relatively low crime rates and that such areas happened to be served by schools with fewer poor children and higher average student performance.

The finding that the schools attended by the MTO children in either the comparison or the experimental group were better than the control group schools in terms of resources, socioeconomic status of the student body, and average outcomes appears solid. But the conclusion that schools attended by the MTO children are no more effective than those attended by the control group children may be more questionable. The empirical and conceptual uncertainties surrounding our value-added measures call for caution. First, our value-added measures rely on school-(rather than student-) level data and make use of pseudo-cohorts to control for a student body's difficult-to-observe characteristics.[18] Second, our value-added measures represent the contribution of each school to student learning, controlling for the effects of the students' socioeconomic characteristics on learning. Hence, the approach may mask some important differences in school effectiveness. For example, schools serving better-off students will likely be better able to recruit and retain well-trained, talented teachers. Accordingly, our value-added measures might understate the difference in instructional effectiveness between schools serving poor and affluent students.

Taken together, the results reported here suggest that assignment to the MTO experimental or comparison groups in Baltimore moves children to schools with more resources and more affluent student bodies. These changes are not as substantial as we would have predicted based on the availability of affordable rental housing throughout the Baltimore area, particularly for the experimental group. The discrepancy between the actual and predicted changes in children's school characteristics appears to be due in large part to the tendency of MTO families to stay within Baltimore City. Our other key finding is that the higher math and reading pass rates found in the schools attended by experimental and comparison group children may be due more to the affluent student bodies in these schools than to the effectiveness of the schools themselves. Whether these improvements in the experimental group's peer groups translate into improved educational outcomes is a question that is taken up in the next chapter.

NOTES

This chapter was written in part while Ludwig was a National Academy of Education/ Spencer Foundation Postdoctoral Fellow in Education and was also supported by grants from the U.S. Department of Housing and Urban Development, the Spencer Foundation, the Georgetown University Graduate School of Arts and Sciences, and the Mellon Foundation. The authors thank Gary Brager, Rohit Burman, Robert Crain, Joe Darden, Dick Doran, Judie Feins, Bob Gajdys, Janice Gentry, Martin Gould, Joseph Hawkins, Rebecca Hawkins, Paul Hirschfield, Laura Hodges, Matthew Kazcmierzak, Jeff Kling, Debbi Magri-McInnis, Juan Carlos Mendoza, Carter Nicely, Terence Trader, Kerry Whitacre, Amy Yost, and Philip Walsh for valuable assistance. Special thanks to Ruth Crystal, Greg Duncan, John Goering, Jennifer Hochschild, Christopher Jencks, Shazia Miller, James Peterson, Steve Pischke, Jim Rosenbaum, Julie Wilson, and seminar participants at the November 1997 HUD MTO Conference and the University of Chicago for helpful comments.

1. Among the Section 8 requirements that landlords may wish to avoid are annual inspections of housing units. In addition, Section 8 paperwork may delay payments, and other tenants may react negatively to Section 8 families.

2. School data come from the Maryland State Department of Education, supplemented by data from the U.S. Department of Education's Common Core of Data.

3. We deleted 24 of these schools because they report no student population; we believe about half of these schools are evening schools. In addition, we deleted another seven schools that report only marginal information because they are "Home and Hospital" schools, kindergartens, or "alternative centers."

4. This choice provides a more accurate measure of economic disadvantage for elementary school students than for high school students because many eligible high school students, for various reasons, do not sign up for subsidized lunches.

5. Average standardized test scores within a school would be preferable to pass rates, but they are not available.

6. For some children living in Baltimore City or in Anne Arundel, Baltimore or Montgomery counties, the schools reported on the follow-up surveys were different from the schools reported by the school districts. Our default was to use the school

names reported by the school districts, though we replicate all of our analysis using the school names listed on the follow-up surveys in such cases as well. The results are generally not sensitive to these decisions.

7. We first calculate p_{ij}, the number of housing units in tract j of size i that had rent levels below the Section 8 payment standard plus $100, divided by the total number of affordable housing units of size i in the entire Baltimore metropolitan area. We then calculate the fraction of the Baltimore area's affordable rental housing located in tract j as $p_j = \Sigma i\ (p_{ij})$ and the fraction of the area's affordable rental housing in each county by summing across both housing unit sizes and census tracts within the county, or $p_c = \Sigma j \Sigma i\ (p_{ij})$.

8. CAN staff informed us that no families rented single-bedroom units because families with children are typically eligible for units with at least two bedrooms. As a result, we did not count any one- or no-bedroom units as "affordable" in our calculations, regardless of the rent prices for these apartments. The maximum voucher payment for a five-bedroom apartment was equal to the four-bedroom payment adjusted upwards by 15 percent, per federal regulations.

9. We also experimented with adjusting for the rental vacancy rate within census tracts. With this adjustment, we found no statistically significant relationships between any of the housing accessibility measures and school quality. This result may reflect the effects of at least two sources of measurement error with the vacancy variable. First, the 1990 vacancy rate within an area's rental market will be, at best, a rough approximation of the area's vacancy rate when MTO families entered the market during 1994 and 1995. Second, the 1990 Census does not provide vacancy rates separately for units in different rent categories, so we are only able to calculate the overall vacancy rate for all rental units within a tract.

10. Note that our average test results for blacks should be viewed as only approximate. Although we have test results disaggregated by race and gender, we do not have the numbers of students in each racial and gender group taking the test. The figures in the table assume that 50 percent of the students are male and 50 percent are female. Further, these weighted results are based on 1993 data on the number of black children by school from the National Center for Education Statistics Common Core of Data.

11. The value of Wilks' Lambda for the full set of means presented across tables 5.9 and 5.10 is equal to 0.735, with an F-statistic equal to 0.97 and probability value of 0.57.

12. Because the value-added results are somewhat surprising, we explored the sensitivity of our findings to the specification of the value-added model. We find that our results are fairly robust to different model specifications. When we use value-added outcome measures that are kept in log-odds form (rather than converted back into pass rates), the results are qualitatively similar to those presented in table 5.9. More parsimonious specifications that control for either previous pass rates or student socioeconomic characteristics, but not both simultaneously, also produce results that are quite similar to those presented in table 5.9, except that the estimated effects of assignment to the comparison group on schools' effectiveness in mathematics become slightly larger (by one-half and one-third a percentage point, respectively) and become statistically significant at the 10 percent level.

13. We produce generally similar results when we estimate separate intent-to-treat effects for MTO families that reported baseline addresses in one of the buildings affected by HOPE VI.

14. Rosenbaum and Popkin (1991) find that suburban relocaters in Chicago's Gautreaux program had higher employment rates, but not higher hourly wages, than those who relocated to other parts of the city of Chicago. In this case, we might expect the greatest benefits of relocation to accrue to unemployed participants in MTO.

15. Alternative specifications of the value-added model do not alter this conclusion. Substituting a probit model for the linear probability model in the first stage also does not significantly change our estimates of the effects of relocating.

16. We predict the school quality for experimental and comparison group relocators by calculating the weighted average of school characteristics for schools in the Baltimore metropolitan area, with each school weighted by the relevant experimental and comparison housing accessibility measure, as described in the next section.

17. Note that the results for the experimental and comparison group relocators shown in table 5.12 do not exactly correspond to those shown in table 5.13. This discrepancy occurs because table 13 presents the actual outcomes for relocating families, while table 5.12 presents the predicted outcomes for relocating families as estimated from the instrumental variables regression described in appendix C.

18. That is, we control for difficult-to-measure characteristics of each group of fifth-graders in 1995 by using the pass rates for third-graders two years earlier, rather than matching each individual fifth-grader in 1995 with his or her own pass rate in third grade.

REFERENCES

Abt Associates. 1997. *Primary Tabulation of Destination Data, Prepared for the November 1997 U.S. Department of Housing and Urban Development Moving to Opportunity Conference.* Cambridge, Mass.: Abt Associates.

Cook, Philip J., and Jens Ludwig. 1997. "Weighing the 'Burden of Acting White': Are There Race Differences in Attitudes Towards Education?" *Journal of Policy Analysis and Management* 16(2): 256–78.

Goering, John, Katherine Carnevale, and Manuel Teodoro. 1996. *Expanding Housing Choices for HUD-Assisted Families: Moving to Opportunity.* Washington, D.C.: HUD.

Hausman, Jerry A., and David Wise. 1979. "Attrition Bias in Experimental and Panel Data: The Gary Income Maintenance Experiment." *Econometrica* 47(2): 455–73.

Jencks, Christopher, and Susan E. Mayer. 1990. "The Social Consequences of Growing Up in a Poor Neighborhood." In *Inner-City Poverty in the United States,* edited by Laurence Lynn and Michael McGeary (111–86). Washington, D.C.: National Academy Press.

Johnson, Richard A., and Dean W. Wichern. 1992. *Applied Multivariate Statistical Analysis.* Englewood Cliffs, N.J.: Prentice Hall.

Ladd, Helen F., Rebecca L. Roselius, and Randall P. Walsh. 1997. "Using Student Test Scores to Measure the Effectiveness of Schools." Paper prepared for the Nineteenth Annual Research Conference of the Association of Public Policy Analysis and Management, Washington, D.C.

Manski, Charles F. 1996. "Learning About Treatment Effects from Experiments with Random Assignment of Treatments." *Journal of Human Resources* 31(4): 707–33.

Rosenbaum, James E., and Susan J. Popkin. 1991. "Employment and Earnings of Low-Income Blacks Who Move to Middle-Class Suburbs." In *The Urban Underclass*, edited by Christopher Jencks and Paul E. Peterson (342–56). Washington, D.C.: Brookings Institution.

Rouse, Cecilia E. 1997. "Private School Vouchers and Student Achievement: An Evaluation of the Milwaukee Parental Choice Program." NBER Working Paper 5964.

APPENDIX 5A

Representativeness of School Sample for MTO Children

Despite our attempts to follow up the addresses and schools of MTO families using several different methods and data sources, address and school information are still missing for some families that participated in the Baltimore demonstration. Conceivably, there may be some systematic differences between children whose schools we could identify versus the ones we could not find schools for. To explore this possibility, we conducted a probit analysis using as our dependent variable an indicator (equal to 1 if we had information about the post-intervention school that the child attended, equal to 0 otherwise) and a set of covariates related to family socioeconomic status and child characteristics. The results are presented in appendix table 5.A1.

Except along two dimensions—age of the child and size of the families—the children in our subsample appear to be very similar to the rest of the children in the MTO program. Compared with the other MTO children, the children for whom we have school data tend to be somewhat older and tend to come from smaller families.

Table 5.A1. *Probit Analysis for Child/School Matched Sample*

	Dependent variable equals 1 if school of attendance available for child, 0 otherwise	
	Full sample[a] (1)	Experimental group sample[a] (2)
Child's age[b]	$.5 \times 10^{-3}$ $(.3 \times 10^{-3})$**	$.5 \times 10^{-3}$ $(.1 \times 10^{-3})$**
Family receives AFDC	−0.22 (0.14)	−0.47 (0.25)*
Last 12 months, householder:		
Went to meeting at school	0.06 (0.14)	0.01 (0.22)
Went to event at school	−0.09 (0.11)	−0.20 (0.17)
Volunteered at school	−0.16 (0.09)*	−0.14 (0.16)
Female-headed household	0.11 (0.29)	0.47 (0.65)
Householder has GED	0.02 (0.12)	−0.07 (0.21)
Householder has h.s. degree	0.04 (0.10)	−0.22 (0.17)
Householder works full-time	0.05 (0.15)	−0.07 (0.24)
Householder married	−0.05 (0.22)	0.45 (0.42)
Householder separated	0.18 (0.14)	0.37 (0.21)*
Householder divorced	−0.13 (0.16)	0.39 (0.23)*
Householder widowed	0.02 (0.25)	0.32 (0.61)
Household income ($1,000s)	−0.01 (0.01)	−0.02 (0.02)
Number of children in HH	0.10 (0.03)**	−0.10 (0.06)*
Someone in HH victimized by crime last 6 months	−0.04 (0.09)	−0.06 (0.14)
Log likelihood	−576.3	−224.7
N	1,532	630

Source: Authors' calculations of Abt baseline surveys of Baltimore families.
Note: Standard errors in parentheses.
AFDC = Aid to Families with Dependent Children
HH = household
a. Samples restricted to those children age 5 and older at the time of the baseline survey.
b. Coded as date of birth measures as number of days after January 1, 1960.
*Difference is statistically significant at $p < 0.10$; **Difference is statistically significant at $p < 0.05$.

Estimating Schools' Value-Added

Measures of each school's value-added are most accurately estimated with longitudinally matched data at the student level (Ladd, Roselius, and Walsh 1997). Because such data are not available for Maryland, we rely on pseudo-cohorts of students at the school level to estimate the contribution of each school to the learning of its students. The dependent variable in each equation is the log of the odds of each school's fifth-grade pass rate on the state reading or math test. Explanatory variables include several measures of a school's student population, including socioeconomic characteristics and withdrawal rates. As a proxy for prior performance, we include pass rates for third-graders in the same school in 1993; the groups of students will differ somewhat because of student mobility, which is particularly high in city schools (where withdrawal rates exceed 20 percent).

We have experimented with many forms of a model to predict fifth-grade test scores. The strongest model, by our estimate, takes the following form:

(B1) $\text{Log}((P5)/(1 - P5)) = f(P3, P3^2, PS3, PS3^2, P3{*}PS3, C, W),$

where

> $P5$ is a pass rate (more precisely, the fraction of students receiving a satisfactory grade or better) for a fifth-grade subject such as reading, math, language arts, or writing:
>
> $P3$ is a pass rate for that same subject for third-graders two years earlier;[1]
>
> $PS3$ is the pass rate of third-graders in a different subject;
>
> C is a vector of student characteristics at the school level, including the logarithm of the percentage of students receiving free or reduced price lunch, and the fractions of students in special education and Chapter 1 programs; and

W is the percentage of students leaving the school during the year.

For example, we predict a school's fifth-grade pass rate in math as a function of the school's third-grade pass rate in math two years before, its third-grade pass rate in language arts and, to allow for nonlinearities, those two variables squared and interacted. In addition, we control for various characteristics of the student body, such as the percentage of students receiving subsidized lunches or with limited proficiency in English and the mobility of students out of the school. We have written the dependent variable in the form of log of the odds of passing to ensure that the predicted pass rates fall in the range of 0 to 1.

As a measure of each school's value-added, we simply use the difference between each school's actual pass rate (for fifth-grade students) and the pass rate predicted by the equation. While this measure is imperfect, it is the best we can do with the available data. Fortunately, the results generally seem reasonable. The main problem arises from the reliance on school-level aggregates (at the fifth-grade level) rather than longitudinally matched student data. To examine the quality of our estimates, we used a dataset on student test scores in North Carolina that were longitudinally matched by student over the period 1993–95. With this North Carolina data we were able to simulate school effectiveness measures for North Carolina schools using a method similar to the one we used for Maryland. We then compared these measures to the best measures of school effectiveness (at the fifth-grade level) that could be estimated with that data. Those best measures, described in Ladd, Roselius, and Walsh (1997), are derived from equations that predict fifth-grade scores for individual students using fourth-grade scores as explanatory variables, with appropriate corrections for measurement error. The correlation between the gold-plated measures and the measures using the methodology for Maryland is 0.55. If we do not make the correction for measurement error (which requires that we use the third-grade test scores as an instrument for fourth-grade scores), we can use the North Carolina data to estimate each school's value-added between third and fifth grade, which is more comparable to the approach we used for Maryland. The correlation between the third- to fifth-grade school effectiveness measures based on the individual data and that based on school level data is 0.77.

Calculation of Program Effects

The results shown in tables 5.9 and 5.11 come from estimating regression equations for both the effect of random assignment on school quality (the intent-to-treat effect) and the effects of relocation. Let y_i represent some dependent variable of interest for parent or child i; for example, the pass rate within a school on a standardized reading or math test, or expenditures per pupil, or some other measure of either school inputs or outputs,[2] and let $z_i(n)$ represent the treatment intended for each family i, where n signifies the group to which families were randomly assigned, with 0 for the control group, 1 for the comparison group, and 2 the experimental group. We assign the value 1 to $z_i(n)$ if family i is assigned to program n and the value 0 otherwise.

We determine the intent-to-treat effect by applying ordinary least squares to equation (C2), using the full sample of Baltimore MTO families.

(C1) $$y_i = \alpha_1 z_i(1) + \alpha_2 z_i(2) + \beta x_i + \varepsilon_i.$$

The parameter α_1 represents the effects of being assigned to the experimental group and α_2 the effects of assignment to the comparison group, compared with the counterfactual of what would have happened to low-income families in the targeted Baltimore census tracts in the absence of MTO (including mobility induced by HOPE VI). We include a vector x_i of socioeconomic characteristics that may be relevant for outcome y_i in the equation to generate more efficient estimates of α_1 and α_2 (that is, to reduce the size of their standard errors). We present Huber/White standard errors to control for the nonindependence of the error terms, since our dataset contains multiple children from some families.

The parameter α_1 estimated from equation (C1) is the product of the proportion of experimental group families who relocate to low-poverty areas (designated by r_1) and the effects of relocation to a low-poverty area on school characteristics, λ (see, for example, Rouse 1997). Because r_1 will be less than one, the intent-to-treat effects estimated in the preceding section will understate the effects on school quality of relocating to a low-poverty area:

(C2) $$\alpha_1 = (r_1) * (\lambda).$$

Our goal is to estimate the effects of relocating to a low-poverty area on various school characteristics y_i as in the following equation:

(C3) $$y_i = \lambda t_i(1) + \beta x_i + \varepsilon_i,$$

where $t_i(1) = 1$ represents the "treatment" of relocating to a low-poverty area (with $t_i(1) = 0$ otherwise) and x_i represents the same set of covariates as in equation (C1). If we were to estimate this equation by ordinary least squares we would obtain a biased estimate of λ, the treatment effect since a family's success at relocating is not a random event and may well be correlated with unobserved family characteristics that are captured by the error term, ε_i. The effects of relocating to a low-poverty area λ can be identified by using the outcome of the random-assignment process as an instrumental variable. This instrument is appropriate since the group to which each family is assigned [$z_i(1) = 1$ for the experimental group and $z_i(2) = 1$ for the comparison group] is exogenous (outside the family's control) and is highly correlated with the likelihood of relocating to a low-poverty area ($t_i(1) = 1$). Hence we first predict the probability that a family relocates to an area with a low poverty rate using either a linear probability model or a probit model of the following form:

(C4) $$t_i(1) = \delta_1 z_i(1) + \delta_2 z_i(2) + \gamma x_i + v_i.$$

We then substitute the predicted probability of relocation to a low-poverty area for the actual probability of treatment in equation (C4), that is, we estimate an equation of the form:

(C5) $$y_i = \lambda t_i(1) + \beta x_i + \varepsilon_i,$$

where $t_i(1)$ represents the predicted probability of relocating to a low-poverty area.

NOTES

1. Because we are missing third-grade pass rates for reading in 1993, we substituted the third-grade pass rates in language arts in the fifth-grade regression equation for reading.

2. In the future we will make use of the longitudinal structure of our dataset, for example from the overlap in questions on our follow-up surveys and the Abt baseline surveys, or the multiple periods of data that we have from state administrative records, to define the outcomes of interest as individual gains. This strategy may increase the power of our evaluation in light of previous findings that individual fixed-effects in the New Jersey NIT experiment were responsible for the majority of the variation in response (Hausman and Wise 1979).

6

The Effects of MTO on Children and Parents in Baltimore

Jens Ludwig
Greg J. Duncan
Helen F. Ladd

oes moving from high- to low-poverty neighborhoods provide families with more productive opportunities and social supports? And if it does, can families take advantage of these environmental changes? In the previous chapter, Helen Ladd and Jens Ludwig raised questions about whether low-poverty areas provide MTO families with access to better opportunities in one important dimension—education. This chapter extends the analysis to examine whether relocating families leads to behavioral changes in three important areas: children's school achievement, an important motivation behind the congressional legislation that authorized MTO; adult labor market outcomes, such as employment, earnings, and welfare use, the focal point for most social policy discussions about poverty; and juvenile delinquency, an important contributor to the substantial costs of crime in the United States—on the order of $1 trillion per year by one recent estimate (Anderson 1999).[1]

The findings from the Baltimore site are generally positive and consistent with those from the other MTO demonstration sites. Helping low-income families move from high- to low-poverty neighborhoods appears to improve children's academic achievement test scores and to reduce their involvement in violent crime. Less clear is whether the offer to move to a lower-poverty area engenders some less desirable changes among children, such as more property offending or disciplinary problems in school.

Because we may expect law enforcement and school authorities to enforce more rigorous behavioral standards in areas with low poverty compared with those with high poverty, increased disciplinary actions or arrests for property crimes among those who move into lower-poverty neighborhoods may simply reflect changes in enforcement rather than in participants' behaviors.

For adults, the evidence suggests that those provided with vouchers and required to move to a low-poverty area (the experimental group) were less likely than families that did not receive a voucher or move (the control group) to be on welfare, a finding that has not been found in the other demonstration sites. Consistent with the other MTO sites, employment or earnings rates, as measured by data from Maryland's unemployment insurance (UI) system, did not change following the moves.

Why Might Neighborhoods Matter?

That MTO's offer to move families from high- to low-poverty neighborhoods should improve their well-being makes sense when we consider the troubled state of much of the nation's public housing. Such moves, at the least, should improve the quality of housing that families occupy. Neighborhoods should also be safer and healthier. Compared with more affluent areas, high-poverty neighborhoods, on average, are characterized by high levels of crime (Sampson, Raudenbush, and Earls 1997) and pollution (Gayer 2000; Hamilton 1995). Consistent with these expectations, data from the Boston MTO site reveals that families that moved experienced fewer injuries or asthma attacks, as well as improvements in other measures of physical and mental health, than families that did not move (see chapter 9 of this volume).

Less clear is whether neighborhood attributes have any impact on family *behaviors*. Anthropological conceptions of poverty in the 1960s viewed the poor as being trapped in a "culture of poverty," with little hope of ever escaping: "By the time slum children are six or seven, they have usually absorbed the basic attitudes and values of their subculture and are not psychologically geared to take full advantage of the changing conditions or increased opportunities that may occur in their lifetime" (Lewis, 1968, 188). Today, most observers—as evidenced by the debate over welfare reform—would reject such a position.

In this chapter we discuss three aspects of neighborhoods that may affect individual behavior: the behaviors of one's neighbors, the sociodemographic or personal characteristics of one's neighbors, and the institutional features of the neighborhood itself (Manski 1993). The social processes implied by the three categories of "neighborhood effects" have different implications for public policy.

Peer Behavior

Casual empiricism strongly suggests that individuals respond to the attitudes and behaviors of those around them. Many high school students who would never wear a coat and tie or formal evening gown to school would also not show up at their proms wearing a sweatshirt, jeans, and sneakers. Decisions about what to wear (and when) show how the expectations of others in the community influence behavior.

In principle, the same phenomenon may generalize to various pro- and antisocial behaviors. Sociologists have long argued that the degree of social support for prosocial behaviors (such as work) and the stigma associated with antisocial activities (such as crime) relates to an area's socioeconomic composition (for example, Wilson 1987). The behaviors and attitudes of one's neighbors may also affect individual behavior more indirectly: Sampson, Raudenbush, and Earls (1997) argue that more socially cohesive communities are better able to enforce prosocial norms. In areas with high degrees of "collective efficacy," they contend, neighbors are more likely to report antisocial behavior to police or to the offender's parents. This greater supervision likely curbs delinquent behavior. Parents living in safe neighborhoods, among neighbors they trust, may also be more likely to go to work and not worry about their children. The key prediction from this social reinforcement process is that moves from high- to low-poverty neighborhoods should lead to more prosocial and fewer antisocial behaviors among movers.

Peer Characteristics

Alternatively, the sociodemographic and personal characteristics of neighbors, rather than their behaviors and attitudes, may matter more in affecting the behavior of individual neighborhood residents. For example teens growing up in neighborhoods with few successfully employed, educated adults may have a more difficult time understanding the value of staying in school (Ludwig 1999; Wilson 1987). Employed neighbors also provide a more useful set of job contacts and referrals than unemployed neighbors (Wilson 1996). These effects need not be positive: As Jencks and Mayer (1990) note, the competition in school or jobs may be greater in more affluent areas and may discourage or alienate some children.

Neighborhood Institutions

A final possibility is that neighborhoods' institutional and structural features may be the most important factor in determining how people act. Obvious examples include the quality of public services, schools, and law enforcement. The traveling distance to lower-skill job opportunities may also affect behavior; the migration of such jobs from the central-city to the suburbs over recent decades has led many labor economists to worry about a "spatial mismatch" between inner-city workers and suburban job opportunities (Holzer 1991; Raphael 1998).

Although more affluent communities generally have better public services and more favorable neighborhood characteristics, not all residents necessarily have equal access to them. The gains to MTO families relocating in such neighborhoods may be mitigated in part by the possibility of variation within neighborhoods in access to those institutions. For example, if poor children attending schools in affluent neighborhoods tend to be sorted into lower-track classes, then the gains that MTO children experience will not be as large as anticipated based on the average school characteristics.

Taken together, these various hypotheses lead us to expect that, on net, moves from high- to low-poverty neighborhoods may improve the life chances of poor families to some degree, although we cannot rule out the possibility of adverse behavioral changes among MTO movers. If behavioral changes are evident, determining which of these three mechanisms explains them will be of interest to social scientists and public policymakers, given the possible implications for other antipoverty interventions.

Suppose, for example, that changes in the behaviors and attitudes of neighbors are responsible for "neighborhood effects." Policymakers could then, in principle, design programs that alter community norms to achieve the same behavioral changes as those brought about through the MTO relocations. If the behaviors and attitudes of people within a community are self-reinforcing, so that pro- and antisocial norms sometimes catch and spread as with an epidemic, then, in principle, even minor alterations to the attitudes or behaviors of a small group could lead to substantial changes in behavior among all neighborhood residents. Similarly, public policymakers can, in principle, improve many of the public services available to poor families in high-poverty neighborhoods without relocating these families, although previous efforts to improve public services such as schools in poor areas have not been on the whole very successful.

On the other hand if the *attributes* of a family's neighbors are what matter for individual behavior, then replicating the behavioral changes achieved by MTO would require policy interventions that increase interactions among people of different social classes or races. Possibilities include school assignment changes, such as magnet school programs; mixed-income housing programs that subsidize the housing costs of working- or middle-class families moving into higher-poverty areas; or mentoring programs that pair working- or middle-class adults with children living in high-poverty neighborhoods.

Because the MTO demonstration changes all of a family's neighborhood attributes simultaneously, it is difficult to determine which processes are responsible for any changes in behavior among program participants. Complicating matters further is the fact that families assigned to the experimental group in Baltimore also received counseling assistance to help them with basic life skills and to become economically self-sufficient. These counseling services provide yet another possible explanation for any behavioral impacts of the MTO program, particularly regarding labor market outcomes among adults. Since the processes described here have different implications for whether policymakers can replicate MTO's effects without residential relocation, efforts to identify the relative importance of these behavioral mechanisms should be a future research priority.

Data

This chapter's main findings are drawn from local and state administrative records on MTO program participants in the areas of schooling outcomes, juvenile crime, labor market earnings, and welfare receipt.

Schooling Outcomes

We measure schooling outcomes for children in the Baltimore MTO demonstration using student-level data from each child's official school transcripts. Because the Maryland State Department of Education does not maintain student-level data, we obtained student records for the 1993–94 through 1998–99 academic years from the six school districts that contained the 1,243 MTO children who were of school age during the sample period: Baltimore City together with Baltimore, Anne Arundel, Howard, Montgomery, and Hartford counties. (Baltimore City and Baltimore County are nonoverlapping, distinct jurisdictions.) Fully 98 percent of MTO children lived in three counties during the postprogram period (Baltimore City, Baltimore County, and Howard County), with Baltimore City accounting for the vast majority (85 percent).

Our main outcome measures come from student performance on two sets of standardized achievement test scores, the Comprehensive Test of Basic Skills (CTBS) for elementary and middle-school students, and the Maryland Functional Tests (MFT) for middle- and high-school students. CTBS scores are available in reading and math and are reported as the student's percentile rank within the national distribution in that year for the given test. Measuring scores as percentile ranks complicates efforts to examine how a given student's achievement changes from one year to the next. However, percentile rank scores are appropriate for comparing the level of academic performance of groups of students at a point in time, as in the MTO analysis. Percentile scores have the added virtue of enabling us to pool together students from different grades, since each student's percentile score is implicitly grade-adjusted. For the MFT, students in Maryland are required to pass tests in reading, math, and, in some years, other subjects as well in order to graduate from high school. Because of problems with the MFT math data, the analysis focuses on reading and relies on a constructed measure indicating whether the student has achieved a passing score on the reading test.

Other available measures of schooling outcomes include the number of school absences, an indicator for disciplinary actions (equal to one if the student has been suspended or expelled from the school during the year), and indicators for whether the student received special education services, dropped out of school, or was retained in grade. One complication is that unlike with standardized achievement tests, the meaning of these other measures may vary across schools. For example, some minor offenses, such as talking back to teachers, that garner suspensions or expulsions in affluent areas may often go unpunished in high-poverty schools, where school violence and gangs pose more pressing problems. If schools in low-poverty areas enforce stricter behavioral standards than do schools in high-poverty neighborhoods, comparing experimental and comparison group children with controls should *understate* any reductions in antisocial behavior and *overstate* any increases in such behaviors.

One final complication is that not all these school measures are available for each MTO child in each year. Some data are missing for reasons that are unlikely to bias the analysis. For example, only students in selected grades are administered the CTBS and MFT. However, data may also be missing for more worrisome reasons. Suppose, for instance, that low-poverty schools are more likely to classify MTO children as special education and then exempt them from testing; in this case, our analysis of average test scores for the experimental and control groups may overstate any positive effects of the experimental treatment on academic achievement. We examine the sensitivity of our estimates to the missing data problem below.

Juvenile Arrests

Juvenile involvement in crime is measured using official arrest histories maintained by the Maryland Department of Juvenile Justice (DJJ). These histories include the charges for which juveniles (under age 18) are arrested, the date and disposition of the arrest, and other information. These data provide us with an average of 3.7 years of postprogram criminal-offending information for MTO juveniles. The analysis focuses attention on the postprogram criminal activity of MTO participants who were between the ages of 11 and 16 at the time of random assignment. This age range is optimal for two reasons: children under the age of 10 or 11 are almost never arrested for crime, and the upper end of the age range includes only participants who were classified as juveniles by the Maryland legal system for at least some of the postrandomization period.

Previous research in criminology suggests that neighborhood characteristics may have different effects on different types of crime. For example, compared with affluent areas, poor neighborhoods have higher average rates of violent crime, but less property crime (Dumanovsky, Fagan, and Thompson 1999; Dunworth and Saiger 1994). Perhaps there are less valuable items to steal in poor neighborhoods. Alternatively, residents in such areas may be less likely to report more minor property offenses to the police. To address the possible heterogeneity in MTO's effects, we divide the arrests of the program population into three crime categories: violent offenses (of which 77 percent are assaults and 16 percent are robberies);

property offenses (of which 55 percent are larcenies/thefts, 25 percent are motor vehicle thefts, and 20 percent are burglaries), and "other" offenses (of which 50 percent are drug offenses and 19 percent are for disorderly conduct or resisting arrest). The MTO sample's arrests are more or less evenly distributed across the three categories.

Focusing on separate crime categories is also advantageous because it helps minimize the problem of variation across neighborhoods in "false arrests." Case studies suggest that police harassment and false arrests are disproportionately associated with resisting arrest and disorderly conduct (Ogletree et al. 1995), crimes that are included in our residual category. The main findings for the specific categories of violent and property offenses should thus be less susceptible to this bias.

Labor Market Outcomes

The Maryland Department of Labor, Licensing, and Regulation (DLLR) maintains complete quarterly employment and earnings histories for people employed in jobs covered by the state's unemployment insurance (UI) system. The UI program covers around 93 percent of all jobs in Maryland (Born 1999); the major exceptions include the self-employed, independent contractors, individuals working for religious organizations or the government, students employed by their schools, and those who work part-time at nonprofit organizations. The UI records also miss "off-the-books work," which ethnographic research has shown to be an important source of income for poor families (Edin and Lein 1997).

The UI data enable us to construct measures of whether a household head is employed in any given quarter and, if so, his or her total quarterly earnings. We also replicated the analysis focusing on whether anyone in the household is employed in a given quarter and total quarterly household earnings and obtained similar results. Our UI data are available for an average of 3.8 years following random assignment, with a minimum of 2.4 years and a maximum of 4.4 years.

Welfare Receipt

The measures of pre- and postprogram welfare receipt come from the Maryland Department of Human Resources (DHR), which maintains records that capture the start and end date of every period a family in the state receives public assistance (PA) cash benefits. The DHR data used in our analysis capture PA receipt through August 1998 for an average of 3.2 years following random assignment for families in the Baltimore MTO demonstration (with a minimum of 1.9 years and a maximum of 3.8 years). We use the start and end dates of each PA spell to construct an indicator of whether a given household head was receiving welfare benefits during a given quarter-year. Replicating our analysis focusing on welfare receipt by anyone in the household yields nearly identical results.

One complication for our welfare analysis comes from the fact that during our sample period, each Maryland county transitioned from the state's old welfare data system to a new data system. Unfortunately, these transitions appear to produce artifactual "spikes" in welfare receipt rates. To address this problem we do not use data from the new welfare data system. We focus our attention on the period that runs through the fourth quarter of 1996, when Baltimore County—behind Baltimore City, the Maryland jurisdiction with the most MTO participants—switched over to the new data system. (When we replicate our analysis using data through the fourth quarter of 1997, when Baltimore County switched over to the new data system, we obtain qualitatively similar results.)

A relatively small number of families (17 experimental group families and 9 in the Section 8-only group) live outside Baltimore City or County in other counties that transitioned to the new data system earlier than the fourth quarter of 1996. To address the missing-data problem that results we calculate upper and lower bounds on the program effect using the methods developed by Manski (1989, 1990, 1995).[2]

Methods

A broad literature has tried to understand "neighborhood effects" on individual behavior by comparing the outcomes of survey respondents living in different types of areas. The primary concern with these studies is that almost all families have at least some degree of choice over where they live. As a result, differences in outcomes between families living in high- versus low-poverty neighborhoods may reflect either the causal effects of neighborhood environment or difficult-to-measure family differences related both to outcomes and how residential decisions are made. It may not be surprising that the children of poor parents living in the affluent suburb of Bethesda, Maryland, have better educational outcomes than poor children living in Washington, D.C. But whether these differences are due to something about living in Bethesda or to whatever caused one set of parents but not another to move out of the city is difficult to determine.

MTO overcomes this "self-selection" problem by randomly assigning families who volunteer for the program into either the low-poverty experimental, Section 8 comparison, or control groups (see chapter 1). Because of random assignment, we can be confident that in the absence of the MTO program the outcomes of families across the three groups would, on average, have been quite similar. Thus, any differences in average outcomes between families assigned to the various MTO groups can be attributed to the causal effects of being assigned to a group that is offered the chance to move to a more affluent neighborhood, known as the "intent-to-treat" (ITT) effect. We estimate this ITT effect using a multivariate regression analysis as in equation (1). The key outcome measures of interest, Y_{it}, are available for most individuals or families, indexed by (i), in multiple postprogram quarters or years, indexed by (t). By regressing these outcomes against binary variables indicating whether the family was assigned to the low-poverty experimental group (E_i equal to 1 if so, equal to 0 otherwise) or Section 8 comparison group (S_i), the parameter estimates for β_1 and β_2 in equation (1) reveal the difference in the average outcomes across these groups over the entire postprogram period for which data are available. We also include a set of baseline survey variables and preprogram measures of the outcome of interest, X_i, to control for chance differences in preprogram characteristics that may arise with the relatively modest sample of MTO families in Baltimore. The standard errors for equation (1) are adjusted to account for the clustering of multiple children within given MTO families for the schooling and crime analyses, and for the fact that we have multiple observations over time for each individual in all of the analyses:

$$(1) \qquad Y_{it} = \beta_0 + \beta_1 E_i + \beta_2 S_i + \beta_3 X_i + \varepsilon_{it}.$$

The idea of comparing average outcomes across MTO groups, regardless of whether a family has moved or not, will strike many readers as counterintuitive. Suppose instead that we had chosen to compare the average outcomes of families that move within the experimental group with the average outcomes of the control group as a whole. This type of analysis may seem a more obvious way to identify the effects of moving from a high- to low-poverty area, but note that the families that move are a self-selected subgroup of the set of families assigned to the experimental group. Because of this, we would expect the outcomes of experimental movers to be systematically different from the average outcomes of the control group as a whole—even if moving had no effect at all.

The ITT calculations from equation (1) provide unbiased estimates of the effects of *offering* low-income families the chance to move through either the MTO experimental or comparison "treatments." These estimates will be proportional to the actual effect of moving on those families who actually move. Assuming that assignment to the experimental or comparison groups has no effect on those families assigned to these groups who do not move, we can derive unbiased estimates for the effects of moving on those who move by simply dividing the ITT estimates by the proportion of experimental and comparison families in the Baltimore site who relocate through MTO.

Consider an example: Suppose that 200 families are randomly assigned to either the experimental or control groups through a flip of a coin, that 50 of the 100 families assigned to the experimental group relocate, and that each family contains one and only one school-age child. Five years later we administer an academic achievement test, and find that the average test scores of the 100 children assigned to the experimental group are 10 points higher than the average scores of the 100 children in the control group. If assignment to the experimental group had no effect on the 50 experimental-group children whose families did not relocate, then it is easy to see that the 50 experimental-group *movers* must have gained 20 percentage points each on the test (10 percentage point ITT effect / 50 percent relocation rate = 20 points).

We focus on the ITT estimates to simplify the discussion, but readers more interested in understanding the effects of moving on the movers can simply divide the ITT effects for the experimental group by 0.54 (the fraction of movers within this group) and the comparison group ITT effect by 0.73. In what follows we often use the terms "offer to move" and "moving" interchangeably because the direction of the effects (and statistical significance) are the same, and differ only in magnitude.

Findings

The findings from Baltimore are largely consistent with evidence from the other MTO sites. Young children in the experimental and comparison groups achieved higher test scores than the controls and experienced fewer arrests for violent criminal behavior. For adults, the evidence from Baltimore seems potentially encouraging—those in the experimental group were less likely to be on welfare than controls—although the UI earnings data reveal no increases in employment or earnings rates, and similar declines in welfare receipt have not been found at the other MTO sites.

Schooling

Table 6.1 summarizes the effects of the Baltimore MTO demonstration on the educational outcomes of young children. The analysis focuses separately on elementary school children (those ages 5 to 12 at random assignment) and middle-school or high-school children (12 and older),

Table 6.1. *MTO Intent-to-Treat Effects on Schooling Outcomes of Young Children*

Item	N	Control mean	Experimental vs. control	Section 8 vs. control
CTBS, reading	458	25.13	7.34	6.39
(percentile score)		(2.47)	(2.75)**	(3.23)**
CTBS, math	404	28.77	7.48	1.48
(percentile score)		(2.69)	(3.67)**	(3.83)
MFT reading	347	.192	.178	.059
(fraction pass)		(.059)	(.083)**	(.093)
Absences	2,200	12.54	0.57	1.10
(days)		(1.02)	(1.16)	(1.31)
Grade retention	1,711	.075	−.013	.002
(fraction retained)		(.010)	(.013)	(.015)
Disciplinary actions	1,123	.150	−.015	.001
(fraction suspended/		(.026)	(.031)	(.039)
expelled during year)				
Special education	2,206	.162	.043	.052
(fraction)		(.024)	(.032)	(.037)

Source: Ludwig, Ladd, and Duncan (2001).

Notes: Sample restricted to MTO children ages ≥ 5 and < 12 at random assignment. Robust standard errors (in parentheses) are adjusted to account for panel structure of data set and presence of multiple children from the same family within our analytic sample. Estimates are calculated controlling for preprogram educational outcomes, as well as baseline family characteristics (see text).

**Statistically significant at $p < 0.05$.

in part because of the possibility of different program effects on young versus older children. More pragmatically, academic achievement scores are primarily available only for younger children, because schools in Maryland do not administer the same types of tests to students in higher grades.

Young children in both the experimental and Section 8 comparison groups had CTBS reading scores that were on average 6 to 7 percentile points higher than those of controls.[3] This large effect is equal to around one-quarter of the control group mean of 25 percentile points and one-quarter of a standard deviation in the national CTBS math distributions. By comparison, evidence from the widely cited Tennessee STAR class-size experiment suggests that moving elementary school children from classes with 22 to 15 students also achieves test score gains of about the same magnitude (Krueger 1999). Children in the experimental group also experienced a gain in CTBS math scores of about the same size, and their pass rates on the MFT reading test were nearly double those of the control group. Children in the comparison group did not see gains on the CTBS math or MFT reading tests.

Results for adolescents, at least at first glance, seem less positive (table 6.2). Compared with their counterparts in the control group, teens in the experimental group—and in some categories teens in the Section 8 comparison group—had higher rates of grade retention, disciplinary action, and school dropout. But as argued earlier, these differences may be due to the enforcement of higher behavioral standards in more affluent schools. Some of the results indirectly support this explanation: there are no statistically significant differences across groups in the two teen measures that are likely to be least sensitive to variation across schools in enforcement activity and standards—school absences and MFT reading status.[4]

Missing data represent the most important caveat, particularly for the CTBS achievement test scores. At least one valid observation was available for the disciplinary action, special education, absence, and grade retention variables for around 90 percent or more of the young children in the sample. CTBS reading and math scores, however, were available for only around half the sample, while MFT reading status was available for only a quarter of the children. Consistent with the hypothesis that preset school testing schedules are an important explanation for missing test-score data, the likelihood of missing test scores is strongly related to the academic year in question and the child's age, not to other student baseline characteristics.

Table 6.2. *MTO Intent-to-Treat Effects on Schooling Outcomes of Adolescents*

Item	N	Control mean	Experimental vs. control	Section 8 vs. control
MFT reading	679	.268	.073	−.009
(fraction pass)		(.063)	(.072)	(.071)
Absences	825	29.85	2.06	1.78
(days)		(2.20)	(2.92)	(3.45)
Grade retention	564	.092	.065	.109
(fraction retained)		(.021)	(.032)**	(.052)**
Disciplinary actions	328	.126	.086	.088
(fraction suspended/		(.033)	(.050)*	(.069)
expelled during year)				
Special education	826	.202	−.017	.013
(fraction)		(.049)	(.050)	(.059)
Dropout	1,384	.187	.062	.019
(fraction)		(.030)	(.036)*	(.043)

Source: Ludwig, Ladd, and Duncan (2001).

Notes: Sample restricted to MTO children 12 years old or older at random assignment. Robust standard errors (in parentheses) are adjusted to account for panel structure of data set and presence of multiple children from the same family within our analytic sample. Estimates are calculated controlling for preprogram educational outcomes as well as baseline family characteristics (see text).

*Statistically significant at $p < 0.10$; **Statistically significant at $p < 0.05$.

If data were missing nonrandomly, the estimates would likely be sensitive to whether we control for baseline characteristics, but this does not appear to be the case. The results are also similar when we replace missing values with the most recent valid observation on that variable for the child (Krueger 1999). While we cannot rule out the possibility that nonrandom patterns of missing data influence our results, the key achievement score results are at least not sensitive to our tests for this problem.

Juvenile Crime

The analysis suggests that the offer to move from a high- to low-poverty neighborhood reduced the proportion of juveniles who are arrested for a violent offense ("prevalence") and the number of arrests per 100 juveniles ("incidence") by around half. As shown in table 6.3, 2.7 percent of control group members were arrested during an average postprogram quar-

Table 6.3. *MTO Intent-to-Treat Effects on Juvenile Arrests*

Crime type	Control mean		Experimental vs. control		Section 8 vs. control	
	Prev.	Incid.	Prev.	Incid.	Prev.	Incid.
Violent crime	.027	3.0	−.013	−1.6	−.012	−1.4
			(.007)*	(0.8)**	(.008)	(0.8)*
Property crime	.018	2.0	.009	1.3	−.003	−0.5
			(.006)	(0.8)	(.007)	(0.8)
Other crime	.028	3.3	−.005	−0.7	−.009	−1.3
			(.008)	(1.0)	(.008)	(1.0)
All crimes	.068	8.3	−.009	−0.9	−.022	−3.1
			(.012)	(1.8)	(.015)	(1.8)*

Source: Ludwig, Duncan, and Hirschfield (2001).

Notes: "Prevalence" refers to the proportion of teens who are arrested per quarter during the postprogram period, while "incidence" refers to arrests per 100 teens per quarter. Sample restricted to MTO children 11 to 16 years old at random assignment. Robust standard errors (in parentheses) are adjusted to account for panel structure of data set and presence of multiple children from the same family within our analytic sample. Estimates are calculated controlling for preprogram criminal records as well as baseline family characteristics (see text).

*Statistically significant at $p < 0.10$; **Statistically significant at $p < 0.05$.

ter, compared with only 1.4 percent of experimental teens ($p < .10$) and 1.5 percent of comparison teens (a difference that is not quite statistically significant). Similarly, the incidence of arrest for violent crime among the control group equaled 3 per 100 teens per quarter, compared with 1.4 among experimental teens ($p < .05$) and 1.6 among the comparison group ($p < .10$). Interestingly, a reduction in robbery arrests accounted for around half the difference between experimental and control teens, even though robberies were only 16 percent of all arrests within the violent-crime category.

The prevalence and incidence of arrest for property offenses among experimental teens is around 50 percent higher than that observed for the control group, although these differences are not statistically significant (table 6.3). But more important, as with in-school disciplinary actions, the increase in property-crime arrests could simply reflect a higher probability of arrest per crime in low-poverty areas compared with high-poverty neighborhoods. If this source of bias held true, the results reported on violent crimes would understate the decline in violent behavior among the experimental teens.

Finally, because teenage boys account for the large majority of all juvenile arrests, differences among boys could potentially account for the bulk of the observed reductions in violent offenses between the experimental and Section 8 comparison group teens, on the one hand, and control group teens, on the other hand. However, the reductions in violent-crime arrests among teenage girls were also quite large in proportional terms, although the differences are not statistically significant.

Welfare Receipt and Earnings

On average, around 44 percent of household heads in the control group were on welfare in a given quarter during the postprogram period (table 6.4). By comparison, the proportion in the experimental group on welfare was around 5 to 7 percentage points lower. Interestingly, much of the decline in welfare receipt rates among the experimental group was already in evidence during the first year following random assignment. This pattern suggests that whatever processes are responsible for these changes—such as social norms in low-poverty neighborhoods that are more supportive of work than welfare, improved access to jobs or job referrals, or improved interview skills or knowledge of the earned income tax credit derived from the experimental group counseling—may not operate with a long lag. In contrast to the experiences of the experimental group, household heads in the Section 8 comparison group did not exhibit a sustained decline in the probability of receiving welfare.

Somewhat surprisingly, the movement of families off welfare is not reflected in higher quarterly earnings or employment rates according to the unemployment insurance data (bottom panel, table 6.4). We have also explored the possibility of an increase in the variance but not the mean of the earnings distribution for experimental families, under the assumption that families may exit welfare only when their earnings exceed some threshold, and have similarly found no statistically significant differences across groups.

One possible explanation for the apparent discrepancy between the UI and the welfare results is that experimental group adults are moving from welfare into government or other jobs not covered by the state's UI system. Some support for this possibility comes from findings that only around half of *all* welfare leavers in the state of Maryland were employed in a UI-covered job in the quarter following their welfare exit (Born 1999). Another explanation is that the UI findings are not necessarily inconsis-

Table 6.4. *MTO Intent-to-Treat Effects on the Labor Market Outcomes of Household Heads*

		Experimental vs. control		Section 8 vs. control	
Outcome	Control mean	Lower bound	Upper bound	Lower bound	Upper bound
Welfare receipt					
Entire postprogram period	−.44	−.054* (.028)	−0.74** (.028)	−.020 (.034)	−0.41 (.033)
Postprogram quarters					
1 to 4	.46	−0.47** (.023)	−.058 (.023)	−.030 (.028)	0.049* (.027)
5 to 8	.47	−.071 (.046)	−.108** (.046)	−.004 (.058)	−.029 (.057)

Outcome	Control mean	Experimental vs. control	Section 8 vs. control
Quarterly employment (entire post)	.45	−.009 (.027)	−.023 (.032)
Quarterly earnings (entire post)	1,020	−10.4 (96.1)	4.5 (112.9)

Source: Ludwig, Duncan, and Pinkston (2002).

Notes: Estimates are calculated controlling for baseline household characteristics; estimates for postprogram welfare receipt also control for preprogram welfare receipt, while estimates for postprogram welfare-to-work transitions earnings control for preprogram earnings and for postprogram employment control for preprogram employment. Upper and lower bounds for welfare findings come from imputing missing data for those experimental and comparison group families living in counties that had switched from Maryland's old to new welfare data system during the sample observation period (see text).

*Statistically significant at $p < 0.10$; **Statistically significant at $p < 0.05$.

tent with the welfare results, given the standard errors around both sets of estimates. For example, based on the UI data in table 6.4, we cannot rule out the possibility of a 5 percentage point increase in employment rates among experimental group adults compared with controls, which fits quite comfortably alongside the 5 to 7 percentage point reduction in welfare receipt rates for the experimental group. A third potential explanation is that welfare offices in the suburbs may be more likely than offices in the city to push families off welfare, even though every Maryland welfare office should ostensibly follow the same set of state rules governing the welfare program. But arguing against this last explanation is our finding of qualitatively similar program impacts when the sample is confined to those MTO families that stay within the city of Baltimore.

Early Impacts

The MTO experiment provides an important opportunity to learn more about the effects of neighborhoods on the life chances of low-income families. MTO overcomes the self-selection problem plaguing most previous studies of neighborhood effects by randomly assigning families into three groups, each of which receives different opportunities to move to lower-poverty areas. Yet even with MTO's experimental design, some challenges to valid inferences remain.

Perhaps the most important challenges for the research reported here stem from the inherent limitations of government administrative data. The Maryland school records do not include achievement test information for each student in every year. Our tests suggest that missing data do not appear to drive our results, but we of course can never be entirely sure. Administrative data on school problems and criminal arrests may confound differences in teen behavior across MTO treatment groups with variation across neighborhoods in behavioral standards and enforcement. Since the probability of sanction for a given behavior should be higher in low-poverty neighborhoods compared with areas with more poverty, this problem will lead us to understate MTO's effects in reducing antisocial behavior and to overstate any increases. And the data used to measure labor market outcomes misses jobs that are not covered by Maryland's unemployment insurance system, which may be a disproportionately important source of employment for less-skilled workers.

Subject to these qualifications, the findings reviewed here suggest that the chance to move from high- to low-poverty neighborhoods through the Baltimore MTO demonstration improves the life chances of children. We find that young school-age children (5 to 12 at random assignment) assigned to the experimental group achieve higher standardized test scores in math and reading than children in the control group. These gains (about a quarter of a standard deviation) are about the same size as those for elementary school students moving from classrooms with 22 students to those with 15 students (Krueger 1999). Children in the comparison group experience gains of about the same magnitude in reading, but do not appear to gain in math. Because similar measures of academic achievement are not available for adolescents in the Baltimore MTO site, we can say little about the program's effects on the achievement of older children.

For adolescents, the evidence suggests that those assigned to either the experimental or comparison groups are arrested for violent crimes at about half the rate as those in the control group. We also find that teens in the experimental group are arrested more often than those in the control group for property crimes and are also disciplined more often in school, although we cannot rule out the possibility that these changes reflect more strict enforcement in affluent areas. As a result we are fairly confident that moving from a high- to low-poverty neighborhood reduces the rate at which Baltimore MTO teens are involved in violence, and we remain uncertain about whether there are any offsetting increases in other forms of antisocial behaviors.

These findings are consistent with those reported from the other MTO demonstration sites. For example evidence from Boston (chapter 7) suggests that children in the experimental and comparison groups experience better mental and physical health than controls, and are also less likely to engage in antisocial behavior. Evidence from New York (chapter 8) finds that the quality of parenting for children in the experimental and Section 8 comparison groups improves. These findings from the Boston and New York sites would lead us to predict that children in the experimental and comparison groups should learn more in school and be arrested less often than controls—consistent with what we find in the administrative data available for the Baltimore site.

For adults, the findings from the Baltimore MTO demonstration are also encouraging, but less consistent with what has been found in the other MTO cities. We find evidence suggesting that welfare receipt rates are 5 to 7 percentage points (about one-seventh) lower among experimental group household heads compared with the control group, although there are no differences in welfare use between Section 8 comparison and control families. However, we do not observe any increase in quarterly employment or earnings rates as measured by state UI data. Survey data from the other MTO sites find no program impact on employment, earnings, or welfare use. The findings from the different MTO sites are not necessarily inconsistent. But in any case we should be cautious in drawing inferences from the Baltimore MTO site about the effects of neighborhoods on labor market outcomes, particularly since the counseling services provided to the experimental group could explain at least part of the observed changes in welfare receipt.

While ultimately it will be important to validate these initial MTO findings over a longer period, what do the results so far, if taken at face value, imply for public policy? The gains experienced by families assigned to the Section 8 comparison group raise the possibility that the federal government's regular Section 8 housing-voucher program, which now serves even more families than the public housing program (Quigley 2000), has improved the life chances of many families. This conclusion should be tempered by the observation that the MTO program population is a self-selected subgroup of eligible low-income families; since families volunteered to participate, these households may believe they have the most to gain from moving. Whether relocation can generate similar gains among a more representative population of poor families remains unclear. Moreover, we would also wish to learn more about the impacts on the families who do not receive vouchers and remain in public housing or high-poverty areas more generally, as well as the impacts on families living in the host neighborhoods into which voucher-holders relocate.

Finally, switching families from public housing to housing vouchers raises a variety of program-design issues, particularly about whether families should be steered toward certain types of neighborhoods, as the MTO experimental group was. While the offer to relocate through the comparison group sometimes generates the same gains as the experimental group relocation offer, on average, the experimental group experiences beneficial changes across a broader set of outcome measures. Since a larger proportion of families assigned to the comparison group relocate, the trade-off appears to be that movers gain more when they are steered toward lower-poverty areas but fewer people move with these restrictions in place. Another complication is introduced by the fact that relatively few comparison group families move into the lowest-poverty neighborhoods. Perhaps housing market constraints are more severe in these areas, which would make a large-scale effort to move poor families into the most affluent areas difficult. On the other hand, poor families may prefer other neighborhoods, in which case steering comes at the cost of reducing the utility of program participants compared with an offer of an unconstrained housing voucher.

NOTES

Research for this chapter was supported by grants from the U.S. Department of Housing and Urban Development; the Georgetown University Graduate School of Arts and Sciences; and the Andrew W. Mellon, Spencer, Smith Richardson, and William T. Grant foundations. It was written in part while Ludwig was a visiting scholar at the Northwestern University/University of Chicago Joint Center for Poverty Research and the Andrew W. Mellon Fellow in Economic Studies at the Brookings Institution.

    1. The results and discussion reported here are drawn from Ludwig, Duncan, and Hirschfield (2001); Ludwig, Ladd, and Duncan (2001); and Ludwig, Duncan, and Pinkston (forthcoming).

    2. The Manski (1989, 1990, 1995) bounding procedure that we employ in our analysis of welfare data consists of calculating the largest and smallest program impacts that are logically possible given the missing observations in the data. For example the upper bound on the experimental treatment's effect on welfare receipt comes from assuming that none of the experimental-group families for whom we are missing welfare data were on welfare during the missing calendar quarters. (Note that data are not missing for any control-group families, so we are not forced to impute any observations for this group.) To calculate the lower bound estimate for the experimental group's effect, we assume that all of the families for whom we are missing welfare observations were on welfare during the missing periods.

    3. The fractions of school-age children in the experimental and Section 8-only comparison groups who relocate through the MTO program equal 0.68 and 0.85, respectively (somewhat higher than the relocation rates observed among all families assigned to each of the two groups). These relocation rates imply an effect of moving on the movers (or the "effect of treatment on the treated" in the evaluation literature) equal to around 11 points for the experimental group and 7 points for the Section 8 comparison group (see Ludwig, Ladd, et al. 2001).

    4. Some readers may reasonably argue that dropout is a fairly objective outcome. However our dropout measure is actually inferred from students essentially disappearing from their school databases before the end of 12th grade. The higher dropout rates among the experimental group reported in table 6.2 could be explained if inner-city schools are less diligent about purging from their rosters students who no longer come to school.

REFERENCES

Anderson, David. 1999. "The Aggregate Burden of Crime." *Journal of Law and Economics* 92: 611–42.

Born, Catherine E. 1999. *Life After Welfare: Fourth Interim Report.* Baltimore: Welfare and Child Support Research and Training Group, School of Social Work, University of Maryland at Baltimore.

Dumanovsky, Tamara, Jeffrey Fagan, and Philip Thompson. 1999. "The Neighborhood Context of Crime in New York City's Public Housing." Working Paper, Mailman School of Public Health, Columbia University.

Dunworth, Terence, and Aaron Saiger. 1994. "Drugs and Crime in Public Housing: A Three-City Analysis." Washington, D.C.: U.S. Department of Justice, National Institute of Justice.

Edin, Kathy, and Laurie Lein. 1997. *Making Ends Meet: How Single Mothers Survive Welfare and Low-Wage Work.* New York: Russell Sage Foundation.

Gayer, Ted. 2000. "Neighborhood Demographics and the Distribution of Hazardous Waste Risks: An Instrumental Variables Estimation." *Journal of Regulatory Economics* 17(2): 131–55.

Hamilton, James T. 1995. "Testing for Environmental Racism: Prejudice, Profits, Political Power?" *Journal of Policy Analysis and Management* 14(1): 107–32.

Holzer, Harry J. 1991. "The Spatial Mismatch Hypothesis: What Has the Evidence Shown?" *Urban Studies* 28(1): 105–22.

Jencks, Christopher, and Susan E. Mayer. 1990. "The Social Consequences of Growing Up in a Poor Neighborhood." In *Inner-City Poverty in the United States,* edited by Laurence Lynn and Michael McGeary (111–86). Washington, D.C.: National Academy Press.

Krueger, Alan B. 1999. "Experimental Estimates of Education Production Functions." *Quarterly Journal of Economics* 114(2): 497–532.

Lewis, Oscar. 1968. "The Culture of Poverty." In *On Understanding Poverty: Perspectives from the Social Sciences,* edited by Daniel P. Moynihan (187–200). New York: Basic Books.

Ludwig, Jens. 1999. "Information and Inner City Educational Attainment." *Economics of Education Review* 18: 17–30.

Ludwig, Jens, Greg J. Duncan, and Paul Hirschfield. 2001. "Urban Poverty and Juvenile Crime: Evidence from a Randomized Housing-Mobility Experiment." *Quarterly Journal of Economics* 116(2): 655–80.

Ludwig, Jens, Greg J. Duncan, and Joshua C. Pinkston. 2002. "Neighborhood Effects on Self-Sufficiency: Evidence from a Randomized Housing-Mobility Experiment." Working paper, Georgetown University.

Ludwig, Jens, Helen F. Ladd, and Greg J. Duncan. 2001. "Urban Poverty and Educational Outcomes." In *Brookings-Wharton Papers on Urban Affairs, 2001,* edited by William G. Gale and Janet Rothenberg Pack (147–202). Washington, D.C.: Brookings Institution.

Manski, Charles F. 1989. "Anatomy of the Selection Problem." *Journal of Human Resources* 24: 343–60.

———. 1990. "Nonparametric Bounds on Treatment Effects." *American Economics Review* 80(2): 319–23.

————. 1993. "Identification of Endogenous Social Effects." *Review of Economic Studies* 150: 531–42.

————. 1995. *Identification Problems in the Social Sciences.* Cambridge, Mass.: Harvard University Press.

Ogletree, Charles J., Mary Prosser, Abbe Smith, and William Talley. 1995. *Beyond the Rodney King Story.* Boston: Northeastern University Press.

Quigley, John M. 2000. "A Decent Home: Housing Policy in Perspective." In *Brookings-Wharton Papers on Urban Affairs, 2000,* edited by William G. Gale and Janet Rothenberg Pack (53–100). Washington, D.C.: Brookings Institution.

Raphael, Steve. 1998. "The Spatial Mismatch Hypothesis and Black Youth Joblessness: Evidence from the San Francisco Bay Area." *Journal of Urban Economics* 43: 79–111.

Sampson, Robert J., Stephen W. Raudenbush, and Felton Earls. 1997. "Neighborhoods and Violent Crime: A Multilevel Study of Collective Efficacy." *Science* (277): 918–24.

Wilson, William Julius. 1987. *The Truly Disadvantaged.* Chicago: University of Chicago Press.

————. 1996. *When Work Disappears: The World of the New Urban Poor.* New York: Knopf.

7

Boston Site Findings

The Early Impacts of Moving to Opportunity

Lawrence F. Katz
Jeffrey R. Kling
Jeffrey B. Liebman

This chapter evaluates the early impacts on safety, health, employment, and other outcomes of the MTO demonstration at the Boston site. We exploit the random-assignment design of the demonstration and compare the outcomes of the experimental and Section 8 comparison groups with those of the control group. These differences in outcomes should be considered estimates of the program's early impacts, because they measure results, on average, about two years after program entry. The analysis draws on information from field observations of the program, qualitative interviews with participants, data on census tract and block group characteristics linked to geocoded initial and current addresses of participants, responses to a survey of 520 MTO Boston participants, and Massachusetts administrative data on earnings and public assistance receipt.

The analysis reveals that 48 percent of the experimental group and 62 percent of the Section 8 comparison group successfully moved through the MTO program. Both groups moved to areas that differed markedly from their origin neighborhoods: The neighborhoods had lower poverty rates, higher education levels, and greater employment rates. A follow-up survey of participants shows that both experimental and Section 8 comparison group households experienced greater safety, fewer behavior problems among boys, and improved health among household heads relative to the control group. The experimental group also had fewer injuries and criminal victimizations among children. Although employment rates for all participants have increased substantially since 1994, neither MTO treatment had a significant short-run impact on the employment or earnings of household heads in Boston.

The MTO Experiment in Boston

The MTO demonstration represents a unique opportunity to identify the causal effects of a housing mobility program on a wide range of outcomes for low-income families. As with the other sites, the interpretation of findings for Boston participants requires an understanding of the specific interventions that occurred at the Boston MTO site.

In Boston, each household assigned to the experimental and Section 8 comparison groups received a Section 8 subsidy, which the household could put toward rent for a private-market apartment, provided the unit met certain inspection standards. In general, the households retain this subsidy for as long as their income remains sufficiently low. Both treatment groups received briefings from Boston Housing Authority staff about program rules and about how to look for an apartment at the time of subsidy issuance.

The experimental group members were also assigned a counselor from the Metropolitan Boston Housing Partnership (MBHP), a local nonprofit. The counselors made home visits to review housing search strategies, explained which neighborhoods the subsidies could be used in (providing a map marked with low-poverty census tracts), helped program participants clean up bad credit histories, found apartment listings in newspapers, provided references to landlords, and sometimes drove participants to see promising apartments. Thus, the counselors played a large role in determining the destination communities of the experimental group members.[1]

The counselors made at least one home visit in the year after the move to each family that successfully moved, or "leased-up" in program terminology. Counselors sometimes resolved problems experienced by participants in their new neighborhoods. For example, they helped mediate disputes between some participants and their landlords, and, on a few occasions, they helped families deal with incidents of racial discrimination. In some cases, MBHP provided small grants to households in the experimental group to purchase furniture or appliances needed in their new apartments.

Aspects of the Boston housing and labor markets during the period of study, along with some changes in government policies that affected the participating families, may also affect our estimates. In qualitative interviews, we found that actual and potential changes to welfare rules and Section 8 produced substantial anxiety among the MTO population. A major change was also made to Section 8 in the middle of MTO. For the first time, Section 8 landlords were permitted to require security deposits from prospective tenants.[2] Major safety improvements in some of the development ments from which MTO families came also occurred during the study.

Data and Methodology

Information about the program came from five sources: (1) field observations of program operations; (2) open-ended qualitative interviews with a random sample of a dozen program participants; (3) a survey of 520 families in all three groups; (4) survey and administrative records on residential addresses—geocoded and merged with the Summary Tape File 3 of the 1990 Census to describe the attributes of the neighborhoods of MTO families; and (5) state administrative data from Massachusetts on the earnings and public assistance receipt of participating families.

Because so much is going on inside the "black box" of the MTO treatments, quantitative comparisons of outcomes by treatment status were complemented by qualitative research. Field work included observing the administration of the baseline survey, attending intake sessions for families after randomization, accompanying counselors on home visits, and interviewing program staff. Qualitative interviews consisted of 12 90-minute open-ended interviews with MTO household heads in the experimental and Section 8 comparison groups. The interviews covered the participants' experiences with the program, their perceptions of their old neighborhoods, and, if they moved, their perceptions of their new neighborhoods.[3]

The sampling frame for the data consisted of household heads randomly assigned in the MTO program in Boston between October 1994 and May 1996. Over these 20 months, 540 families were enrolled; new cohorts were assigned approximately once a month, for an average of 27 families per month. This study uses data from two surveys: First, each household head completed a survey before enrolling in the MTO program, referred to here as the MTO baseline survey. Our sampling universe of 540 Boston households consists of 240 in the experimental group, 120 in the Section 8 comparison group, and 180 in the control group.

We also conducted our own survey of household heads, referred to here as the MTO-Boston follow-up survey.[4] The survey focuses on safety, criminal victimization, adult and child health, child social behaviors and school experiences, family social interactions, and the employment and income sources of the household head. The questions were modeled after questions on established national surveys. For example, the employment questions were drawn from the Current Population Survey, and the questions on criminal victimization were drawn from the National Criminal Victimization Survey.

During June and July 1997, 340 telephone interviews took place. Between November 1997 and April 1998, an additional 180 in-person interviews occurred, for an overall survey response rate of 96.3 percent.[5] Although families in Boston continued to enroll in MTO through 1996–97, the sample of this study is limited to families who had up to 120 days to find a new residence and at least nine months to live in the new residence as of June 1997. The monthly enrollments of new families and different survey completion dates combined yield an average time between random assignment and the follow-up survey of 2.2 years, for a range of 1.0 to 3.5 years. Administrative data on earnings and welfare usage for the Boston MTO families were obtained from the Massachusetts Department of Revenue. The earnings data originated in the Department of Revenue Wage Reporting System. All state employers, including those that do not participate in the Unemployment Insurance system, are required to report quarterly earnings to the state. The welfare records originated in the Massachusetts Department of Transitional Assistance. Members of MTO households were matched to their earnings records using Social Security numbers and names and to the welfare records using their Social Security numbers, names, and dates of birth.

Our basic empirical approach is to use the data from our follow-up survey and administrative records to compare a wide range of socioeconomic and health outcomes of treatment-group families (the experimental or Section 8 comparison groups) to those of the control group families. All of these groups were originally living in the same set of public housing projects. The random-assignment design of the demonstration means that differential outcomes for the experimental and Section 8 comparison groups relative to the control group (occurring after program entry) can be interpreted as estimates of treatment effects of eligibility for these programs (commonly known as intention-to-treat effects).

In interpreting the results, it is worth emphasizing that they reflect the overall impact of the program on the entire experimental and Section 8 treatment groups, including those who did not move through the program. Under the plausible assumption that the program had little or no impact on those not moving with program subsidies, the impact on the program movers within the experimental and Section 8 comparison groups would be substantially larger than the average differences between groups reported here. In this case, the simple mean differences in outcomes for the experimental and control groups should by inflated by a factor of 2.1 to produce the impact on program movers in the experimental group (known as the impact of treatment on the treated). The reported estimates should be inflated by 1.6 for the Section 8 comparison group.[6]

Characteristics of the MTO-Boston Families

The characteristics at time of program entry of the 540 Boston sample households are presented in table 7.1. As shown in the last column of the first panel, the majority of these families are headed by a single mother who received public assistance; 27 percent of the household heads were employed (either part-time or full-time) at the time of the baseline survey, and 22 percent owned an automobile. While the participating families have young children (63 percent of households have a child between ages 0 and 5), 66 percent of the household heads were at least 30 years old at the time of random assignment. These patterns are not surprising given that eligibility for the program was restricted to families with children living in public housing (or project-based assisted housing) in high-poverty, inner-city census tracts.[7] Indeed, MTO participants at all five sites are largely minority, female-headed households (Goering et al. 1999). The Boston site has one of the more ethnically diverse groups of participants: 45 percent are Hispanic and 37 percent are black.[8]

According to the baseline survey, conducted at the time of program enrollment, the main reason a majority of Boston families (56 percent) wanted to move was fear of crime ("to get away from drugs and gangs"). Improvements in housing ("to get a bigger or better apartment") and school quality ("better schools for my children") were the next most

Table 7.1. *MTO-Boston Descriptive Statistics from Baseline Survey
for Households Enrolled through May 1996*

	Experimental	Section 8	Control	All
Household head characteristics				
Age < 30	.33	.37	.35	.34
Female	.92	.92	.89	.91
Black	.36	.40	.35	.37
Hispanic	.44	.39	.48	.45
Never married	.55	.63	.60	.59
High school graduate	.45	.44	.40	.43
Employed	.25	.26	.28	.27
Receiving AFDC	.62	.68	.64	.64
Car that runs	.25	.19	.19	.22
Any children, 0–5 years	.61	.63	.64	.63
Any children, 6–17 years	.81	.78	.76	.79
Most important reason wanted to move				
Drugs and gangs	.62	.47	.53	.56
Bigger and better apartment	.27	.31	.31	.29
Better schools for children	.06	.13	.07	.08
To be near job or to get job	.00	.03	.01	.01
Recent criminal victimization				
Purse, wallet, jewelry snatched in past six months	.12	.13	.16	.14
Threatened by knife or gun in past six months	.11	.20	.17	.15
Beaten or assaulted in past six months	.13	.20	.16	.15
Stabbed or shot in past six months	.06	.06	.09	.07
Attempted break-in in past six months	.15	.24	.16	.18
Housing and neighborhood conditions				
Apartment in poor condition	.28	.28	.27	.28
Too little space in apartment is a problem	.78	.79	.74	.77
Somewhat or very dissatisfied with neighborhood	.59	.50	.55	.55
Feels unsafe or very unsafe during the day	.51	.44	.46	.48
Drug dealers are a big problem in the neighborhood	.75	.74	.73	.74
Origin census tract				
Poverty rate	.41	.41	.42	.41
If white	.34	.36	.35	.35
If black	.46	.42	.44	.45

Table 7.1. *Continued*

	Experimental	*Section 8*	*Control*	*All*
If Hispanic	.26	.28	.27	.27
If English not first language	.34	.37	.35	.35
If high school dropout (25 years and older)	.46	.46	.46	.46
Unemployment rate	.09	.09	.09	.09
If households on welfare	.33	.33	.33	.33
Sample size	240	120	180	540

Source: Data are from the MTO baseline survey for universe of participants enrolling in MTO in Boston between October 1994 and May 1996.

Notes: Origin census tract data are based on geocoded addresses linked to 1990 Census data. Missing data are imputed at nonmissing mean. Estimates are weighted as described in the text.

important factors motivating moves (second panel, table 7.1). Employment concerns ("to get a job" or "to be near my job") were listed as the main reason to move by only 1 percent of all participants.[9]

Fear of crime was also listed as the main factor motivating participants' desire to move out of public housing in all other MTO sites (Goering et al. 1999).[10] The concern about crime may also have been the direct result of having been victimized recently. Boston participants reported quite high rates of criminal victimization over the six months prior to the baseline survey (third panel, table 7.1). For example, in 14 percent of households someone had their purse, wallet, or jewelry snatched in the prior six months; in 15 percent of the households, someone had been threatened by a knife or gun; and in 15 percent, someone had been beaten or assaulted over the preceding six months. The reported victimization rates of MTO families were about four times higher than those computed from a recent national survey of public housing households in family developments (Zelon et al. 1994).[11]

At the time that MTO families applied for the program, a large proportion of the household heads were dissatisfied more generally with their apartments and neighborhoods (fourth panel, table 7.1). For example, 28 percent reported their apartment was in poor condition, and 77 percent said it contained too little space. Also, 55 percent reported they were somewhat or very dissatisfied with their neighborhood, and 74 percent said that drug dealers were a big problem.

Some characteristics of the origin (baseline) neighborhoods of our Boston sample are presented in the bottom panel of table 7.1.[12] As expected, given the demonstration's eligibility rules, the typical family lived in a census tract with a very high poverty rate (more than 41 percent on average) and with approximately one-third of the households receiving public assistance in 1990. The diversity of the racial and ethnic composition of the mean origin census tracts for the Boston families belies the substantial racial and ethnic residential segregation they face. More than half the black families in the sample lived in origin census tracts in which more than 70 percent of the residents were black and in tracts where less than 15 percent of residents were white. The median white (non-Hispanic) family resided in an origin census tract with more than 94 percent white residents. The Hispanic (nonblack) families lived in the most racially and ethnically diverse origin census tracts.

Under random assignment to one of three groups in MTO, the baseline survey characteristics should be the same, on average, across the groups, except for variation due to sampling. The baseline characteristics of the three groups are consistent with successful random assignment (first three columns of table 7.1).[13] One additional factor to keep in mind when comparing groups: the randomization proportions were changed after the first 450 households were randomly assigned; all statistics reported in this study are weighted to account for this change.[14]

Program Moves in the Boston MTO Demonstration

To realize expected location improvements, the experimental and Section 8 comparison groups in Boston had to successfully use program subsidies to move to private-market apartments. Table 7.2 presents the program move rates (or "take-up" rates) and shares of families using the program to move to the suburbs (out of Boston) for the experimental and Section 8 comparison groups and for various subgroups. A substantial fraction of families in both treatment groups—48 percent of the experimental group and 62 percent of the Section 8 comparison group—were able to successfully move using program housing vouchers (or certificates).[15] In the experimental group, 30 percent, compared with 16 percent of the Section 8 comparison group, used program subsidies to move out of the city of Boston. According to an analysis not shown in this table, program movers in the experimental group concentrated in eligible, low-poverty tracts in Boston (38 percent of the movers) and in the suburbs just south of Boston (35 percent); 3 percent of the experimental program movers left Massachusetts.

Table 7.2. *MTO-Boston Program Moves by Baseline Survey Characteristics*

Baseline survey characteristics	Experimental			Section 8		
	Program move	Program move beyond Boston	N	Program move	Program move beyond Boston	N
All	.481	.296	240	.634	.156	120
All (and geocoded follow-up survey location)	.479	.298	235	.619	.134	114
If dissatisfied with neighborhood	.577	.391	138	.697	.236	59
If satisfied with neighborhood	.355	.164	100	.572	.077	61
Difference by satisfaction	.223**	.227**		.125	.159**	
	(.067)	(.058)		(.090)	(.067)	
If too little space in apt. is problem	.502	.302	189	.694	.172	96
If space in apt. is not big problem	.433	.267	50	.404	.096	24
Difference by problems with space	.069	.043		.289**	.076	
	(.086)	(.077)		(.115)	(.076)	
If previously lived in mostly white area	.667	.517	75	.692	.230	37
If have not previously lived in a mostly white neighborhood	.401	.192	161	.606	.109	81
Difference by previous neighborhood	.266**	.325**		.086	.121	
	(.075)	(.071)		(.098)	(.080)	
If race/ethnicity is black	.429	.347	88	.630	.050	44
If race/ethnicity is Hispanic	.483	.192	106	.680	.222	50
If race/ethnicity is not black or Hispanic	.577	.442	46	.557	.233	26

Sources: Data on program moves are from Abt Associates, within 120 days of random assignment. Data on characteristics are from the MTO baseline survey.
Note: Estimates are weighted as described in the text.
**Statistically significant at $p < 0.05$.

Families reporting dissatisfaction with their neighborhood in the base-line survey were more likely to make a program move (second panel, table 7.2). For example, in the experimental group, those who were dissatisfied saw a 22 percentage point increase in overall program move rates over those who were satisfied. They saw a 23 percentage point increase in program move rates to locations outside Boston city limits. Similarly, the overall program move rate was 29 percentage points higher among Section 8 comparison group households who reported that too little space in their apartment was "a big problem" at the time of the baseline survey (third panel, table 7.2). The program move rates (both overall and outside of Boston) for the experimental group were much higher among the roughly one-third of households that reported they had lived at one time in a "mostly white" area at baseline (fourth panel, table 7.2).

Program move rates were modestly lower for blacks than for non-blacks in the experimental group (fifth panel, table 7.2). But the black families that did take advantage of the subsidies in the experimental group were the most likely to move out of Boston. In contrast, Hispanics in the experimental group were less likely than others to use the program to move to the suburbs. In fact, the program move rate to the suburbs for Hispanics was actually lower in the experimental group with restricted vouchers than in the Section 8 comparison group. These differences may reflect racial attitudes in the neighborhoods of Boston eligible for MTO moves and the distribution of Hispanic-speaking families in the Boston area, as well as differences in the emphasis of the MTO counselors handling black and Hispanic participants at the Boston MTO site.

In results not shown in the table, we also analyzed the differences between initial program moves and locations at the time of the MTO-Boston follow-up survey (1.0 to 3.5 years later). Among those who moved through the MTO program, about 26 percent had moved at least once more by the time of the follow-up survey.[16] Similarly, about 27 percent of those in all three MTO groups who did not move through the MTO program had also moved from their baseline location by the time of the follow-up survey. Although these overall mobility rates are quite similar, the experiences of experimental group families that moved through the MTO program did differ somewhat from other groups.

Nearly all experimental program movers initially moved to census tracts with less than a 10 percent poverty rate, as required by program rules. These families, however, were allowed to move again after one year without a restriction on the census tract characteristics of their next loca-

tion. By the time of the follow-up survey, 85 of the experimental program movers had not moved again from their program move location,
and 32 experimental program movers did move again. Of these 32 families, 22 (or 19 percent of all experimental program movers) were located
in a census tract at the time of the follow-up survey with a poverty rate at
least 10 percentage points higher than the tract to which they had made
their initial program move. Notably, however, these changes were not initial moves to the suburbs followed by a return to high-poverty neighborhoods. Only 11 of the 22 movers had initially relocated outside of Boston,
and only 6 of the 11 chose to move back into Boston. None of the 22 participants moved to a census tract with a poverty rate of 40 percent or
higher. Among the other groups, only 1 of the 16 Section 8 comparison
program movers and 3 of the 92 nonprogram movers who had moved
again by the follow-up survey increased their tract poverty rate by
more than 10 percentage points.

Mobility Outcomes and Neighborhood Characteristics

We next turn to an analysis of the impacts of the experimental and Section 8 comparison treatments on the overall residential mobility rates
and neighborhood attributes of the Boston MTO families. The MTO
program had a substantial impact on the residential location of households offered subsidies to relocate to private apartments. The top panel
of table 7.3 summarizes the residential mobility outcomes for the treatment and control group families at the time of our MTO-Boston follow-
up survey.[17] It should be noted that the format of this table, and of those
that follow, differs from that of the earlier tables. The control group mean
is presented in the first column of numbers. The next two columns show
the *difference* in means between the experimental group and the control
group and between the Section 8 comparison group and the control
group. Therefore, the mean for the experimental group can be obtained
from the table by adding the experimental-control difference to the control group mean, and the mean for the Section 8 comparison group can
be obtained by adding the Section 8-control difference to the control
group mean.

The experimental and Section 8 comparison treatments both greatly
increased the rate at which families moved out of their original housing
projects. During the 1.0–3.5 years that elapsed before the follow-up survey,

Table 7.3. *Impact of MTO-Boston on Mobility and Neighborhood Characteristics*

	Control	Experimental–control	Section 8–control
Mobility rates			
Program move	0	.479**	.619**
Move out of project	.271	.325**	.414**
Living outside Boston	.049	.234**	.069**
Census tract characteristics			
Poverty rate	.359	−.122**	−.100**
If poverty rate < 10%	.018	.344**	.116**
If poverty rate < 20%	.128	.347**	.237**
If poverty rate < 30%	.318	.308**	.352**
If poverty rate < 40%	.407	.288**	.341**
If income > 2× poverty level	.415	.170**	.122**
If race is white	.380	.146**	.060
If race is black	.218	−.095**	−.057
If race is Hispanic	.449	−.056**	−.018
If English not first language	.315	−.053**	.012
If English almost not spoken at all	.097	−.025**	.000
If immigrant	.148	−.001	.042**
If family female-headed	.632	−.172**	−.112**
If public assistance	.294	−.097**	−.066**
If person in renter-occupied unit	.827	−.197**	−.112**
If workers using public transportation	.387	−.104**	−.071**
Unemployment rate	.086	−.018**	−.011**
Full-time, full-year worker	.327	.072**	.064**
If managerial/professional worker	.206	.029**	.022**
If has at least some college (25 years and older)	.289	.064**	.066**

Sources: Data on residential location are taken from the MTO-Boston follow-up survey, one to three years after random assignment, and geocoded to link to 1990 Census data on area characteristics.

Note: The total sample size is 525 (235 experimental, 114 Section 8, and 176 control).

**Statistically significant at $p < 0.05$.

a substantial share of control households (27 percent) had moved out of the housing project or other census block group in which they were living at the time of the baseline survey. Among the experimental group, 60 percent had moved out of their original location (48 percent through MTO and 12 percent independently). Among the Section 8 comparison group, a total share of 69 percent had moved (62 percent through MTO and 7 percent independently). Further analysis of the locations of households at the time of the follow up survey reveals that few control (5 percent) and Section 8 comparison households (12 percent) were living outside the city of Boston, while the experimental group households (28 percent) were much more likely to reside outside the city limits.[18]

To assess the impact of MTO on neighborhood attributes, we compare the mean neighborhood characteristics (based on 1990 Census tract data) at the time of the follow-up survey of households in the two treatment groups with those of the controls. The areas in which experimental and Section 8 comparison households were living at the time of the follow-up survey were significantly different, on average, from the control households across many dimensions (bottom panel, table 7.3). The treatment groups resided in census tracts with lower poverty rates, lower welfare receipt, a lower prevalence of female-headed households, a higher fraction of full-time/full-year workers, a higher proportion of managerial and professional workers, higher education levels, and a higher share of owner-occupied units. Notably, the Section 8 comparison group did not significantly differ from the control group in the racial composition of the census tracts or in the prevalent use of the English language. Results (not shown in the table) are similar for census block group comparisons.

The fact that the differences in the average tract characteristics for the experimental and Section 8 comparison groups versus the control group are similar on many dimensions does not fully convey the differences in the underlying distribution of the tract characteristics. For example, the experimental-control difference in the average poverty rate was 12 percentage points, and the Section 8 comparison-control difference was 10 percentage points. However, the experimental group members were substantially more likely to end up in tracts with very low poverty rates than the Section 8 comparison and control groups. This greater likelihood is to be expected, given the initial restriction on MTO rental assistance for the experimental group to units in census tracts with a poverty rate of no more than 10 percent. The overall share of the experimental group living in low-poverty (less than 10 percent) census tracts was about

23 percentage points greater at the time of the follow-up survey than for the Section 8 comparison group. In contrast, more families in the Section 8 comparison group (with its higher take-up rate) moved out of census tracts with 40 percent or greater poverty rates.

Safety and Criminal Victimization

The previous section documents that the residential environments of those who moved through the MTO program changed on many dimensions. The qualitative interviews suggested that the neighborhood characteristics most salient to the participating families are those affecting the exposure to violence and overall safety of their children. Furthermore, in the baseline survey, 56 percent of MTO families reported the main reason they wanted to move was "drugs and gangs." To investigate the extent to which perceptions of neighborhood safety changed for those afforded the chance to move through the MTO program, the follow-up survey asked various questions about safety.

In the baseline survey, 48 percent of household heads reported feeling unsafe or very unsafe on the streets near home during the day. This level declined to 39 percent in the control group in the follow-up survey, as shown in the first row of table 7.4. The experimental group saw a further

Table 7.4. *Impact of MTO-Boston on Safety*

	Control	Experimental–control	Section 8–control	N
Streets near home are unsafe or very unsafe during the day	.386 (.038)	−.163** (.047)	−.078 (.059)	509
Household head or child has seen people using or selling drugs once a week or more	.359 (.038)	−.203** (.045)	−.134** (.056)	507
Household head or child has seen or heard gunfire once a month or more	.205 (.032)	−.132** (.036)	−.106** (.044)	513

Source: MTO-Boston follow-up survey.
Notes: Estimates are weighted as described in the text; robust standard errors are reported in parentheses.
**Statistically significant at $p < 0.05$.

decline of 16 percentage points, which is statistically significant, and also an estimate of a modest (but not statistically significant) decline for the Section 8 comparison group. To assess the specific issues of drugs and guns, we asked several additional questions. Both the experimental and Section 8 comparison groups reported a substantially lower prevalence of seeing people using or selling drugs and of seeing or hearing gunfire (table 7.4).

Since a shocking 37 percent of the Boston MTO households reported having experienced some criminal victimization (threat, break-in, purse snatching, assault, stabbing, or shooting) in the six months prior to the baseline survey, the follow-up survey asked detailed questions about victimization incidents to assess the extent of any changes.[19]

The results show that only 26 percent of households in the control group reported that at least one crime incident occurred in the six months prior to the follow-up survey, as shown in the first row of table 7.5. The reductions in victimization rates and improvements in neighborhood safety from the time of the baseline survey to that of the follow-up survey may be due to the well-documented sharp decline in Boston's crime rates over this period (Piehl, Kennedy, and Braga 2000).[20] Victimization was 12 percentage points lower in both the experimental and Section 8 comparison groups than in the control group, indicating highly significant declines.

Table 7.5. *Impact of MTO-Boston on Criminal Victimization*

	Control	Experimental–control	Section 8–control	N
If any crime	.255	−.118**	−.115**	519
	(.033)	(.041)	(.047)	
If property crime	.134	−.057*	−.087**	519
	(.026)	(.032)	(.033)	
If personal crimes: at least one child involved	.127	−.059*	−.023	519
	(.026)	(.031)	(.039)	
If personal crimes: household head involved	.073	.003	−.042*	519
	(.020)	(.031)	(.025)	

Sources: MTO-Boston follow-up survey.

Notes: Personal crimes are assault, rape, robbery, or pickpocketing (attempted or completed). Property crimes are theft, household, or motor vehicle burglary (attempted or completed). Robust standard errors are reported in parentheses.

*Statistically significant at $p < 0.10$: **Statistically significant at $p < 0.05$.

In the control group, 13 percent reported a property crime. The prevalence of property crimes declined by 6 percentage points in the experimental group and 9 percentage points in the Section 8 comparison group, with the statistical significance marginal for the former and strong for the latter. There was also a marginally statistically significant decline in the prevalence of personal crimes involving children for the experimental group and a similar decline among household heads for the Section 8 comparison group. In analyses not reported here, we find the same pattern of results by crime type when the outcome is average number of incidents, instead of probability of at least one incident.

Overall, both the experimental and Section 8 comparison group household heads reported substantially fewer criminal victimizations than the controls and found their neighborhoods to be less dangerous—similar to the findings for the Los Angeles MTO site (see chapter 9). The families who moved through the MTO program, especially those in the experimental group, did succeed in accomplishing one of their main goals: relocating to substantially safer neighborhoods.

Children's Social Behavior and School Experiences

The results of previous housing mobility programs, such as the Gautreaux program in Chicago (Rosenbaum 1995), suggest that residential location changes can affect children's developmental processes. These changes, in turn, ultimately can affect outcomes later in life. To assess the early impact of MTO on children's social behavior and school experiences, we asked household heads a number of questions about up to two randomly selected children per household in the MTO-Boston follow-up survey (table 7.6).

Clinical researchers have suggested that living in a violent, stressful environment may lead children to exhibit various negative behaviors (Augustyn et al. 1995). To assess such behaviors, the survey included several follow-up survey questions drawn from items in the National Health Interview Survey Child Supplement and the National Longitudinal Survey of Youth Child Supplement. The questions largely focused on observable "external" behaviors rather than "internal" feelings of children, which would be more difficult for the household head to judge.

In general, boys exhibit substantially more behavioral problems than girls. For example, in the control group, boys had higher prevalence of all

Table 7.6. *Impact of MTO-Boston on Social Behavior Outcomes for Children Age 6–15*

		Control	Experimental–control	Section 8–control	N
Child behavioral problems					
Has trouble getting along with teachers	Boys	.353 (.053)	−.113* (.067)	−.041 (.087)	267
	Girls	.156 (.034)	.018 (.049)	.036 (.060)	291
Is disobedient at home	Boys	.316 (.048)	−.104* (.061)	−.029 (.082)	273
	Girls	.174 (.040)	−.047 (.049)	−.080 (.053)	299
Is disobedient at school	Boys	.455 (.054)	−.077 (.075)	−.124 (.088)	274
	Girls	.333 (.053)	.038 (.073)	−.137* (.071)	300
Hangs around with kids who get into trouble	Boys	.221 (.047)	−.095 (.058)	−.100 (.066)	273
	Girls	.115 (.032)	−.047 (.040)	−.021 (.052)	297
Is cruel or mean to others	Boys	.190 (.044)	−.137** (.048)	−.123* (.065)	274
	Girls	.076 (.026)	−.024 (.033)	−.033 (.037)	298
Is restless or overly active	Boys	.468 (.055)	−.038 (.076)	−.117 (.088)	273
	Girls	.263 (.044)	.003 (.062)	.032 (.076)	299
Is unhappy, sad, or depressed	Boys	.284 (.049)	−.125** (.061)	−.163** (.067)	274
	Girls	.232 (.042)	−.015 (.061)	−.026 (.068)	298
Child social behavior					
At least one close friend in neighborhood	Boys	.747 (.054)	.018 (.075)	.056 (.077)	272
	Girls	.823 (.042)	−.134** (.064)	−.160** (.077)	295

(*continued*)

Table 7.6. *Impact of MTO-Boston on Social Behavior Outcomes for Children Age 6–15 (Continued)*

		Control	Experimental– control	Section 8– control	N
Participated in extracurricular activities	Boys	.428 (.056)	−.050 (.077)	−.091 (.089)	274
	Girls	.473 (.054)	−.137* (.072)	−.031 (.087)	290

Sources: MTO-Boston follow-up survey.
Notes: Estimates are weighted as described in the text; robust standard errors are reported in parentheses, adjusted for household clustering.
*Statistically significant at $p < 0.10$; **Statistically significant at $p < 0.05$.

seven behavior problems measured, though the boy-girl difference for "unhappy, sad, or depressed" is small and statistically insignificant. When we look at the improvements in behavior problems for the MTO treatment groups, the boys saw larger improvements than the girls for five out of seven behavior problems in the Section 8 comparison group and for seven out of seven problems in the experimental group.

Specifically, statistically significant reductions were evident in the incidence of boys being "cruel or mean to others" and being "sad, unhappy, or depressed" in both the experimental and Section 8 comparison groups relative to the control group. Declines for "trouble getting along with teachers" and for "disobedient at home" were marginally statistically significant in the experimental group and negative for the Section 8 comparison group. For the remaining three behaviors, "disobedient at school," "hangs around with kids who get into trouble," and "restless or overly active," the sign of the estimates indicated a reduction in problems for both treatment groups, although the differences were not statistically significantly different from zero.

For girls in the Section 8 comparison group, the reduction in disobedience at school was marginally statistically significant, and the point estimates were negative for five of the seven problems. In the experimental group, only four of the seven estimated effects for girls were negative, and none were significant. These findings are consistent with those of the recent New Hope experiment in Wisconsin (providing earnings supplements, health insurance, and child subsidies to low-income families), which found significant improvements in child behaviors among boys and not girls (Bos et al. 1999).

One reason for the differential effect between boys and girls is that girls appear to have had more difficulty socially integrating into their new neighborhoods. As shown in the second panel of table 7.6, girls in both the experimental and Section 8 comparison groups were significantly less likely to have at least one close friend in the neighborhood, whereas boys in both groups were more likely to have at least one close friend in the neighborhood. Girls in the experimental group were also less likely to participate in extracurricular activities after school, although this difference is only marginally statistically significant, and the contrast with boys is not as large as in the analysis of neighborhood friends.

Children's Health

MTO families are greatly concerned with the many types of danger facing children living in a public housing project. The qualitative interviews not only revealed criminal victimizations, but also injuries from broken glass in nearby courtyards and falls on concrete in local playgrounds. A burgeoning medical literature also shows that living in an inner city is associated with higher rates of accidents, injuries, and asthma for children (Quinlan 1996; Sarpong 1996; Sharfstein and Sandel 1998). Field work suggested that MTO families may have safer places for their children to play and less exposure to the high-stress environments and housing conditions that may trigger asthma attacks.

The follow-up survey asked household heads about injuries and asthma attacks during the past six months for up to two randomly selected children. Table 7.7 reports results for children age 6–15. In analyzing injuries, we focused on nonsports injuries, which turned out to come primarily from falls, fights, or dangerous external factors, such as broken glass or needles.[21] For the experimental group, the proportion with injuries was cut in half, more than 4 percentage points lower than the injury rate of 8 percent in the control group. The results reported here are marginally statistically significant. Katz, Kling, and Liebman (2001) incorporate additional information about the children to increase statistical precision, and the results for injuries become strongly statistically significant.[22]

For asthma attacks, we had suspected that known asthma triggers, such as cockroach allergens, dust mites in carpets (Gelber et al. 1993), and stress (Wright 1988) may have been less prevalent in the housing

Table 7.7. *Impact of MTO-Boston on Physical Health Outcomes, Children Age 6–15*

	Control	Experimental–control	Section 8–control	N
If nonsports injury in past six months requiring medical attention	.078 (.019)	−.043* (.022)	−.025 (.029)	569
If asthma attack in past month requiring medical attention	.098 (.023)	−.038 (.029)	−.007 (.026)	570

Source: MTO-Boston follow-up survey.
Notes: Estimates are weighted as described in the text; robust standard errors are reported in parentheses, adjusted for household clustering.
*Statistically significant at $p < 0.10$.

families may have moved to through the MTO program. The prevalence of asthma attacks may have been reduced in the experimental group by a substantively important magnitude, but the estimate is not statistically significant (table 7.7). As with injuries, in tests adding additional covariates to improve estimation precision (Katz, Kling, and Liebman 2001), the difference between the experimental and control groups is marginally statistically significant.

Adult Health

Some of the most striking results from the MTO-Boston follow-up survey are based on self-reported health status. Fieldwork results suggested that the reduction in anxiety from moving to a neighborhood with fewer guns, drug dealers, and violent behavior had the potential to be one of the most salient changes in the lives of adults in families that moved through MTO. The experimental and Section 8 comparison groups do appear to have moved to neighborhoods that were safer and less violent. On the other hand, movers may be socially isolated in their new neighborhoods. Several questions on the follow-up survey assessed the impact of these changes on health, with results reported in table 7.8.[23]

Regarding overall health, 58 percent of the control group responded that their health was good or better. The fraction in the experimental

Table 7.8. *Impact of MTO-Boston on Adult Health*

	Control	Experimental– control	Section 8– control	N
Overall health is good or better	.578	.113**	.180**	511
	(.038)	(.050)	(.056)	
Calm and peaceful "a good bit	.465	.100*	.136**	508
of the time" or more often	(.039)	(.052)	(.062)	
during the past four weeks				
Happy "a good bit of the time"	.561	.069	.035	506
or more often during the	(.039)	(.052)	(.062)	
past four weeks				

Source: MTO-Boston follow-up survey.

Notes: Estimates are weighted as described in the text; robust standard errors are reported in parentheses.

*Statistically significant at $p < 0.10$; **Statistically significant at $p < 0.05$.

group was 11 percentage points higher, and 18 percentage points higher in the Section 8 comparison group. Not surprisingly, given the very large magnitude of the differences, the results are highly statistically significant.

Fieldwork suggested that impacts on overall health of MTO in the short run were more likely to be through mental health than physical health. Changes in physical health cannot be ruled out, but strong increases in calmness and peacefulness do suggest that at least part of the large impact on general health occurred through positive changes in mental health. In the control group, 47 percent responded that they were calm and peaceful a good bit of the time or more often. The fraction was 10 percentage points higher in the experimental group, and 14 percentage points higher in the Section 8 comparison group. Again, the results are statistically significant and of substantively large magnitude. The results also indicate that members of the two treatment groups were happier, but these differences are smaller in magnitude and not statistically significant.

Social Relations

One of the potential drawbacks to living in a new neighborhood could be the disruption of established social ties, potentially leading to social isolation. As noted, there does not appear to have been a negative effect on mental health in the MTO treatment groups. This section presents direct evidence that social contact itself does not appear to be appreciably lower either. Overall, the analysis reveals remarkably little evidence that households in the experimental and Section 8 comparison groups were more socially isolated than the control group.

Household heads in the experimental and Section 8 comparison groups were less likely than those in the control group to report having had a friend to their homes in the past week, but more likely to report having visited a friend or relative at their homes (table 7.9). For both outcomes, these differences are not statistically significant between any of the groups. Similarly, the treatment group household heads talk even more frequently by telephone with close friends and relatives than control group heads, although this difference too is insignificant. Virtually the same fraction, 57 percent, of the experimental and control groups

Table 7.9. *Impact of MTO-Boston on Social Relations*

	Control	Experimental– control	Section 8– control	N
Visited with friend or relative at your home at least once a week in the past month	.482 (.039)	−.056 (.053)	−.055 (.062)	509
Visited with a friend or relative at their home at least once a week in the past month	.422 (.038)	.082 (.053)	.055 (.062)	512
On the telephone with close friends or relatives 4 times or more in the past week	.561 (.038)	.018 (.053)	.075 (.061)	508
Went to church or place of worship at least once in the past 30 days	.573 (.038)	−.007 (.053)	−.060 (.062)	510
Agree with: "Most people can be trusted" versus "You can't be too careful in dealing with people"	.078 (.022)	.065* (.033)	.035 (.038)	499

Source: MTO-Boston follow-up survey.
Notes: Estimates are weighted as described in the text; robust standard errors are reported in parentheses.
*Statistically significant at $p < 0.10$.

attended church at least once in the past 30 days. The share of attendees in the Section 8 comparison group is lower, but the difference is statistically insignificant.

As one final measure of social relations, the survey asked about social trust, which has been shown to be correlated with membership in local organizations and other measures of civic engagement (Putnam 1995). In theory, people living in neighborhoods where they were more likely to be a racial or linguistic minority may exhibit lower social trust. The question itself, taken from the General Social Survey, is "Which of the following do you agree with—'Most people can be trusted' or 'You can't be too careful in dealing with people'?" The fraction in the control group who said they feel most people can be trusted was only 8 percent, but somewhat surprisingly, the experimental group fraction was 6.5 percentage points higher, a marginally statistically significant difference. The difference for the Section 8 comparison group was also positive, but not statistically significant.

Welfare and Employment

The decline of the inner-city labor market has been well-documented (see, for example, Wilson 1996). A move through MTO may increase the accessibility of employment and introduce different neighborhood social expectations about work and welfare. Alternatively, a move may disrupt the informal networks through which people find jobs, particularly in the short run, before new social networks can be established. The most directly relevant previous research is probably the initial short-term study of the Gautreaux housing mobility program, which found no significant employment effects after about one year following relocation to the suburbs relative to placement in a central-city location (Peroff et al. 1979). In a study of a sample of Gautreaux families about five years after their initial move, Rosenbaum (1995) found significantly higher employment among household heads who had been placed in suburban areas in comparison with city placements. The response rate for the early study was 81 percent versus 67 percent for the later study, a difference that may have affected the results. If employed movers were less likely to move over time and therefore easier to locate and survey, the later results may be biased towards finding higher employment among movers. Still, these two sets of results suggest that there may be differences between short-run and long-run effects.

From 1994 to 1998, striking changes in the levels of welfare receipt and employment for the entire MTO-Boston sample occurred. Over this period, public assistance receipt fell by almost one-half, and employment increased by more than one-half. Several sources supply information about these outcomes. First, we can use the MTO-Boston baseline survey (administered between October 1994 and May 1996), which reflects the status of families as they entered the MTO program, and the MTO-Boston follow-up survey, which was administered between June 1997 and April 1998. (Results from the follow-up survey are shown in the top panel of table 7.10.) Second, we can use administrative data from the commonwealth of Massachusetts, including records on welfare usage from the Department of Transitional Assistance and quarterly earnings data from the Department of Revenue. Results from these administrative data are shown in the second panel of table 7.10. For the administrative data, the time periods are expressed as calendar quarters. For example, the third quarter of 1994 is denoted as 94:3.

At the time of the baseline survey, 64 percent of households reported receiving welfare (see first panel of table 7.1). In the follow-up survey, only 47 percent of control households were receiving welfare. Similarly, 73 percent of the MTO sample were receiving welfare in 94:3, according to administrative records, and this level had decreased to 51 percent by 97:3 among the controls. As shown in the top two panels of table 7.10, the differences among the three MTO groups are not statistically significant for either the follow-up survey or for the 97:3 administrative records. One important reason for this overall decline was undoubtedly the changes in welfare eligibility during this period. In December 1996, Massachusetts implemented time limits on benefits, such that approximately one-third of the statewide caseload was restricted to 24 months of assistance in a 60-month cycle.[24] Indeed, 76 percent of those receiving welfare benefits at the time of the follow-up survey acknowledged they had been notified that they could only receive their benefits for a certain number of months. The strong economy, the expansion of the earned income tax credit, and increases in parental work associated with children entering school likely played a role as well.

The level of welfare receipt appears to have continued to decline over time. In 98:3, welfare receipt in the control group was only 40 percent, statistically indistinguishable from the experimental and Section 8 comparison groups. Some evidence, not shown in the table, suggests that welfare receipt may have decreased relatively more among the Section 8

Table 7.10. *Impact of MTO-Boston on Welfare and Work*

	Control	Experimental–control	Section 8–control	N
MTO-Boston follow-up survey				
Receiving welfare benefits	.472	.030	−.008	519
(AFDC/TANF)	(.039)	(.053)	(.062)	
Notified of a time limit on	.415	.018	−.019	519
welfare benefits	(.038)	(.052)	(.061)	
Receiving aid for disabled or	.242	.030	−.015	516
needy elderly	(.033)	(.046)	(.053)	
(Supplemental Security				
Income)				
Receiving food stamps	.520	.019	−.020	517
	(.039)	(.053)	(.062)	
Worked for pay last week	.434	−.071	.001	520
	(.038)	(.052)	(.062)	
Worked at job with health or	.149	−.001	.058	520
other benefits	(.027)	(.038)	(.049)	
Average hourly wages among	.46	.493	.153	186
workers	(0.43)	(.619)	(.581)	
Average quarterly earnings	1455	−252	−85	520
	(169)	(222)	(261)	
Massachusetts administrative records				
Received TANF in 1997,	.505	−.001	−.017	540
3rd quarter	(.038)	(.052)	(.061)	
Received TANF in 1998,	.399	.027	−.067	540
3rd quarter	(.035)	(.050)	(.058)	
If any earnings in 1997,	.436	−.017	−.007	540
3rd quarter	(.037)	(.051)	(.060)	
If any earnings in 1998,	.494	−.002	−.026	540
3rd quarter	(.038)	(.052)	(.060)	
Average quarterly earnings	1572	−101	121	540
in 1997, 3rd quarter	(193)	(253)	(305)	
Average quarterly earnings	2045	−328	−278	540
in 1998, 3rd quarter	(226)	(281)	(325)	

Sources: MTO-Boston follow-up survey, the Massachusetts Department of Transitional Assistance, and the Massachusetts Department of Revenue.

Notes: Estimates are weighted as described in the text; robust standard errors are reported in parentheses.

AFDC = Aid to Families with Dependent Children

TANF = Temporary Assistance for Needy Families

comparison group by the very end of 1998. Out-of-state moves were unlikely to have had much effect on our results from the administrative data. Of the 540 members of our sample, all but 23 were confirmed to be still living in Massachusetts.

Regarding other types of public assistance, food stamps were received by 68 percent of households in the baseline survey and 52 percent in the follow-up survey, among controls, with no distinguishable differences between groups. Supplemental Security Income (SSI) was received by 17 percent of households in the baseline survey and by 25 percent of all MTO households in the follow-up survey. This change over time in SSI receipt is statistically significant and may indicate some substitution of SSI benefits for welfare benefits over time among this population, as welfare eligibility became more restrictive.

In addition to questions about public assistance, the follow-up survey asked about employment. Employment increased from 27 percent in the baseline survey (as reported in table 7.1) to 43 percent in the follow-up survey for controls. These results correspond to those from the data obtained from tax records, in which 29 percent had reported earnings during 94:3 and 44 percent of controls had reported earnings in 97:3. As shown in table 7.10, the differences among the three MTO groups are statistically insignificant for employment. Moreover, the moderately large point estimate of −7 percent for the experimental-control difference appears unlikely to be indicative of a systematic difference, both because it is not statistically significant and because for 97:3 or 98:3 the point estimates for this difference based on administrative data are not nearly so large, as shown in 7.10, or for any other quarter in between. Differences between the groups' participation in training or job search assistance since the time of random assignment also are not statistically significant.

As with the analysis of welfare, the analysis of Massachusetts tax records may be influenced by families that have moved out of state. Yet, even the most extreme assumptions about differential employment between MTO groups among families not confirmed to be living in Massachusetts would not generate differences between MTO groups greater than the sampling error on the estimates on employment differences. Therefore, use of state administrative data is extremely unlikely to be driving these results.

To assess the quality of the jobs at which MTO households were working, the follow-up survey asked about various aspects of their employment situation. Again, no statistically distinguishable differences between the three MTO groups turned up. Only 15 percent of control households worked in jobs in which health insurance or other fringe benefits were provided. Average wages among controls working were $8.46 per hour. From the administrative data, we can compute total earnings in each calendar quarter. The administrative data on earnings appear to roughly agree with the implied usual earnings (based on wages and hours) for controls, in that the follow-up survey quarterly earnings were $1,455 and the tax data earnings were $1,572 for 97:3. In results not reported in the table for the administrative data, average earnings were $921 in the fourth quarter of 1994 and $1,838 by 98:3 (adjusted for inflation to 1998 dollars) for all three MTO groups. Given that the official poverty threshold for a family of three in 1998 was about $3,400 per quarter (based on a $13,650 annual threshold), these average earnings levels are still quite low, despite the strong increase in labor earnings over time.

In sum, while welfare receipt declined substantially and employment rose over time for all three MTO groups, the differences among the groups were much less dramatic. We found no solid evidence of meaningful differences between MTO groups in employment or earnings for the Boston site, which is consistent with evidence on employment for the Baltimore MTO site (Ludwig, Duncan, and Pinkston 2000) and the short-term Gautreaux experience. The possibility that experimental or Section 8 comparison group members will increase their employment rates relative to the control group in the longer run remains an open question for further research.

Early Impacts

This chapter presents evidence on the early impacts of the Moving to Opportunity demonstration in Boston. Among households assigned to the experimental group, 48 percent used an offered subsidy and moved through the program to a new apartment. In the Section 8 comparison group, 62 percent moved through the program. At the time of the follow-up survey, 1.0–3.5 years after random assignment to an MTO group, the experimental families were living in neighborhoods that differed from those of the control group families on many dimensions, including poverty rates, racial composition, and employment rates. The magnitude of the differences for Section 8 comparison program movers, while substantial, were typically not as large. Both the experimental and Section 8 comparison groups had, on average, moved to neighborhoods with less drug dealing and less gunfire. Moreover, the families in these two groups were less likely to be victims of property crimes, and children in the experimental group were less likely to be the victims of personal crimes.

These location differences appear to have had significant beneficial influences on the social behavior of boys, the physical health of boys and girls, and the overall and mental health of household heads. For example, we found that boys were less likely to be cruel to others or to be depressed in both the experimental and Section 8 comparison groups than in the control group. We also present evidence here (and stronger evidence in Katz, Kling, and Liebman 2001) that the prevalence of injuries and asthma attacks fell in the experimental group relative to the control group. Household heads in the experimental and Section 8 comparison groups reported that they were more calm and peaceful and that their overall health was better than did similar adults in the control group. In principle, program movers could have been more socially isolated, but there does not appear to be noticeably less social interaction with friends or relatives in the experimental or Section 8 comparison group families relative to the control group.

The changes in residential location experienced by the experimental and Section 8 comparison groups do not appear to have had a systematic impact on welfare receipt or employment in either the follow-up survey or in commonwealth administrative records. There is some indication that the prevalence of welfare receipt may have decreased by the end of 1998 for the Section 8 comparison group relative to the control group, but additional data need to be collected and analyzed to see if this difference persists over time.

The contrasting results for the Section 8 comparison group and the control group on outcomes such as safety, child behavior problems, and adult mental health are of potential relevance to current policy discussions about increasing the number of Section 8 vouchers available. This option seems particularly promising for households currently receiving project-based assistance, especially as projects are renovated and the total number of units in the project decreases. The Section 8 comparison results for Boston suggest that marked improvements in neighborhood quality and adult health may result from offering Section 8 subsidies to public housing residents in high-poverty neighborhoods.

The treatment received by the experimental group, which is a combination of housing mobility counseling and a geographically restricted subsidy, does not align with policies under consideration. To the extent that related counseling initiatives, such as HUD's Regional Opportunity Counseling, emphasize information and client visits to low-poverty census tracts to a greater degree, their outcomes might be similar to the experimental group's. In particular, participating families may experience less criminal victimization among children and lower rates of injuries and asthma attacks than families participating in Section 8 that do not receive additional moving assistance.[25] The experimental group's outcomes on most dimensions were at least as good as the Section 8 comparison group's; their outcomes on other dimensions, including some that are highly valued by participants (such as child safety and health), were better. These outcomes, despite the restrictions on individual choice when moving, suggest that regular Section 8 participants may not have sufficient information about the full set of opportunities (and potential benefits) available to them. Counselors could be integral to providing such information.

Another factor to consider when assessing the policy relevance of the MTO results is the scale of the potential policy under consideration. MTO is a relatively small program, and the lessons from it are most directly applicable to other incremental programs, such as adding several hundred Section 8 vouchers in various cities. Families that move to new neighborhoods through the MTO program are too few in number, for the most part, to substantially change the character of the new neighborhoods. A large-scale program, such as the complete elimination of all public housing projects and the issuance of vouchers to all former tenants, might have different effects than a smaller-scale program.

The results reported in this chapter represent the beginning of the research effort needed to reach stronger conclusions about the nature of neighborhood effects and the efficacy of housing mobility policies from the MTO demonstration. Results cover only the early impacts of MTO in Boston. In addition, we have no information on the impact of the moves on very young children. Since the youngest children will likely be exposed to the new neighborhoods the longest, they may eventually show the strongest results. Nonetheless, early outcomes, such as improvements in mothers' mental health and fewer problem behaviors among children, are promising because they may be important factors in improving long-run child educational and economic outcomes. The demonstration is intended to study the experiences of families over 10 years. Only time, further data collection, and in-depth research will reveal the full extent of MTO's long-term impacts.

Although the long-term effects of MTO will be a crucial issue for future research, the short-term impacts on adult and child circumstances described here are of substantial importance. Many of the hopes of MTO family members concerning increased safety, reduced stress, and "a better life" for their children do seem to have been realized through the moves. By many measures, the Moving to Opportunity program has already significantly improved the well-being of many families in Boston.

NOTES

The authors thank the U.S. Department of Housing and Urban Development, the National Science Foundation (SBE-9876337), the National Institute on Aging, National Bureau of Economic Research, Harvard University, and the Center for Economic Policy Studies at Princeton University for research support. The authors are grateful to Yvonne Gastelum for collaborating on qualitative interviews in Spanish, Ying Qian for conducting pilot survey interviews and for compiling family contact information, Adriana Mendez for translating the survey into Spanish, Humberto Reynosa for editing the Spanish translation, Beth Welty for processing the administrative earnings and welfare data, and to Patrick Wang, Lorin Obler, and Ali Sherman for excellent research assistance. We thank all of the members of the MTO teams at MBHP, BHA, Abt, and Westat for making our research possible and Carol Luttrel for facilitating our access to Massachusetts administrative data. We have also benefited from conversations with numerous colleagues.

    1. It turned out, for example, that one African-American counselor believed in moving families as far away from the city of Boston as possible and developed extensive ties to landlords in suburban communities. A second African-American counselor tried to discourage his clients from moving to the suburbs immediately south of Boston and instead urged them to move to the northern suburbs. He told his clients that the southern suburbs are "where all of the people you are trying to get away from are moving to." The two Latino counselors were less directive about where families should move and appeared to have stronger ties to closer-in suburbs. Thus, in interpreting differential move rates between Latino and African-American participants, it is important to be aware that the Spanish-speaking participants were assigned to the Hispanic counselors.

    2. This requirement could be extremely burdensome for a tenant. For example, a security deposit of one month's rent for a tenant whose share of the rent was 10 percent (and HUD's share was 90 percent) would be equivalent to the amount of rent that the tenant would normally pay over 10 months. Conversations with housing counselors indicated that the security deposits were not major obstacles to mobility, but it is possible that some of the drop-off in move rates we observe in later cohorts of enrollees was due to the change in security deposit rules.

    3. The interviews, which took place in the respondents' homes, were taperecorded. Interviews in English were jointly conducted by Jeffrey Kling and Jeffrey Liebman, two of the authors of this chapter. Interviews in Spanish were conducted by Liebman and Yvonne Gastelum, a doctoral student in clinical psychology at Boston University. Further details on this qualitative research can be found in Kling, Liebman, and Katz (2001).

4. The survey was written by our research team and administered in mixed modes (by telephone and in person) by Westat Inc. The survey was administered in both Spanish and English. The complete survey instrument is available at http://www.wws.princeton.edu/~kling.

5. Interviews with 20 household heads could not be completed. In 13 of these cases, we located the household, but were unable to complete an interview because the sample member was deceased, avoided our interviewer, or refused to be interviewed. In seven cases, we did not locate the household head, although in five of those cases we were in touch with friends or family members of the household head and might ultimately have been able to locate the household head or other members of the MTO household with additional efforts. While our overall survey response rate is very high, the different dates of survey completion (the lag between our telephone and in-person surveys and the six months we spent tracing the most difficult-to-find families) are not ideal.

6. The adjustment factors to convert the simple mean differences of treatment and control groups into estimates of the treatment on the treated are the inverse of the program-move probabilities for each of the treatment groups. Katz, Kling, and Liebman (2001) present a more formal analysis of the derivation of intent-to-treat and treatment-on-the-treated estimates.

7. Compared with other tenants in the same public housing development in which the MTO families lived, Goering et al. (1999) found that MTO and non-MTO households were very similar in household size and in number of children under 18. MTO households (pooling across all five sites) were more likely to be female-headed (93 percent versus 78 percent), receiving Aid to Families with Dependent Children (75 percent versus 51 percent), not working (88 percent versus 70 percent), and younger (median age 33 versus 39).

8. The New York and Los Angeles sites contain roughly equal percentages of blacks and Hispanics. In contrast, the Baltimore and Chicago sites are nearly 100 percent black.

9. Employment opportunities were rarely listed as people's second most important reason for wanting to move. In total, drugs and gangs were listed as either the first or second most important reason for wanting to move for 75 percent of the sample, while getting a bigger and better apartment was listed for 58 percent of the sample. In contrast, better schools for children was the first or second most important reason for only 29 percent, and being near a job or getting a new job was listed as the first or second reason by only 3 percent of household heads.

10. In contrast to the emphasis on crime as a motivation for wanting to move among current public housing residents in high-poverty areas, participants in the Gautreaux housing mobility program in Chicago in the late 1970s (Peroff et al. 1979) indicated that good schools (34 percent) and quality of housing (26 percent) were more important considerations than crime (23 percent). The increased concern about crime among inner-city public housing residents likely reflects the increase in violent crime rates that occurred in many urban areas in the late 1980s and early 1990s.

11. Note that the victimization rates may be somewhat exaggerated in the baseline survey. Despite explicit instructions that the survey was being conducted by outside researchers and that the housing authority would not receive copies of individual responses, fieldwork revealed that some respondents assumed their answers could influence their acceptance into the program. This may have encouraged them to overreport criminal victimization. The high victimization rates could also be caused by respondents

including events that occurred before the time frame of the questions into the six-month period.

12.   Neighborhood characteristics are obtained by geocoding the street address and linking the resulting location to 1990 Census data on areas such as tracts (contiguous geographic areas with an average of 4,000 inhabitants) and block groups (subdivisions of tracts). In interpreting these neighborhood characteristics, it is worth remembering that census tract characteristics may have changed between 1990 and the time at which the MTO families were surveyed, and that census tracts do not necessarily correspond to the concept of a "neighborhood."

13.   In Katz, Kling, and Liebman (2001), we also conducted a variety of statistical tests, which indicated that the distribution of baseline survey characteristics is consistent with random assignment.

14.   The randomization proportions were adjusted after it became apparent that more experimental families and fewer Section 8 comparison families were taking up the offered subsidy than had been projected. For the earlier 450 sample households, the exp: Sec 8: control random assignment ratio was 225:85:140. For the later 90 households, from March–May 1996, the ratio was 15:35:40. To account for this change, all statistical estimates presented in this study are computed using weights. This weighting allows us to abstract from the change and address the counterfactual question of what our results would look like if the randomization probabilities had remained constant throughout our time period at the overall sample ratio of 240:120:180, or 4:2:3. For example, fewer control households fall in the earlier period than in the overall sample, so these observations are upweighted by $(180/540)/(140/450) \approx 1.07$. Without weighting, simple mean differences will not accurately estimate an average causal effect of the MTO program if the average level of any outcome is changing over time within any of the groups.

15.   Note that the experimental group take-up rate of 48 percent substantially exceeded the HUD's expectation of 30 percent, while the Section 8 comparison group take-up rate of 62 percent was lower than the anticipated 80 percent (Feins et al. 1994).

16.   In our qualitative interviews, a number of families explained that they took one of the first apartments they were shown in order to be assured of leasing-up within the time limit of 120 days necessary to obtain the Section 8 certificate or voucher. Once they had the Section 8 subsidy, they were able to look at a more leisurely pace for another apartment and often found a better apartment after talking to people in their new neighborhoods.

17.   We were able to obtain accurate geocoded information on the current residential locations of 525 of the 540 target families at the time of our MTO-Boston follow-up survey: 235 experimental, 114 from the Section 8 comparison group, and 176 controls. The first two rows of table 7.2 indicate that the program move rates for both the experimental and Section 8 comparison groups are almost identical for the full sampling universe and the geocoded subsample.

18.   Nearly all of those outside the city limits were living in Boston's surrounding communities, although seven experimental and two control households moved to other states. In addition, there were three Section 8 comparison households living in Puerto Rico with whom we completed interviews but from whom we were unable to obtain street addresses that could be matched to census tracts; these households are therefore not included in table 7.3.

19. Our questions were modeled on the National Criminal Victimization Survey and designed to evoke recollections of incidents involving the household head or a child that occurred in the prior six months. Table 7.5 reports results for personal crimes (assault, robbery, and pickpocketing) and property crimes (theft, and household or motor vehicle burglary), with classifications based on descriptions of the incidents.

20. Different reporting behavior by respondents in the baseline and follow-up surveys may also have played a role, since the follow-up survey did not appear to be viewed be respondents as having the potential to influence their chance of selection for Section 8 in the way that the baseline survey appears to have been. The wording of the questions also differed in the follow-up survey, although the newer questions (Bureau of Justice Statistics 1994) have generally been shown to increase the reporting of incidents.

21. We had hypothesized that sports injuries may have increased for families who moved through the MTO program, since the children were potentially more likely to spend recreational time playing sports in safer neighborhoods. In fact, only about 2 percent of children experienced sports injuries requiring medical attention, and the frequency of sports injuries does not appear to differ substantially among the groups.

22. Katz, Kling, and Liebman (2001) estimate linear probability models of treatment effects, including variables from the baseline survey to reduce residual variation and improve efficiency of estimation. We also present evidence that these results on children's health outcomes are not being spuriously driven by changes in access to medical care.

23. These questions were originally developed for analysis of the Rand Health Insurance Experiment (Manning et al. 1987) and are now commonly used in the SF-36 Health Survey (Ware et al. 1994). First, we asked: "In general, would you say that your health is excellent, very good, good, fair, or poor?" Second, we asked: "How much of the time during the past four weeks have you felt calm and peaceful—all of the time, most of the time, a good bit of the time, some of the time, a little of the time, or none of the time?" Third, we asked: "How much of the time have you been a happy person?" with the same response choices.

24. For details see Massachusetts Department of Transitional Assistance. 2002. "Chapter 5: Where we've been and where we're going." http://www.magnet.state.ma.us/dta/dtatoday/reform

25. The mechanisms that are the source of these differences between the experimental and Section 8 comparison groups remain a subject for further research. On one hand, families may need to move to neighborhoods that are much different, rather than moderately different, as was the case for the Section 8 comparison group. Alternatively, the results for the two groups may differ because the composition of families that moved through the MTO program in the two groups is not the same. For instance, there may be some families that moved through MTO when assigned to the Section 8 comparison group, but would not have moved if they had been assigned to the experimental group. If the injury rates of children in these particular families were only minimally affected by the move, then such families could be driving the difference between the experimental and Section 8 comparison results by lowering the estimated average effect for the Section 8 comparison group. Under either of these alternatives, however, a counseling program that resulted in more placements in low-poverty census tracts and resulted in a lower probability of actually moving through the program could have the potential to emulate the outcomes of the experimental group in the MTO program.

REFERENCES

Aaronson, Daniel. 1998. "Using Sibling Data to Estimate the Impact of Neighborhoods on Children's Educational Outcomes." *Journal of Human Resources* 33 (fall): 915–46.

Augustyn, Marilyn, S. Parker, B. Groves, B. Zuckerman. 1995. "Silent Victims: Children Who Witness Violence." *Contemporary Pediatrics* (August): 35–57.

Bos, Johannes, Aletha Huston, Robert Granger, Greg Duncan, Tom Brock, and Vonnie McLoyd. 1999. *New Hope for People with Low Incomes: Two-Year Results of a Program to Reduce Poverty and Reform Welfare.* New York: Manpower Demonstration Research Corporation.

Bureau of Justice Statistics. 1994. *Technical Background on the Redesigned National Crime Victimization Survey: NCJ-151172.* Washington, D.C.: U.S. Department of Justice.

Duncan, Greg J., James P. Connell, and Pamela K. Klebanov. 1997. "Conceptual and Methodological Issues in Estimating Causal Effects of Neighborhoods and Family Conditions on Individual Development." In *Neighborhood Poverty. Volume 1: Context and Consequences for Children,* edited by Jeanne Brooks-Gunn, Greg Duncan, and J. Lawrence Aber (219–50). New York: Russell Sage Foundation.

Feins, Judith D., Mary Joel Holin, and Antony A. Phipps. 1994. "Moving to Opportunity for Fair Housing Demonstration: Program Operations Manual." HUD-006483. Rockville, Md.: HUD USER, July.

Gelber, L. E., L. H. Seltzer, J. K. Bouzoukis, S. M. Pollart, M. D. Chapman, and T. A Platts-Mills. 1993. "Sensitization and Exposure to Indoor Allergens as Risk Factors for Asthma among Patients Presenting to Hospital." *American Review of Respiratory Disease* 174: 573–78.

Goering, John M., Joan Kraft, Judith Feins, Debra McInnis, Mary Joel Holin, and Huda Elhassan. 1999. *Moving to Opportunity for Fair Housing Demonstration Program: Current Status and Initial Findings.* Rockville, Md.: HUD USER, September.

Jencks, Christopher, and Susan E. Mayer. 1990. "The Social Consequences of Growing Up in a Poor Neighborhood." In *Inner-City Poverty in the United States,* edited by Laurence Lynn and Michael McGeary (111–86). Washington, D.C.: National Academy Press.

Katz, Lawrence F., Jeffrey R. Kling, and Jeffrey B. Liebman. 2001. "Moving to Opportunity in Boston: Early Results of a Randomized Mobility Experiment." *Quarterly Journal of Economics* 116(2, May): 607–54.

Kling, Jeffrey R., Jeffrey B. Liebman, and Lawrence F. Katz. 2001. "Bullets Don't Got No Name: Consequences of Fear in the Ghetto." Northwestern University/University of Chicago Joint Center for Poverty Research Working Paper 225.

Ludwig, Jens O., Greg J. Duncan, and Joshua C. Pinkston. 2000. "Neighborhood Effects on Economic Self-Sufficiency: Evidence from a Randomized Housing-Mobility Experiment." Northwestern University/University of Chicago Joint Center for Poverty Research Working Paper 159.

Manning, Willard et al. 1987. "Health Insurance and the Demand for Medical Care: Evidence from a Randomized Experiment." *American Economic Review* 77 (June) 251–77.

Manski, Charles F. 1993. "Identification of Endogenous Social Effects: The Reflection Problem." *Review of Economic Studies* 60: 531–42.

Peroff, Kathleen A., Coteal L. Davis, Ronald Jones, Richard T. Curin, and Ronald W. Marans. 1979. *Gautreaux Housing Demonstration: An Evaluation of Its Impact on Participating Households.* Washington, D.C.: U.S. Department of Housing and Urban Development.

Piehl, Anne M., David Kennedy, and Anthony A. Braga. 2000. "Problem Solving and Youth Violence: An Evaluation of the Boston Gun Project." *American Law and Economics Review* 2 (spring, 1): 58–106.

Putnam, Robert D. 1995. "Bowling Alone: America's Declining Social Capital." *Journal of Democracy* 6(1): 65–78.

Quinlan, Kyran P. 1996. "Injury Control in Practice." *Archives of Pediatrics Adolescent Medicine* 150: 954–7.

Rosenbaum, James E. 1995. "Changing the Geography of Opportunity by Expanding Residential Choice: Lessons from the Gautreaux Program." *Housing Policy Debate* 6: 231–69.

Sarpong, Sampson B. 1996. "Socioeconomic Status and Race as Risk Factors for Cockroach Allergen Exposure and Sensitization in Children with Asthma." *Journal of Allergy and Clinical Immunology* 97: 1393–401.

Sharfstein, Joshua, and Megan Sandel, eds. 1998. *Not Safe at Home.* Boston: Boston Medical Center.

Ware, John E. Jr., Kristin K. Snow, Mark Kosinski, Barbara Gandek. 1994. *SF-36 Health Survey: Manual and Interpretation Guide.* Boston: New England Medical Center.

Wilson, William Julius. 1996. *When Work Disappears.* New York: Alfred A. Knopf.

Wright, Rosalind J. 1988. "Review of Psychosocial Stress and Asthma: An Integrated Biopsychosocial Approach" *Thorax* LIII: 1066–74.

Zelon, Harvey, Bill Rhoe, Sam Leaman, and Steve Williams. 1994. *Survey of Public Housing Residents: Crime and Crime Prevention in Public Housing.* Research Triangle Park, N.C.: Research Triangle Institute.

8

New York City Site Findings
The Early Impacts of Moving to Opportunity on Children and Youth

Tama Leventhal
Jeanne Brooks-Gunn

The New York City MTO evaluation was conducted approximately three years after baseline interviews (mover families had lived in their new neighborhoods for approximately two years), a relatively short time frame in which to expect program effects on child and adolescent outcomes. While there is growing evidence from nonexperimental studies that neighborhood residence is associated with child and adolescent well-being (Brooks-Gunn et al. 1997 a, b; see Leventhal and Brooks-Gunn 2000 for a review), this research does not provide much information on how long individuals must reside in neighborhoods for changes in behavior to occur. In our own work looking at children during the first three years of life (not in the context of a housing experiment), we have found that neighborhood effects on children's cognition do not appear until children are three years old (Klebanov et al. 1998). This pattern has been interpreted as suggesting that some level of exposure to neighborhood contexts is necessary for neighborhoods to influence well-being and, more important, that neighborhoods primarily affect young children indirectly through processes such as parental behavior and quality of the home environment (see also Chase-Lansdale et al. 1997; Klebanov et al. 1997). Neighborhood influences on older children and adolescents, while primarily thought of as indirect, may in some ways operate more directly because these youths have greater exposure to neighborhood contexts than do younger children. Indirect neighborhood effects (e.g., transmitted through parenting behavior or peer groups) may take longer to influence outcomes than direct neighborhood effects (e.g., neighborhood violence). See Duncan and Brooks-Gunn (1997) for an examination of the indirect effects of family income on child and adolescent development.

Three theoretical models help us understand the pathways through which neighborhood effects may be transmitted to children and youth (Leventhal and Brooks-Gunn 2000, 2002; see also Jencks and Mayer 1990). The first, the institutional resources model, posits that neighborhood influences operate by means of the quality, quantity, and diversity of community resources. The relationships and ties model focuses on the family as a mediator of neighborhood effects, including parental attributes, social networks, and behavior as well as home environment characteristics; this model draws heavily from research on family stress and economic hardship (Conger et al. 1992, 1993, 1994; McLoyd 1990). The final model, norms/collective efficacy, based on social disorganization theory (Sampson and Groves 1989; Sampson, Raudenbush, and Earls 1997), postulates that neighborhood effects are accounted for by the extent of formal and informal community institutions present to monitor residents' behavior and physical threats to them. The utility of each model depends partly on the age of the individual and partly on the outcome under investigation. Although the experimental design of MTO does permit us to identify specific mechanisms that might transmit program effects to children and youth, these theoretical models offer further guidance on expectations for and interpretation of MTO results.

This research has implications for MTO program effects on child and adolescent well-being. First, we anticipate that health, behavior, and social outcomes may be altered prior to achievement and educational outcomes. Health, behavior, and social outcomes are likely to be affected more directly by an improvement in neighborhood social conditions (although indirect effects through community social organization are posited); achievement and educational outcomes are most likely to be influenced primarily indirectly through quality of available resources, such as schools. Second, we expect that program effects may vary by children's sex and age; however, these differential effects may depend on the outcome under investigation. For example, neighborhood influences on delinquency are thought to be greater for boys than for girls. On the other hand, sex differences in program effects on future aspirations are less clear. As such, we explore potential subgroup differences in program effects.

This chapter provides a first look at the families in the New York City MTO program. It finds that the MTO program achieved its goal of moving families to better neighborhoods. While moving to less poor neighborhoods had very modest beneficial effects on family economic well-being (compared with remaining in high-poverty neighborhoods), moving to less poor neighborhoods resulted in large improvements in boys' mental health, especially among experimental boys who moved to low-poverty neighborhoods. Program effects on positive indicators of children's well-being—participation in school activities and future expectations—however, were small and mixed. Finally, although program impacts on adolescent problem behavior—delinquency and substance use—were negligible, findings revealed that, compared with peers who stayed in high-poverty neighborhoods, experimental boys appeared to have peers who were less likely to engage in problem behavior, but experimental girls were more likely to have delinquent peers.

Study Overview

Design

The New York City MTO study was designed to examine the experiences of three categories of families: (1) those who moved out of public housing into low-poverty neighborhoods, (2) those who moved out of public housing into poor and near-poor urban neighborhoods, and (3) those who did not move out of public housing in high-poverty neighborhoods. The New York City MTO evaluation goes beyond considering just the effects of moving on employment, income, and welfare use. The focus is on child and family well-being—family members' health, children's and youths' achievement and behavior, and parent-child relationships. Of the 794 families that participated in the New York City MTO program,[1] 550 were located and interviewed, for a 69 percent response rate (comprising 220 experimental group families, 181 Section 8 families, and 149 in-place control families).

The 244 families that did not participate in the New York City MTO follow-up did not differ significantly from the sample of 550 families on any of the 11 baseline parental and family characteristics examined, including parental education, employment, race/ethnicity, welfare receipt, household income, and composition. However, there was a trend level difference, suggesting that families that participated in the follow-up evaluation, on average, had marginally higher per person incomes than families that did not participate.[2] Together, these findings suggest that the 550 families that participated in the follow-up evaluation are representative of the larger sample.

Program Take-Up

Overall, 40 percent of families in the present sample took up the randomly assigned treatment they were offered (42 percent of the experimental group and 38 percent of the Section 8 group). For the entire New York City sample, the take-up rate for the experimental group was 45 percent and 49 percent for the Section 8 group (Goering et al. 1999). The take-up rates in New York were, generally, lower than in the four other MTO sites. The follow-up sample slightly underrepresents the families that took up the treatment, somewhat attenuating our ability to estimate treatment effects.

Families that took up the treatment (i.e., successfully moved) in the sample differed significantly from families that did not take up the treatment on five of the eleven baseline parental and family characteristics examined.[3] Families that took up the treatment were more likely to have younger and more educated parents than families that did not take up the treatment. These families also had lower household and per person incomes and greater levels of welfare receipt than comparable families that did not take up the treatment. In addition, families that took up the treatment had marginally more unemployed and African-American heads of households. Thus, families that took up the treatment appear to be somewhat more disadvantaged than families that did not. This chapter focuses on all 550 families that participated in the follow-up evaluation, including those that did and did not move within the MTO program.

Procedure

BASELINE
Baseline interviews were conducted with families from 1994 to 1999; most housing placements/random assignment designations occurred between 1995 and 1996 in New York City. Applicants were initially recruited through the New York City Public Housing Authority and invited to group orientations. For families that signed up for the program, heads of households completed lengthy questionnaires with the assistance of trained research staff from Abt Associates. The same infor-

mation was collected in all five MTO sites. The interviews focused on demographic information and obtained limited data on parenting, child health, behavior, and school/child care. Parents also reported on their housing and neighborhood conditions.

Families in the New York City MTO were drawn from approximately 14 housing projects in Manhattan and the Bronx. Families assigned to the experimental group received counseling and assistance with their moves from the Northern Manhattan Improvement Corporation (for additional details, see Goering et al. 1999).

THREE-YEAR FOLLOW-UP
Follow-up interviews were conducted with families in the New York City MTO demonstration approximately three years after baseline interviews were completed.[4] For all located families, in-home interviews were conducted with primary caregivers and up to two randomly selected children per household (an effort was always made to target children that lived in baseline households and that were three years of age or older). For a small subset of families that moved out of the New York City metropolitan area, telephone interviews were conducted with primary caregivers and one child age 11 or older per household ($n = 14$). The measures used in this study were drawn largely from national surveys (Baker and Mott 1989), the Abt baseline survey, other MTO site evaluations, and several neighborhood-based studies, including the Project on Human Development in Chicago Neighborhoods (Earls and Buka 1997) and the Yonkers Project (Briggs 1997). During the parent interview, household demographic information was obtained, in addition to information on housing, neighborhood conditions, education, employment, work and family issues, parent mental and physical health, children's schooling/child care, childrearing issues, parent-child relationships, the home environment, and children's behavior problems, temperament, and physical health. Reading/verbal and mathematics assessments were administered in English or Spanish to all children age three or older by trained interviewers, and children between age eight and eighteen were also interviewed. These youths reported on their schooling, peer group, behavior problems, delinquency, substance use, exposure to violence, self-efficacy, employment, routine activities, and future expectations. All parents and children were compensated for their participation.

At the time of the follow-up, almost all families (96 percent) continued to reside in New York City—even experimental and Section 8 families that had moved within the program (a majority moved to or within the Bronx and the remainder moved to Manhattan, Brooklyn, Staten Island, and Westchester County, a suburban region just north of the Bronx).

Profile of Families at Baseline

What was the initial profile of the 550 families in 1995–96, when they enrolled in the MTO program? Findings are reported for parents, children, and families (see table 8.1).

Table 8.1. *Baseline Parental, Child, and Family Characteristics, by Condition* (percent, except where noted)

	Experimental (n = 220)	Section 8 (n = 181)	Control (n = 149)	Total (N = 550)
Parental age (years)	35.77 (10.13)	35.43 (9.13)	34.96 (9.67)	35.44 (9.67)
Parent sex (female)	91.3	96.1	92.6	93.2
Parental race/ethnicity				
African American	48.6	50.5	51.0	49.9
Hispanic	48.6	45.1	45.6	46.6
Other	2.8	4.4	3.4	3.5
Parent high school graduate/GED	66.5	67.4	58.4	64.6
Married	12.1	7.7	12.3	10.7
Child age[a] (years)	7.78 (4.18)	8.00 (4.18)	7.71 (4.15)	7.84 (4.17)
Child sex (male)[a]	50.7	44.0	49.3	48.0
Main reason want to move				
Get away drugs and gangs	49.5	48.5	53.6	50.3
Get bigger/better apartment	29.5	31.7	25.0	29.0
Better schools for children	16.8	18.6	18.6	17.9
Other	4.2	1.2	2.9	2.8

Source: Abt MTO baseline data.

Note: Table presents means (standard deviation). Descriptive statistics weighted by date of random assignment because assignment ratio for the three groups changed throughout randomization period. No significant group differences found.

a. N = 806.

PARENTS

At the time of baseline interviews, parents in the New York City MTO program were in their mid-30s, with more than two-thirds holding a high school degree or an equivalency diploma. Approximately half the sample was African American and the remainder was Hispanic (a very small number reported "other" for race/ethnicity). Notably, almost all households were headed by an unmarried woman.

CHILDREN

The three-year follow-up assessed 806 children in the 550 households (one child was interviewed in 38 percent of households, and two children were interviewed in 62 percent of households). On average, children were seven years old at baseline, and approximately half were boys. At follow-up, children were, on average, 11 years old.

FAMILIES

When asked the primary reason for wanting to move from their neighborhood of residence, a majority of families reported safety (i.e., "getting away from drugs and gangs"); this sentiment was consistent across MTO sites (Goering et al. 1999). The other major reason for wanting to move, cited by approximately one-third of the sample, was to get a larger or better apartment. Very few families said that employment opportunities were the major impetus for signing up for the MTO program.

Only about one-quarter of parents was employed at baseline; three-quarters of families were receiving welfare at that time. At baseline, approximately four people lived in each household. Average household income was just over $10,000, well below the poverty level of $15,911 for a family of four in 1996 (two adults and two children). Across the three groups, household income per person was approximately $3,000.

As would be expected because of random assignment, the three groups did not differ significantly on any of the baseline parental, child, and family characteristics presented in tables 8.1 and 8.2.

Changes from Baseline to Follow-Up

What changes in parental, family, and neighborhood characteristics occurred between baseline and follow-up, and did the three groups' pattern of changes differ? Findings are reported for employment, welfare, income, and household size (table 8.2) as well as for neighborhood conditions (table 8.3).

EMPLOYMENT, WELFARE, AND INCOME

At the three-year follow-up, almost half the parents were employed with no significant differences across the groups. However, notable differences in change patterns occurred across groups. Specifically, more parents saw increased employment in the Section 8 group than the in-place controls. Approximately 7 percent more of the unemployed Section 8 parents at baseline had entered the workforce at follow-up compared with in-place control parents.

At the time of the follow-up, more than half the families were receiving welfare, with no reported group differences. However, the decrease in welfare receipt from baseline to follow-up was largest for the Section 8 families.

At the three-year follow-up, family income was approximately $12,200, with per person household income of about $4,000; no significant group differences were found. Notably, income rose more for experimental and Section 8 families than for in-place control families (although the difference within and across groups was not significant). This trend is consistent with the increase in employment observed among these groups. From baseline to follow-up, per person income rose significantly for all groups, particularly experimental families, whose increase was significantly different from that of the in-place controls.

HOUSEHOLD SIZE

Approximately three to four persons lived in each household at the time of the follow-up. No significant differences emerged across groups; however, declines in household size from baseline to follow-up were notably larger for the mover groups. This change largely reflected a decrease in the number of children in mover households (although the number of adults declined as well). Among movers, it appears that some household members might have remained in their original neighborhoods. At this point in time, it is unclear why these reductions in household members occurred. Some older children may have remained behind, female relatives coresiding with families may not have moved, families in public housing might have been more likely to "double up" than families that moved, or male partners may have chosen not to move. Only further analysis can reveal which factors created the reductions.

Table 8.2. *Economic Well-Being at Baseline and Follow-Up, by Condition*

	Experimental (n = 220)	*Section 8* (n = 181)	*Control* (n = 149)	*Total* (N = 550)
% parent employed				
Baseline	22.3	26.6	28.1	25.3
Follow-up	43.6	50.6	44.8	46.2
Difference[a]	21.3***	24.0***	16.7***	20.9***
% receive welfare				
Baseline	71.6	72.8	70.3	71.6
Follow-up	58.5	53.6	55.4	56.1
Difference[a]	−13.1***	−19.2***	−14.9***	−15.5***
Household size				
Baseline	3.90 (1.53)	4.18 (1.89)	4.04 (1.83)	4.03 (1.74)
Follow-up	3.34 (1.53)	3.58 (1.65)	3.61 (1.70)	3.50 (1.62)
Difference[a]	−0.56***	−0.60***	−0.43***	−0.53***
Household income ($)				
Baseline	10,405 (4,731)	10,358 (4,811)	11,204 (5,395)	10,610 (4,953)
Follow-up	12,264 (8,983)	12,341 (9,988)	12,096 (8,606)	12,243 (7,207)
Difference[a]	1,859*	1,983**	892	1,633***
Per person income ($)				
Baseline	2,920 (1,558)	2,789 (1,431)	3,063 (1,549)	2,916 (1,515)
Follow-up	4,443 (4,257)	3,813 (3,334)	3,726 (2,818)	4,041 (3,621)
Difference[a]	1,523***[b]	1,024***	663*	1,125

Source: Abt MTO baseline data and New York City MTO follow-up evaluation.

Note: Table presents percentages and means (standard deviations) weighted by date of random assignment because assignment ratio for the three groups changed throughout assignment period. For each treatment condition, rows present status at baseline, follow-up, and difference between follow-up and baseline, respectively.

a. For difference scores, significance levels indicate significant change over time for the respective group.

b. Difference score from follow-up to baseline is marginally significantly different from in-place controls.

*p < .05; **p < .01; ***p < .001.

Table 8.3. *Parent-Reported Neighborhood Characteristics at Baseline and Follow-Up, by Condition*

	Experimental (*n* = 220)	Section 8 (*n* = 181)	Control (*n* = 149)	Total (*N* = 550)
Physical and social disorder (trash, graffiti, public drinking, public drug use, and abandoned buildings)[c]				
Baseline	2.63 (0.38)	2.66 (0.31)	2.67 (0.32)	2.65 (0.34)
Follow-up[a]	2.03 (0.73)***	2.16 (0.66)**	2.39 (0.57)	2.17 (0.68)
Difference[b]	−0.60***[d]	−0.50***[d]	−0.28***	−0.48***
Exposure to violence (mugged, threatened, beaten, and stabbed/shot)[e]				
Baseline	0.98 (1.22)	1.02 (1.29)	0.94 (1.25)	0.98 (1.25)
Follow-up	0.22 (0.62)	0.28 (0.69)	0.28 (0.70)	0.26 (0.67)
Difference	−0.76***	−0.74***	−0.66***	−0.72***
Satisfaction[f]				
Baseline	1.74 (0.96)	1.67 (0.94)	1.77 (1.07)	1.73 (0.98)
Follow-up[a]	3.06 (1.43)***	2.81 (1.33)	2.57 (1.38)	2.85 (1.40)
Difference[b]	1.32***[d]	1.14***	0.80***	1.12***

Source: Abt MTO baseline data and New York City MTO follow-up evaluation.

Note: Table presents percentages and means (standard deviations) weighted by date of random assignment because assignment ratio for the three groups changed throughout assignment period. For each treatment condition, rows present status at baseline, follow-up, and difference between follow-up and baseline, respectively.

a. For experimental and Section 8 groups, significance levels indicate significant difference from in-place control group.

b. For difference scores, significance levels indicate significant change over time for the respective group.

c. Parents reported how big of a problem five events in the neighborhood were on a three-point scale, rating them "a big problem" (3 points) to "not a big problem" (1 point). For disorder scale, range = 1–3.

d. Difference score from follow-up to baseline is significantly different from in-place controls.

e. For exposure to violence, range = 0–4.

f. For satisfaction, range = 1–5.

**p < .01; ***p < .001.

NEIGHBORHOOD CONDITIONS
Physical and social disorder, our first proxy of neighborhood conditions, was measured as the mean of five items rated by respondents. Respondents rated how big a problem several objects or events (trash, graffiti, public drinking, public drug use or dealing, and abandoned buildings) were in their neighborhoods, from 1 ("not a big problem") to 3 ("a big problem"). Overall, respondents rated neighborhood physical and social disorder as very high at the time of both baseline and follow-up interviews. At the three-year follow-up, significant group differences in reports of neighborhood disorder were found. These differences also translated into significant group differences in patterns of change from baseline to follow-up. Specifically, both experimental and Section 8 parents reported significantly less disorder than the in-place control parents. Consequently had significantly larger declines in neighborhood disorder, particularly the experimental group (i.e., 23 percent, 19 percent, and 10 percent declines in disorder for the experimental, Section 8, and in-place control groups, respectively).

The exposure-to-violence scale asked whether any family member had been exposed to several violent incidents in the past six months (mugged, threatened with gun or knife, beaten or assaulted, and stabbed/shot). Exposure to violence was low over time (approximately 1 incident at baseline and 0.3 at follow-up), and all families experienced more than a 70 percent decline in exposure to violence.

Neighborhood satisfaction, rated "1" for "very satisfied" to "5" for "very dissatisfied" (and reverse coded so higher scores represented greater satisfaction), was also low at baseline, but it was moderate at follow-up. At the three-year follow-up, only experimental families reported significantly greater satisfaction with their neighborhoods relative to the in-place controls, resulting in significantly larger increases in neighborhood satisfaction for these families.

Table 8.4 reports selected 1990 Census measures of neighborhood conditions at the three-year follow-up. According to almost all these neighborhood indicators, experimental families lived in the most advantaged neighborhoods. Their neighborhoods had higher median incomes, fewer poor residents, more affluent residents, fewer unemployed residents, and fewer rental units than the in-place control families' neighborhoods. Notably, experimental families' neighborhoods did not significantly differ from in-place control families' neighborhoods in terms of the percentage of African Americans, but they did differ in percentage of Latinos and

Table 8.4. *Neighborhood Characteristics as Measured by 1990 Census Data at Follow-Up, by Condition*

	Control (n = 149)	Experimental–control[a] (n = 220)	Section 8–control[a] (n = 181)
Median family income ($)	14,808 (6531)	8,469 (14684)***	3,114 (9283)*
Fraction poor	0.45 (.12)	−0.11 (.20)***	−0.05 (.14)*
Fraction households w/income > $50k	0.01 (.01)	+0.15 (.14)***	0.00 (.01)
Fraction unemployed	0.17 (.05)	−0.03 (.07)***	0.01 (.05)
Fraction rental units	0.94 (.15)	−0.12 (.25)***	−0.02 (.15)
Fraction black	0.41 (.21)	0.04 (.25)	−0.01 (.24)
Fraction Latino	0.51 (.20)	−0.10 (.25)***	−0.03 (.23)
Fraction white	0.06 (.16)	0.06 (.21)*	0.03 (.18)

Source: New York City MTO follow-up evaluation.

Note: Table presents means (standard deviations) weighted by date of random assignment because assignment ratio for the three groups changed throughout assignment period.

a. For experimental and Section 8 groups, significance levels indicate significantly different from in-place controls.

*p < .05; ***p < .001.

whites. Thus, families moved predominately to more affluent and racially mixed neighborhoods in the northeast Bronx.[5]

As shown in table 8.4, Section 8 families' neighborhoods had significantly higher median incomes and fewer poor residents than in-place control families' neighborhoods; their neighborhoods did not significantly differ from the those of in-place control families on any other neighborhood demographic measures. Section 8 families lived in neighborhoods that can be characterized as "near poor."

Health and Behavior of Children Age 8 to 18

This section focuses on information collected during follow-up interviews with 512 children age 8 to 18. Children were approximately 11 years old and about half were boys. In the public health domain, large discrepancies in child health outcomes by neighborhood socioeconomic status have been widely reported at the aggregate or neighborhood level (e.g., Collins and David 1990; Durkin et al. 1994). These studies point to neighborhood disadvantage as a major contributor to poor health outcomes among children. In related work, we have found that living in a poor neighborhood is associated with lower-quality physical home environments, a condition theoretically linked to child health (Klebanov, Brooks-Gunn, and Duncan 1994). A growing body of research also has documented a link between neighborhood poverty and child and adolescent behavior and emotional problems (Leventhal and Brooks-Gunn 2000).

The short-term effects of the MTO program are likely to have a positive impact on mover children's health and behavior. Reductions in neighborhood danger are likely to improve mover children's well-being relative to the in-place control group. In addition, higher levels of neighborhood social organization in the new neighborhoods (compared with baseline neighborhoods) are likely to be associated with greater community regulation of negative peer group activities and threats to physical well-being. We expect program effects on child health and behavior to be larger for experimental than for Section 8 children, since the former moved to the most affluent neighborhoods.

Program effects may vary by child sex and age. Specifically, moving to less poor neighborhoods may have more pronounced effects for boys than for girls, because research suggests that boys may benefit more from advantaged neighborhoods than girls (Leventhal and Brooks-Gunn 2000). Boys' greater susceptibility to neighborhood contexts may result, at least in part, from their increased access to neighborhood influences (e.g., peers and resources). Additionally, given the higher prevalence of behavior problems among boys than girls (Zahn-Waxler 1993), such behaviors may vary more across neighborhoods for boys than for girls, resulting in larger program effects for boys. Finally, children may display more beneficial outcomes than adolescents. Moving may be more difficult for teenagers than children because of the disruption of peer groups, which play an especially prominent role in adolescent development (Steinberg and Sheffield-Morris 2001).

Do the health and behavior of children age 8 to 18 differ by group? The questions used to assess child health (National Health Interview Survey Child Health Supplement 1988) and behavior (Zill 1985) have been widely used in national surveys. The measure of child health was based on parental reports, and behavior problems were reported by children. Program effects were examined across the full sample and separately by child sex and age (8 to 13 years versus 14 to 18 years).

Overall Health

Parents were asked to rate their children's health on a scale of 1 ("excellent") to 5 ("poor"); scores were recoded to reflect the percentage of parents who reported their children's health as excellent or very good (compared with "good," "fair," or "poor"). There were no significant group differences in children's health. Two-thirds of parents reported their children's health as very good or excellent.

Behavior Problems

Behavior problems are a commonly used measure of children's mental health. In this study, children reported how true a series of behaviors were for them over the past six months on a scale from 0 ("not true") to 2 ("often true"). Scores were recoded to indicate whether the behavior was reported as sometimes or often true (compared with "not true"). To allow some cross-site replication, we first examined six of the seven behavior problems defined here that corresponded with behaviors examined in the Boston MTO evaluation (trouble getting along with teachers; disobeying parents; disobeying at school, teasing others; trouble sitting still; and being unhappy, sad, or depressed). For the full sample, the most frequent behavior reported during the past six months was having trouble sitting still (42 percent), while the least common behavior reported was disobeying at school (26 percent). Similar to the Boston evaluation, boys were more likely than girls to report each of these behaviors, except being unhappy, sad, or depressed. Similarly, children age 14 to 18 were more likely than children age 8 to 13 to report each of the behaviors, except difficulty sitting still.

For these six items, significant group differences were found only for reports of feeling unhappy, sad, or depressed in the past six months. Among boys, experimental children were less likely to report this behavior than in-place control boys (27 percent versus 39 percent, respectively; see table 8.5), representing a 30 percent reduction in feelings of unhappiness/sadness among experimental boys relative to boys in the control group. No significant group differences between Section 8 and control boys were found. However, among children age 8 to 13, Section 8 children displayed a 36 percent reduction in reports of feeling unhappy, sad, or depressed, compared with their in-place control peers. No significant program effects were found for girls or for older children age 14 to 18.

Table 8.5. *Behavior of Children Age 8 to 18 at Follow-Up, by Condition* (means and robust standard errors)

	Control (n = 146)	Experimental– control[a] (n = 195)	Section 8– control[a] (n = 171)
Unhappy, sad, or depressed (total)	.40 (.04)	−.08 (.04)	−.08(.04)
Boys	39 (.05)	−.12 (.06)†	.08 (.06)
Girls	.40 (.06)	−.02 (.06)	−.08 (.06)
Age 8–13	.42 (.05)	−.10 (.05)	−.15 (.05)*
Age 14–18	.35 (.07)	−.02 (.05)	.03 (.06)
Too fearful or anxious (total)	.42 (.04)	−.06 (.04)	−.05 (.04)
Boys	.43 (.06)	−.15 (.05)*	−.14 (.06)
Girls	.40 (.05)	.05 (.05)	.05 (.06)
Age 8–13	.48 (.05)	−.16 (.05)*	−.08 (.06)
Age 14–18	.31 (.06)	.09 (.06)	.03 (.06)
Need to be near adults (total)	.43 (.04)	−.07 (.04)	−.09 (.04)
Boys	.49 (.06)	−.17 (.05)*	−.17 (.06)†
Girls	.38 (.06)	.01 (.05)	−.03 (.05)
Age 8–13	.50 (.06)	−.15 (.05)*	−.16 (.05)†
Age 14–18	.33 (.06)	.04 (.06)	.01 (.06)
Depend too much on others (total)	.38 (.04)	−.06 (.04)	−.10 (.04)†
Boys	.44 (.06)	−.15 (.05)†	−.19 (.05)*
Girls	.32 (.06)	.02 (.06)	−.02 (.05)
Age 8–13	.39 (.06)	−.07 (.05)	−.09 (.05)
Age 14–18	.36 (.07)	−.05 (.06)	−.11 (.06)

Source: New York City MTO follow-up evaluation.

Note: Each child reported during past six months, how true each behavior was of him/her on a 3-point scale, and scale was recoded to reflect "not true" (scored 0) or "sometimes/often true"(scored 1). Estimates weighted by date of random assignment because assignment ratio for the three groups changed throughout randomization period. Robust standard errors adjust for multisibling households.

a. Significance levels indicate significantly different from in-place controls.

†$p < .10$; *$p < .05$.

Several other behavior problems reported by children might be affected by moving from poor to less-poor neighborhoods, including being too fearful or anxious, needing to be near adults, and depending too much on others (table 8.5).[6] Similar to the cross-site analyses, significant program effects were limited to boys and to children age 8 to 13. Among experimental boys, a 35 percent reduction in reports of feeling too fearful or anxious in the past six months (compared with in-place controls) was found. In addition, both experimental and Section 8 boys were significantly less likely than in-place control boys to report needing to be near adults or depending too much on others. The magnitude of these reductions was similar across the two mover groups (34 percent to 43 percent).

For children age 8 to 13, experimental children displayed a significant, 33 percent reduction in reports of feeling too fearful or anxious relative to in-place controls. Finally, both experimental and Section 8 children age 8 to 13 were significantly less likely to report needing to be near adults than in-place control peers—approximately a 30 percent reduction.

Participation in School Activities and Future Expectations of Children Age 8 to 18

This section turns to more positive indicators of children's and youths' adjustment—participation in school activities and future expectations. One way children and youth may integrate into their new neighborhoods is through participation in extracurricular school activities. One of the most likely avenues for peer acceptance may be athletics. Other skills could also facilitate social integration into new schools, such as theater, art, and music. Children and youth without special skills or interests may have more difficulty forming peer networks in their new schools. Participation in school activities may also be fostered by additional opportunities to engage in such activities, since schools in more-advantaged neighborhoods tend to have more resources (Jencks and Mayer 1990).

Experimental and Section 8 children may display higher levels of participation in school activities than in-place control children because of a desire to integrate into their new schools and form peer networks. They may also have more opportunity to participate in extracurricular activities, particularly in low-poverty neighborhoods. (However, because many youths did not change schools, these positive effects might not fully show up).[7] Further, social isolation should not be highly problematic for New York City children that moved through MTO, because families generally relocated to racially integrated neighborhoods.

Program effects may vary by child sex and age. Differences between boys and girls in program effects may depend, at least in part, on the activity. For example, boys that moved may participate more in sports than boys in the control group, whereas girls that moved may participate more in theater and music activities than girls in the control group. In terms of differential age effects, potentially larger effects may be seen for youth than for children because of the greater availability of extracurricular activities in high schools compared with middle and elementary schools.

Changes brought about by moving from high- to low-poverty neighborhoods will likely not only alter children's school experiences but also affect many aspects of their daily lives. Consequently, children may modify their expectations for the future. Studies focusing on low-income children suggest that their expectations about the opportunities available to them are shaped by the immediate neighborhood context (Ogbu 1991; Paulter and Lewko 1987). In some instances, however, these expectations may be quite unrealistic. We anticipate that mover children may display higher expectations about college and work relative to in-place control children because of changes in their neighborhood context (e.g., more resources, opportunities, and role models). It is unclear whether sex and age differences will affect future expectations outcomes.

Do participation in school activities and future expectations of children age 8 to 18 differ by group? Participation in school activities during the past year was assessed using a series of questions that have been used in several studies of urban youth (Furstenberg et al. 1999). Future expectations were assessed by measures developed for national studies (National Center for Education Statistics 1988). Again, outcomes were examined for the full sample and for child sex and age subgroups. The findings are reported in table 8.6.

Participation in School Activities

Program effects on children's participation in four activities—music/theater, sports, student government, and academic clubs—during the past year were investigated, as well as a summary score of total participation. Among all children age 8 to 18, approximately 25 percent had participated in sports and in music/theater activities in the past year, while approximately 10 percent of children participated in student government and in academic clubs. For the four activities examined, program effects were mixed and generally small. For the full sample, the only significant group difference was for student government; experimental children were more likely than in-place control children to be involved in this activity (10 percent versus 4 percent). Among boys, however, experimentals were less

Table 8.6. *Self-Reported Participation in School Activities and Future Life Expectations of Youth Ages 8 to 18 at Follow-Up, by Condition* (means and robust standard errors)

	Control (n = 146)	Experimental– control[a] (n = 195)	Section 8– control[a] (n = 171)
School activity participation past year			
Orchestra, band, theater, drama, dance, or choir (total)	.25 (.04)	−.03 (.03)	.00 (.04)
Boys	.31 (.06)	−.12 (.04)[†]	−.12 (.05)
Girls	.19 (.05)	.08 (.05)	.11 (.06)
Age 8–13	.25 (.05)	−.06 (.04)	.07 (.06)
Age 14–18	.25 (.06)	.02 (.06)	−.09 (.05)
Organized sports teams or athletics (total)	.24 (.04)	.00 (.03)	.04 (.04)
Boys	.30 (.06)	−.03 (.05)	.02 (.06)
Girls	.18 (.04)	.03 (.05)	.06 (.05)
Age 8–13	.24 (.05)	−.08 (.04)	.06 (.06)
Age 14–18	.24 (.06)	.14 (.06)	.00 (.05)
Student government or council (total)	.04 (.02)	.06 (.03)[†]	.04 (.02)
Boys	.03 (.02)	.04 (.03)	.03 (.03)
Girls	.06 (.03)	.07 (.05)	.04 (.04)
Age 8–13	.06 (.03)	.02 (.03)	.00 (.03)
Age 14–18	.02 (.02)	.11 (.05)*	.09 (.04)*
Academic clubs (honor society, language, or business) (total)	.10 (.03)	−.02 (.02)	.01 (.03)
Boys	.10 (.04)	.00 (.03)	.03 (.05)
Girls	.11 (.04)	−.05 (.04)	−.02 (.03)
Age 8–13	.09 (.04)	−.04 (.02)	.04 (.04)
Age 14–18	.13 (.05)	.01 (.05)	−.06 (.03)
Future expectations[b]			
To complete college (total)	.88 (.03)	−.07 (.03)[†]	−.06 (.03)[†]
Boys	.82 (.05)	−.03 (.04)	−.06 (.05)
Girls	.94 (.03)	−.12 (.04)*	−.08 (.04)[†]
Age 8–13	.91 (.03)	−.06 (.04)	−.05 (.04)
Age 14–18	.83 (.06)	−.09 (.05)	−.07 (.05)

Table 8.6. *(Continued)*

	Control (n = 146)	Experimental– control[a] (n = 195)	Section 8– control[a] (n = 171)
Find stable well-paid job as adult (total)	.90 (.03)	−.03 (.03)	−.08 (.03)[†]
Boys	.84 (.05)	.04 (.03)	−.04 (.05)
Girls	.96 (.02)	−.10 (.04)*	−.13 (.04)*
Age 8–13	.93 (.03)	−.04 (.03)	−.10 (.04)[†]
Age 14–18	.85 (.05)	−.01 (.05)	−.05 (.05)

Source: New York City MTO follow-up evaluation.

Note: Estimates weighted by date of random assignment because assignment ratio for the three groups changed throughout randomization period. Robust standard errors adjust for multisibling households.

a. Significance levels indicate significantly different from in-place controls.

b. Child asked to report in future, what are chances that each respective event will occur on a 5-point scale from 1 "very low" to 5 "very high." Scores coded to reflect percentage of children who reported chances as high or very high (compared with very low, low, or about 50–50).

$^{†}p < .10; *p < .05$

likely to participate in music/theater activities than in-place control children (19 percent versus 31 percent).

The age subgroup analyses reveal that among children age 14 to 18, both experimental (13 percent) and Section 8 (11 percent) youth were significantly more likely to be involved in the student government than their in-place control peers (2 percent). Finally, experimental youth age 14 to 18 participated in significantly more activities overall than in-place control youth (0.9 activities versus 0.6).[8] No significant group differences were found for girls or for children age 8 to 13.

Future Expectations

Children were asked to rate on a scale from 1 ("very low") to 5 ("very high") their expectations for two significant future events—completing college and finding a stable well-paid job as an adult. Scores were recoded to reflect the percentage of children who reported their chances of meeting these expectations as high or very high (compared with "very low," "low," or "about 50-50"). Almost all children had high expectations for the future, with approximately 85 percent anticipating that they would complete college and find stable jobs as adults. In terms of program effects, in-place control children were significantly more likely to expect to complete college than both mover groups (81 percent versus 82 percent versus 88 percent, for the experimental, Section 8, and control groups, respectively) as well as significantly more likely than Section 8 children to expect to find stable jobs in adulthood (82 percent versus 90 percent, for Section 8 and control, respectively). Moreover, girls in both mover groups reported significantly lower future expectations for both outcomes than the in-place control girls. Among children age 8 to 13, Section 8 children were also less likely to anticipate finding a stable job than their in-place control peers. These findings may reflect a growing awareness of social class differences among mover children who are likely to have greater exposure to individuals from more diverse economic backgrounds in their neighborhoods than control peers in high-poverty neighborhoods. No significant group differences were found for boys or for older children age 14 to 18.

Adolescent Problem Behavior

Finally, we consider problem behavior—delinquency and substance use— for the subsample of youth age 11 to 18 as well as their peers' engagement in problem behavior ($N = 376$). Adolescents, on average, were 14 years old and divided equally between girls and boys. Research indicates that adolescent participation in delinquent and criminal behavior is higher in low-socioeconomic-status neighborhoods than in high-socioeconomic-status neighborhoods (Elliott et al. 1996; Loeber and Wikstrom 1993; Peeples and Loeber 1994; Sampson and Groves 1989). Early results from the Baltimore MTO site provide experimental evidence that moving out of public housing, high-poverty neighborhoods leads to a reduction in violent crimes among adolescent boys (Ludwig, Duncan, and Hirschfield 2001). According to social disorganization theory, neighborhood structural characteristics, such as income, ethnic heterogeneity, and residential instability, are associated with the extent of neighborhood institutions present to monitor residents' behavior, particularly youths' activities (deviant and antisocial peer group behavior) and the presence of physical risk (violence and harmful substances) to residents, especially children and youth. Several recent studies indicate that at both the community and individual levels, mechanisms of social control, particularly surrounding peer group behavior, are linked to rates of adolescent problem behavior (Elliott et al.

1996; Sampson 1997; Sampson and Groves 1989; Sampson et al. 1997). Moreover, exposure to aggressive and antisocial peers is most likely to occur in an adolescent's neighborhood of residence (Briggs 1997; Dishion, Andrews, and Crosby 1995; Sinclair et al. 1994). Participation in delinquent activities is highly correlated with having a peer group that is delinquent (Osgood et al. 1996).

Very little data can link neighborhood conditions to adolescents' substance use. In nonexperimental studies of older children, school rates of alcohol use were higher in residentially stable neighborhoods than in residentially unstable neighborhoods (Ennett et al. 1997). Studies examining the roots of substance use, more generally, point to peer drug use as an important predictor of adolescent substance use (Kandel 1998).

Together, these findings have some implications for the short-term effects of the MTO program on adolescent problem behavior. Program effects on adolescent delinquent behavior are likely to result from changes in neighborhood economic and social conditions. Less delinquent behavior among mover adolescents and less affiliation with delinquent peers may result because of greater community control. On the other hand, two factors may thwart these effects. First, adolescents may have access to old neighborhoods and peers (which is true for most mover families in New York) and/or children may not change schools (the case for a majority of mover youth). Second, poor youth may attach to more deviant peer groups in their new setting. Program effects on youth and peer delinquency may be larger for boys than for girls because, as earlier research has documented, there are stronger links between neighborhood disadvantage and such behavior for boys than for girls. It is unclear if moving will lead to a drop in substance use among movers. (It may depend on the peer group to which the youths attach.)

Do adolescent and peer problem behavior among youths age 11 to 18 differ by group? Measures of adolescent delinquency were drawn from the Project on Human Development in Chicago Neighborhoods, which focuses, in part, on criminal and antisocial behavior (Huizinga, Esbensen, and Weiher 1991). The substance use outcomes were based on questions from national surveys (National Institute on Drug Abuse 1991). These measures were obtained by means of a self-administered questionnaire to improve reliability (Turner et al. 1998). Measures of peer problem behavior also were drawn from the Project on Human Development in Chicago Neighborhoods. Program effects were examined for the full sample and by sex.

Delinquency

Delinquency was assessed by whether adolescents reported engaging in six behaviors during the past year: graffiti, trespassing, hitting someone, stealing, purposely destroying property, and carrying a hidden weapon/ something that could hurt someone. A summary score of the total number of events in which adolescents engaged was also examined. At least 20 percent of adolescents reported engaging in each of the behaviors, except for trespassing (9 percent) and graffiti (14 percent), which occurred less frequently. Overall, adolescents reported engaging in just over one of the events, suggesting relatively low rates of delinquency among this sample. Boys were more likely than girls to engage in each of the activities, except for graffiti, in which boys and girls were equally likely to have taken part. No significant group differences were found for the full sample or for boys or girls.

Substance Use

Program effects on adolescents' use of cigarettes and alcohol during the past year revealed that 13 percent of youth reported having smoked cigarettes in the past year, with the same amount reporting alcohol use during that time. Use of these substances was similar for both boys and girls. The only significant group difference found was for girls' alcohol use; experimental girls were significantly more likely to have used alcohol in the past year than in-place control girls (20 percent versus 4 percent, respectively).[9] No significant group differences were found for the full sample or for boys.

Peer Problem Behavior

To the extent possible, activities that corresponded with youths' reported problem behaviors were considered, including whether peers stole, attacked others with weapons, destroyed/damaged property, used cigarettes, and/or used alcohol during the past year. Adolescents' reports of peer theft and weapon use were similar to reports of their own delinquent behavior (i.e., in the 20 percent range). However, rates of peer destruction of property and cigarette and alcohol use during the past year were approximately twice as high as adolescents' own reported behavior during the period (38 percent, 30 percent, and 34 percent, respectively). For boys, behavior among peers was similar to youths' own behavior. Boys' peers engaged in more delinquent activities than girls' peers, but rates of peer substance use were similar for boys and for girls. In terms of significant group differences, experimental boys were about half as likely as control boys to have peers who had smoked cigarettes in the past year (19 percent versus 38 percent). By contrast, experimental girls were almost twice as likely as control girls to have peers who had stolen in the past year (35 percent versus 18 percent).[10]

Early Impacts

This study provides a first look at the well-being of children and families that participated in the New York City MTO experiment, approximately three years after the baseline interviews (and two years since families in the mover groups relocated to their new neighborhoods). Notably, in the New York City site sample, only about 40 percent of families offered vouchers (experimental and Section 8 groups) used the subsidy to move. This low take-up rate limits our ability to detect program effects. Further, the analysis captures family responses after a relatively short period of exposure to their new neighborhoods. Despite these caveats, the MTO program appears to have improved child health and behavior, the two primary areas examined in this chapter, in important ways.

Almost all parents reported a strong desire to move to neighborhoods without drugs and gangs, and most families in the mover groups improved their neighborhood conditions considerably. In accordance with the program design, experimental families moved to more economically and socially advantaged neighborhoods than their old neighborhoods. Experimental families also reported less disorder and higher satisfaction with their current neighborhoods at follow-up (compared with the control group). Likewise, Section 8 families' neighborhoods appeared more advantaged than the baseline neighborhoods of in-place control families on both objective census measures and more subjective report measures. The relative differences, however, were more modest than those observed for experimental families.

On family economic and social indicators, patterns of change from baseline to follow-up did not differ significantly across groups, except in one area—per person household income. By this measure, experimental families' resources rose more than the in-place control families' resources.

Generally, the outcomes reflected greater improvements among the experimental and Section 8 groups, with Section 8 families in particular entering the workforce and leaving public assistance in greater numbers relative to in-place families. Together, these findings provide early evidence that MTO had begun achieving its goal of improving the economic circumstances of families in the experimental and Section 8 groups.

The MTO program also positively affected children's and youths' well-being within the relatively short period studied. Findings for children's and youths' behavior problems generally were consistent with those reported in the Boston MTO evaluation, though our data were self-reported by children instead of assessed by mothers (Katz, Kling, and Liebman, this volume). Specifically, experimental boys had better mental health than in-place control boys, particularly fewer internalizing (anxious/depressive and dependency) problems. Section 8 boys' behavior also improved. Across both mover groups, no significant program effects on girls' behavior problems were found. In addition, the results suggest that children age 8 to 13 who moved to less poor neighborhoods displayed superior emotional health than in-place control peers (no program effects were found for children age 14 to 18). Program effects on behavior problems ranged from a 30 percent to 43 percent reduction in problems compared with in-place controls, a large drop. These effects were most pronounced for experimental children who moved to low-poverty neighborhoods. In contrast to the Boston MTO site, however, no program effects were found for children's health (Katz, Kling, and Liebman, this volume).

MTO's short-term effects on positive indicators of child well-being were only modest. The few significant differences found for children's participation in school activities suggest that experimental children, particularly older children, may be more involved in some activities, notably student government, compared with their peers in the in-place control group families. The Los Angeles and Boston MTO evaluations also found weak program effects on children's participation in school activities (Hanratty, McLanahan, and Pettit, this volume; Katz, Kling, and Liebman, this volume). Although all the youths had high expectations for their future education and employment, in-place control children and teenagers, especially girls, had the most favorable expectations.

The analysis reveals limited evidence that the short-term effects of the MTO program had altered adolescent delinquency and substance use. Despite low levels of substance use, some experimental girls appeared more likely than their in-place control peers to have used alcohol in the prior year. The findings on adolescent delinquency do not concur with the Baltimore MTO evaluation, which found dramatic program effects on violent crime among youths that had moved (Ludwig et al. 2001). However, it is important to note that our analysis drew from adolescent self-reported data rather than from juvenile and criminal records. In addition, problem behaviors occurred fairly infrequently within the New York City MTO sample. Although moving out of high-poverty, public housing neighborhoods into low-poverty neighborhoods did not generally correlate with adolescent problem behaviors, the findings suggest that peer engagement in problem behavior may differ across groups, with more beneficial effects showing up for boys and more detrimental effects resulting for girls.

Overall, the magnitude of program effects reported varied across the outcomes examined as well as by children's sex and age. It is also important to note that across the outcomes, the effects of the experimental treatment were, typically, more pronounced than those observed for the Section 8 condition. The largest effects were reported for behavior problems, but program benefits were restricted to boys and children age 8 to 13. Program effects on children's participation in school activities were, generally, positive but modest and limited to experimental children age 14 to 18, and the program had negative effects on girls' future expectations. Among adolescents, negative program effects were also seen for experimental girls' alcohol use and peer delinquency; however, experimental adolescent boys had peers who engaged in less controlled substance use than the in-place control boys. These effects on adolescent and peer problem behavior were small to modest.

The pattern of results suggests that different underlying processes may be at play, depending on the outcome. The finding that MTO program activity affected boys' but not girls' mental health suggests that improvements in neighborhood disorder and related conditions, such as violence and gang activity, brought about by moving to less poor neighborhoods, may account for observed program effects. In fact, adolescent boys in the experimental group were less likely than in-place controls to report having peers who engaged in delinquency. On the other hand, negative program effects on experimental girls' future expectations, alcohol use, and peer theft, suggest that these girls may be experiencing difficulties integrating into their new neighborhoods, particularly in forming peer networks (or at least attaching to nondelinquent peers).

Beneficial program effects on the emotional well-being of children age 8 to 13 may reflect, at least in part, the mover parents' superior mental health (reported in a subsequent study[11]), given the importance of family context for this age group. The lack of program effects for the mental health of children age 14 to 18 may reflect their ability to travel back to their old, high-poverty neighborhoods and/or from the disruption of peer networks, which are particularly important during adolescence. On the contrary, greater participation in school activities observed among older experimental youth (compared with the control) suggests that they are able to take advantage of additional school resources found in affluent neighborhoods. Overall, the benefits of residing in more economically advantaged communities translated into sizable improvements, particularly in children's mental health, within a relatively brief period of exposure to the new neighborhoods.

The neighborhood effects found for the New York MTO site appear much larger than those reported in other (nonexperimental) neighborhood studies, which typically explain about 5 to 10 percent of the variance in child outcomes. This finding likely reflects, at least in part, the nature of program, which led to dramatic changes in neighborhood conditions. Experimental families moved from neighborhoods that were 40 percent poor to 10 percent poor. Such drastic changes in neighborhood through residential moves are rare, especially among low-income families (Leventhal and Brooks-Gunn 2001). In addition, the experimental design of MTO overcomes the self-selection problem in non-experimental neighborhood research (Tienda 1991).

What are the policy implications of these short-term findings? First, the treatment offered by the MTO program can affect parental employment, welfare use, and income (although they were not the focus of this chapter and effects were modest at best). In addition, moving out of public housing, high-poverty neighborhoods can improve children's well-being, especially mental health. Behavior problems in children can be an indicator of future emotional and social problems, including crime and delinquency (McCord 1990). The positive program impacts often emerged independent of whether vouchers were used to purchase housing in low-poverty neighborhoods or neighborhoods of residents' choice (poor and near-poor neighborhoods). This finding suggests that providing families with Section 8 vouchers that enable them to move out of the most distressed neighborhoods can lead to enhanced well-being among male children and youth—a group at high risk for crime, delinquency, and high school dropout.

At the New York City site, most experimental and Section 8 families relocated to neighborhoods that were near their old neighborhoods (resulting in few disruptions of ties), a pattern that may account for some of the similarity in program effects across groups. At the same time, children and youth who moved to more-advantaged neighborhoods displayed superior mental health and greater participation in school activities, but not necessarily higher future expectations and less problem behavior than peers who stayed in high-poverty neighborhoods. Accordingly, the findings reported here (as well as in studies of other MTO sites) suggest that enabling more families to move out of public housing through expanded voucher programs is a worthwhile investment. Moreover, without requiring families moving out of high-poverty public housing projects to relocate to low-poverty neighborhoods (with the help of counseling and other services), such moves are not likely to occur.

NOTES

The authors would like to thank the United States Department of Housing and Urban Development (HUD) and the Russell Sage Foundation for their support. We are also grateful to the National Science Foundation, the National Institute of Child Health and Human Development, and the NICHD Research Network on Child and Family Well-Being. We are especially thankful to John Goering for his support throughout this project. We also would like to thank the staff at Schulman, Ronca, and Bucuvalas, Inc., for their role in data collection and preparation, particularly Al Ronca and Matthew Moffre. We are indebted as well to Judith Feins and Debi McInnis of Abt Associates, Inc., for technical assistance throughout this project. In addition, we are grateful to Greg Duncan, Tom Cook, Bob Crain, and Phil Thompson for their comments and suggestions throughout the study. Finally, we would like to thank Rebecca Fauth and Christina Borbely for assistance with manuscript preparation.

1. We initially planned to see about 70 families, but were able to increase our sample size by combining our funds with those received by Robert Crain, also at Teachers College, and additional support from the Russell Sage Foundation.

2. The mean per person income for families who participated in the follow-up was $2,916 (SD = $1,515), compared with $2,719 (SD = $1,272) for families that did not participate (F $[1,740]$ = 2.92, $p < .10$).

3. The mean age of parents for families that took up the treatment was 33.22 (SD = 9.85), compared with 37.25 (SD = 9.44) for families that did not take up the treatment (F $[1,396]$ = 17.21, $p < .001$). For families that complied with the program, 76 percent of parents had graduated from high school or obtained a GED at baseline, compared with 62 percent of parents in families who did not comply with the program (χ^2 $[1, N = 360]$ = 7.47, $p < .01$). The mean household income for families that took up treatment was $8,829 (SD = $37701), compared with $11,503 (SD = $5,048) for families that did not take up the treatment (F $[1, 371]$ = 30.84, $p < .001$), and the mean per person income for families that took up the treatment was $2,451 (SD = $1244), compared with $3,156 (SD = $1598) for

families that did not take up the treatment (F [1, 371] = 21.08, $p < .001$). Seventy-eight percent of families that took up the treatment received welfare at baseline compared with 68 percent of families that did not take up the treatment (χ^2 [1, $N = 377$] = 4.86, $p < .05$). For families that took up the treatment, 20 percent of parents were employed at baseline compared with 27 percent of parents in families that did not take up the treatment (χ^2 [1, $N = 366$] = 2.53, $p < .10$), and 56 percent of parents whose families complied with the program were African American compared with 47 percent of parents whose families did not comply with the program (χ^2 [1, $N = 368$] = 2.68, $p < .10$).

4. All families were contacted and interviewed by trained research field staff from Schulman, Ronca, and Bucuvalas, a survey research firm in New York City. Families were sent an informative letter explaining the study and the interview procedures. If the letter was returned or we received no response, the interviewer called the family at a telephone number provided by Abt Associates (which conducts periodic canvassing) to set up an appointment. If a family could not be located at this point, several search strategies were initiated, including the use of directory assistance and several professional search/location databases. Interviewers were also sent out to investigate addresses. In addition, we also worked with the New York City Housing Authority to locate families still residing in public housing or receiving housing vouchers. Finally, all families that were located were recontacted several times.

5. When looking at just the families that actually moved in the MTO program, the percentage of African Americans in the neighborhood is still 50 percent, and the poverty rate is 16 percent, closer to the program criterion of 10 percent.

6. In a subsequent study (Leventhal and Brooks-Gunn forthcoming), we have examined subproblem scores derived from the Behavior Problems Index (Zill 1985) and run regression analyses controlling for baseline characteristics. Results indicate that the experimental boys reported significantly fewer anxious/depressive problems than the in-place control boys and that both experimental and Section 8 boys reported fewer dependency/withdrawn problems than the in-place control boys.

7. Among families that moved within the program, only 28 percent of both experimental and Section 8 children changed schools when families relocated.

8. F [1, 181] = 3.54, $p = .06$.

9. χ^2 [1, $N = 96$] = 4.71, $p < .05$.

10. For boys' reported peer cigarette use: χ^2 [1, $N = 116$] = 4.47, $p < .05$, and for girls' reported peer theft: χ^2 [1, $N = 105$] = 3.00, $p < .10$.

11. In Leventhal and Brooks-Gunn (forthcoming), we examined parental depressive and anxiety/distress symptoms and found that, after accounting for baseline characteristics, experimental parents reported significantly less distress than in-place control parents.

REFERENCES

Baker, Paula C., and Frank Mott. 1989. *NLSY Child Handbook 1989: A Guide and Resource Document for the National Longitudinal Survey of Youth 1986 Child Data.* Columbus, Ohio: Center for Human Resources Research, Ohio State University.

Briggs, Xavier de Souza, ed. 1997. *Yonkers Revisited: The Early Impacts of Scattered-Site Public Housing on Families and Neighborhoods.* Report submitted to the Ford Foundation. New York: Teachers College.

Brooks-Gunn, Jeanne, Greg J. Duncan, and J. Lawrence Aber, eds. 1997a. *Neighborhood Poverty. Volume 1: Context and Consequences for Children.* New York: Russell Sage Foundation.

——. 1997b. *Neighborhood Poverty. Volume 2: Policy Implications in Studying Neighborhoods.* New York: Russell Sage Foundation.

Chase-Lansdale, P. Lindsay, Rachel Gordon, Jeanne Brooks-Gunn, and Pamela K. Klebanov. 1997. "Neighborhood and Family Influences on the Intellectual and Behavioral Competence of Preschool and Early School-Age Children." In *Neighborhood Poverty. Volume 1: Context and Consequences for Children,* edited by Jeanne Brooks-Gunn, Greg J. Duncan, and J. Lawrence Aber (79–118). New York: Russell Sage Foundation.

Collins, James W., and Robert J. David. 1990. "The Differential Effect of Traditional Risk Factors on Infant Birthweight among Blacks and Whites in Chicago." *American Journal of Public Health* 80(6): 679–81.

Conger, Rand D., Xiaojia Ge, Glen H. Elder Jr., Fred O. Lorenz, and Ronald L. Simons. 1992. "A Family Process Model of Economic Hardship and Adjustment of Early Adolescent Boys." *Child Development* 63(2): 526–41.

——. 1993. "Family Economic Stress and Adjustment of Early Adolescent Girls." *Developmental Psychology* 29(2): 206–19.

——. 1994. "Economic Stress, Coercive Family Process, and Developmental Problems of Adolescents." *Child Development* 65(2): 541–61.

Dishion, Thomas J., David W. Andrews, and Lynn Crosby. 1995. "Antisocial Boys and Their Friends in Early Adolescence: Relationship Characteristics, Quality, and Interactional Process." *Child Development* 66: 139–51.

Duncan, Greg J., and Jeanne Brooks-Gunn, eds. 1997. *Consequences of Growing Up Poor.* New York: Russell Sage Foundation.

Durkin, Maureen S., Leslie L. Davidson, Louise Kuhn, Patricia O'Connor, and Barbara Barlow. 1994. "Low-Income Neighborhoods and the Risk of Severe Pediatric Injury: A Small-Area Analysis in Northern Manhattan. *American Journal of Public Health* 84: 587–92.

Earls, Felton, and Steve L. Buka. 1997. *Project on Human Development in Chicago Neighborhoods: Technical Report.* Rockville, Md.: National Institute of Justice.

Elliott, Delbert, William J. Wilson, David Huizinga, Robert Sampson, Amanda Elliott, and Bruce Rankin. 1996. "The Effects of Neighborhood Disadvantage on Adolescent Development." *Journal of Research in Crime and Delinquency* 33(4): 389–426.

Ennett, Susan T., Robert L. Flewelling, Richard C. Lindrooth, and Edward C. Norton. 1997. "School and Neighborhood Characteristics Associated with School Rates of Alcohol, Cigarette, and Marijuana Use." *Journal of Health and Social Behavior* 38: 55–71.

Furstenberg, Frank F. Jr., Thomas D. Cook, Jacquelynne Eccles, Glenn H. Elder Jr., and Arnold Sameroff. 1999. *Managing to Make It: Urban Families and Adolescent Success.* Chicago: University of Chicago Press.

Goering, John, Joan Kraft, Judith Feins, Debra McInnis, Mary Joel Holin, and Huda Elhassan. 1999. *Moving to Opportunity for Fair Housing Demonstration Program:*

Current Status and Initial Findings. Washington, D.C.: U.S. Department of Housing and Urban Development.

Huizinga, David, Finn-Aage Esbensen, and Anne W. Weiher. 1991. "Are There Multiple Paths to Delinquency?" *The Journal of Criminal Law and Criminology* 82: 83–118.

Jencks, Christopher, and Susan Mayer. 1990. "The Social Consequences of Growing Up in a Poor Neighborhood." In *Inner-City Poverty in the United States,* edited by Laurence Lynn and Michael McGeary (111–86). Washington, D.C.: National Academy Press.

Kandel, Denise B. 1998. "Persistent Themes and New Perspectives on Adolescent Substance Use: A Lifespan Perspective." In *New Perspectives on Adolescent Risk Behavior,* edited by Richard Jessor (43–89). New York: Cambridge University Press.

Klebanov, Pamela K., Jeanne Brooks-Gunn, and Greg J. Duncan. 1994. "Does Neighborhood and Family Poverty Affect Parents' Parenting, Mental Health, and Social Support?" *Journal of Marriage and the Family* 56(2): 441–55.

Klebanov, Pamela K., Jeanne Brooks-Gunn, P. Lindsay Chase-Lansdale, and Rachel Gordon. 1997. "Are Neighborhood Effects on Young Children Mediated by Features of the Home Environment?" In *Neighborhood Poverty. Volume 1: Context and Consequences for Children,* edited by Jeanne Brooks-Gunn, Greg J. Duncan, and J. Lawrence Aber (119–45). New York: Russell Sage Foundation.

Klebanov, Pamela K., Jeanne Brooks-Gunn, Cecelia McCarton, and Marie C. McCormick. 1998. "The Contribution of Neighborhood and Family Income to Developmental Test Scores over the First Three Years of Life." *Child Development* 69: 1420–36.

Leventhal, Tama, and Jeanne Brooks-Gunn. 2000. "The Neighborhoods They Live In: The Effects of Neighborhood Residence upon Child and Adolescent Outcomes." *Psychological Bulletin* 126(2): 309–37.

———. 2001. "Changing Neighborhoods: Understanding How Children May Be Affected in the Coming Century." *Advances in Life Course Research* 6: 263–301.

———. Forthcoming. "Moving to Opportunity: An Experimental Study of Neighborhood Effects on Mental Health." *American Journal of Public Health.*

Loeber, Rolf, and Per-Olof H. Wikstrom. 1993. "Individual Pathways to Crime in Different Types of Neighborhoods." In *Integrating Individual and Ecological Aspects of Crime,* edited by D. P. Farrington, Robert J. Sampson, and Per-Olof H. Wikstrom (169–204). Stockholm: National Crime Council of Sweden.

Ludwig, Jens, Greg J. Duncan, and Paul Hirschfield. 2001. "Urban Poverty and Juvenile Crime: Evidence from a Randomized Housing-Mobility Experiment." *Quarterly Journal of Economics* (May): 655–79.

McCord, Joan. 1990. "Problem Behaviors." In *At the Threshold: The Developing Adolescent,* edited by Shirley S. Feldman and Glen R. Elliott. Cambridge, Mass.: Harvard University Press.

McLoyd, Vonnie C. 1990. "The Impact of Economic Hardship on Black Families and Development." *Child Development* 61: 311–46.

National Center for Education Statistics. 1988. *National Education Longitudinal Study.* Washington, D.C.: National Center for Education Statistics.

National Health Interview Survey. 1988. "Child Health Supplement." National Center for Health Statistics. DAAPPP Date Set 13–14. Washington, D.C.: U.S. Department of Health and Human Services.

National Institute on Drug Abuse. 1991. *National Household Survey on Drug Abuse: Population Estimates, 1991.* Rockville, Md.: National Institute on Drug Abuse.

Ogbu, John U. 1991. "Minority Coping Responses and School Experience." *Journal of Psychohistory* 18(4): 433–56.

Osgood, D. Wayne, Janet K. Wilson, Patrick M. O'Malley, Jerald G. Bachman, and Lloyd D. Johnston. 1996. "Routine Activities and Deviant Behavior." *American Sociological Review* 61: 635–55.

Paulter, Katherine J., and John H. Lewko. 1987. "Children's and Adolescents' Views of the Work World in Times of Economic Uncertainty." In *How Children and Adolescents View the World of Work: New Directions for Child Development* (no. 35), edited by John H. Lewko (21–31). San Francisco: Jossey-Bass Inc.

Peeples, Faith, and Rolf Loeber. 1994. "Do Individual Factors and Neighborhood Context Explain Ethnic Differences in Juvenile Delinquency?" *Journal of Quantitative Criminology* 10(2): 141–57.

Sampson, Robert J. 1997. "Collective Regulation of Adolescent Misbehavior: Validation Results from Eighty Chicago Neighborhoods." *Journal of Adolescent Research* 12(2): 227–44.

Sampson, Robert J., and W. Byron Groves. 1989. "Community Structure and Crime: Testing Social-Disorganization Theory." *American Journal of Sociology* 94(4): 774–80.

Sampson, Robert J., Stephen W. Raudenbush, and Felton Earls. 1997. "Neighborhoods and Violent Crime: A Multilevel Study of Collective Efficacy." *Science* 277: 918–24.

Sinclair, Jamie J., Gregory S. Pettit, Aamada W. Harrist, Kenneth A. Dodge, and John E. Bates. 1994. "Encounters with Aggressive Peers in Early Childhood: Frequency, Age Differences, and Correlates of Risk Behaviour Problems." *International Journal of Behavioral Development* 17(4): 675–96.

Steinberg, Laurence, and Amanda Sheffield-Morris. 2001. "Adolescent Development." *Annual Review of Psychology* 52: 83–110.

Tienda, Marta. 1991. "Poor People and Poor Places: Deciphering Neighborhood Effects on Poverty Outcomes." In *Macro-Micro Linkages in Sociology,* edited by Joan Huber (244–62). Newberry, Cal.: Sage.

Turner, C. F., Leighton Ku, S. M. Rogers, L. D. Lindberg, J. H. Pleck, and Freya S. Sonenstein. 1998. "Adolescent Sexual Behavior, Drug Use, and Violence: Increased Reporting with Computer Survey Technology." *Science* 280: 867–73.

Zahn-Waxler, Carolyn. 1993. "Warriors and Worriers: Gender and Psychopathology." *Development and Psychopathology* 5(1–2): 79–89.

Zill, Nicholas. 1985. *Behavior Problem Scales Developed from the 1981 Child Health Supplement to the National Health Interview Survey.* Washington, D.C.: Child Trends, Inc.

9

Los Angeles Site Findings

Maria Hanratty
Sara McLanahan
Becky Pettit

This chapter examines the impacts of the Los Angeles site of the MTO program on short-run measures of family well-being. Using a sample of 285 families that entered the program between March 1995 and December 1996, it measures the short-run effects of the MTO program on residential mobility and neighborhood characteristics, access to neighborhood resources, and the extent of social integration within the neighborhood. This chapter also uses administrative data to assess somewhat longer-term impacts of the program on parental employment and welfare receipt.

The analysis shows that both the MTO and Section 8 groups moved to neighborhoods with much higher socioeconomic levels than the control group. Although on average MTO and Section 8 neighborhoods were similar, the MTO group was both more likely to move to low-poverty neighborhoods (58 percent vs. 1 percent) and more likely to remain in high-poverty neighborhoods (32 percent vs. 17 percent) than the Section 8 group.

Both the MTO movers to low-poverty neighborhoods and the Section 8 movers achieved substantial reductions in neighborhood crime rates as well as substantial increases in perceived neighborhood safety levels relative to the control group. In addition, the point estimates suggest that parents in both treatment groups used more center-based child care and less hospital emergency care; however, these estimates were not statistically significant.

On social capital the evidence is mixed. Parents in both the MTO experimental and the Section 8 groups reported reductions in church activity and in the number of friends and family in their neighborhoods compared with parents in the control group. However, these parents were no less likely to be involved in their children's activities and their children were just as likely to have friends in the neighborhood.

On employment and earnings, this analysis found that all three groups in the experiment achieved substantial increases in employment and earnings, and decreases in welfare receipt, during the first three years after they entered the MTO program. However, it failed to find significant increases in employment and earnings or decreases in welfare receipt for the two treatment groups relative to the control group.

Los Angeles Follow-Up Survey Design

The analysis of the short-run impacts of the MTO program is based on a phone survey of families that entered the Los Angeles Moving to Opportunity Program between March 10, 1995, and December 18, 1996. For families that entered the program before April 1996, interviews were completed by phone between September and December 1996. If families could not be reached by telephone, local interviewers went to respondents' homes to conduct the interviews in person. Interviews were conducted in both English and Spanish, and families were paid $20 to participate in the survey.

An additional set of interviews, conducted between August 1997 and October 1997, gathered data for families that entered the program between April 24, 1996, and December 18, 1996. Owing to resource limitations, these families were contacted by phone only. Members of the control group were excluded from this sample because obtaining their updated contact information proved too difficult.[1]

For the initial sample, comprising 259 families, 95 percent were located and 92 percent completed interviews.[2] The second sample, conducted by phone only, had a much lower response rate. Of the 95 families, 48 were contacted by phone and 47 were interviewed.

While there are some differences in baseline characteristics of MTO and Section 8 group participants from the two sets of interviews (e.g., the second sample had a higher proportion of black, never-married, and employed household heads), most of the results that follow are not sensitive to the inclusion of the second sample.

Promoting Housing Search and Mobility

Two key features of the MTO program encourage families to move to low-poverty neighborhoods. First, families were required to move to a low-poverty neighborhood to qualify for a housing voucher. This requirement may have encouraged some families that would have likely preferred moving elsewhere to relocate to a low-poverty neighborhood. Second, the program offered extensive housing search and relocation services. These services may have helped participants overcome barriers in moving to low-poverty neighborhoods, such as limited information about low-poverty neighborhoods, landlord resistance to renting to low-income families, and lack of accessible transportation. (See box 9.1 for a short description of the supportive services offered.) Did participants view these components as help or hindrance? And how might their perceptions have affected mobility rates?

Low-Poverty Requirement

To assess how MTO participants viewed the requirement that they move to a low-poverty neighborhood, MTO movers were asked where they would have moved if they could have relocated anywhere and still have received the voucher.[3] As shown in table 9.1, nearly half said that they would have moved to their current neighborhood; most of the remainder said they would have moved to some place other than their original neighborhood. While many MTO families indicated that they would have chosen other neighborhoods, the MTO "low-poverty requirement" does not appear to have affected anticipated future mobility rates. As shown, the MTO experimental group was no more likely than the Section 8 group to report that they were "very likely" or "somewhat likely" to move within the next year.

Supportive Services

MTO supportive services could play a critical role in helping families locate housing in low-poverty neighborhoods if they increase the information

---

Box 9.1. Helping Families Move

Until October 1996, two nonprofit organizations provided services to help families in the MTO group locate housing and make the transition to a low-poverty neighborhood. The Fair Housing Congress of the City of Los Angeles helped with the housing search process by recruiting landlords, providing information on housing search techniques, and driving participants to visit up to three apartments in low-poverty neighborhoods. A second organization, Beyond Shelter, helped families adjust to their new neighborhoods by helping families access resources in their new communities, by providing families with furniture and appliances for their new apartments, and by conducting workshops on financial management[a] and on child development. Effective October 1996, the responsibilities of these two organizations were consolidated and taken over by the nonprofit organization On Your Feet.

---

a. This seminar was critical because moving costs could be substantial. In addition to paying their moving costs, MTO (and Section 8) participants could be required to pay a security deposit and first month's rent at the unsubsidized rate. In addition, participants were liable for any rent exceeding the amount reimbursed by the voucher.

---

available to families about housing options in other neighborhoods. As shown in table 9.2, prior to the MTO program there were substantial informational barriers to finding housing in low-poverty neighborhoods. Over three-quarters of MTO movers reported that they were "unfamiliar" with their destination neighborhood prior to their move, compared with half of Section 8, and one-twelfth of control group movers.

The MTO treatment group reported that MTO housing search activities played a critical role in their search for housing. MTO housing referrals were by far the most common search method employed by MTO participants, with eight out of ten participants using MTO housing referrals. The MTO treatment group was also much more likely to rank MTO housing referrals as their "most useful" housing search method. By contrast, both Section 8 and control group respondents were most likely to report that newspaper ads were most productive.

Table 9.1. *Los Angeles MTO Participants' Neighborhood Preference and Future Mobility Plans*

	Experimental	Section 8	Control
MTO movers who would have moved:			
to current neighborhood	.471		
	(.050)		
some place near old neighborhood	.049		
	(0.021)		
to other neighborhood	0.480		
	(0.050)		
How likely you are to move in next year (movers only):			
Very likely	0.256	0.345	0.246
	(0.035)	(.063)	(0.052)
Somewhat likely	0.353	0.276	0.246
	(0.038)	(.059)	(0.052)
Unlikely	0.372	0.328	0.464
	(0.039)	(0.062)	(0.060)

Source: Follow-up survey of families that entered the Los Angeles MTO program from March 10, 1995, to December 18, 1996.

Note: Standard errors are in parentheses.

While the intensity of housing search activity for the MTO group and the Section 8 group was about the same, the MTO group was somewhat less likely than the Section 8 group to find an apartment that would have qualified for a housing voucher under the program. Thus, even with additional program services, families in the MTO group appear to have had somewhat more difficulty locating housing that met program requirements.

Residential Mobility Rates

Estimates of Mobility Rates

Estimates of mobility rates—or how often families moved—may be sensitive to how one adjusts for "nonresponse bias"—or for the potential differences between families that could be located and those that could not be located at the time of the survey. For this reason, table 9.3 presents a range of mobility estimates. The "lower bound" estimates assume

Table 9.2. *Housing Search Methods Employed
by Los Angeles MTO Program Demonstration Participants*

	Experimental	Section 8	Control
How well you knew neighborhood before moving (movers only)			
Very familiar	0.127	0.106	0.583
	(0.033)	(0.045)	(0.148)
Somewhat familiar	0.108	0.362	0.333
	(0.031)	(0.071)	(0.142)
Unfamiliar	0.765	0.532	0.083
	(0.042)	(0.074)	(0.083)
Search methods used			
Section 8 housing listing	0.535	0.444	NA
	(0.042)	(0.068)	
MTO counselor referral	0.791	NA	NA
	(0.035)		
Friend/Relative	0.426	0.370	0.643
	(0.042)	(0.066)	(0.075)
Newspaper ad	0.614	0.704	0.619
	(0.041)	(0.063)	(.076)
Real estate agent	0.296	0.167	0.381
	(0.038)	(0.051)	(0.076)
Yellow Pages	0.100	0.057	0.190
	(0.025)	(0.032)	(0.061)
"For rent" notice on building	0.493	0.444	0.429
	(0.042)	(0.068)	(0.077)
Other	0.256	0.255	0.262
	(0.039)	(0.062)	(0.069)
Search method rated "most useful" by those who used multiple search methods			
Section 8 housing office listing	0.096	0.173	NA
	(0.025)	(0.053)	
MTO counselor referral	0.441	NA	NA
	(0.043)		
Friend/Relative	0.051	0.058	0.194
	(0.019)	(0.033)	(0.067)

Table 9.2. *Continued*

	Experimental	Section 8	Control
Newspaper ad	0.243	0.385	0.389
	(0.037)	(0.068)	(0.082)
Real estate agent	0.000	0.038	0.111
	(0.000)	(0.027)	(0.053)
Yellow Pages	0.015	0.000	0.028
	(0.010)	(0.000)	(0.028)
"For rent" notice on building	0.059	0.173	0.139
	(0.020)	(0.053)	(0.058)
Other	0.096	0.173	0.139
	(0.025)	(0.053)	(0.058)
Search intensity			
Searched	0.910	0.932	0.609
	(0.023)	(0.033)	(0.059)
Visited one or more places	0.865	0.932	0.449
	(0.027)	(0.033)	(0.060)
Average number of places visited by	6.91	6.58	4.00
those who visited one or	(0.70)	(1.12)	(0.74)
more places			
Found a place you could have moved	0.814	0.932	0.333
into that qualified for a voucher	(0.031)	(0.033)	(0.057)
Average number of places found	3.20	4.04	1.65
by those that found a place that	(0.30)	(0.70)	(0.24)
qualified for a voucher			

Source: Follow-up survey of families that entered the Los Angeles MTO program from March 10, 1995, to December 18, 1996.

Note: Standard errors are in parentheses.

that all families that could not be located moved at the same rate as families identified by the survey, while the "upper bound" estimates assume that all families that could not be located had moved.

Both sets of estimates suggest that mobility rates for the Section 8 group (0.80 to 0.85) were higher than for the MTO group (0.64 to 0.67) and that both rates were higher than those of the control families (0.17 to 0.27).

While the MTO group was on average less likely to move than the Section 8 group, this difference appears to have decreased with time (see top and middle panels of table 9.3). For the group that entered the program between April 24, 1996, and December 18, 1996, approximately four out of

Table 9.3. *Los Angeles MTO Site Residential Mobility Rates*

	Experimental	Section 8	Control
Initial sample			
Reported move	0.602	0.804	0.174
	(0.044)	(0.059)	(0.046)
Reported move or imputed to move	0.614	0.813	0.274
	(0.043)	(0.057)	(0.049)
Second sample			
Reported move	0.794	0.769	
	(0.070)	(0.122)	
Reported move or imputed to move	0.810	0.884	
	(0.080)	(0.143)	
Total sample			
Reported move	0.643	0.797	0.174
	(0.038)	(0.053)	(0.046)
Reported move or imputed to move	0.671	0.846	0.274
	(0.039)	(0.074)	(0.049)

Source: Los Angeles follow-up survey.
Notes: "Initial sample" represents 259 families that entered the MTO program between March 10, 1995, and April 24, 1996. "Second sample" represents 95 MTO and Section 8 families that entered the program between April 24, 1996, and December 18, 1996. Imputation assumes that all families that could not be located at follow-up survey had moved. Standard errors are in parentheses.

five MTO treatment group families moved—a mobility rate that was not statistically different from that of the Section 8 comparison group. This finding may reflect the fact that MTO housing services may have become more effective as the program became more fully operational. In addition, it may reflect a shift in the nonprofit organizations responsible for implementing the program in October 1996.

Neighborhood Socioeconomic Characteristics

Neighborhood demographic and economic characteristics at the time of the follow-up survey reveal that the MTO program met its stated goal of increasing the proportion of families moving to low-poverty neighborhoods: nearly 6 in 10 MTO respondents moved to a census tract with poverty rates below 10.5 percent compared with only 1 in 100 control group respondents. Compared with the Section 8 group, the MTO group was much more likely to move to a low-poverty neighborhood, and it was also more likely on average to remain in neighborhoods with high concentrations of poverty.

As shown in table 9.4, both the MTO and Section 8 groups lived in neighborhoods with significantly higher socioeconomic levels at the time of the follow-up survey than did the control group. Both groups lived in neighborhoods with higher levels of education and employment, lower rates of public assistance receipt, higher owner occupancy rates, and higher housing values than the control group.

The most striking difference between MTO and Section 8 neighborhoods is their racial and ethnic composition. MTO families moved to neighborhoods with much higher proportions of non-Hispanic whites and much lower proportions of Hispanics and non-Hispanic blacks than either the Section 8 or the control groups. In contrast, race and ethnic

Table 9.4. *Characteristics of Los Angeles Census Tracts of Residence at Follow-Up*

	Experimental	Section 8	Control
Share of census tracts with poverty rates:			
Below 10.5%	0.583	0.011	0.014
	(0.039)	(0.016)	(0.014)
Below 20.5%	0.621	0.338	0.057
	(0.038)	(0.062)	(0.028)
Below 30.5%	0.641	0.542	0.159
	(0.038)	(0.065)	(0.044)
Below 40.5%	0.679	0.830	0.202
	(0.037)	(0.049)	(0.048)
Average racial/ethnic composition			
Non-Hispanic white	0.293	0.082	0.025
	(0.022)	(0.017)	(0.060)
Non-Hispanic black	0.230	0.316	0.410
	(0.024)	(0.035)	(0.036)
Hispanic	0.395	0.552	0.529
	(0.022)	(0.030)	(0.030)
Share of residents that speak Spanish	0.354	0.508	0.508
	(0.021)	(0.028)	(0.028)
Single-parent families as a share of all	0.382	0.402	0.589
families with children	(0.016)	(0.016)	(0.021)

(*continued*)

Table 9.4. *Characteristics of Los Angeles Census Tracts of Residence at Follow-Up (Continued)*

	Experimental	Section 8	Control
Education level of census tract residents			
Not a high school graduate	0.408	0.551	0.655
	(0.021)	(0.021)	(0.016)
High school graduate	0.213	0.200	0.197
	(0.005)	(0.007)	(0.008)
Some college	0.225	0.181	0.115
	(0.009)	(0.010)	(0.007)
College graduate	0.152	0.064	0.031
	(0.010)	(0.006)	(0.004)
Male employment rate	0.630	0.615	0.462
	(0.012)	(0.013)	(0.017)
Female employment rate	0.471	0.419	0.278
	(0.013)	(0.012)	(0.013)
Share of households with public	0.198	0.235	0.428
assistance income	(0.015)	(0.014)	(0.023)
Housing characteristics			
Share owner-occupied	0.348	0.316	0.178
	(0.020)	(0.020)	(0.020)
Median housing value (1990 $)	195,215	137,452	114,684
	(7,575)	(5,617)	(5,817)
Median rent (1990 $)	569	498	339
	(17)	(12)	(13)

Source: Based on 1990 Census data geocoded to the addresses of families in Los Angeles follow-up survey.

Notes: Sample includes 156 MTO, 59 Section 8, and 69 control group respondents that entered the program from March 10, 1995, to December 18, 1996. Standard errors are reported in parentheses.

characteristics of the Section 8 neighborhoods were much more similar to those of the control group.

Crime Rates and Perceived Neighborhood Safety

Crime Rates

One critical goal of most families that entered the MTO program was achieving greater neighborhood safety. At the time they applied for the program, 59 percent of families in the sample said that getting away from drugs and gangs was their main reason for entering the program. These families also reported high rates of victimization by crime: 11 percent reported that someone in their household had been stabbed or shot in the past six months, 23 percent reported that a household member had been beaten or assaulted, 29 percent reported that a household member had been threatened with a knife or a gun, and 46 percent reported that some-one had tried to break into their home. Given these extreme levels of vio-lent crime, neighborhood safety is arguably one of the most important metrics of the program's impact on family well-being.

Table 9.5 shows average crime rates by treatment group at baseline and at the time of the follow-up survey. Not surprisingly, there are few signif-icant differences at baseline between the groups. There are, however, striking differences in crime rates between the MTO treatment group and the control group at the time of the follow-up survey. Respondents in the MTO treatment group lived in census tracts with nearly 30 percent fewer burglaries than respondents in the control group. Murder rates in MTO census tracts were 40 percent of the rates found in control tracts. Both rape and assault rates in the MTO treatment group were just over half of the rates found in control tracts.

The one exception to this pattern is property crimes, which were somewhat higher for MTO than for control group neighborhoods. These results confirm that the MTO group was able to achieve substantially lower neighborhood crime rates than the control group. In addition, while the MTO program does not appear to have reduced average total neighborhood crime rates for MTO families relative to Section 8 families, it has resulted in reductions in both murder and assault rates.

Perceptions of Neighborhood Safety

Both MTO and Section 8 respondents reported much higher levels of perceived neighborhood safety than the control group: 61 percent of MTO and 57 percent of Section 8 group families reported their neigh-borhood was either "very safe" or "safe" at night compared with 21 per-cent of the control group (table 9.6). The two treatment groups were also much more likely to report that drug dealers and gangs were not a prob-lem than the control group. Of the two treatment groups, the MTO respondents were more likely to report their neighborhood was either

Table 9.5. *Los Angeles Census Tract Average Crime Rates per 100,000*

	Experimental	Section 8	Control
Baseline			
Burglary	1,507.46	1,339.06	1,409.62
	(83.30)	(117.97)	(115.23)
Murder	81.34	68.24	75.04
	(3.87)	(6.52)	(6.15)
Rape	103.51	101.19	109.15
	(5.42)	(8.69)	(8.79)
Assault	2,995.58	2,831.36	2,983.94
	(122.26)	(189.77)	(178.17)
Theft	251.78	386.86	270.74
	(16.90)	(94.44)	(19.94)
Total	8,401.83	8,092.22	8,281.66
	(245.08)	(407.75)	(350.96)
Follow-up			
Burglary[a,b,c]	968.45	753.71	1,359.79
	(52.94)	(52.67)	(128.88)
Murder[a,b,c]	29.57	41.52	73.97
	(3.53)	(5.95)	(6.11)
Rape[a,b]	54.25	57.58	104.40
	(4.25)	(4.57)	(8.67)
Assault[a,b,c]	1,450.32	1,663.19	2,830.17
	(101.84)	(102.67)	(182.74)
Theft[a]	605.45	480.11	362.04
	(72.72)	(96.10)	(55.39)
Total[a,b]	6,137.25	5,984.21	8,018.40
	(234.58)	(268.83)	(362.52)

Source: Based on published crime data from the Los Angeles Police Department for 1995 and 1990 Census population data geocoded to the addresses of families in the Los Angeles follow-up survey.

Notes: Sample includes 154 MTO, 57 Section 8, and 68 control group respondents that entered the program between March 10, 1995, and December 18, 1996. Standard errors are reported in parentheses.

a. Significant two-sided test of differences in means between MTO and control at $p < .05$.
b. Significant two-sided test of differences in means between Section 8 and control at $p < .05$.
c. Significant two-sided test of differences in means between MTO and Section 8 at $p < .05$.

Table 9.6. *Los Angeles MTO Participants Perceptions of Neighborhood Safety*

	Experimental	Section 8	Control
Very unsafe neighborhood[a,b]	0.198	0.101	0.521
	(0.032)	(0.039)	(0.060)
Unsafe neighborhood	0.179	0.288	0.260
	(0.030)	(0.059)	(0.053)
Safe neighborhood[a,b,c]	0.346	0.508	0.115
	(0.038)	(0.065)	(0.038)
Very safe neighborhood[a,c]	0.275	0.067	0.101
	(0.035)	(0.033)	(0.036)
Drug dealers and gangs are a big problem[a,b]	0.403	0.372	0.695
	(0.039)	(0.063)	(0.055)
Drug dealers and gangs are a small problem[c]	0.134	0.288	0.173
	(0.027)	(0.059)	(0.045)
Drug dealers and gangs are not a problem[a,b]	0.455	0.338	0.130
	(0.039)	(0.062)	(0.040)

Source: Based on follow-up survey of 156 MTO, 59 Section 8, and 69 control group respondents that entered the Los Angeles MTO program between March 10, 1995, and December 18, 1996.

Notes: Standard errors are reported in parentheses.

a. Significant two-sided test of differences in means between MTO and control at $p < .05$.

b. Significant two-sided test of differences in means between Section 8 and control at $p < .05$.

c. Significant two-sided test of differences in means between MTO and Section 8 at $p < .05$.

"very safe" or "very unsafe," while the Section 8 group had more moderate responses. These results are consistent with those described earlier.

Parents' Access to Community Resources

Besides living in safer environments, we might expect MTO and Section 8 respondents to have greater access to community services than respondents in the control group. At the same time, we also might expect the two treatment groups to have less *social capital* than the control group, since moving almost always breaks old social ties and new ones take time to develop. Of particular concern was whether MTO respondents would have trouble making friends in their new communities because of the small proportion of poor families and lack of racial diversity. To examine

these issues, we asked respondents about their employment; use of community services; participation in voluntary organizations, including children's schools; and the availability of family and friends.

Employment and Education

Respondents answered several questions about their employment, including whether they worked, the number of hours they worked, and their
total earnings (table 9.7).[4] Just over a quarter of all respondents reported
working for pay. Employed respondents, on average, worked just over 30
hours per week and earned just under $200 per week. There are no signif-
icant differences in employment rates among MTO, Section 8, and control
group respondents. However, among those who did work, average weekly
earnings were significantly higher for both treatment groups, with both
groups earning between $48 and $78 more than the control group. Average hours were also significantly higher for the Section 8 group, at 37 hours
per week compared with 27 hours for the control group.

Child Care

Quality child care is an important community resource, especially for
single mothers and low-income families. Not only does the availability of
child care affect whether or not a parent works, it also affects the child's
health and school readiness. Respondents were asked about their use of
child care and the type of child care they used.[5] Only 142 respondents said
that they had a child under age 5, and fewer than 40 percent of respondents
indicated that they had a regular source of child care. Of those with regular arrangements, nearly one half of parents took their children to child
care centers or Head Start programs. Our estimates suggest that the MTO
group was significantly less likely to use nonrelative care than the control
group (6 percent versus 50 percent). They also suggest that the MTO group
was more likely to use Head Start programs or child care centers than the
control group, although these estimates were not statistically significant.

Medical Care

Another important community service is the quality and accessibility of
medical care. Not only is access to health care a valuable resource, but
the location at which care is provided also matters. Low-income families

Table 9.7. *Parents' Access to Community Resources Reported in Los Angeles Follow-Up Survey*

	Experimental	Section 8	Control
Work	0.269	0.271	0.260
	(0.035)	(0.058)	(0.053)
Weekly hours[b]	33.1	37.2	26.8
(workers only)	(10.7)	(5.1)	(3.1)
Weekly earnings[a,b]	206.4	236.4	158.2
(workers only, $)	(16.7)	(20.7)	(24.1)
Have a place for child care	0.402	0.448	0.333
	(0.056)	(0.093)	(0.079)
Child care center/Head Start program	0.483	0.306	0.250
	(0.091)	(0.128)	(0.130)
Relative	0.483	0.538	0.333
	(0.091)	(0.143)	(0.142)
Nonrelative[a]	0.064	0.153	0.500
	(0.044)	(0.104)	(0.150)
Have a regular place for medical care	0.845	0.864	0.913
	(0.029)	(0.044)	(0.034)
Hospital	0.076	0.080	0.129
	(0.023)	(0.038)	(0.042)
Clinic	0.572	0.620	0.571
	(0.043)	(0.069)	(0.062)
Doctor	0.312	0.220	0.238
	(0.040)	(0.059)	(0.054)

Source: Based on follow-up survey of 156 MTO, 59 Section 8, and 69 control group respondents that entered the Los Angeles MTO program between March 10, 1995, and December 18, 1996.

Notes: Standard errors are reported in parentheses.

a. Significant two-sided test of differences in means between MTO and control at $p < .05$.

b. Significant two-sided test of differences in means between Section 8 and control at $p < .05$.

are much more likely than middle-income families to use hospital emergency rooms as their main source of medical care, a practice that is both costly for providers and time-consuming for patients.[6]

Almost 90 percent of all respondents reported that they had a regular place for medical care, although control group respondents were somewhat more likely to answer yes to this question than MTO respondents. Looking at where respondents were likely to receive care suggests that MTO and Section 8 respondents went to doctors' offices more often, whereas control group respondents were more likely to go to hospitals.

Again, owing to the small size of our sample, these estimates were not statistically significant.

Participation in Community Organizations

Community organizations such as churches, children's schools, and other organizations[7] provide residents with information and emotional support while reinforcing social norms. Parents' connections with teachers and schools are particularly important.

More than half of all respondents in the survey reported belonging to a church, with nearly 80 percent of this group going to church at least once a week. As shown in table 9.8, respondents in both the Section 8 and the MTO groups were less likely to belong to a church than respondents in the control group (54 percent of MTO, 46 percent of Section 8, and 65 percent of control respondents). MTO and Section 8 respondents also reported that they attended church less frequently than the control group. Note that MTO families were much more likely than the other two groups to attend church in their old neighborhood (16 percent MTO, 3 percent Section 8, and 1 percent control). These differences suggest that MTO respondents face barriers to becoming integrated in their new communities, especially in religious organizations, which tend to be more intimate than schools or other voluntary organizations.

Between one-half and three-fifths of respondents reported attending events at their child's school. MTO and Section 8 families were just as likely to be involved in their child's school as control families, a somewhat surprising finding given that the families in the treatment group were much more likely to have moved in the past year.

Friends and Family

A final set of questions asked about access to family and friends[8] to investigate whether respondents in the treatment groups had fewer friends and family in their current neighborhoods than respondents in the control group. Just over half of all respondents in the survey reported having friends in their neighborhoods, and less than a third reported having family. As expected, respondents in both the MTO and Section 8 groups were less likely than respondents in the control group to live near friends or family: Control group respondents were nearly twice as likely as MTO and Section 8 respondents to report having friends in their neighborhood. The same pattern appears for family members.

Table 9.8. *Los Angeles Parents' Access to Social Capital*

	Experimental	Section 8	Control
Belong to church[b]	0.544	0.457	0.652
	(0.039)	(0.065)	(0.057)
Attend frequently[a,b]	0.378	0.372	0.550
	(0.038)	(0.063)	(0.060)
Attend very frequently	0.192	0.152	0.231
	(0.031)	(0.047)	(0.051)
Current neighborhood[a]	0.192	0.203	0.318
	(0.031)	(0.052)	(0.056)
Old neighborhood[a,c]	0.160	0.033	0.014
	(0.029)	(0.023)	(0.014)
Go to programs at child's school	0.615	0.524	0.550
	(0.039)	(0.065)	(0.060)
Belong to other organizations	0.070	0.050	0.057
	(0.020)	(0.028)	(0.028)
Friends in neighborhood[a,b]	0.429	0.355	0.724
	(0.039)	(0.062)	(0.054)
Many friends	0.102	0.084	0.101
	(0.024)	(0.036)	(0.036)
Family in neighborhood[a,b]	0.205	0.220	0.420
	(0.032)	(0.054)	(0.059)
Many family	0.044	0.000	0.043
	(0.016)	(0.000)	(0.024)

Source: Based on follow-up survey of 156 MTO, 59 Section 8, and 69 control group respondents that entered the Los Angeles MTO program between March 10, 1995, and December 18, 1996.

Notes: Standard errors are reported in parentheses.

a. Statistically significant two-sided test of differences in means between MTO and control at $p < .05$.

b. Statistically significant two-sided test of differences in means between Section 8 and control at $p < .05$.

c. Statistically significant two-sided test of differences in means between MTO and Section 8 at $p < .05$.

Summary

In summary, differences in community resources show some early signs of success among respondents in both treatment groups, compared with controls, for both employment opportunities and access to quality community services. Respondents in both treatment groups reported higher earnings than respondents in the control group, and MTO parents reported more use of center-based child care and Head Start programs, which generally can provide more comprehensive services.

On social connections and social capital, the evidence is mixed. On the one hand, MTO and Section 8 groups reported being just as involved as the control group in their children's school activities, and just as likely to belong to "other organizations"—both positive signs. On the other hand, the treatment groups reported having fewer friends and family in their neighborhood and slightly lower levels of church membership and attendance.

Finally, based on comparisons of MTO families and Section 8 families, requiring families to move to a low-poverty neighborhood does not appear to reduce the overall level of social involvement among these families.

Children's Outcomes

Elementary-Age Children (Age 6–11)

During the telephone interviews, we selected up to two children from each family from two age groups (6–11 and 12–17) and asked adult respondents a number of questions about these children's activities and friendships. The survey included specific questions about child participation in after-school activities, after-school supervision, and friends.

AFTER-SCHOOL ACTIVITIES

Parents, asked about their child's participation in activities after school and during the summer, reported information on whether the child participated in any activity, the total number of activities, and specific activities.[9] Just over three-quarters of all 6- to 11-year-olds participated in at least one of the specified activities (table 9.9). On average, children participated in 1.7 of the 7 listed activities.

Children in MTO families were somewhat less likely to participate in any activity, and they appear to have participated in fewer activities overall than children in Section 8 families or control families (1.5 for MTO, 2.0 for Section 8, and 2.0 for control families). Children in MTO families may have participated in fewer activities over the period because their families faced more severe financial pressures as a result of their moves.

When families moved through the MTO or Section 8 program, their expenditures were likely to increase because their monthly out-of-pocket contributions to rent often increased.[10] In addition, these families had to make larger up-front payments for the security deposit and the first month's rent. To the extent that rental costs are higher in the neighborhoods into which MTO families moved, these families may have had greater financial constraints than Section 8 or control families.

AFTER-SCHOOL SUPERVISION

Parental supervision generally improves children's chances of success in school. It also reduces the risk that children will become involved in delinquent behavior. When asked about how the experiment affected children's supervision,[11] nearly all parents reported that their children were being supervised after school (table 9.9). Of those being supervised, most were being supervised at home. There is no evidence that children in the MTO or Section 8 groups were more or less likely than control group children to have supervision after school or to have supervision at home.

FRIENDS

To find out if children were adjusting to their new neighborhoods, parents were asked, "How many friends does your child have in this neighborhood?" According to parents, almost all children age 6 to 11 had at least one friend in the neighborhood, and over half of all children had three friends or more. Although the same proportion of children in all three groups reported having at least one friend in the neighborhood, children in the two treatment groups—especially children in the Section 8 group—had fewer friends than children in the control group.

Finally, to find out if parents were becoming acquainted with other parents in their neighborhoods, we asked them how often they talked to the parents of their children's friends. Although more than three-quarters of parents reported talking with the parents of their child's friends, less than 40 percent reported talking to them once a week or more. Despite the fact that the differences are not statistically significant, the point estimates suggest that, if anything, parents in the two treatment groups are somewhat *more* likely to talk frequently with other parents than parents in the control group. These results are consistent with the qualitative interviews we conducted with a few selected families, which suggested that having a child in elementary school facilitated parents' becoming involved in their new neighborhoods.

Table 9.9. *Los Angeles Child Outcomes for Children Age 6–11*

	Experimental	Section 8	Control
Any activities	0.716	0.888	0.769
	(0.043)	(0.061)	(0.058)
Total activities[a,c]	1.490	2.037	2.000
	(0.139)	(0.140)	(0.228)
Activities			
Art[a,c]	0.188	0.407	0.385
	(0.038)	(0.096)	(0.067)
Sports	0.349	0.481	0.404
	(0.046)	(0.097)	(0.068)
Tutoring	0.245	0.370	0.308
	(0.041)	(0.094)	(0.064)
Military	0.009	0.000	0.000
	(0.009)	(0.000)	(0.000)
Religious activities	0.292	0.259	0.327
	(0.044)	(0.085)	(0.065)
Camp	0.188	0.222	0.173
	(0.038)	(0.081)	(0.052)
Other activities	0.132	0.185	0.231
	(0.033)	(0.076)	(0.058)
Supervised after school	0.952	1.000	0.962
	(0.020)	(0.000)	(0.027)
Home after school	0.716	0.740	0.731
	(0.043)	(0.085)	(0.062)
Elsewhere after school	0.273	0.222	0.269
	(0.043)	(0.081)	(0.062)
Friends in neighborhood	0.905	0.888	0.903
	(0.028)	(0.061)	(0.041)
Many friends[b]	0.537	0.370	0.692
	(0.048)	(0.094)	(0.064)
Parents talk with other parents	0.735	0.777	0.788
	(0.043)	(0.081)	(0.081)
Talk frequently	0.396	0.481	0.307
	(0.047)	(0.097)	(0.064)

Source: Based on follow-up survey of respondents that entered the Los Angeles MTO program between March 10, 1995, and December 18, 1996.

Note: Standard errors are reported in parentheses.

a. Statistically significant two-sided test of differences in means between MTO and control at $p < .05$.

b. Statistically significant two-sided test of differences in means between Section 8 and control at $p < .05$.

c. Statistically significant two-sided test of differences in means between MTO and Section 8 at $p < .05$.

Adolescent Children (Age 12–17)

AFTER-SCHOOL ACTIVITIES

Most (84 percent) of all 12- to 17-year-olds participated in at least one of the specified activities. On average, they participated in 1.76 of the 7 listed activities (table 9.10). The MTO group, and to a lesser extent the Section 8 group, reported greater involvement in art and tutoring activities than the control group, although these differences were not statistically significant.

Table 9.10. *Los Angeles Child Outcomes for Children Age 12–17*

	Experimental	Section 8	Control
Any activities	0.864	0.807	0.795
	(0.038)	(0.078)	(0.065)
Total activities	1.864	1.423	1.769
	(0.142)	(0.229)	(0.234)
Activities			
Art	0.222	0.230	0.154
	(0.046)	(0.084)	(0.058)
Sports	0.555	0.461	0.564
	(0.055)	(0.099)	(0.079)
Tutoring	0.271	0.230	0.154
	(0.049)	(0.084)	(0.058)
Military	0.012	0.000	0.026
	(0.001)	(0.000)	(0.025)
Religious activities	0.333	0.307	0.308
	(0.052)	(0.092)	(0.074)
Camp	0.185	0.115	0.205
	(0.043)	(0.063)	(0.065)
Other activities[b,c]	0.172	0.000	0.179
	(0.004)	(0.000)	(0.061)
Earn money	0.342	0.272	0.200
	(0.077)	(0.140)	(0.091)
Supervised after school	0.925	1.000	0.923
	(0.002)	(0.000)	(0.043)
Home after school	0.827	0.846	0.897
	(0.042)	(0.072)	(0.049)
Elsewhere after school	0.160	0.153	0.103
	(0.041)	(0.072)	(0.049)

(*continued*)

Table 9.10. *Los Angeles Child Outcomes for Children Age 12–17 (Continued)*

	Experimental	Section 8	Control
Friends in neighborhood	0.814	0.769	0.795
	(0.043)	(0.084)	(0.065)
Many friends	0.518	0.384	0.564
	(0.055)	(0.097)	(0.079)
Parents talk with other parents	0.716	0.615	0.666
	(0.050)	(0.097)	(0.076)
Talk frequently	0.283	0.384	0.307
	(0.050)	(0.097)	(0.074)

Source: Based on follow-up survey of respondents that entered the Los Angeles MTO program between March 10, 1995, and December 18, 1996.

Note: Standard errors are reported in parentheses.

Parents of children age 15 and older were also asked about their child's work activities.[12] These comparisons reveal that children in the MTO group and Section 8 groups were more likely to earn money than children in the control group (34 percent for MTO, 27 percent for Section 8, and 20 percent for controls).

AFTER-SCHOOL SUPERVISION
More than 90 percent of children age 12 to 17 had supervision after school, with no important supervision differences reported across the three groups. These high rates of supervision may reflect parental concern about the safety of their neighborhoods. Children in both treatment groups were less likely to have supervision at home than the controls, suggesting that their parents may be willing to give them more freedom to visit friends in their new neighborhoods.

FRIENDS
According to parents, four-fifths of children age 12 to 17 had at least one friend in their neighborhood and more than half had three or more friends. For this group of older children, there is little evidence that children in the MTO and Section 8 groups have fewer friends in the neighborhood than children in the control groups.

Parents of children age 12 to 17 reported talking to other parents even more frequently than parents of children age 6 to 11.[13] Although more than 68 percent of parents said they talk to parents of their child's friends, only 31 percent of parents talked to other parents frequently (once a week or more). Very similar proportions of parents in each group reported talking with other parents (72 percent MTO, 62 percent Section 8, and 67 percent control) and that they talk with other parents frequently (28 percent MTO, 38 percent Section 8, and 31 percent control).

Summary

Children in the experimental groups were not isolated, and they reportedly made friends in their new neighborhoods. This finding holds for adolescents as well as elementary-age children. There is some evidence, however, that younger children in the two treatment groups may have experienced a small deficit in total activities, as compared with control children. But parents reported establishing contact with other parents in the neighborhood, a good sign, and one that, along with the estimates presented in table 9.8, suggests residential mobility did *not* result in a major loss of social capital.

Medium-Term Effects on Employment, Earnings, and Welfare Receipt

This paper draws upon state administrative records to examine the impact of the Los Angeles MTO program on welfare receipt and labor market outcomes. Information on utilization of Aid to Families with Dependent Children/Temporary Assistance for Needy Families (AFDC/TANF) came from the California Department of Social Security's "MEDS/Medi-Cal" recipient database. These data give information on all Medi-Cal recipients by basis of eligibility. Since one of the key eligibility categories for Medi-Cal is AFDC/TANF receipt, it is possible to determine whether someone has received AFDC or TANF from the "eligibility codes" in this database.

A sample of 1,003 household heads that entered the Los Angeles MTO program between March 1995 and July 1998 was merged to the MEDS database on the basis of Social Security number. (After the initial match, first and last names recorded in each database were compared to verify the match.) On this basis, eight individuals were excluded from the sample, leaving a final sample size of 995. The MEDS data include information on welfare receipt for all months from January 1994 to September 2000. These data were aggregated to quarterly participation data by recording a household head as having received welfare if he or she received welfare for at least one month during each quarter.

Data on quarterly employment and earnings were drawn from the California Employment Development Department's (EDD) quarterly unemployment insurance records. The sample includes all adults age 16 to 55, as of 1994, who entered the Los Angeles MTO program between March 1995 and July 1998. The sample was matched to the EDD data on the basis of Social Security number and was further checked on the basis of name. In this case, 85 individuals (6 percent of the sample) were excluded from the data due to inconsistencies with the EDD data.[14] The remaining sample contained 1,253 adults and included information on quarterly earnings from the first quarter of 1994 to the third quarter of 2000.

Table 9.11 presents regression estimates of the effect of entering the MTO and Section 8 programs on AFCD/TANF receipt, employment, and quarterly earnings. These regressions control for demographic characteristics and for quarter effects. The first row of each panel presents estimates of the cumulative effect of entering the program. The following four rows present estimates from a separate regression model that allows the effect of the program to vary with the time spent in the program.

Table 9.11. *MTO Effects on Los Angeles Adult Earnings and Welfare Receipt*

Outcome	Control group mean	MTO minus control	Section 8 minus control
AFDC/TANF receipt (household heads)			
Entire postprogram period	0.52	−0.001	0.039
		(0.030)	(0.029)
Time since program entry			
Quarters 1–4	0.62	0.001	0.027
		(0.025)	(0.023)
Quarters 5–8	0.55	0.030	0.049
		(0.032)	(0.030)
Quarters 9–12	0.47	−0.008	0.030
		(0.037)	(0.034)
Quarters 13+	0.42	−0.021	0.049
		(0.047)	(0.048)

Table 9.11. *(Continued)*

Employment (adults)			
Entire postprogram period	0.43	−0.020	−0.069
		(0.025)	(0.027)
Time since program entry			
Quarters 1–4	0.38	−0.025	−0.051
		(0.025)	(0.024)
Quarters 5–8	0.44	−0.033	−0.062
		(0.030)	(0.029)
Quarters 9–12	0.45	−0.011	−0.074
		(0.033)	(0.035)
Quarters 13+	0.45	−0.015	−0.099
		(0.043)	(0.049)
Earnings (employed adults, $)			
Entire postprogram period	3,406	33.8	−130.4
		(162.1)	(188.0)
Time since program entry			
Quarters 1–4	3,129	−162.3	−194.2
		(155.3)	(184.4)
Quarters 5–8	3,266	89.1	−121.0
		(185.3)	(204.2)
Quarters 9–12	3,566	47.4	−69.6
		(201.2)	(240.3)
Quarters 13+	3,750	53.6	−141.9
		(280.5)	(312.2)

Source: Based on regression estimates using administrative data from the California Department of Social Security and the California Employment Development Department from the first quarter of 1994 to the third quarter of 2000.

Notes: Welfare sample includes 995 household heads that entered the Los Angeles MTO program from March 1995 to July 1998. Employment and earnings sample includes 1,253 adults age 16–55 in 1994 who entered the program from March 1995 to July 1998. Regressions control for demographic characteristics and quarter effects. Robust standard errors that adjust for multiple observations on the same individual are in parentheses. The first line of each panel presents regression estimates of the cumulative effect of the program. The next four lines present estimates from a separate regression that allows the effect of the program to vary with time since program entry.

As shown, there were substantial increases in employment and quarterly earning and decreases in AFDC/TANF receipt throughout the measurement period. For example, the share of the control group receiving AFDC/TANF in each quarter decreased from 0.62 in the first four quarters after entering the program to 0.42 after three years in the program. During the same period, the quarterly employment rate increased from 0.38 to 0.45 and the average quarterly earnings of those who worked increased from $3,100 to $3,750. The increase in earnings outpaced the increase in prices over this period.

However, despite the general improvement in the economic position of the total sample throughout this period, there is little evidence that either the MTO group or the Section 8 group experienced larger decreases in welfare receipt, or larger increases in quarterly employment rates or quarterly earnings than did the control group.[15] This may be due to the relatively small size of the sample that may make it difficult to determine the impact of the program.

Early Impacts

Although it is still too early to assess the long-term effects of the Moving to Opportunity program, the results presented point to several tentative conclusions.

Mobility Rates

Both the MTO and Section 8 groups had substantially higher mobility rates than controls. MTO mobility rates were lower than Section 8 group mobility rates, indicating that the more stringent requirements associated with the MTO voucher may have discouraged some MTO families from moving. Overall, 67 percent of MTO families moved, compared with 85 percent of Section 8 and 27 percent of control group families. However, there is some evidence that MTO mobility rates relative to the Section 8 group improved as the program became more fully operational.

Poverty Rates and Socioeconomic Levels

Both the MTO and Section 8 groups moved to neighborhoods with substantially lower poverty rates and higher socioeconomic levels than the control group. While on average the MTO and Section 8 neighborhoods were similar on a number of dimensions, we found important distributional differences. These differences occurred because the MTO program participants were both more successful than Section 8 participants in moving to very low poverty neighborhoods and less successful in moving out of very high poverty neighborhoods. At the time of the follow-up survey, 58 percent of the MTO group lived in low-poverty neighborhoods, compared with only 1 percent of both the the Section 8 and the control groups. By contrast, 32 percent of MTO families remained in very high poverty neighborhoods, compared with 17 percent of the Section 8 and 80 percent of the control groups.

Crime and Safety

Both MTO and Section 8 groups achieved notable reductions in neighborhood crime rates and increases in perceived neighborhood safety. At the time of the follow-up survey, neighborhood violent crime rates for the combined MTO and Section 8 sample were between 45 percent and 67 percent of those for the control group. In addition, parents in the two treatment groups were much less likely than parents in the control group to report that their neighborhood was very unsafe (20 percent MTO, 10 percent Section 8, and 52 percent controls). Since most parents claimed that getting out of violent neighborhoods was the main reason they had participated in the MTO program, that they succeeded must be given a great deal of weight in assessing the success of the program.

Community Resources

There is some evidence that parents in the MTO and Section 8 groups were more likely to use center-based care or Head Start programs, which tend to be well structured and education-oriented, and were less likely than controls to seek medical care in a hospital emergency room. However, these differences were not statistically significant.

Social Capital

On social connections, or *social capital*, the evidence is mixed. On the one hand, parents in the treatment groups appear to have lost some types of social capital. They were less likely than control group parents to belong to a church and to attend church regularly and they were less likely to have many friends and relatives in their neighborhood. Nevertheless, parents in the two treatment groups were just as likely as the control group to be involved in their children's school activities and to know the parents of their children's friends. In addition, their children appeared to have formed connections in their new neighborhoods. A high share of children in all three treatment groups reported that they had friends in their neighborhood; moreover, MTO children age 12 to 17 were just as likely as control group children to report that they had many friends in the neighborhood.

Employment, Earnings, and Welfare Receipt

An analysis of administrative data suggests that during the first three years in the program, there were no noticeable increases in the employment and earnings, or decreases in the use of AFDC/TANF, for the MTO and Section 8 groups relative to the control group. However, the economic position of all groups improved substantially over this period, probably in large part due to the changes in the welfare program and the economic opportunities that occurred simultaneously with this program.

NOTES

The research was sponsored by the U.S. Department of Housing and Urban Development and by the Smith Richardson Foundation. Staff at the Housing Authority of the City of Los Angeles, Beyond Shelter, and the Fair Housing Congress of the City of Los Angeles provided invaluable information on the implementation of the program and up-to-date client contact information. The authors would like to thank participants in a working group at the Industrial Relations Section of Princeton University for helpful comments and suggestions.

1. Because most Section 8 and MTO families remain in subsidized housing when they move, the housing authority can obtain up-to-date information on the phone numbers and addresses for families in the two treatment groups. By contrast, the housing authority has no way of tracking families who move out of public housing to nonsubsidized housing.

2. It was possible to verify whether a family had moved in 98 percent of all cases, since interviewers went to the homes of respondents who could not be reached over the phone.

3. The question was, "As you probably know, the Moving to Opportunity program is designed to help people move to areas where there are low levels of poverty. If you could have moved anywhere, and not just to a low-poverty neighborhood, would you have moved to the neighborhood where you live now, someplace near the neighborhood you lived in when you enrolled in MTO, or someplace else?"

4. First, respondents were asked, "During most of last week, were you working for pay?" Then they were asked "How much do you usually earn?" and "How many hours do you usually work in a week?" Finally, they were asked, "Did you take any classes or participate in any training programs during the past month?"

5. The questions were, "Do you have someone else care for [name(s) of child(ren) age 5 or younger] on a regular basis?" If the respondent answered yes, he or she was asked, "What type of care do you use? Child care center/preschool, Head Start program, relative, baby-sitter who is not a relative, or other?"

6. The initial question was, "Do you have a place where you usually take your children for medical care?" If the respondent answered yes, he or she was asked "Is this a private doctor's office, a hospital outpatient room, a health clinic, or some other place?" and the distance of the place from his or her current home.

7. Respondents were asked, "Last spring, did you attend any kind of program at your children's school, such as a PTA meeting or a special program for parents or anything like that?" They also were asked, "Do you belong to a church or other religious organization?" If the answer was yes, they were asked a series of follow-up questions about the location of the church and how often they attended services. Finally, they were asked, "Do you belong to any groups or organizations (other than your church)?"

8. Respondents were asked "How many of your friends currently live in this neighborhood? Would you say none, a few, or many?" and "How may of your family members currently live in this neighborhood? Would you say none, a few, or many?"

9. Respondents were asked, "During the past six months, did [child's name] participate in any of the following activities after school or in the summer: art, music, band or drama lessons or clubs; sports lessons or sports teams, including swimming; Scouts, Big Brothers or Big Sisters, or Boys and Girls clubs; academic courses, tutoring, or literacy training; military training, such as Junior ROTC; religious activities supervised by an adult; camp or other supervised recreation; some other supervised activity?"

10. Families in both the Section 8 and the MTO groups must pay a specified fraction of their income toward rent; the housing authority will pay the remainder up to a maximum amount specified by the fair market rent in the area. However, if the rent for an apartment exceeded the maximum voucher amount, families could make up the difference with their own contributions.

11. The initial question read, "After school, is [child's name] usually supervised by an adult, that is, someone 18 years of age or older?" Then the respondent was asked, "After school, where does [child's name] usually go? Would you say home, or somewhere else?"

12. The question read, "During the past month, did [child's name] do anything to earn money, such as baby-sit, help out with yard work, or have a part-time job?"

13. These groups are not mutually exclusive. Some parents have focal children in each age group.

14. In particular, individuals were excluded from the sample if two or more individuals with different names appeared to have the same social security number in the EDD data, or if the name of the individual in the MTO sample did not match the name reported in the EDD data. The estimates included here are not sensitive to this exclusion of these individuals from the sample.

15. These estimates are based on linear regressions that include controls for age, race, ethnicity, sex, family size, age of children, marital status, education, disability status, the presence of friends or family in the neighborhood, family experience with neighborhood violence, whether the family has a car that runs, and prior family mobility. They also include quarter effects. The regressions were weighted to reflect the changing probabilities associated with selection into the program for each of the three treatment groups. They also present standard errors that are adjusted to account for multiple observations for the same individual over time.

REFERENCES

Jargowsky, Paul A. 1997. *Poverty and Place: Ghettos, Barrios, and the American City.* New York: Russell Sage Foundation.

Rosenbaum, James E., and Susan J. Popkin. 1991. "Employment and Earnings of Low-Income Blacks Who Move to Middle-Class Suburbs." In *The Urban Underclass,* edited by Christopher Jencks and Paul E. Peterson (342–56). Washington, D.C.: Brookings Institution.

Rosenbaum, James E., Nancy Fishman, Alison Brett, and Patricia Meaden. 1993. "Can the Kerner Commission's Housing Strategy Improve Employment, Education, and Social Integration for Low-Income Blacks?" *North Carolina Law Review* 71: 1519–56.

U.S. Department of Housing and Urban Development, Office of Policy Development and Research. 1997. *A Picture of Subsidized Households in 1997.* Washington, D.C.: HUD.

10

New Places, New Faces

An Analysis of Neighborhoods and Social Ties among MTO Movers in Chicago

Emily Rosenbaum
Laura Harris
Nancy A. Denton

C hicago is a city known for its high levels of residential segregation and concentrated poverty (Massey and Denton 1993; Wilson 1987, 1996). Over the years, both journalists and researchers have documented the harsh realities of everyday life in the city's public housing projects—especially for children (e.g., Garbarino, Kostelny, and Dubrow 1991; Jones and Newman 1997; Kotlowitz 1991; Popkin et al. 2000).[1] Of all the MTO sites, Chicago residents, in particular, are likely to see drastic neighborhood changes in moving from public housing complexes to low-poverty areas.

This chapter investigates how much housing and neighborhood quality among Chicago MTO participants improved. It measures differences in improvements for the experimental and comparison groups and explores the factors that facilitate or inhibit program participants' ability to adjust, in the short term, to their new homes. It finds that all participating families were able to improve their housing and neighborhood conditions as a result of moving, but that families in the experimental group experienced greater improvements. Experimental families also were adjusting better to their new neighborhoods, partly as a result of their greater success at meeting their preferences for racially mixed neighborhoods. Multivariate analyses indicate that the most important factor in predicting positive adjustment was the greater feeling of safety that all families felt in their new neighborhoods.

Research Questions

The extent to which origin and destination neighborhoods differ for program participants warrants serious study for several reasons. First, MTO mandated that the experimental group relocate to low-poverty neighborhoods. The comparison group, however, could choose any neighborhood and was thus constrained only by the housing market. Thus, a pertinent question is how the two sets of destination neighborhoods differ in the opportunities they offer the new residents. In other words, did the requirement that experimental families move to low-poverty neighborhoods boost how much they gained in neighborhood and housing quality? Or did the counseling received only by experimental movers make a difference in the movers' gains in housing and neighborhood quality?

Second, all movers must adjust to their new surroundings, and successfully adjusting is necessary to achieve any long-term benefits from the neighborhood environment. How do experimental and comparison families compare in their ability to adjust, in the short term, to their new neighbors and their new neighborhoods? Do certain characteristics of the neighborhoods impede or enhance the adjustment process? And, if so, do these characteristics differ across the neighborhoods chosen by experimental and comparison families?

One important factor contributing to adjustment is the receptivity of new neighbors. Given the presumed (and, as we document later, real) differences between the destination neighborhoods chosen by the two groups of families, did program participants receive different receptions? Do the extent and type of neighborhood interactions differ among experimental and comparison families? Such differences need examining because they could conceivably affect a family's desire to stay in the new neighborhood (since few people would want to live in a place where they encountered deliberate hostility), and because it is *social interaction* rather than aggregate characteristics that produce neighborhood effects (Briggs 1997; Jencks and Mayer 1990; Tienda 1991).

Third, almost by definition, moving implies some disruption of social ties and family networks. Previous research has shown that some ties, such as help with child care and periodic financial assistance, are very important in poor neighborhoods (e.g., Edin and Lein 1997; Leavitt and Saegert 1990; Stack 1974; Williams and Kornblum 1994). However, other ties, such as gang membership, might be better broken. Which ties are broken, how well the movers handle the disruptions, and whether new ties are being formed are important questions. Indeed, movers' ability to form new ties in their new neighborhoods may be a key factor in enabling families to adjust to their new surroundings. While the MTO program's long-term goals center on achieving positive labor force and educational outcomes, these goals are more attainable if participants are able to adjust to, and successfully live in, new locations that offer them more opportunities than their old neighborhoods.

Answering questions about how neighborhoods improved and about the movers' ability to adjust is fairly complicated. First, the fact that many will consider simply not being in public housing a major improvement predisposes all findings to be positive. Statements of public housing residents, the poor condition of much public housing (Donaldson 1993; Kotlowitz 1991; Kozol 1995; Lemann 1991; Popkin et al. 2000), and the length of the waiting lists to receive housing assistance outside of public housing (Davis 1993) all support this point. To avoid this bias, we must derive objective indicators of the neighborhoods as well as of the respondents' views of their new neighborhoods.

Second, previous research has shown that adjustment issues decrease over time (Rosenbaum et al. 1996). Many of the people studied here have only been in their new neighborhoods a few months. Thus, we may be simultaneously overestimating the positive effects (of not being in public housing) and overestimating the negative effects (of the initial adjustment problems). Last, both the experimental and control groups moved with Section 8 certificates/vouchers. The extent to which families can find housing at the mandated rents, and the extent to which landlords will accept Section 8 tenants, may influence the degree to which the families (especially those in the comparison group) can actually find housing. Because they are still limited to low-income housing units, families might not be able to relocate in neighborhoods with very many opportunities (Apgar 1993; Coulton et al. 1996; Harris 1999; Newman and Schnare 1997).

Data Sources

The analysis draws on three data sources. The first is the Urban Institute's Under Class Database, which provides 1990 Census indicators for the

origin (or pre-move) and destination (or post-move) tracts for all households in our sample. The second data source is HUD's pre-move baseline
survey of all participating families. The third source is our own post-
move survey of 120 households (67 experimental group families that we
refer to as "MTO families" and 53 in the comparison group, who we term
Section 8 families) that moved under the Chicago MTO program. Our
original plan was to conduct two separate surveys, but data problems and
administrative issues limited us to one "merged" survey based on three
waves of contact with participants.[2] Our survey questions focus on adjustment issues and the effects of the new neighborhoods on families' lives.
Thus, we only interviewed households that had successfully moved as
part of the MTO program. This choice, which was partly motivated by
resource limitations, restricted our possible sample, eliminating households in the control group and households in the MTO and Section 8
groups that did not move from public housing as part of MTO.

The goal for the number of households successfully leasing-up in
Chicago was 285 (143 in the experimental group and 142 in the Section 8
comparison group). We received the first round of contact information in
June 1996 ($N = 66$), the second round in September 1997 ($N = 130$ for both
rounds), and the last round in July 1998 ($N = 234$ for all three rounds). In
each round, the percentage of households with telephone numbers was
less than 30 percent. To obtain the missing numbers, we contacted relatives and friends, researched local telephone directories, and wrote letters
to participating households. Using the first round of contact information, one researcher went to Chicago to locate participants in person.
This effort yielded complete in-person interviews with two participants
who did not have telephones as well as eight telephone interviews. All told,
we completed interviews with 120 households (22 for survey 1; 55 for
surveys 1 and 2; 43 for the merged survey), for an overall response rate of
51.3 percent.[3]

Our limited success at finding the Chicago movers largely reflects the
administrative problems at the Chicago site. For example, in 1994, shortly
after the Chicago MTO program began, HUD took over the Chicago
Housing Authority (CHA), and CHAC, a private organization, took over
the administration of the Section 8 program (where MTO was
housed). Additionally, in 1996 the Leadership Council for Metropolitan
Opportunities, the organization that had provided the counseling and
search assistance to experimental group families, decided not to continue
in this role. CHAC also took over that part of the program. All these

changes slowed down the initial pace of participant enrollment and, subsequently, our receipt of contact information. The difficulty in contacting families also highlights the problems inherent in doing telephone surveys with a poor, mobile population.

Most important, our inability to locate some families raises an important methodological question: Did the mover families we did interview differ significantly from those we were unable to contact? If so, our results may not adequately reflect outcomes for all movers. To determine whether our sample contains major differences, we compared interviewed families with noninterviewed families, according to program group, using attitudinal variables from the baseline survey. (We chose attitudinal variables over demographic or socioeconomic variables, because of the homogeneity of the sample along the latter two dimensions.) Using simple two-tailed t-tests, we found no significant differences for MTO families. But for the Section 8 families, interviewed householders differed from their non-interviewed counterparts in three ways. Specifically, as shown in table 10.A1, among Section 8 families, interviewed householders were more likely to feel good/very good about sending their children to majority white schools, to feel good/very good about living in a neighborhood where most of their neighbors earned more than they did and to feel sure/very sure that they would like living in a new neighborhood. In sum, the comparisons suggest that the results reported here for MTO families are representative of those of all MTO mover families in Chicago, but that any positive findings uncovered for Section 8 families may be overstated, given that our sample appears biased in favor of those families with the most optimistic outlook on their potential new neighbors and neighborhoods.

Results

Overview of Sample Characteristics

Before proceeding with the analyses of housing and neighborhood outcomes and short-term adjustment, we provide a brief profile of the interviewed participants based on the baseline survey data collected by HUD. Almost all (97 percent) household heads were women, and all (except for three MTO household heads) were non-Hispanic African Americans. The two groups of household heads were similar ages: On average, MTO household heads were 33 years old and Section 8 household heads were

32 years old. Very few household heads were married at the time of the baseline survey (five from MTO and four from Section 8), and most had never been married (63 percent of MTO and 68 percent of Section 8 household heads). All but four of the families had children and, on average, comparison families had slightly more children (3.24) than the experimental families (2.75). While 19 percent of MTO and 16 percent of Section 8 household heads reported being in school at the time of the baseline survey, experimental household heads reported slightly higher levels of high school completion (including GED) than did comparison household heads (67 percent versus 58 percent). Slightly more than 1 in 4 household heads reported that they worked for pay during the week prior to the baseline survey, yet 66 percent of MTO household heads and 71 percent of Section 8 household heads reported that they were looking for work. Despite the fact that almost all household heads received welfare at the time of the baseline (12 from each group did not), prior work experience was nearly universal: Only eight MTO and five Section 8 household heads reported they had *never* worked for pay. The high prevalence of work experience and welfare reliance may at first appear contradictory. But research has shown that, while work is a primary route off of welfare, it is not sufficient to *keep* women off welfare, and many low-income families tend to cycle in and out of the system (Edin and Harris 1999; Harris 1996; Pavetti 1993).

According to the baseline survey, household heads were unanimous in their desire to move to a different neighborhood (100 percent of MTO and 98 percent of Section 8) and in their very positive feelings about moving, yet relatively few household heads (31 percent of MTO and 16 percent of Section 8) had *ever* applied for a Section 8 voucher or certificate before enrolling in the program. Our data do not reveal why these respondents have relatively few experiences with Section 8, given their strong desire to move and the program's design as a feasible way for poor families to access the private market. It may be that long waiting lists depress the motivation to apply for Section 8 certificates and vouchers,[4] that respondents had little information about how to move, or that they may have thought that expressing a strong desire to move would help them in the MTO program.

As for their reasons for moving, nearly 8 in 10 household heads from each group cited "getting away from drugs" and "crime" as their first or second most important reason. Next in importance were "better schools for their children" and "getting a bigger or better apartment" (mentioned by slightly less than half the women in each group). This ranking of reasons for moving matches that for the other four MTO sites (Goering et al. 1999). When asked where they would like to move, more than half of each group (61 percent of the MTO and 74 percent of the Section 8 respondents) chose a different neighborhood in the city; only 28 percent of the MTO and 14 percent of the Section 8 respondents chose the suburbs. This strong desire to remain in or near Chicago likely stems from the respondents' previous experiences; only 22 percent of household heads reported they had ever lived outside of Chicago. Indeed, only six MTO families and three Section 8 families wanted to leave the Chicago area entirely; two families did so, one by relocating to Milwaukee and the other to California.

Experience in different types of neighborhoods can be an important factor in helping families adjust to their new neighborhoods. The baseline survey asked respondents if they had ever lived in various types of racially or ethnically mixed neighborhoods. About half the families in each group had lived in areas that were mixed African American and white; 28 percent of each group had lived in areas populated only by African Americans and Hispanics, by Hispanics and whites (eight MTO and six Section 8 families), and by all three groups (27 percent of MTO and 23 percent of Section 8 families). Only two MTO families and six Section 8 families had previously lived in mostly white areas. These findings fit with what other research has shown about neighborhoods in Chicago and Chicago's high residential segregation (Denton and Anderson 1995). That is, given that Chicago has few mixed neighborhoods, it is not surprising that these families, who are perhaps among the most disadvantaged in the housing market, have not lived in them.

In summary, as one might expect from the experimental design of the program, the families assigned to the MTO and Section 8 groups generally were quite similar in demographic and socioeconomic background characteristics. They were also similar in their overall motivations to move, their stated reasons for moving, and their previous experiences with neighborhoods of varying racial/ethnic compositions. While these data capture respondents' lifetime experience with different neighborhood compositions, the next section compares the objective (i.e., census-based) characteristics of their origin tracts with those of their destination tracts. Our goal is twofold: On the one hand, we seek to evaluate the gains made by each group of families as a result of moving. On the other hand, we seek to compare the two groups by the characteristics of their new neighborhoods.

Objective Neighborhood Differences

We compare the origin neighborhoods with the destination neighborhoods chosen by the comparison and experimental groups using 1990 Census data. For this portion of the analysis, neighborhoods are defined by census tract.[5] We focus on three areas: racial and ethnic composition, economic status, and social context. We measure social context using proxy indicators of education and labor force opportunities. Summary statistics for the three groups of census tracts (i.e., origin tracts, destination tracts for Section 8 families, and destination tracts for MTO families) are presented in table 10.1.[6]

The origin tract neighborhoods were essentially racially homogeneous, suggesting that the families, while they lived in these areas, had limited contact with persons of other racial/ethnic backgrounds. In addition, taken as a whole, the measures of economic status reveal a consistent story of extreme poverty. Beyond the very high average poverty rate (75 percent) and the low average median income ($6,212), nearly 60 percent of households, on average, received public assistance, and less than 3 percent owned the homes they lived in. Thus, these tracts not only were extremely poor, but they also contained very little *wealth* (Oliver and Shapiro 1995), indicating a high degree of economic marginalization. Finally, these data suggest that the neighborhoods had relatively few adult role models who worked or had high school or college degrees (Wilson 1987, 1996). In addition, nearly all families and subfamilies in the origin neighborhoods were headed by women. Thus, the families wanted to leave census tracts that were racially, socially, and economically isolated and that offered few, if any, opportunities for socioeconomic advancement.

How do the destination tracts of Section 8 and MTO families compare with their origin tracts? Among the Section 8 families, while the racial composition of the *average* destination tract was virtually the same as in the origin tract (on average, 90 percent of residents were black), the variation across tracts was substantial. This finding suggests that Section 8 families relocated to neighborhoods with a variety of racial compositions. Indeed, the percentages of whites and Hispanics in the destination neighborhoods of Section 8 households greatly exceeded those in the origin neighborhoods. The tracts to which Section 8 families moved also varied according to measures of economic status. For example, while the average tract had a fairly high poverty rate (37 percent), some families found new homes in low-poverty tracts (minimum poverty rate of 4 percent), while

Table 10.1. *Summary Statistics Based
on Selected Census Tract Characteristics (1990)*

| | | Destination tracts | |
| | Origin tracts | Section 8 | MTO |
Tract characteristic	(118)[a]	(53)[a]	(67)[a]
Racial/ethnic composition			
Percent non-Hispanic black	99.29	90.00	57.22
	(0.79)	(20.51)	(38.32)
Percent non-Hispanic white	0.11	5.99	34.10
	(0.20)	(14.25)	(32.05)
Percent Hispanic	0.60	3.21	7.17
	(0.70)	(8.53)	(11.82)
Economic status			
Percent of tract population in poverty	74.99	36.61	10.60
	(13.70)	(15.76)	(8.84)
Percent of households receiving	58.61	31.15	10.15
public assistance	(16.06)	(13.34)	(8.66)
Median household income	$6,211.92	$17,041.19	$33,716.12
	($1,678.38)	($8,736.85)	($8,702.38)
Percent of homes owner-occupied	2.82	26.22	66.17
	(4.81)	(21.61)	(19.88)
Social context			
Percent of female-headed families	84.72	65.54	36.99
and subfamilies	(5.97)	(16.94)	(16.89)
Percent of adolescents age 16–19	17.03	18.11	9.49
neither enrolled nor graduated	(10.93)	(10.72)	(8.47)
from high school			
Percent of adult population (25+)	25.94	27.27	27.93
with high school degree	(4.01)	(5.85)	(6.96)
Percent of adult population (25+)	8.07	15.39	23.02
with college degree	(3.43)	(10.36)	(13.05)
Percent of population age 16 and	38.13	55.57	67.94
older in the civilian labor force	(7.25)	(11.41)	(6.78)
Male employment rate	26.10	46.34	65.44
	(13.42)	(13.08)	(11.97)

Source: Urban Underclass database.

Notes: All figures reported are means; standard deviations appear in parentheses. All differences between MTO and Section 8 destination tracts are significant at the $p \leq .05$ level or above.

a. Number of unique tracts.

others moved to extremely poor tracts (maximum poverty rate of 70 percent). These higher-income tracts have, on average, more positive role models of two-parent families and subfamilies, economically active adults, and college graduates than the Section 8 families' origin tracts.

Not surprisingly, the MTO families wound up in the most potentially advantageous environments. The tracts are economically well-off; they have the highest median household incomes, the highest levels of home ownership, and the highest labor force participation and male employment rates of the three groups of tracts.[7] Moreover, the smaller standard deviation suggests that labor force activity is the *rule* more than the *exception.* For racial/ethnic composition, MTO families also appear to have moved to the most diverse census tracts; while the average tract was approximately 57 percent black, the variation in racial composition was extremely high, and whites made up the majority of the nonblack population.

In summary, while all the families originated in tracts that were highly isolated, in terms of racial composition, and social and economic opportunities, the tracts to which they moved appear to differ greatly depending on the group they were assigned to. While the Section 8 families moved to tracts that, on average, offer more diversity (in race and ethnicity) and opportunity than those they left behind, the variation on all the measures examined indicates that some Section 8 families moved to areas that were similar to the ones they left behind. In contrast, MTO families moved to the most potentially advantageous environments, as measured by the proportion of their neighbors who graduated from college, work, and earn income rather than receive public assistance. Furthermore, the MTO families moved to the most racially and ethnically diverse census tracts, with tract populations that were, on average, only slightly more than half black.

Neighborhood Preferences

Presumably, families participating in MTO wanted to move to more resource-rich neighborhoods. But did they wish to move to more *racially* mixed neighborhoods? Moreover, did composition preferences differ across the two groups, and were both groups as likely to satisfy their preferences? To determine whether families met their stated preferences, we compared respondents' baseline survey responses to questions about the type of neighborhood they would most *prefer* to live in with responses to our survey questions asking about the racial/ethnic composition of the neighborhoods they *actually* moved to.

The MTO families that were required to move to low-poverty neighborhoods received counseling and had access to listings of landlords in low-poverty neighborhoods compiled by their counselors. Accordingly, we might expect the areas in which they searched for housing, and those to which they eventually moved, will differ from those areas evaluated and chosen by Section 8 families. In addition, we would expect a family's ability to match its preferences to vary by group, with the MTO families demonstrating the greatest ability to meet their goals.

Equally, if not more, important, the disappointment among some families that do not attain their preferences could influence their evaluations of their new neighborhoods and affect their motivation to adjust to, and remain in, their new neighborhoods. For example, research has linked evaluations of neighborhood conditions to neighborhood racial composition (St. John and Bates 1990). A family seeking an integrated neighborhood that is limited by housing market forces to a mostly black area may not judge the new neighborhood objectively. The family's evaluation of the new area's quality may reflect *expectations* for low quality more than family members' *experiences* with the neighborhood's conditions. Similarly, disappointed families may not be committed to remaining in a neighborhood that differs from their preferences. Thus, we conceptualize the match between preferences and the actual destination neighborhoods to be a key intervening variable.

Overall, the results from the baseline survey suggest that most families would like to live in mixed neighborhoods: 56 percent of the MTO families and 40 percent of the Section 8 families preferred neighborhoods populated by a mix of African Americans, Hispanics, and whites; 28 percent of MTO and 44 percent of Section 8 families preferred areas with a mix of African Americans and whites; and only four MTO and six Section 8 families chose mostly African-American areas. The strong preference among black families to live in mixed neighborhoods parallels findings in other studies on neighborhood preferences (Farley 1993; Farley, Fielding, and Krysan 1997; Farley et al. 1994; Zubrinsky and Bobo 1996).

Most families preferred to move to racially mixed areas. But were some families in the sample more able to acquire housing in racially and ethnically mixed neighborhoods? Apparently, the answer is yes. According to our survey, MTO families were far less likely than Section 8 families to report having moved to a mostly black neighborhood (22 percent versus 68 percent), and they were far more likely to describe their destination neighborhood as containing a mix of black and white residents (37 percent versus 19 percent of Section 8 families) or to say it fell in the "other" category (27 percent versus 9 percent of Section 8 families).[8] Moreover, 41 percent of all families stated they preferred moving to mixed areas but ended up in mostly black areas, an experience more prevalent among Section 8 families (68 percent) than among MTO families (19 percent). We considered this group of families as potentially disappointed with the destination neighborhoods.

Overall, MTO families were more likely than Section 8 families to move to neighborhoods with a mixture of racial/ethnic groups. Section 8 families were more likely to move to mostly black neighborhoods, despite their stated preference to live in mixed areas. Given the extensive literature documenting the persistence of housing market discrimination (Yinger 1995), the extreme levels of racial segregation and poverty concentration in Chicago (Denton 1994; Massey and Denton 1993), the geographic concentration of affordable housing units (Apgar 1993; Harris 1999), and the fact that the Section 8 families were left to navigate the housing market on their own, it seems reasonable to conclude that persistent market barriers constrained families' housing choices to mostly black areas, regardless of their stated preference.[9] Indeed, Turner (1998) demonstrates that housing vouchers and certificates alone do not always enable central-city minority families to move to low-poverty, racially mixed neighborhoods. However, when a program complements vouchers or certificates with search assistance and housing counseling, assisted households' locational outcomes improve (Turner 1998). Identifying the causes of the Section 8 families' ability to satisfy their preferences for mixed neighborhoods is beyond the scope of this chapter. Notably, however, relatively higher disappointment levels among Section 8 families may help explain the differences in MTO and Section 8 families' capacity to adjust positively, an issue addressed later in this chapter. We next review the families' subjective evaluations of their housing and neighborhoods.

Housing Quality and Neighborhood Perceptions

This section analyzes families' ability to meet their desire to find better-quality housing and safer neighborhoods through the MTO program. Like our analysis of census-tract indicators, the section compares not only the relative success of MTO and Section 8 families in achieving their goals for better housing and safer neighborhoods, but also how the families' current housing and neighborhood conditions differ from those they left behind. The comparisons focus on the respondents' pre- and post-move reports on housing quality and condition, neighborhood problems, and neighborhood safety.

In general, both the experimental and control groups saw substantial improvements in housing and neighborhood quality as a result of moving. However, on some quality indicators, gains were about the same for the MTO and Section 8 groups, while on other quality indicators, the two groups reported substantial differences. It is important to note that when we compare participants' responses to our survey with their responses on the baseline survey, we are limited, by methodology, to our 120 respondents. We do not have matching data for all Chicago families accepted into the program.

Housing Conditions

Starting with the most general housing conditions, before moving, 68 percent of respondents reported their housing to be in fair or poor (rather than good/excellent) condition. After the move, only 19 percent of the experimental and 26 percent of the comparison group characterized their housing as fair or poor (top panel, table 10.2). Moreover, among the MTO and Section 8 families that rated the quality of their pre-move housing as fair or poor, a respective 81 percent and 71 percent rated the units they moved to as of good/excellent quality, a difference that is significant at the $p \leq .10$ level (second panel, table 10.2). Thus, while most MTO and Section 8 families were able to move to housing they rated as high quality, MTO families were significantly more successful in improving their housing condition.

To gain more specific measures of housing quality, the baseline survey and our survey asked respondents to evaluate whether each of five conditions (peeling paint, plumbing, rats, locks, and space) was a problem.[10] Problems related to these housing conditions can annoy residents, but more important, each can have serious effects on residents' health, safety, and well-being, especially among children.

Overall, both MTO and Section 8 households experienced dramatic improvements in their housing conditions. For example, before the move, 67 percent of all household heads reported problems with peeling paint.

Table 10.2. *Pre- and Post-move Housing Conditions and Improvements in Housing Conditions among MTO and Section 8 Families in Chicago*

		Post-move	
Characteristic	Pre-move	MTO	Section 8
Housing condition			
Overall condition is fair/poor	.68	.19	.26
	(.47)	(.40)	(.44)
Peeling paint is a problem	.67	.16	.38***
	(.47)	(.37)	(.49)
Nonfunctional plumbing is a problem	.53	.19	.23
	(.50)	(.40)	(.42)
Rats/mice are a problem	.57	.18	.26
	(.50)	(.39)	(.45)
Broken locks/no locks are a problem	.47	.01	.14**
	(.50)	(.29)	(.35)
Inadequate space is a problem	.77	.33	.34
	(.42)	(.47)	(.48)
Improvements in housing conditions[a]			
Overall condition improved		.81	.71*
		(.39)	(.46)
Peeling paint is no longer a problem		.80	.63*
		(.40)	(.49)
Nonfunctional plumbing is no longer a problem		.83	.71
		(.38)	(.46)
Rats/mice are no longer a problem		.85	.66**
		(.36)	(.48)
Broken locks/no locks are no longer a problem		.96	.84*
		(.19)	(.37)
Inadequate space is no longer a problem		.68	.62
		(.47)	(.49)

Source: HUD baseline survey and survey of Chicago MTO participants.

Notes: All figures are means; standard deviations in parentheses.

a. The percentage of respondents who report the condition as not a problem in their post-move housing units among those who reported the condition a problem in their pre-move housing units.

* $p \leq .10$; ** $p \leq .05$; *** $p \leq .01$ (one-tailed tests of differences between MTO and Section 8).

After their moves, only 16 percent of MTO and 38 percent of Section 8 household heads reported problems with peeling paint ($p \leq .01$). Among families that had reported a problem with peeling paint in their old apartments, MTO households were significantly more successful than Section 8 households in moving to housing units where peeling paint was no longer a problem (second panel, table 10.2). Similarly, while slightly more than half of all respondents reported problems with the plumbing and with rats or mice in their pre-move housing units, at most, 26 percent in each group had the same complaints after their moves. In addition, while MTO and Section 8 families were about as likely to move from units with plumbing problems to units without plumbing problems, MTO families were significantly more successful at moving from units with rodent problems to units without such problems. About half the families overall reported having problems with broken locks or no locks in their old apartments, yet only 1 percent of the MTO households and 14 percent of the Section 8 households reported such problems after their moves. Moreover, MTO families were much more likely than Section 8 families to move from units with lock-related problems to units without such problems.

Finally, families from both groups appear to have had fewer problems with inadequate space in their new apartments. However, the data suggest that inadequate space is the most difficult housing-related problem to eliminate; after the move, about one-third of MTO and Section 8 families reported having inadequate space in their new units. Thus, participation in the program, in general, appears to have helped families satisfy their desire for well-maintained housing. But the persistent space problems suggest that the stock of affordable units available to participating families does not match their needs for more space, perhaps because larger units generally cost more.

Neighborhood Conditions

The baseline survey and our survey contained two sets of identical questions on neighborhood quality. The first set of questions addressed safety issues: Respondents were asked to rate the safety of the parking lots and sidewalks near the local school, the safety of the streets near their home during the day and the night, and how safe they felt while home alone at night.[11] The second series of questions asked respondents to evaluate whether five conditions (litter/trash on the streets/sidewalks, graffiti/writing on the walls, people drinking in public, drug dealers/users, and

abandoned buildings) were problems.[12] These indicators of social disorder and physical deterioration have been associated with neighborhood
decline (Skogan 1990) and lack of neighborhood cohesion (Anderson
1990). Thus, they are important measures of a family's overall housing situation and the potential for new neighborhoods to contribute to successful life outcomes (Elliott et al. 1996; Wilson 1996).

The safety measures tell a fairly simple story. In the baseline survey, a
minority of all families reported that the parking lots and sidewalks near
the local school were safe (19 percent), that the streets near their homes
were safe during the day (31 percent) and at night (12 percent), and that
they felt safe at home alone (39 percent). These findings fit well with the
finding, reported earlier, that the majority of families wanted to move to
escape crime and drugs. After moving, the overwhelming majority in
each group (ranging from 75 percent to 97 percent) reported these same
conditions as safe (top panel, table 10.3). Two of the post-move differences in feelings of safety are significant: MTO respondents were significantly more likely than Section 8 respondents to report that the parking
lots and sidewalks near the local school were safe and that the streets near
their homes were safe at night. In moving from unsafe to safe neighborhoods, MTO families were significantly more successful than Section 8
families on two dimensions: the safety of the streets near their homes
during the day and at night (second panel, table 10.3). Because fear of
crime prompted many families to join MTO, the greater feelings of safety
among all participating families should be considered one of the program's major successes. The findings that MTO families feel significantly
safer than Section 8 families on two dimensions, and that MTO families
were more successful at improving their sense of safety on two dimensions,
however, suggest that moves to low-poverty neighborhoods produce
greater benefits.

On indicators of social disorder and physical deterioration, the respondents were virtually unanimous in reporting that their origin neighborhoods had problems with trash, graffiti, drinking, drugs, and abandoned
buildings (93 to 99 percent; third panel, table 10.3). After moving, these
conditions improved enormously for all families, but the difference was
significantly greater for MTO families. Section 8 families' neighborhood
problems eased in all areas. The percentage of families reporting problems
in their new neighborhoods ranged from a low of 23 percent for graffiti to
a high of 55 percent for both trash/litter and drug dealers/users. In contrast, the most frequent post-move problem mentioned among MTO

Table 10.3. *Pre- and Post-move Neighborhood Conditions and Improvements in Neighborhood Conditions among MTO and Section 8 Families in Chicago*

		Post-move	
Characteristic	Pre-move	MTO	Section 8
Feelings of safety			
In parking lots and on sidewalks near	.19	.97	.88*
neighborhood school	(.39)	(.18)	(.33)
At home alone at night	.40	.94	.89
	(.49)	(.24)	(.32)
On the streets near home during the day	.31	.92	.87
	(.47)	(.27)	(.34)
On the streets near home at night	.12	.88	.75*
	(.33)	(.33)	(.44)
Improvements in feelings of safety [a]			
In parking lots and on sidewalks near		.96	.92
neighborhood school		(.20)	(.27)
At home alone at night		.93	.87
		(.27)	(.34)
On the streets near home during the day		.95	.84*
		(.22)	(.37)
On the streets near home at night		.88	.72*
		(.33)	(.45)
Neighborhood problems			
Trash/litter on the street	.97	.28	.55**
	(.16)	(.45)	(.50)
Graffiti/writing on the walls	.99	.10	.23*
	(.09)	(.31)	(.43)
People drinking in public	.97	.10	.43***
	(.18)	(.31)	(.50)
Drug dealers/users	.99	.21	.55***
	(.09)	(.41)	(.50)
Abandoned buildings	.93	.01	.32***
	(.26)	(.27)	(.47)
Improvements in neighborhood conditions [b]			
Trash/litter on the street		.74	.45***
		(.44)	(.50)
Graffiti/writing on the walls		.89	.76*
		(.31)	(.43)

(*continued*)

Table 10.3. *Continued*

Characteristic	Pre-move	Post-move	
		MTO	Section 8
People drinking in public		.90	.56***
		(.30)	(.50)
Drug dealers/users		.80	.45***
		(.41)	(.50)
Abandoned buildings		.91	.67***
		(.29)	(.47)

Source: HUD baseline survey and survey of Chicago MTO participants.

Notes: All figures are means; standard deviations appear in parentheses.

a. Percentage of respondents who report feeling safe in the situation in their post-move neighborhoods among those who reported feeling unsafe in the situation in their pre-move neighborhoods.

b. Percentage of respondents who report the condition as not a problem in their post-move neighborhoods among those who reported the condition as being a problem in their pre-move neighborhoods.

*$p \leq .05$; **$p \leq .01$; ***$p \leq .0001$ (one-tailed test for differences between MTO and Section 8).

families was trash/litter. Still, almost half as many MTO families, compared with Section 8 families, reported this problem (28 percent versus 55 percent). Moreover, *thirty times* more Section 8 families than MTO families reported problems with abandoned buildings after their moves (32 percent versus 1 percent). Not only were MTO families far less affected by neighborhood problems after their moves, they were also far more successful at moving from neighborhoods with problems on all five dimensions to neighborhoods free of social and physical disorder (fourth panel, table 10.3). To the extent that these neighborhood problems correlate with other negative life outcomes, the experimental group clearly did much better than the comparison group in improving their opportunities.

In summary, our analysis reveals that MTO and Section 8 movers saw important improvements in housing and neighborhood quality. Before the moves, almost all families reported housing problems, neighborhood problems, and fears for personal safety. These problems eased dramatically after families moved to their new neighborhoods.

Several open-ended survey questions asked respondents what they liked most about their new neighborhoods. In response to these questions, several families mentioned the quiet atmosphere of their new neighborhoods, in particular, the absence of gunfire, gang activity, and drug dealing. For example, one respondent said, "Quiet. It's quiet. I can go to bed without hearing the bottles breaking and loud radios." Others also mentioned that in their new areas, people minded their own business, but "it's more like a family thing. They [the neighbors] look out for each other and their kids." Respondents also repeatedly mentioned the convenience of shopping and public transportation, services that may have been lacking in their old neighborhoods.

The survey findings suggest that, for housing and neighborhood conditions and feelings of safety, experimental families gained more than comparison families by moving. Moreover, the relatively greater improvements experienced by MTO families were most dramatic in the area of neighborhood conditions. Specifically, MTO families were far less likely than Section 8 families—and at very high levels of statistical significance—to report problems with trash/litter on the street, drug users/dealers, people drinking in public, and abandoned buildings in their new neighborhoods. At this stage, the extent to which these differences are correlated with families' abilities to perceive and to take advantage of opportunities in their new neighborhoods remains unclear. Yet, what matters now, both from an academic and a policy perspective, is determining how these differences may influence families' abilities to adjust to—and their desire to remain in—their new surroundings.

Adjusting to a New Neighborhood

Our analysis of personal adjustment looks at how the respondents and their children liked their new neighborhoods and at how receptive movers found their new neighbors to be. This section also examines how moving affected kin and friendship networks and reports qualitative data on good and bad events experienced by movers in their new neighborhoods.

The analysis of short-term adjustment addresses four general questions, with a true-false response format, on feelings about the new neighborhood (table 10.4). Overall, the results paint a somewhat contradictory story. On the one hand, a majority of respondents answered affirmatively to the statements, "This neighborhood is a good place for me to live" and "I feel at home in this neighborhood." These positive responses suggest that families, both in the experimental and the comparison groups, were initially adjusting well to their new surroundings. But answers to the two remaining general statements—"It is important for me to live in this

Table 10.4. *Percentages of MTO and Section 8 Families Exhibiting Positive Adjustment to Their New Neighborhoods*

Survey statement	Percent indicating that the statement is true	
	MTO	Section 8
This neighborhood is a good place for me to live	91	72***
I feel at home in this neighborhood	93	92
It is important for me to live in this neighborhood	71	43***
I expect to live in this neighborhood for a long time	62	45*

Source: Survey of Chicago MTO participants.

*$p \leq .05$; ***$p \leq .0001$ (one-tailed test for differences between MTO and Section 8).

neighborhood" and "I expect to live in this neighborhood for a long time"—were more mixed. A majority of MTO household heads, but less than half of Section 8 household heads, answered "true" to each question. It may be that respondents were referring to the poor state of their old neighborhoods when reacting to these statements. If so, their answers suggest that it is important for them to be living outside the projects, not in that *particular* destination neighborhood.

The significantly higher proportions of MTO families reporting positive news—that their chosen destination neighborhoods are good places for them to live, places they consider important to live in, and places they expect to remain in for a long time—may reflect the differences, reported earlier, in perceived levels of social disorder and neighborhood quality. Alternatively, the responses may reflect the experimental movers' greater ability to satisfy their preferences for living in mixed neighborhoods. Given that Section 8 families were more likely than MTO families to see problems in the social fabric of their new neighborhoods, and less likely to have satisfied their preferences, they may be less likely to consider it important for them to live in, or remain in, their new neighborhoods.

The reception of movers' neighbors likely affect how comfortable newcomers feel. Past housing relocation programs suggest that neighbors' reception may be especially relevant when movers are low-income families. Families that moved from the projects under the auspices of the Gautreaux program, MTO's precursor, reported that, at least initially, they encountered a certain amount of hostility from their new neighbors (Rosenbaum et al. 1996).

To assess how families felt about their reception in the new neighbor-hoods, we asked a series of questions about the degree to which they were greeted with friendly gestures, indifference, or outright hostility. The results were, in general, positive. Only nine respondents overall reported that their new neighbors were either "somewhat unfriendly" or "very unfriendly" to them when they moved in. In contrast, 42 percent of MTO families and 34 percent of Section 8 families said that their new neighbors were very friendly, while 50 percent and 59 percent, respectively, said that their new neighbors were somewhat friendly (differences not significant). The similarity in the two groups' responses was somewhat unexpected. Because the comparison group moved to neighborhoods that, on aver-age, tended to house more people with similar characteristics, we might expect them to have an easier time making friends and getting along in their new neighborhoods (Briggs 1997).

Although the general story is that new neighbors were, for the most part, friendly, the majority of our respondents reported that their neigh-bors did not generally go out of their way to help them settle in (59 per-cent of MTO and 62 percent of Section 8 families, though differences were not statistically significant). Open-ended questions asked about neighbors' friendly gestures. In general, the friendliness of neighbors involved a lot of practical advice about bus routes and where to shop, help moving furniture, and neighborly favors, gestures that can enhance feel-ings of being welcomed. For example, one MTO respondent reported that "neighbors will accept UPS packages so that they don't get sent back." Another reported that a "welcoming committee of five or six neighbors came over and brought lots of food. I was shocked. I had only seen things like this on TV." Only three MTO and two Section 8 families reported specific incidents of unfriendliness. However, none of these instances involved extreme hostility. For example, one respondent spoke of an "older lady downstairs [who] called the police when [she] had family over for a housewarming." Another mentioned that her son had a fight with another child (who was about 5 years old). Thus, our data turned up little evidence of hostile reactions for either group of families.

When asked about routine interactions (i.e., how often a mover gets together with new neighbors) the comparison and experimental groups responded quite differently, likely because Section 8 families tended to live among families more like them: 23 percent of the comparison group reported getting together with neighbors several times a week or more; only 9 percent ($N = 6$) of the experimental group reported interacting with their new neighbors as often (difference is significant at $p \leq .05$). Although the Section 8 families reported a higher degree of frequent "neighboring," MTO families generally were not socially marginalized in their new environments. Indeed, about 28 percent reported getting together with their neighbors between once a week and once a month, compared with 26 percent of Section 8 families, a difference that is not statistically significant.

The higher degree of very frequent neighboring we find among comparison families may reflect the greater similarity between these families and their new neighbors. One such factor may be the average distance moved by families in each group, and thus how geographically strained ties to family and friends become after the move. We asked a series of questions to try to assess how far families moved from their family members and friends, and how this distance affected their ability to see their friends and family. Not surprisingly, after moving, MTO respondents were significantly more likely to report that they lived farther from their family (64 percent) and friends (89 percent) than did Section 8 respondents (34 percent for family and 59 percent for friends; $p \leq .001$ for both comparisons). However, respondents in both the MTO and the Section 8 groups did not report being overly distressed about the increased distances from friends and family. In fact, one respondent said, "I feel good [about being farther away] . . . they might want to move in."

Because Section 8 families were less likely to move further away from friends and family, the "neighbors" they had in mind when responding more likely consisted of the same people they got together with before their moves. Indeed, when questioned about whether they see their friends and family members more or less frequently after moving, the Section 8 respondents said they were slightly more likely to see family and friends more often (41 percent see family more often, 18 percent see friends more often, versus 22 percent and 10 percent of MTO respondents for each question; the difference for seeing family is significant at $p \leq .05$; the difference for visiting with friends just missed being significant at $p \leq .10$). Similarly, Section 8 respondents were more likely than MTO respondents to report that the people they confide in, borrow money from, relax with, and receive help from lived in their current neighborhood, while MTO families were more likely to report that the people they confide in and receive help from lived in their old neighborhoods (table 10.5). However, on each of these dimensions, respondents said the people they relied on lived "someplace else" (i.e., neither the

Table 10.5. *Type and Location of Social Ties among MTO and Section 8 Mover Families in Chicago*

Type and location	MTO	Section 8
People you seek advice from:		
Current neighborhood	.03	.17**
Old neighborhood	.30	.15*
Someplace else	.67	.66
People who will lend you money:		
Current neighborhood	.11	.24*
Old neighborhood	.25	.16
Someplace else	.60	.55
People you relax with:		
Current neighborhood	.19	.23
Old neighborhood	.20	.17
Someplace else	.56	.56
People who will help:		
Current neighborhood	.15	.29**
Old neighborhood	.23	.08**
Someplace else	.52	.52

Source: Survey of Chicago MTO participants.

Notes: Figures may not sum to 100 percent because some respondents provided answers indicating that they had no ties at all.

*p ≤ .05; **p ≤ .01 (one-tailed test for differences between MTO and Section 8).

new nor the old neighborhood), suggesting that moving someplace new does not directly affect the viability of social ties. Thus, our data initially suggest that the "new" neighboring relationships being forged by Section 8 respondents may be strengthened versions of previously existing social ties to friends and family. In contrast, MTO respondents were more likely to rely on ties in their old neighborhoods. Still, the fact that more than half of all respondents indicated that their social networks were located someplace other than the new or the old neighborhood complicates matters. We cannot simply conclude that social ties keep MTO respondents strongly linked to their old neighborhoods. Furthermore, without being able to better determine which ties benefit program participants (for example, ties that "help you to get by" and those that "help you get ahead" [Briggs 1997]), it is impossible to evaluate the importance of this finding at this stage.

An important factor in respondents' adjustment to their new neighborhoods would likely be how their children dealt with the move. Our survey data suggest that most children wanted to move and were getting along well with the other children in their new neighborhoods. For example, most respondents in both the experimental and comparison groups reported that their children had wanted to move (79 percent and 91 percent, respectively; $p \leq .05$). Similarly high percentages reported their children were currently satisfied or very satisfied with the neighborhood (90 percent and 96 percent; results not statistically significant). Part of children's overall satisfaction with their new neighborhoods may reflect the apparent ease they feel in making friends; only 12 percent of all families reported it was harder for their children to make friends in the new neighborhood, and less than 13 percent reported that it was hard or very hard for their children to find someone to hang out with. Indeed, in open-ended questions, most mothers reported positive things about their children's abilities to make friends and the sense of added safety, which allowed children to play outside more often. For example, one mother talked about how many more activities her children had become involved in after moving. By contrast, her children had stayed indoors all the time in the old neighborhood to avoid fights. She summed it up by saying she was "astonished at how children in different environments behave. It's really, really been an uplift." Cases where children did not adjust well or make friends typically involved older children still going to their old schools and still attached to friends in their old neighborhoods.

Explaining Short-Term Adjustment

According to our descriptive analyses, MTO families expressed a higher degree of positive feelings of adjustment in their new neighborhoods than did Section 8 families. The logical question, then, is what explains this difference? To what extent do adjustment differences reflect the fact that MTO families had to move to low-poverty neighborhoods, that MTO families' counseling may have eased their adjustment, or that Section 8 families were much less likely to translate their preferences for mixed neighborhoods into living in such neighborhoods? To what extent does the creation of new ties in the new neighborhood help families adjust? To what extent do neighborhood problems impede the adjustment process? Regression analysis allows an initial—and essentially exploratory—attempt at answering these questions (table 10.6).

The dependent variable measuring positive adjustment is an index created as the mean score on three of the four true-false statements on respondents' feelings about their neighborhoods (range from 0 [not adjusting] to 1 [positively adjusting], mean = .6556, standard deviation [s.d.] = .3766, α = .7464). The three statements used are, "This neighborhood is a good place for me to live," "It is important for me to live in this neighborhood," and "I expect to live in this neighborhood for a long time."[13]

The model includes a total of five independent variables: a dummy variable for assignment group status (1 = MTO, 0 = Section 8); an index of "feelings of safety" created as the mean score on the four safety-rating variables discussed above, with scores ranging from 1.25 (very unsafe) to 4.00 (very safe) (mean = 3.2215, s.d. = .5773); a sum of four possible social ties reported for the new neighborhood (created from the variables indicating the location of persons respondents confide in, relax with, borrow money from, and receive help from; range from 0 to 4,

Table 10.6. *Results of Regression Models Predicting Adjustment to New Neighborhoods by MTO and Section 8 Families in Post-Move Survey, Chicago*

Independent variable	Bivariate	Full model
MTO (versus Section 8)	.217**	.066
	(.067)	(.071)
Index of feelings of safety	.385***	.346***
	(.048)	(.056)
Number of social ties in new neighborhood	−.007	.011
	(.034)	(.028)
Number of neighborhood problems	−.091***	−.029
	(.021)	(.021)
Preferences for mixed areas not met:	−.219**	−.042
moved to mostly black area	(.071)	(.069)
Intercept		−.454
Adjusted R^2		.363

Source: Survey of Chicago MTO participants.

Notes: Figures are unstandardized coefficients; standard errors appear in parentheses. Results are based on a sample of 116 families.

**$p \leq .01$; ***$p \leq .001$.

mean = .6555, s.d = 1.0369); the total number of neighborhood problems, created as the sum of the five indicators described earlier (trash/litter, drug dealers/users, people drinking in public, graffiti, and abandoned buildings), with scores that range from 0 (indicating no neighborhood problems) to 5 (indicating that all five conditions are considered problems) (mean = 1.3500, s.d. = 1.5592); and a dummy variable that measures whether or not the family's preference for a particular neighborhood was met (mean = .3596, s.d. = .4820). Specifically, this variable is coded 1 if the preference was for a mixed neighborhood but the destination neighborhood proved to be "mostly black" and 0 if the family's preferences were either met or the members wanted a mixed neighborhood and moved to some other type of mixed neighborhood.[14]

While essentially an exploratory analysis, we expect that having social ties in the new neighborhood and having a sense of safety will enhance adjustment. In contrast, we expect that living in a neighborhood that did not match the family's preference (i.e., a family preferring a mixed setting moves to a mostly black neighborhood) will impede the adjustment process, as will the number of neighborhood problems. The first column of table 10.6 presents bivariate regression coefficients that, by and large, support our expectations. At the bivariate level, MTO families were significantly more adjusted to their new areas ($p \leq .01$), as were respondents with higher scores on the safety scale ($p \leq .001$). In contrast, families whose preferences for mixed neighborhoods were not satisfied scored significantly lower on our measure of adjustment than did families whose preferences were satisfied ($p \leq .01$). The number of neighborhood problems is also negatively associated with adjustment ($p \leq .001$). Contrary to expectations, at the bivariate level, the coefficient for social ties is negative (although very small in size) and not significantly related to our index of positive adjustment.

The second column of table 10.6 reports results for the full model. In the presence of the full range of controls, program-group status no longer bears a statistically significant relationship to adjustment, and only feelings of safety significantly predict adjustment. Other analyses (not shown) indicate that the significantly lower levels of adjustment among Section 8 families at the bivariate level weaken in strength and significance when we only control for the unmet preferences variable, suggesting that the higher level of "disappointment" experienced by Section 8 families may contribute to the differences in the two groups' adjustment.[15] However, additional models (not shown) that jointly control for feelings of safety and neighborhood problems, absent other controls, eliminate the significant difference in adjustment between MTO and Section 8 families. The finding that the unmet preferences variable loses significance in the full model suggests that the positive changes occurring in new neighborhoods, in particular the enhanced feelings of safety, may counter the negative impact that the "disappointment" they may feel has on their ability to positively adjust and to feel good about their new neighborhoods.

Early Impacts

This chapter evaluates the gains in housing and neighborhood quality achieved by families participating in the Chicago MTO site, the extent to which participating families have positively adjusted to their new neighborhoods, and the factors associated with families' ability to positively adjust. Overall, MTO families reported higher levels of housing quality after moving than did Section 8 families. In addition, MTO families were significantly more able to exchange their low-quality units for units they rated as high in quality. MTO families' greater success in finding quality housing likely reflects the requirement that they move to low-poverty neighborhoods and to the counseling and landlord lists they received. Significantly, when poor families are given housing subsidies and other assistance in moving to low-poverty neighborhoods, they substantially improve their housing status, a key (although often overlooked) indicator of overall well-being (Rosenbaum 1996).

In evaluating neighborhood quality, we found that almost all MTO families and Section 8 families reported housing problems, neighborhood problems, and fears for personal safety while residing in Chicago's public housing projects. Reports of such problems dramatically declined after the families moved to their new neighborhoods. Even more important, MTO families were much less likely than Section 8 families to report problems of social disorder and physical deterioration in their new neighborhoods. Our analysis of census data corroborates these findings; on all available measures, MTO families moved to tracts that had higher overall economic status, more racially and ethnically diverse populations, and more opportunities for socioeconomic advancement.

According to our analysis of how movers adjusted to their new neighborhoods, MTO families tended to do better than Section 8 families, a difference that may reflect MTO families' greater success at relocating to their preferred type of neighborhood (i.e., racially mixed) and the overall higher-quality rating they provided for their new neighborhoods. Families that felt safer in their new neighborhoods, and those that succeeded in establishing new social ties, would likely adjust more easily. Our regression models, while essentially exploratory, tended to bear out these expectations. In particular, in the full model, the index of feelings of personal safety proved to be the sole significant predictor of positive adjustment. The increased ease that comes with feeling safe and knowing that your children are safe may have helped mothers feel more positively about their new neighborhoods. In addition, it could encourage them to stay and to take advantage of the opportunities available in their new neighborhoods.

Despite these encouraging findings, we also find that controlling for the unmet preferences variable greatly weakened the strength and significance of the differences in adjustment exhibited by MTO and Section 8 families. This effect suggests that disappointment among Section 8 families, who often failed to move to their preferred types of neighborhoods, hurt their ability to feel positively about, and thus adjust to, their new neighborhoods. If correct, this interpretation raises important policy issues about the persistent housing market barriers that prevent poor and minority families from accessing preferred neighborhoods. Surveyed Section 8 families, who stated clear preferences for mixed neighborhoods, received subsidies enabling them to access the private rental market. Left to navigate that market on their own, however, a disproportionate share moved to mostly black neighborhoods. This failure to fulfill preferences suggests that external forces can predetermine the types of neighborhoods available to poor and minority households (Rosenbaum 1992, 1994; Turner 1993). MTO families' greater ability to satisfy their preferences for living in mixed neighborhoods may stem from the program's requirement that they relocate to low-poverty neighborhoods. The housing counseling and search assistance received by MTO families also likely played a key role in enabling these families to satisfy their preferences. Such an interpretation is consistent with evidence that families receiving Section 8 certificates/vouchers along with supportive services had better locational outcomes than families that had to navigate the housing market on their own (Turner 1998). This finding suggests that supportive services should be an integral part of future housing mobility programs.

NOTES

1. However, a growing amount of evidence also points to the existence of positive social ties and social capital in very poor communities and how residents and communities benefit from being tied into such networks (Leavitt and Saegert 1990; Williams and Kornblum 1994).

2. Our original research plan was to conduct two telephone surveys with MTO participants who moved. The first survey would be conducted as soon after the move as we could obtain the participants' contact information, and the second would be conducted three to six months later. For a wide range of reasons, including the administrative problems detailed in the text, our original research plan proved impossible to carry out.

3. Of the 77 households responding to survey 1, we were able to recontact 55, or 71.4 percent. For survey 2, only two of the 77 [2.6 percent] refused to be reinterviewed; another two [2.6 percent] were ill and unable to be reinterviewed; and 18 [23.3 percent] were lost to follow-up. Of the 114 households we could not interview at all, only three (1.3 percent of 234) refused to participate outright. Another three (1.3 percent) were ill or were not in the program. We were unable to locate a total of 108 households (46.2 percent of 234), despite all our efforts. The fact that outright refusals overall were very rare suggests that if we had access to better or more timely contact information, our overall sample sizes would have been much closer to the target goal for lease-ups.

4. In fact, the waiting lists for Section 8 participation in Chicago were so long that the lists were closed for a period of time.

5. To evaluate purely "objective" neighborhood characteristics, we must rely on census data, although we fully recognize that our program participants likely do not conceptualize their own neighborhoods along those lines. Thus, it is unwise to directly compare the comparison based on census-based indicators with that of the reports of neighborhood and housing quality made by our respondents (see next section).

6. The destination tracts used to compute the summary statistics in table 10.1 are the tracts in which we found the respondents for our post-move survey. Twenty-one households (10 MTO and 11 Section 8) had moved away from their first program-related new housing unit by the time we were able to contact them. About half the MTO households in this group moved to new tracts with substantially higher poverty rates, while the other half moved either to low-poverty or moderate-poverty (10–19 percent) tracts. Thus, in table 10.A2 we replicate table 10.1 but use as the destination tracts the first tracts to which participating families moved.

7. The average poverty rate for MTO destination tracts in table 10.1, 10.6 percent, exceeds the level one would expect if all MTO households were, in fact, in low-poverty tracts. As indicated in the previous note, a number of MTO households had moved away from their first program-related housing unit before we were able to contact them. When we use the first tracts to which the households in our sample moved (table 10.A1), the average poverty rate for MTO destination tracts is 8.32 percent.

8. "Other" likely indicates a mixture of three or more groups. When asked to specify what they meant by "other," four respondents said a "mix of everything," while others listed specific groups, such as "black, white, Puerto Rican," and a "mix of black, white, Hispanic, Jamaican, and Puerto Rican."

9. Clearly, the mandate that MTO families move to low-poverty neighborhoods also makes them more likely to find housing in mixed, rather than predominantly black, neighborhoods.

10. Respondents could choose from three response categories: the condition was a "big problem," a "small problem," or "not a problem at all." To simplify the analysis, we divided responses into "problem" and "not a problem."

11. The original scale consisted of four points (from "very safe" to "very unsafe"), which we recoded into one "safe" category, and one "unsafe" category.

12. Again, while the original coding had three categories ("big problem," "small problem," "no problem at all"), we divided responses into "problem" and "no problem."

13. We eliminated the statement, "I feel at home in this neighborhood," because in both groups, the overwhelming majority responded affirmatively (93 percent and 92 percent of MTO and Section 8 respondents). This decision did not greatly affect the underlying reliability of the scale of adjustment; when the four measures are used, $\alpha = .7506$.

14. Because we did not repeat the same categories of racial/ethnic composition as were used on the baseline survey, it is impossible to tell if a given category of mixed composition from one survey really differs from another category of mixed composition on the second survey. Still, unmet expectations seem clear when a household's preferences were for mixed composition but the respondent described the new area as mostly black.

15. While the impact of this variable may well reflect the "disappointment" that may arise when preferences are not satisfied, this variable may also be picking up differences in the racial/ethnic and poverty concentration of the destination neighborhoods chosen by families. We control for that to a degree in the full model by controlling for number of neighborhood problems.

REFERENCES

Anderson, Elijah. 1990. *Streetwise.* Chicago: University of Chicago Press.

Apgar, William. 1993. "An Abundance of Housing for All but the Poor." In *Housing Markets and Residential Mobility,* edited by G. Thomas Kingsley and Margery Turner (99–124). Washington, D.C.: Urban Institute Press.

Briggs, Xavier de Souza. 1997. "Moving Up Versus Moving Out: Neighborhood Effects in Housing Mobility Programs." *Housing Policy Debate* 8(1): 195–234.

Coulton, Claudia, Julian Chow, Edward Wang, and Marilyn Su. 1996. "Geographic Concentration of Affluence and Poverty in 100 Metropolitan Areas." *Urban Affairs Review* 32: 186–97.

Davis, Mary. 1993. "The Gautreaux Assisted Housing Program." In *Housing Markets and Residential Mobility,* edited by G. Thomas Kingsley and Margery Austin Turner (243–53). Washington, D.C.: Urban Institute Press.

Denton, Nancy. 1994. "Are African Americans Still Hypersegregated in 1990?" In *Residential Apartheid: The American Legacy,* edited by Robert Bullard, Charles Lee, and J. Eugene Grigsby III (49–81). Los Angeles: UCLA Center for African American Studies.

Denton, Nancy, and Bridget Anderson. 1995. "A Tale of Five Cities: Neighborhood Change in Philadelphia, Chicago, Miami, Houston, and Los Angeles, 1970–1990." Paper presented at annual meeting of the Population Association of America, San Francisco, Apr. 6–8.

Donaldson, Greg. 1993. *The Ville*. New York: Anchor/Doubleday.

Edin, Kathryn, and Kathleen Mullan Harris. 1999. "Getting Off and Staying Off: Differences in the Work Route Off Welfare." In *Latinas and African American Women at Work*, edited by Irene Brown (270–301). New York: Russell Sage Foundation.

Edin, Kathryn, and Laura Lein. 1997. *Making Ends Meet*, New York· Russell Sage Foundation.

Elliott, Delbert, William Julius Wilson, David Huizinga, Robert Sampson, Amanda Elliott, and Bruce Rankin. 1996. "The Effects of Neighborhood Disadvantage on Adolescent Development." *Journal of Research in Crime and Delinquency* 33(4): 389–426.

Farley, Reynolds. 1993. "Neighborhood Preferences and Aspirations among Whites and Blacks." In *Housing Markets and Residential Mobility*, edited by G. Thomas Kingsley and Margery Turner (161–91). Washington, D.C.: Urban Institute Press.

Farley, Reynolds, Elaine Fielding, and Maria Krysan. 1997. "The Residential Preferences of Blacks and Whites: A Four-Metropolis Analysis." *Housing Policy Debate* 8(4): 763–800.

Farley, Reynolds, Charlotte Steeh, Maria Krysan, Tara Jackson, and Keith Reeves. 1994. "Stereotypes and Segregation: Neighborhoods in the Detroit Area." *American Journal of Sociology* 100(3): 750–80.

Goering, John, Joan Kraft, Judith Feins, Debra McInnis, Mary Joel Holin, and Huda Elhassan. 1999. *Moving to Opportunity for Fair Housing Demonstration Program: Current Status and Initial Findings*. Washington, D.C.: U.S. Department of Housing and Urban Development.

Harris, Kathleen Mullan. 1996. "Life after Welfare: Women, Work, and Repeat Dependency." *American Sociological Review* 61(3): 407–26.

Harris, Laura. 1999. "A Home Is More Than Just a House: A Spatial Analysis of Housing for the Poor in Metropolitan America." Ph.D. Dissertation, State University of New York at Albany.

Jencks, Christopher, and Susan Mayer. 1990. "The Social Consequences of Growing Up in a Poor Neighborhood." In *Inner-City Poverty in the United States*, edited by Laurence Lynn and Michael McGeary (111–86). Washington, D.C.: National Academy Press.

Kotlowitz, Alex. 1991. *There Are No Children Here*. New York: Anchor Books.

Kozol, Jonathan. 1995. *Amazing Grace*. New York: Harper Collins.

Leavitt, Jacqueline, and Susan Saegert. 1990. *From Abandonment to Hope*. New York: Columbia University Press.

Lemann, Nicholas. 1991. *The Promised Land*. New York: Vintage.

Massey, Douglas, and Nancy Denton. 1993. *American Apartheid: Segregation and the Making of the Underclass*. Cambridge, Mass.: Harvard University Press.

Newman, Sandra, and Ann Schnare. 1997. " '. . . And a Suitable Living Environment': The Failure of Housing Programs to Deliver on Neighborhood Quality." *Housing Policy Debate* 8(4): 703–42.

Oliver, Melvin, and Thomas Shapiro. 1995. *Black Wealth/White Wealth: A New Perspective on Racial Inequality.* New York: Routledge.

Pavetti, LaDonna. 1993. "The Dynamics of Welfare and Work: Exploring the Process by Which Young Women Work Their Way Off Welfare." Ph.D. Dissertation, Harvard University, John F. Kennedy School of Government.

Popkin, Susan, Victoria Gwiasda, Lynn Olson, Dennis Rosenbaum, and Larry Buron. 2000. *The Hidden War: Crime and the Tragedy of Public Housing in Chicago.* New Brunswick, N.J.: Rutgers University Press.

Rosenbaum, Emily. 1992. "Race and Ethnicity in Housing: Turnover in New York City, 1978–1987." *Demography* 29(3): 467–86.

———. 1996. "Racial/Ethnic Differences in Homeownership and Housing Quality, 1991." *Social Problems* 43(4): 201–24.

Rosenbaum, James, Nancy Fishman, Alison Brett, and Patricia Meaden. 1996. "Can the Kerner Commission's Housing Strategy Improve Employment, Education, and Social Integration for Low-Income Blacks?" In *Race, Poverty, and American Cities,* edited by John Charles Boger and Judith Welch Wegner (273–308). Chapel Hill: University of North Carolina Press.

St. John, Craig, and N. Bates. 1990. "Racial Composition and Neighborhood Evaluation." *Social Science Research* 19: 44–61.

Skogan, Wesley. 1990. *Disorder and Decline.* Berkeley: University of California Press.

Stack, Carol. 1974. *All Our Kin.* New York: Harper and Row.

Tienda, Marta. 1991. "Poor People and Poor Places: Deciphering Neighborhood Effects on Poverty Outcomes." In *Micromacro Linkages in Sociology,* edited by Joan Huber (244–62). Newbury Park, Calif.: Sage Publishing.

Turner, Margery Austin. 1993. "Limits on Neighborhood Choice: Evidence of Racial and Ethnic Steering in Urban Housing Markets." In *Clear and Convincing Evidence: Measurement of Discrimination in America,* edited by Michael Fix and Raymond Struyk (118–47). Washington, D.C.: Urban Institute Press.

———. 1998. "Moving Out of Poverty: Expanding Mobility and Choice through Tenant-Based Housing Assistance." *Housing Policy Debate* 9(2): 373–94.

Williams, Terry, and William Kornblum. 1994. *Uptown Kids.* New York: Putnam.

Wilson, William Julius. 1987. *The Truly Disadvantaged.* Chicago: University of Chicago Press.

———. 1996. *When Work Disappears.* New York: Knopf.

Yinger, John. 1995. *Closed Doors, Opportunities Lost: The Continuing Costs of Housing Discrimination.* New York: Russell Sage Foundation.

Zubrinsky, Camille, and Lawrence Bobo. 1996. "Prismatic Metropolis." *Social Science Research* 25: 335–74.

Table 10.A1. *Comparisons of Interviewed and Noninterviewed Mothers, According to Program-Group Assignment*

	Interview status	
Program group/characteristic	Interviewed	Not interviewed
Section 8		
Social distance attitudes		
Proportion feeling good or very good about:		
Having children attend a school where more than half of the children are white	78.13	57.63***
	(41.67)	(49.84)
Having children attend a school where almost all of the children are white	56.25	31.67***
	(50.00)	(46.91)
Living in a neighborhood where more than half of the people earn more	64.62	48.33*
	(48.19)	(50.39)
Living in a neighborhood where almost all of the people earn more	44.62	33.90
	(50.10)	(47.74)
Outlook		
Proportion feeling sure or very sure that they would:		
Be able to find an apartment in a different area	78.13	75.81
	(41.67)	(43.18)
Like living in a neighborhood they had never lived in	89.23	75.81**
	(43.41)	(43.18)
Get along with their neighbors after they move	80.00	80.65
	(40.31)	(39.83)

(continued)

Table 10.A1. *Comparisons of Interviewed and Noninterviewed Mothers, According to Program-Group Assignment (Continued)*

	Interview status	
Program group/characteristic	*Interviewed*	*Not interviewed*
Like living in a neighborhood with people who earn more	75.38	62.30
	(43.41)	(48.87)
Have a job after they move	66.15	74.19
	(47.69)	(44.11)
Keep their children from hanging around with kids who get in trouble after they move	90.77	91.94
	(29.17)	(27.45)
$N \geq$	64	59
MTO		
Social distance attitudes		
Proportion feeling good or very good about:		
Having children attend a school where more than half of the children are white	76.47	78.26
	(42.84)	(41.70)
Having children attend a school where almost all of the children are white	33.33	50.00
	(47.61)	(50.55)
Living in a neighborhood where more than half of the people earn more	52.94	60.87
	(50.41)	(49.34)
Living in a neighborhood where almost all of the people earn more	43.14	45.65
	(50.02)	(50.36)

Outlook

Proportion feeling sure or very sure that they would:

Be able to find an apartment in a different area	76.47	76.09
	(42.84)	(43.13)
Like living in a neighborhood they had never lived in	82.35	82.61
	(38.50)	(38.32)
Get along with their neighbors after they move	86.00	86.96
	(35.05)	(34.05)
Like living in a neighborhood with people who earn more	74.00	76.09
	(44.31)	(43.13)
Have a job after they move	64.71	71.74
	(48.26)	(45.52)
Keep their children from hanging around with kids who get in trouble after they move	94.12	97.83
	(23.76)	(14.74)
$N \geq$	51	46

Source: Survey of Chicago MTO participants.

*$p \leq .10$; **$p \leq .05$; ***$p \leq .01$; two-tailed t-test.

Table 10.A2. *Summary Statistics Based on Selected Census Tract Characteristics (1990)* (percent)

Tract characteristic	Origin tracts (118)[a]	Destination tracts	
		Section 8 (51)[a]	MTO (66)[a]
Racial/ethnic composition			
Percent non-Hispanic black	99.29	89.35	54.08
	(0.79)	(21.13)	(37.87)
Percent non-Hispanic white	0.11	6.04	38.25
	(0.20)	(13.21)	(32.42)
Percent Hispanic	0.60	3.58	6.09
	(0.70)	(8.95)	(8.96)
Economic status			
Percent of tract population in poverty	74.99	34.83	8.31
	(13.70)	(15.69)	(5.47)
Percent of households receiving public assistance	58.61	30.14	8.61
	(16.06)	(13.66)	(6.16)
Median household income	$6,211.92	$18,076.85	$35,476.06
	($1,678.38)	($8,903.05)	($7,381.40)
Percent of homes owner-occupied	2.82	27.56	69.52
	(4.81)	(22.58)	(17.34)
Social context			
Percent of female-headed families and subfamilies	84.72	64.75	34.00
	(5.97)	(16.68)	(14.17)
Percent of adolescents age 16–19 neither enrolled nor graduated from high school	17.03	17.27	8.59
	(10.93)	(10.74)	(8.08)
Percent of adult population (25+) with high school degree	25.94	27.17	27.79
	(4.01)	(5.63)	(7.38)
Percent of adult population (25+) with college degree	8.07	16.13	24.80
	(3.43)	(11.14)	(13.59)
Percent of population age 16 and older in the civilian labor force	38.13	56.66	68.98
	(7.25)	(11.28)	(5.96)
Male employment rate	26.10	47.29	67.44
	(13.42)	(12.91)	(10.03)

Source: Urban Underclass database.
Notes: All figures are means; standard deviations appear in parentheses.
a. Number of unique tracts.

PART III
Research and
Policy Implications

11

Do Neighborhoods Matter and Why?

Ingrid Gould Ellen
Margery Austin Turner

Social scientists have wondered about the effects of neighborhoods on families and children since at least the 1940s (Shaw and McKay 1942). But interest has grown in recent years, a growth many trace to the publication of William Julius Wilson's *The Truly Disadvantaged* in 1987. Over the past two decades, researchers from a wide range of social science disciplines have used nonexperimental data to investigate whether neighborhood environments have an impact on the lives of families and children. While most of these studies find evidence that neighborhoods matter, they suffer from data limitations that make it difficult to pinpoint causality. Most critically, none can say with certainty whether neighborhoods actually shape behavioral outcomes or whether the apparent link between neighborhood and outcomes simply reflects self-selection. Moreover, the evidence about why neighborhoods may matter is even less clear. Yet understanding what is inside the "black box" of neighborhood effects is critical to evaluate and make policy recommendations.

The research in this volume advances our understanding of neighborhood effects, and future study of the MTO demonstration outcomes will undoubtedly push it further still. This chapter places the contributions of MTO in the context of other social science research. It begins by exploring whether neighborhoods matter, summarizing what we now know about the impacts of neighborhoods across different life stages and highlighting the particular contributions of the MTO research. The second part of the chapter explores why, and how, neighborhoods make a difference. It outlines a number of theories explaining the role that neighborhoods play in shaping social outcomes and summarizes the empirical evidence—both from MTO studies and other research—behind these possible mechanisms.

Do Neighborhoods Matter?

While many empirical studies have found evidence of neighborhood effects, data limitations raise doubts about their findings. Two key limitations stand out. First, it is difficult to capture the neighborhood characteristics that may be most critical to individual and family outcomes, potentially leading to attenuation bias (that is, unduly weak estimates). The second issue is that neighborhood choice is endogenous, that is, households choose the neighborhoods they live in, and the same factors that lead them to choose certain neighborhoods may also lead them to particular individual outcomes. Thus, the links we observe between neighborhood characteristics and outcomes may not be causal ones.

Relevant Neighborhood Characteristics

A fundamental challenge in studying neighborhood effects is defining appropriate neighborhood boundaries. Empirical researchers typically measure neighborhoods by census tracts, well-defined units of spatial analysis through which much data are reported. However, census tracts may fail to accurately represent the neighborhood boundaries that make a difference in people's lives. In some cases, conditions on a family's block, such as crime or vandalism, may most affect them. In others, conditions in a larger geographic area, such as a school enrollment area, might be the key influence. In general, if researchers are measuring neighborhood characteristics at the wrong scale, they are likely to understate the importance of neighborhood conditions in affecting individual outcomes.

A related challenge is getting the measures right. Most studies of neighborhood effects use one or more proxies to represent neighborhood conditions, such as the poverty rate, the average income level, or the proportion of adults in managerial or professional jobs.[1] But these proxies may not accurately reflect the neighborhood attributes that really matter, and if they do, they might not tell us how policy interventions should be targeted. For example, high crime rates or poor school quality (not simply high poverty) may make a neighborhood an unhealthy place to live. Unfortunately, because many symptoms of neighborhood distress are highly correlated, researchers have had much difficulty differentiating their effects empirically. Moreover, a growing number of analysts argue that neighborhoods that appear similar on standard socioeconomic indicators vary significantly in their social capital or civic infrastructure. These differences, in turn, may play a major role in determining the impact of the community environment on neighborhood and individual outcomes (Coulton and Pandey 1992; Putnam 1995; Temkin and Rohe 1997).

Finally, with only a few exceptions, empirical research on neighborhood effects has typically used data that describe neighborhood characteristics at a single point in time. But neighborhoods change over time. Thus, point-in-time measures may not capture neighborhood conditions for the period in which they actually make a difference in a person's life. More specifically, a point-in-time measure (such as poverty rate or unemployment rate) may not accurately reflect the environment that a person was exposed to during the time he or she lived in a neighborhood.

The MTO demonstration was designed to measure the impact of moves from high-poverty to low-poverty census tracts. Accordingly, the first round of data analysis naturally focused on census tracts as the neighborhood unit and on poverty as a key indicator of neighborhood conditions. However, researchers can assemble other data about both origin and destination locations for MTO and comparison households, drawing on 1990 and 2000 census data, as well as other locally available data. Several recent studies have used survey data to create more flexible neighborhood definitions and to capture more nuanced neighborhood characteristics.

The Project on Human Development in Chicago Neighborhoods stands out as one such study (Sampson and Raudenbush 1999). For a few months in 1995, observers drove slowly down every street in selected Chicago neighborhoods and videotaped more than 20,000 block-faces. Trained observers recorded notes at the same time. While studies like this one provide nuanced neighborhood data and allow for flexible neighborhood definitions, they are clearly expensive and difficult to replicate on a large scale. A more affordable strategy would be to employ trained observers to walk through neighborhoods and record descriptions of physical and social conditions. A survey of residents could then complement their observations.

In the area of identifying relevant boundaries, Sampson, Morenoff, and Earls (1999) have used survey data to get information about how individuals define their neighborhoods, a method that also proves relatively expensive. Grannis (1998) uses the geography of street boundaries to define neighborhoods. He finds that residents are more likely to interact with people who live on blocks accessible to pedestrians. Residents are less likely to socialize or interact if they have to cross major thoroughfares. This study suggests that geographic information systems tools can be used to define more meaningful neighborhood boundaries, without having to conduct extensive surveys.

Increasingly available geocoded administrative data make it far easier to use these alternative neighborhood boundaries (Ellen, Schill, et al. 2001). More and more researchers are obtaining current and historical data on crime, schools, vital statistics, school performance, property values, welfare receipt, and other important neighborhood attributes from state and local administrative data systems. Because these data are often available at the address level, they can be aggregated to almost any set of neighborhood boundaries, and they often provide more current and flexible evidence of neighborhood conditions and trends than decennial census data (Kingsley 1998, 1999).

Disentangling Neighborhood and Family Effects

Researchers across the board agree that the well-being of families and children varies across neighborhoods. Ample evidence shows that residents of poor, inner-city neighborhoods are less likely to complete high school and go to college, more likely to be involved in crime (either as victim or as perpetrator), more likely to be a teenage parent, and less likely to hold a decent-paying job (Coulton et al. 1995; Ricketts and Sawhill 1988). Numerous studies also show that residents of poor neighborhoods experience worse health outcomes on average than those living in more prosperous areas (see Ellen, Mijanovich, and Dillman 2001 for review). However, demonstrating that neighborhood conditions actually cause, or magnify, these differences is difficult. It's impossible to tell whether group behavior affects individual behavior or whether group behavior is simply the aggregation of individual behaviors (Manski 2000).[2]

The key methodological challenge is one of isolating the relevant effects. Many of the family and individual attributes that influence a person's life chances may also play a critical role in determining where that person chooses to live. If studies of neighborhood effects fail to adequately control for these individual and family characteristics, they may falsely attribute the effects of the family's own strengths and limitations to the effects of neighborhood conditions. The problem is that while many relevant family characteristics, such as income, education, and race, can be measured easily, other pertinent family characteristics are harder to observe and capture empirically. For example, parents who place a high value on education might choose a neighborhood with well-regarded public schools. These same parents would probably make sure their children attend school and complete their homework, reward them for good grades, and provide greater learning opportunities at home. If their children then performed well in school, their high grades might be the result of either good schools (a neighborhood characteristic) or the parents' demands (a family characteristic), or of some combination of the two.

Most analysts assume that studies failing to adequately control for unobserved (but influential) family characteristics overstate neighborhood effects. As Duncan, Connell, and Klebanov (1997) note, however, omitting these characteristics may sometimes lead one to *understate* the effects of neighborhood. Some parents, for instance, may choose to live in inferior neighborhoods because more affordable housing permits them to work fewer hours and spend more time with their children. In this case, omitting measures of time spent with children will likely bias the estimated neighborhood effect downward. Whatever the direction of the bias, it is clearly important to control for family characteristics and to try to account for these unobserved attributes.

To date, researchers tackled the issue of unobserved family characteristics using three approaches. First, some studies have used nontraditional data sources to attempt to control for the critical parental characteristics that may be correlated with neighborhood location but typically go unobserved, such as assessments of parental warmth, observation of the home-learning environment provided by parents, and incidence of parental separations and remarriages (Brooks-Gunn et al. 1993; Duncan, Brooks-Gunn, and Klebanov 1994; Ginther, Haveman, and Wolfe 2000). While the estimates of neighborhood effects tend to diminish as an analysis broadens its set of family background variables, at least some effects appear to persist, in the case of educational outcomes (Ginther et al. 2000). While efforts to capture a wide set of variables should continue, it seems unlikely that one could ever find data that effectively measure all the parenting factors—such as the quality of time spent with children or the values and morals taught—critical to child outcomes.

Second, researchers have tried using instrumental variables to control for family characteristics. This approach replaces the neighborhood measure with a variable that is highly correlated with the neighborhood characteristic of interest but is not correlated with any unobserved aspects of parenting. For example, Evans, Oates, and Schwab (1992) estimate the proportion of disadvantaged students in a school as a function of conditions in the metropolitan area. They then use the predicted proportions of disadvantaged students, rather than the actual shares, in estimating neighborhood effects. The drawback of this approach, however, is that it is difficult to find a variable that determines neighborhood location but not children's outcomes.[3]

Third, researchers have used fixed-effects models to get around unobserved family characteristics. For instance, some have restricted their analysis to siblings, since children in the same household will presumably be exposed to identical family conditions. The problem, of course, is that most siblings will also be exposed to the same neighborhoods. But both Plotnick and Hoffman (1996) and Aaronson (1997) find sufficient variation across siblings in neighborhood environments to justify such an analysis. Moreover, Weinberg, Reagan, and Yankow (2000) successfully estimated an individual fixed-effects model using Panel Study of Income Dynamics data by observing moves across neighborhoods. These are innovative and important studies, but questions remain about the fixed-effects approach. Most notably, for studies restricted to siblings, unobserved sibling differences may influence parents' decisions to move to new environments. Moreover, other unobserved family changes, such as job changes or changes in marital status, may also prompt moves.

A more promising alternative for dealing with unobserved family characteristics is random assignment. If families are randomly assigned to neighborhoods, any unobserved characteristics will be uncorrelated with their community's attributes. The Moving to Opportunity demonstration comes close to this ideal methodology.

Through MTO, poor families living in public and assisted housing projects in high-poverty neighborhoods were invited to apply for rental vouchers to move to private homes and apartments. As chapter 1 of this volume describes, eligible applicants were randomly assigned to one of three groups:

1. *MTO experimental, or treatment, group.* The MTO experimental group received assistance to move only to low-poverty neighborhoods;

2. *The comparison group.* These families could use their vouchers to move anywhere in the metropolitan area; and
3. *The control group.* These families received no assistance to leave their current public or assisted housing projects.

Over 10 years, families in all three groups are being tracked and monitored to assess their long-term employment, income, and educational outcomes.

Not all families in either the treatment or comparison groups have been successful in finding a suitable house or apartment in a qualifying neighborhood, and some have remained in their original high-poverty environments. Moreover, some of the families that did move to low-poverty neighborhoods moved again fairly quickly, sometimes returning to higher-poverty communities. Finally, some of the comparison or control families undoubtedly found their way to low-poverty neighborhoods on their own, without the help of the MTO treatment. Thus, rather than randomly assigning families to neighborhoods, MTO randomly assigned them to a "treatment" that helped them gain access to different types of neighborhoods.

Thus, comparing relative outcomes across the three MTO groups should answer an important question: Are MTO experimental families (who received vouchers, along with housing search assistance and counseling, and were required to move to a low-poverty area) better-off than comparison families (who received unrestricted vouchers) or control families (who received no assistance in leaving their high-poverty housing projects)? It is important to note that MTO assessments all measure the average effect of the treatment for all families—both those who were successful in moving to low-poverty neighborhoods and those who were unsuccessful and never left their original public housing units. The only way to preserve the power of MTO's random-assignment experimental design is to pool outcomes for all the families receiving a particular treatment. If the analyses focused only on "successful" families (i.e., experimental families that actually moved to a low-poverty neighborhood and stayed there for more than a year), the built-in controls for possible family and individual effects vanish, because successful MTO families may systematically differ from families that failed to use their assistance to move to a low-poverty neighborhood.

Given certain assumptions, however, it is possible to arrive at unbiased estimates of the program's effects on families that actually moved to, and stayed in, a low-poverty area (Bloom 1984). This approach, used in the

Baltimore and Boston studies, effectively compares the outcomes of the families that moved with the outcomes of the control group families that would have moved, had they been offered the treatment (Ludwig, Duncan, and Ladd, this volume; Katz, Kling, and Liebman, this volume). For these estimates to be unbiased, we must make a few assumptions. First, we must assume that assignment to the treatment or Section 8–only group had no effect on families that did not relocate. In other words, we have to assume that any counseling received after initial assignment would have no effect on nonmovers' long-term outcomes. This assumption is unlikely to be entirely true, as Katz, Kling, and Liebman (this volume) point out. But the effects of such counseling are likely to be small relative to the effects of a residential move. Perhaps more troubling is the required assumption that none of the families in the control group received the applicable treatment. While technically true, since none of the control families received counseling and vouchers through the MTO program, some families may have moved into private-market housing in low-poverty neighborhoods on their own. Plus, in the case of the Baltimore site, some families in the control group may have received a voucher through the HOPE VI program (Ludwig, Duncan, and Ladd, this volume).

In short, while the MTO research design does not entirely overcome the endogeneity problem in identifying the actual effects of neighborhood environments, it does allow researchers to arrive at unbiased estimates of the effects of being invited to participate in the MTO program. It also pushes researchers far closer to obtaining unbiased estimates of neighborhood effects.

Available Evidence

This section briefly summarizes existing empirical evidence about the importance of neighborhood across different life stages, highlighting the contributions of MTO analysis. It organizes the evidence by four major life-stages: infancy and preschool, elementary school, adolescence, and adulthood.[4]

INFANTS AND PRESCHOOL CHILDREN

Several studies find evidence that having more affluent neighbors is associated with having a higher IQ among preschool children (Brooks-Gunn et al. 1993; Chase-Lansdale and Gordon 1996; Chase-Lansdale et al. 1997; Duncan et al. 1994). These studies, however, reach mixed conclusions about neighborhood effects on young children's emotional and behavioral problems.

The MTO research in New York City provides the best evidence to date that neighborhoods may shape parenting styles. For example, after moving to low-poverty neighborhoods, mothers' parenting was found to be less strict in the treatment and comparison groups than in the control group. Warmth and affection levels, however, remained unchanged (Leventhal and Brooks-Gunn, this volume).

ELEMENTARY SCHOOL CHILDREN

As children reach school age, their daily frame of reference broadens beyond parents to include teachers, classmates, coaches, and the parents and families of classmates and friends. By observing the social relationships around them, they begin to develop conceptions about what is normal, appropriate behavior. Thus, while families are likely to remain children's dominant source of information and influence during the elementary school years, the broader neighborhood environment should begin to play an increasingly important role.

Nonetheless, few studies have dealt with neighborhood impacts at this stage, perhaps because the outcomes believed to be most important, such as high school completion, employment, and teenage pregnancy, do not occur until after the elementary school years. Halpern-Felsher et al. (1997) consider school performance and find modest evidence that neighborhood matters. Kupersmidt et al. (1995) examine aggressive behavior in a sample of second- through fifth-graders and find some evidence that children living in middle-class neighborhoods display less aggression (as reported by peers) than children from low-socioeconomic-status neighborhoods.

The MTO research contributes to our knowledge of neighborhood impacts on children of this age in several ways. First, the MTO research provides solid evidence that neighborhood environments affect children's health. Both the Boston and New York researchers find that children moving to low-poverty neighborhoods experienced fewer injuries, fewer asthma attacks, and improved mental health. Second, according to these researchers, children moving to low-poverty areas also had fewer behavior problems (such as bullying and disruptive behavior at school). Third, Ludwig, Duncan, and Ladd (this volume) find evidence that moving to low-poverty neighborhoods improves the educational achievement of elementary school children, as measured by reading and math test scores.

ADOLESCENTS

According to one study, adolescents spend twice as much time with peers as with their parents and other adults (Connell and Halpern-Felsher 1997). Not surprisingly, then, most of the research on neighborhood effects has focused on teenagers and young adults. In general, studies have explored one or more of four broad outcomes: educational attainment, employment, sexual activity and teen pregnancy, and criminal involvement.

The literature generally supports the notion that neighborhoods play a role in shaping educational outcomes (Aaronson 1997; Brooks-Gunn et al. 1993; Case and Katz 1991; Clark 1992; Crane 1991; Datcher 1982; Duncan 1994; Duncan et al. 1997; Garner and Raudenbush 1991; Haveman and Wolfe 1996; Rosenbaum 1991). But two recent studies caution that most of these analyses have not fully controlled for the endogeneity of neighborhood location (Evans et al. 1992; Plotnick and Hoffman 1996).[5] The evidence on labor market outcomes for adolescents is somewhat weaker, but of the seven quantitative studies we reviewed, five found some relationship between neighborhood characteristics and labor market success (Case and Katz 1991; Corcoran et al. 1989; Datcher 1982; Massey, Gross, and Eggers 1991; O'Regan and Quigley 1996).

Many studies find evidence to support a relationship between neighborhood environment and sexual activity or pregnancy among adolescents (Brewster 1994; Brewster, Billy, and Grady 1993; Brooks-Gunn et al. 1993; Crane 1991; Hogan and Kitagawa 1985; Hogan, Astone, and Kitagawa 1985; Ku, Sonenstein, and Pleck 1993; Mayer 1991; South and Baumer 2000). But papers by Evans et al. (1992) and Plotnick and Hoffman (1996) suggest some caution. These studies find that after making an effort to control for unobserved family effects that may be correlated with locational choice, neighborhood environment has no independent effect on either pregnancy or teenage births.[6]

Finally, the ethnographic literature strongly suggests that neighborhood environment and social context—along with individual and family characteristics—play an important role in pushing an adolescent toward (or away from) criminal activities (Anderson 1990; Sullivan 1989). Several quantitative studies also find a strong link between a neighborhood's social environment and crime, but they rely on aggregate neighborhood data, making the causality somewhat murky (Glaeser, Sacerdote, and Scheinkman 1995; Sampson and Groves 1989; Sampson, Raudenbush, and Earls 1997). As for the few studies that combine individual and contextual data, the results have been fairly inconclusive (Johnstone 1978; Reiss and Rhodes 1961). Still, Case and Katz (1991), who attempt to control for simultaneity, find strong evidence that teenagers are more likely to commit crimes and use illicit drugs if a greater proportion of the youth who live near them engage in similar activities.[7]

The MTO Baltimore site provides new research findings on both education and crime. For education, Ludwig, Duncan, and Ladd (this volume) find no neighborhood effects on test scores. They do, however, find that movers were more likely to repeat a grade and were more likely to be suspended or expelled. These findings may reflect higher standards in their new schools or perhaps transitional difficulties. In the area of criminal behavior, Ludwig, Duncan, and Hirschfield (2001) examine the frequency of criminal activity among teenagers in Baltimore. They find that youths that move to low-poverty neighborhoods were less likely to be arrested for violent crimes than either their counterparts in the control group or in the comparison-only group. But they also find some evidence suggesting that arrests for property crimes were higher for the youths that move to low-poverty neighborhoods, an outcome that may reflect more vigilant policing in wealthier areas.

ADULTS

Studies on whether neighborhoods affect adults focus on health and employment outcomes. For health, the literature provides only weak evidence that neighborhoods matter to specific illnesses, but several studies report a link between neighborhood socioeconomic status and overall mortality levels (Anderson et al. 1997; Haan, Kaplan, and Camacho 1987; Waitzman and Smith 1998).[8] There is also reasonably sound evidence that neighborhood conditions—especially crime or violence levels in neighborhoods—shape health-related behaviors (Diehr et al. 1993; Ganz 2000; Kleinschmidt, Hills, and Elliott 1995; Robert 1999).

For employment outcomes, studies of the Gautreaux program in Chicago (see chapter 1) provide evidence that neighborhood generally matters to adult employment opportunities—although the effects were modest. Participating Gautreaux families that moved to the suburbs enjoyed both higher employment rates and higher earnings (Rosenbaum and Popkin 1991). Our search turned up few other studies that explore the link between a neighborhood's socioeconomic characteristics and adult labor-market outcomes. The most methodologically persuasive,

Weinberg et al. (2000), uses an individual fixed-effects model to study the impact of neighborhood residence on labor market outcomes. The authors find that the employment rate in a community is associated with an individual's employment status. The extensive literature on spatial mismatch, meanwhile, provides some support for the notion that a neighborhood's proximity to employment opportunities shapes resident employment levels (see discussion below).

In sum, before MTO, research provided tentative evidence that neighborhood conditions and location may influence adult employment and health outcomes. But all of this earlier research, to some degree, is hampered by causality limitations. What does MTO tell us? The chapters in this volume provide mixed evidence for the effects of neighborhoods on employment outcomes, and final conclusions about the effects of moves on these outcomes will have to await the next round of research. The effects on health outcomes, however, are strikingly consistent and provide powerful evidence that neighborhood environments can shape health outcomes. In Boston and New York, household heads in both treatment groups experienced improvements in mental health. Moreover, in Boston, the heads of household in both treatment groups experienced improvements in self-rated health.

Why Might Neighborhoods Matter?

Most existing research has focused on the question of whether neighborhood matters. More specifically, most of the studies, including the MTO research, were designed to test whether living in a high-poverty, or low-socioeconomic-status, neighborhood influences various outcomes. As described earlier, the MTO research as well as other creative, nonexperimental studies are providing growing evidence that neighborhood poverty levels have an effect. But as Sampson, Morenoff, and Gannon-Rowley (forthcoming) point out, any number of social processes may account for this result.

This section explores the question of why and how neighborhoods matter. It identifies several mechanisms through which neighborhood conditions may influence individual outcomes and then reviews what the empirical evidence, including the MTO research, can tell us about why neighborhoods matter.

Causal Mechanisms

Several researchers have offered different typologies of neighborhood effects (Jencks and Mayer 1990; Manski 2000; Sampson et al. forthcoming). While these studies all have the same goal—dissecting social interactions and institutional effects—the way they categorize social interactions differs. This section divides social interactions into three distinct effects: norms and collective efficacy, peer effects, and social networks. These categories encompass the variety of social effects described in the empirical and theoretical literature. Unlike prior research, the analysis here posits that a community's violence and crime levels can have a distinct effect on residents' outcomes.[9]

QUALITY OF LOCAL SERVICES AND INSTITUTIONS

An individual's well-being may be significantly affected by the availability and quality of services delivered at the neighborhood level. The most obvious example is public school quality, especially in the elementary grades, when children are most likely to attend schools in the immediate neighborhood. But other services and institutions whose availability and quality vary across neighborhoods may also have a significant impact on individual outcomes. Examples include child care centers and preschools, health care facilities, and after-school activities for children and teens. The condition of local playgrounds and infrastructure more generally may also affect health and safety.

NORMS AND COLLECTIVE EFFICACY

Sampson et al. (1997) use the term "collective efficacy" to capture the ability of a neighborhood to realize the common values of residents and maintain effective social controls. Examples include a willingness to confront local teenagers who are skipping school, hanging out on street corners, or acting disorderly. A neighborhood's collective efficacy may also extend to political action (e.g., protesting the closing of a local fire station), and thus in a broader sense, can help shape the outcomes of adults as well as those of teenagers and children. Still, collective efficacy may have particularly strong effects on children. Adults in the neighborhood can be critical in helping parents monitor and discipline their children. Adults, through their actions and words, also communicate values about the importance of work, education, and civility. Children learn a lot about norms and expectations from the adults they encounter in the community.

Peer Influences

The behaviors and attitudes of peers can lure a person into destructive or criminal behavior. Conversely, positive behaviors can challenge a person to reach new levels of athletic or academic achievement.[10] The conventional view is that peer effects are strongest for adolescents, but peer effects are also likely to influence adult behavior. It is important to note that peer groups are not solely determined by one's neighborhood. Indeed, recent evidence from a court-ordered desegregation program in Yonkers suggests that teenagers who moved tended to return to their old neighborhoods to hang out with their old friends (Briggs 1997). Still, neighborhood is likely to have a significant impact on the choice of peer group.

Manski (2000) and Durlauf (2001) distinguish between endogenous and contextual peer effects. Endogenous effects, a notion akin to peer pressure, describes the extent to which peer behavior leads people to behave in a similar manner. Teenagers in high-crime neighborhoods, for instance, may be more likely to commit crimes because their peers do and because it is more socially acceptable. Contextual effects, by contrast, describe the extent to which the characteristics of others in the neighborhood (such as neighbors' poverty levels or employment patterns) influence behavior. When studying the behavior of teenagers, the presence of strong neighborhood role models could create contextual effects (Durlauf 2001).

Social Networks

Several researchers have theorized that the very existence of dense, neighborhood social networks can benefit residents, since people living in a more socially cohesive community are more apt to look out for their neighbors' interests; to help them weather hard times; and to share community news, resource tips, and job information (Coleman 1990; Coulton and Pandey 1992; Furstenberg 1993; Putnam 1995; Sampson and Groves 1989; Sampson et al. 1997; Temkin and Rohe 1997). The composition of local networks may matter as well. People living in a neighborhood with high unemployment or poor work opportunities are less likely to hear about available openings. They are also less likely to know employed people who can assure employers that they are reliable and trustworthy.

Exposure to Crime and Violence

People who live in high-crime neighborhoods face higher risks of being victimized, injured, and possibly even killed than people who live in safer neighborhoods. In addition, young children (and possibly adolescents and adults as well) who witness violent crime firsthand may suffer significant and even lasting emotional trauma (Martinez and Richters 1993). Simply witnessing crimes or knowing people who have been victimized may profoundly affect children's outlooks, leading them to see the world as fundamentally violent, dangerous, and unjust. Parents living in high-crime areas may also feel extraordinary stress levels and be more protective and strict with their children.

PHYSICAL DISTANCE AND ISOLATION
Finally, perhaps the most straightforward neighborhood impact is physical proximity and accessibility to economic opportunities, particularly jobs. Residents of neighborhoods that are far from job opportunities or public transportation may be unable to get decent work, even if they possess adequate skills and motivation. John Kain, in his seminal 1968 article, first noted the problem of a spatial divide between neighborhood and opportunity, which other researchers have coined "spatial mismatch." He argued that housing discrimination confines blacks to a few central-city neighborhoods, where jobs have become increasingly scarce as employers (especially manufacturing firms) have relocated to the suburbs. Ihlanfeldt and Sjoquist (1989) have since extended Kain's hypothesis to include poor whites, whose families, they argue, are unable to move to suburban areas offering greater job opportunities because of those areas' high housing prices.

Evidence

Most of the literature on neighborhood effects has focused on the role of peer influence in shaping behavior. According to Ginther et al. (2000), who reviewed many empirical studies of neighborhood effects, the most consistent relationships appear when outcomes are closely linked to neighborhood characteristics. For instance, an individual's likelihood of graduating from high school is most strongly affected by the community's average education level. Similarly, in a study of health-related behaviors, Diehr et al. (1993) find that the most critical community characteristic in determining a particular behavior appears to be the prevalence of that behavior in the community. While these findings seem to suggest that peer effects are important, the strong correlation across many neighborhood conditions makes causality unclear. Moreover, selection effects might explain the greater correlation between closely linked neighborhood characteristics and individual outcomes. Finally, several studies have found that other neighborhood measures also matter. In looking at hours worked, for instance, Weinberg et al. (2000) find that other neighborhood characteristics and neighborhood employment rates have an equally strong effect on behavior as neighborhood employment rates.

Nonetheless, most researchers believe that peers play an important role in people's lives and that this effect may explain much of the apparently negative effects of high poverty levels on behavior. In a study that attempts to more directly address the importance of peers, South and Baumer (2000) find that roughly a third of the correlation between neighborhood socioeconomic status and a teenage girl's risk of premarital childbearing can be attributed to the attitudes and behaviors of her peers.

Fear and people's perceptions of safety and levels of crime—factors that are highly correlated with poverty levels—also appear to play a role in explaining poverty effects. The strongest evidence that neighborhoods affect mental health and health-related behaviors, for instance, comes from studies examining the impact of neighborhood safety and crime levels. Qualitative research has also linked residence in more dangerous neighborhoods to more restrictive parenting styles (Furstenberg 1993; Jarrett 1997).

Sampson, Raudenbush, and Earls (1997) find that the key factor in explaining the correlation of poverty and violent behavior is collective efficacy. Similarly, Morenoff, Sampson, and Raudenbush (2001) find collective efficacy to be an important predictor of criminal behavior, although their findings show it does not explain much of the effect of neighborhood socioeconomic status. Few studies have considered the effects of collective efficacy on other outcomes. In one example, Aneshensel and Sucoff (1996) find that social cohesion explains a large proportion of the apparent relationship between the socioeconomic status of a neighborhood and adolescent depression.

Most empirical research examining the relationship between neighborhood residence and labor market outcomes has emphasized the importance of physical distance, rather than social composition. Of six literature reviews on this topic, three find substantial support for the importance of "spatial mismatch" (Ihlanfeldt 1992, 1999; Kain 1992), two find moderate support (Holzer 1991; Mayer 1996), and one finds the literature too mixed to reach a firm conclusion (Jencks and Mayer 1990).[11] A more recent study, which uses an individual fixed-effects model, finds fairly strong evidence that a neighborhood's proximity to jobs is linked to hours worked (Weinberg et al. 2000). Nonetheless, studies that have tried to distinguish the effects of job access from the effects of social influences typically find social influences to be more important (Cutler and Glaeser 1997; O'Regan and Quigley 1996; Weinberg et al. 2000).

Compared with evidence on the other mechanisms, the case that local institutions and social networks play a role in outcomes is fairly weak. But methodological challenges and data limitations may explain this lack of empirical support. Morenoff et al. (2001), after surveying residents on the number of local institutions available to them, found no evidence that the number of institutions had an effect on violence levels. But this finding may reflect the study's reliance on residents' perceptions about institutions, or more fundamentally, its focus on the quantity, rather than the quality, of local institutions. Few other studies have systematically studied the role of local institutions in shaping neighborhood outcomes. Of course, an enormous literature covers the issue of whether school resource levels, and the school's types of resources, affect student achievement, with little consensus on the results. One of the earliest studies by Coleman et al. (1966) found that family background was more important than school inputs in determining achievement. Since then, researchers have reached conflicting conclusions. Burtless (1996) summarizes much of this literature.

In the case of social networks, qualitative evidence suggests they are important. For example, many adults and adolescents learn about employment opportunities by word-of-mouth (Kasinitz and Rosenberg 1996; Sullivan 1989; Wial 1991). But little quantitative evidence tying social networks to outcomes has emerged, perhaps because social network effects are so difficult to measure.

The emerging MTO research sheds some new light on the mechanisms through which neighborhood conditions influence outcomes for families and children. First, the experience of many of the MTO study families has highlighted the importance of crime and violence. Victimization and fear of violent crime were the primary reasons people gave for participating in the demonstration. Not only were they afraid for their own and their children's safety, mothers also worried that their children would join gangs if they stayed in their original neighborhoods. Although crime rates have declined in most urban communities in the years since MTO's launch, evidence consistently confirms that MTO families moved to dramatically safer communities and that they see the greater security as a major improvement in their lives (Popkin, Harris, and Cunningham 2002). This greater safety and security may be what explains the preliminary findings in this volume: that moves lead to reduced anxiety and stress, contribute to better health outcomes, and enable parents to be calmer and more patient with their children.

Qualitative research conducted as a first step in the formal evaluation of MTO suggests that families in the treatment group are also influenced by their new social networks. Participants report that their neighbors have been welcoming and friendly, that the new neighborhood environment opened their eyes to opportunities for a better life, and that the fact that most people in the neighborhood work provides an important source of motivation. However, some MTO families have found that language, race, and class barriers prevent them from forming relationships in their new neighborhoods, results that can contribute to isolation and loneliness. And some movers (including both adults and children) have maintained very close ties to their old neighborhoods. This raises questions about how much they will benefit from their new neighborhood's social environment (Popkin et al. 2002).

One of the original expectations for MTO was that moving to new neighborhoods would automatically put children in better schools, ultimately leading to better educational outcomes. And there is some evidence emerging from MTO that children whose families moved into suburban school districts are attending higher-performing schools (Ladd and Ludwig 1997). But qualitative research also suggests that in some of the MTO sites, children were already attending high-quality magnet or charter schools, which may have been superior to the schools in their new origin communities. In addition, not all movers changed school districts, and some chose to keep their children in their original schools (even if these schools were not of especially high quality). Finally, in some MTO families, one or more children had already exhibited either learning disabilities or disruptive behavior and were attending special schools for these reasons. Thus, the link between residential location and school quality may not be as strong as originally anticipated (Popkin et al. 2002).

Qualitative research on MTO also highlights the important interactions between neighborhood environment and an individual's, or a family's, strengths and weaknesses. Not all MTO families appear able to take advantage of opportunities offered by their new neighborhoods. Some face physical and/or mental disabilities that make working, attending school, or participating in community life difficult. And some of those who have experienced the biggest benefits from moving appear to be highly moti-vated (Popkin et al. 2002). The varying experiences of MTO families in their new neighborhoods corroborate other empirical research that shows neighborhood conditions alone do not determine the life chances of fam-ilies or individuals.

Next Task: Getting Inside the Black Box

The research emerging from the MTO demonstration has already advanced the existing empirical evidence that neighborhoods profoundly affect the well-being and life chances of their residents. And we can expect rigorous research on household outcomes to continue to be generated by studies of MTO. In addition, however, MTO also has the potential to expand our understanding about why and how neighborhoods affect dif-ferent types of residents at different stages in their lives.

Without an understanding of what happens inside the "black box" of neighborhood effects, it is difficult to make recommendations about pol-icy interventions designed to counter the effects of neighborhood envi-ronment. Policymakers and practitioners in both government and the nonprofit sector need reliable research findings that can help them design and implement more effective interventions for both poor families and poor neighborhoods—about how to give families the information and assistance they need to make prudent residential choices, how to improve existing neighborhoods to better support families and children, and how to help residents of distressed neighborhoods avoid or overcome the problems that surround them. Thus, a priority for future research should be to move beyond the question of *whether* neighborhood matters and to attack the more difficult questions of *how* they make a difference and *for whom*.

NOTES

1. A smaller set of studies has also examined the influence of such neighborhood characteristics as residential stability, homeownership rates, and ethnic heterogeneity (Sampson, Morenoff, and Gannon-Rowley forthcoming).

2. Manski (2000) provides a useful discussion of the challenges of identifying neighborhood effects.

3. Evans, Oates, and Schwab (1992) acknowledge that their metropolitan area instruments may be imperfect. They point out, for instance, that the difference between a teenager's school and the socioeconomic characteristics of the overall metropolitan area may be the most relevant factor. In this case, metropolitan area characteristics are surely inappropriate instruments.

4. For more comprehensive reviews of the neighborhood effects literature, see Ellen and Turner (1997), Ginther, Haveman, and Wolfe (2000), and Leventhal and Brooks-Gunn (2000).

5. Notably, three other researchers that have attempted to control for the endogeneity of location—either through an instrumental variables approach or a family fixed effects model—find that significant neighborhood effects persist (Aaronson 1997; Case and Katz 1991; Duncan, Connell, and Klebanov 1997).

6. Using a two-stage model that considers school choice to be endogenous, Evans et al. (1992) find that the effect of school composition (in particular, the proportion of disadvantaged students) on teenage pregnancy disappears. Plotnick and Hoffman (1996) examine sets of sisters to control for unobserved family effects, and find that the apparent link between pregnancy and neighborhood conditions largely disappears.

7. Case and Katz (1991) find that this effect persists in a two-stage model that attempts to control for the endogeneity of peer group.

8. See Ellen, Schill, et al. (2001) for a review.

9. This terminology differs slightly from that used in our earlier work (Ellen and Turner 1997). The key substantive difference is the replacement of adult socialization with the somewhat broader notion of collective efficacy, which describes how neighborhood norms and expectations about collective behavior can affect adult outcomes as well as children.

10. Jencks and Mayer (1990) suggest that when people's peers are significantly better-off—economically or socially—they may feel discouraged by their peers' many advantages and actually do worse.

11. Weinberg et al. (2000) point out that intercity tests of the mismatch hypothesis (e.g., Cutler and Glaeser 1997; Ihlanfeldt and Sjoquist 1989; Weinberg 2000) have generally found more supportive results than those that exploit neighborhood variation within a given metropolitan area.

REFERENCES

Aaronson, Daniel. 1997. "Sibling Estimates of Neighborhood Effects." In *Neighborhood Poverty. Volume 2: Policy Implications in Studying Neighborhoods,* edited by Jeanne Brooks-Gunn, Greg J. Duncan, and J. Lawrence Aber (80–93). New York: Russell Sage Foundation.

Anderson, Elijah. 1990. *Streetwise: Race, Class, and Change in an Urban Community.* Chicago: University of Chicago Press.

Anderson, Roger T., Paul Sorlie, Eric Backlund, Norman Johnson, and George A. Kaplan. 1997. "Mortality Effect of Community Socioeconomic Status." *Epidemiology* 8(1): 42–47.

Aneshensel, Carol S., and Clea A. Sucoff. 1996. "The Neighborhood Context of Adolescent Mental Health." *Journal of Health and Social Behavior* 37(December): 293–310.

Bloom, Howard S. 1984. "Accounting for No-Shows in Experimental Evaluation Designs." *Evaluation Review* 8: 225–46.

Brewster, Karin. 1994. "Race Differences in Sexual Activity among Adolescent Women: The Role of Neighborhood Characteristics." *American Sociological Review* 59(3): 408–24.

Brewster, Karin L., John O. G. Billy, and William R. Grady. 1993. "Social Context and Adolescent Behavior: The Impact of Community on the Transition to Sexual Activity." *Social Forces* 71(3): 713–40.

Briggs, Xavier de Souza. 1997. "Moving Up vs. Moving Out: Researching and Interpreting Neighborhood Effects in Housing Mobility." *Housing Policy Debate* 8(1): 195–234.

Brooks-Gunn, Jeanne, Greg J. Duncan, Pamela Kato Klebanov, and Naomi Sealand. 1993. "Do Neighborhoods Influence Child and Adolescent Development?" *American Journal of Sociology* 99(2): 353–95.

Burtless, Gary. 1996. "Introduction and Summary." In *Does Money Matter? The Effect of School Resources on Student Achievement and Adult Success,* edited by Gary Burtless. Washington, D.C.: Brookings Institution Press.

Case, Anne, and Lawrence Katz. 1991. "The Company You Keep: The Effects of Family and Neighborhood on Disadvantaged Youth." NBER Working Paper 3705. Cambridge, Mass.: National Bureau of Economic Research.

Chase-Lansdale, P. Lindsay, and Rachel A. Gordon. 1996. "Economic Hardship and the Development of Five- and Six-Year-Olds: Neighborhood and Regional Perspectives." *Child Development* 67: 3,338–67.

Chase-Lansdale, P. Lindsay, Rachel A. Gordon, Jeanne Brooks-Gunn, and Pamela K. Klebanov. 1997. "Neighborhood and Family Influences on the Intellectual and Behavioral Competence of Preschool and Early School-Age Children." In *Neighborhood Poverty. Volume 1: Context and Consequences for Children,* edited by Jeanne Brooks-Gunn, Greg J. Duncan, and J. Lawrence Aber (79–118). New York: Russell Sage Foundation.

Clark, Rebecca. 1992. "Neighborhood Effects of Dropping Out of School among Teenage Boys." Urban Institute Working Paper. Washington, D.C.: The Urban Institute.

Coleman, James S. 1990. *Foundations of Social Theory.* Cambridge, Mass.: Harvard University Press.

Coleman, James S., Ernest Q. Campbell, Carol J. Hobson, James McPartland, Alexander M. Mood, Frederic D. Weinfeld, and Robert L. York. 1966. *Equality of Educational Opportunity.* Washington, D.C.: U.S. Government Printing Office.

Connell, James P., and Bonnie Halpern-Felsher. 1997. "How Do Neighborhoods Affect Educational Outcomes in Middle Childhood and Adolescence? Conceptual Issues and an Empirical Example." In *Neighborhood Poverty. Volume 1: Context and Consequences for Children,* edited by Jeanne Brooks-Gunn, Greg J. Duncan, and J. Lawrence Aber (174–99). New York: Russell Sage Foundation.

Corcoran, Mary, Roger H. Gordon, Deborah Laren, and Gary Solon. 1989. "Effects of Family and Community Background on Men's Economic Status." NBER Working Paper No. 2896. Cambridge, Mass.: National Bureau of Economic Research.

Coulton, Claudia J., and Shanta Pandey. 1992. "Geographic Concentration of Poverty and Risk to Children in Urban Neighborhoods." *American Behavioral Scientist* 35: 238–57.

Coulton, Claudia J., Jill E. Korbin, Marilyn Su, and Julian Chow. 1995 "Community-Level Factors and Child Maltreatment Rates." *Child Development* 66: 1262–76.

Crane, Jonathan. 1991. "The Epidemic Theory of Ghettos and Neighborhood Effects on Dropping Out and Teenage Childbearing." *American Journal of Sociology* 96(5): 1226–59.

Cutler, David, and Edward Glaeser. 1997. "Are Ghettos Good or Bad?" *Quarterly Journal of Economics* 112(3): 827–72.

Datcher, Linda. 1982. "Effects of Community and Family Background on Achievement." *Review of Economics and Statistics* 64: 32–41.

Diehr, Paula, Thomas Koepsell, Allen Cheadle, Bruce M. Psaty, Edward Wagner, and Susan Curry. 1993. "Do Communities Differ in Health Behaviors?" *Journal of Clinical Epidemiology* 46(10): 1141–49.

Duncan, Greg. 1994. "Families and Neighbors as Sources of Disadvantage in the Schooling Decisions of White and Black Adolescents." *American Journal of Education* 103: 20–53.

Duncan, Greg, Jeanne Brooks-Gunn, and Pamela Klebanov. 1994. "Economic Deprivation and Early Childhood Development." *Child Development* 65(2): 296–318.

Duncan, Greg J., James P. Connell, and Pamela K. Klebanov. 1997. "Conceptual and Methodological Issues in Estimating Causal Effects of Neighborhoods and Family Conditions on Individual Development." In *Neighborhood Poverty. Volume 1: Context and Consequences for Children,* edited by Jeanne Brooks-Gunn, Greg J. Duncan, and J. Lawrence Aber (219–50). New York: Russell Sage Foundation.

Durlauf, Steven N. 2001. "A Framework for the Study of Individual Behavior and Social Interactions." *Sociological Methodology* 31(1): 47–87.

Ellen, Ingrid Gould, and Margery Austin Turner. 1997. "Does Neighborhood Matter? Assessing Recent Evidence." *Housing Policy Debate* 8(4): 833–66.

Ellen, Ingrid Gould, Tod Mijanovich, and Keri-Nicole Dillman. 2001. "Neighborhood Effects on Health: Exploring the Links and Assessing the Evidence." *Journal of Urban Affairs* 23(3–4): 391–408.

Ellen, Ingrid Gould, Michael H. Schill, Amy Ellen Schwartz, and Scott Susin. 2001. "Building Homes, Reviving Neighborhoods: Spillovers from Subsidized Construction of Owner-Occupied Housing in New York City." *Journal of Housing Research* 12(2): 185–216.

Evans, William N., Wallace E. Oates, and Robert M. Schwab. 1992. "Measuring Peer Group Effects: A Study of Teenage Behavior." *Journal of Political Economy* 100(51): 966–91.

Furstenberg, Frank F. Jr. 1993. "How Families Manage Risk and Opportunity in Dangerous Neighborhoods." In *Sociology and the Public Agenda,* edited by W. J. Wilson. Newbury Park, Calif.: Sage Publications.

Ganz, Michael. 2000. "The Relationship between External Threats and Smoking in Central Harlem." *American Journal of Public Health* 90(3): 367–71.

Garner, Catherine L., and Stephen Raudenbush. 1991. "Neighborhood Effects on Educational Attainment: A Multilevel Analysis." *Sociology of Education* 64: 251–62.

Ginther, Donna, Robert Haveman, and Barbara Wolfe. 2000. "Neighborhood Attributes as Determinants of Children's Outcomes: How Robust Are the Relationships?" *Journal of Human Resources* 35(4): 603–42.

Glaeser, Edward L., Bruce Sacerdote, and Jose A. Scheinkman. 1995. "Crime and Social Interactions." NBER Working Paper No. 5026. Cambridge, Mass.: National Bureau of Economic Research.

Grannis, Rick. 1998. "The Importance of Trivial Streets: Residential Streets and Residential Segregation." *American Journal of Sociology* 103(6): 1530–64.

Haan, Mary, George A. Kaplan, and Terry Camacho. 1987. "Poverty and Health: Prospective Evidence from the Alameda County Study." *American Journal of Epidemiology* 125(6): 989–98.

Halpern-Felsher, Bonnie, James P. Connell, Margaret Beale Spencer, J. Lawrence Aber, Greg J. Duncan, Elizabeth Clifford, Warren E. Crichlow, Peter A. Usinger, Steven P. Cole, LaRue Allen, and Edward Seidman. 1997. "Neighborhood and Family Factors Predicting Educational Risk and Attainment in African-American and European-American Children and Adolescents." In *Neighborhood Poverty. Volume 1: Context and Consequences for Children,* edited by Jeanne Brooks-Gunn, Greg J. Duncan, and J. Lawrence Aber (146–73). New York: Russell Sage Foundation.

Haveman, Robert, and Barbara Wolfe. 1996. *Succeeding Generations: On the Effects of Investments in Children.* New York: Russell Sage Foundation.

Hogan, Dennis, and Evelyn Kitagawa. 1985. "The Impact of Social Status, Family Structure, and Neighborhood on the Fertility of Black Adolescents." *American Journal of Sociology* 90(4): 825–55.

Hogan, Dennis P., Nan Marie Astone, and Evelyn M. Kitagawa. 1985. "Social and Environmental Factors Influencing Contraceptive Use among Black Adolescents." *Family Planning Perspectives* 17: 165–69.

Holzer, Harry J. 1991. "The Spatial Mismatch Hypothesis: What Has the Evidence Shown?" *Urban Studies* 28(1): 105–22.

Ihlanfeldt, Keith R. 1992. *Job Accessibility and the Employment and School Enrollment of Teenagers.* Kalamazoo, Mich.: W. E. Upjohn Institute for Employment Research.

———. 1999. "The Geography of Economic and Social Opportunity within Metropolitan Areas." In *Governance and Opportunity in Metropolitan America,* edited by Alan Altshuler, William Morrill, Harold Wolman, and Faith Mitchell (213–52). Washington, D.C.: National Academy Press.

Ihlanfeldt, Keith R., and David L. Sjoquist. 1989. "The Effect of Job Access on Black Youth Employment: A Cross-Sectional Analysis." *Journal of Urban Economics* 26: 110–30.

Jarrett, Robin L. 1997. "Bringing Families Back In: Neighborhoods' Effects on Child Development." In *Neighborhood Poverty. Volume 2: Policy Implications in Studying Neighborhoods,* edited by Jeanne Brooks-Gunn, Greg J. Duncan, and J. Lawrence Aber (48–64). New York: Russell Sage Foundation.

Jencks, Christopher, and Susan Mayer. 1990. "Residential Segregation, Job Proximity, and Black Job Opportunities." In *Inner-City Poverty in the United States,* edited by Laurence Lynn and Michael McGeary (187–222). Washington, D.C.: National Academy Press.

Johnstone, John. 1978. "Social Class, Social Areas, and Delinquency." *Sociology and Social Research* 63: 49–72.

Kain, John. 1968. "Housing Segregation, Negro Employment, and Metropolitan Decentralization." *Quarterly Journal of Economics* 82(2): 175–92.

———. 1992. "The Spatial Mismatch Hypothesis: Three Decades Later." *Housing Policy Debate* 3(2): 371–460.

Kasinitz, Philip, and Jan Rosenberg. 1996. "Missing the Connection: Social Isolation and Employment on the Brooklyn Waterfront." *Social Problems* 43(2): 180–96.

Kingsley, G. Thomas. 1998. *Neighborhood Indicators: Taking Advantage of the New Potential.* Washington, D.C.: The Urban Institute.

———. 1999. *Building and Operating Neighborhood Indicator Systems: A Guidebook.* Washington, D.C.: The Urban Institute.

Kleinschmidt, Immo, Michael Hills, and Paul Elliott. 1995. "Smoking Behaviour Can Be Predicted by Neighbourhood Deprivation Measures." *Journal of Epidemiology and Community Health* 49(Supplement 2): s72–s77.

Ku, Leighton, Freya L. Sonenstein, and Joseph H. Pleck. 1993. "Neighborhood, Family, and Work: Influences on the Premarital Behaviors of Adolescent Males." *Social Forces* 72(2): 479–503.

Kupersmidt, Janis B., Pamela C. Griesler, Melissa E. DeRosier, Charlotte J. Patterson, and Paul W. Davis. 1995. "Childhood Aggression and Peer Relations in the Context of Family and Neighborhood Factors." *Child Development* 66: 360–75.

Ladd, Helen F., and Jens Ludwig. 1997. "Federal Housing Assistance, Residential Relocation, and Educational Opportunities: Evidence from Baltimore." *American Economic Review* 87(2): 272–77.

Leventhal, Tama, and Jeanne Brooks-Gunn. 2000. "The Neighborhoods They Live In: The Effects of Neighborhood Residence on Child and Adolescent Outcomes." *Psychological Bulletin* 126: 309–37.

Ludwig, Jens, Greg J. Duncan, and Paul Hirschfield. 2001. "Urban Poverty and Juvenile Crime: Evidence from a Randomized Housing-Mobility Experiment." *Quarterly Journal of Economics* 116(2): 655–79.

Manski, Charles F. 2000. "Economic Analysis of Social Interactions." *Journal of Economic Perspectives* 14(3): 115–36.

Martinez, Pedro, and John Richters. 1993. "The NIMH Community Violence Project: Children's Distress Symptoms Associated with Violence Exposure." *Psychiatry* 56: 22–35.

Massey, Douglas S., Andrew B. Gross, and Mitchell L. Eggers. 1991. "Segregation, the Concentration of Poverty, and the Life Chances of Individuals." *Social Science Research* 20: 397–420.

Mayer, Christopher J. 1996. "Does Location Matter?" *New England Economic Review* May/June: 26–40.

Mayer, Susan. 1991. "How Much Does a High School's Racial and Socioeconomic Mix Affect Graduation and Teenage Fertility Rates?" In *The Urban Underclass,* edited by Christopher Jencks and Paul E. Peterson. Washington, D.C.: Brookings Institution Press.

Morenoff, Jeffrey D., Robert J. Sampson, and Stephen W. Raudenbush. 2001. "Neighborhood Inequality, Collective Efficacy, and the Spatial Dynamics of Homicide." *Criminology* 39(3): 517–60.

O'Regan, Katherine, and John Quigley. 1996. "Spatial Effects upon Employment Outcomes: The Case of New Jersey Teenagers." *New England Economic Review* (May/June): 41–58.

Plotnick, Robert, and Saul Hoffman. 1996. "The Effect of Neighborhood Characteristics on Young Adult Outcomes." Institute for Research on Poverty Discussion Paper No. 1106-96. Madison: University of Wisconsin.

Popkin, Susan J., Laura E. Harris, and Mary K. Cunningham. 2002. "Families in Transition: A Qualitative Analysis of the MTO Experience." Report Prepared for the U.S. Department of Housing and Urban Development.

Putnam, Robert D. 1995. "Bowling Alone." *Journal of Democracy* 6: 65–78.

Reiss, Albert, and Albert Rhodes. 1961. "The Distribution of Juvenile Delinquency in the Social Class Structure." *American Sociological Review* 26: 720–32.

Ricketts, Erol R., and Isabel V. Sawhill. 1988. "Defining and Measuring the Underclass." *Journal of Policy Analysis and Management* 7: 316–25.

Robert, Stephanie A. 1999. "Neighborhood Socioeconomic Context and Adult Health. The Mediating Role of Individual Health Behaviors and Psychological Factors." *Annals of New York Academy of Science* 896: 465–8.

Rosenbaum, James. 1991. "Black Pioneers: Do Moves to the Suburbs Increase Economic Opportunity for Mothers and Children?" *Housing Policy Debate* 2: 1179–213.

Rosenbaum, James, and Susan Popkin. 1991. "Employment and Earnings of Low-Income Blacks Who Move to Middle-Income Suburbs." In *The Urban Underclass*, edited by Christopher Jencks and Paul E. Peterson. Washington, D.C.: Brookings Institution.

Sampson, Robert, and W. Byron Groves. 1989. "Community Structure and Crime: Testing Social-Disorganization Theory." *American Journal of Sociology* 94: 774–802.

Sampson, Robert J., and Stephen W. Raudenbush. 1999. "Systematic Social Observation of Public Spaces: A New Look at Disorder in Urban Neighborhoods." *American Journal of Sociology* 105(3): 603–51.

Sampson, Robert J., Jeffrey D. Morenoff, and Felton Earls. 1999. "Beyond Social Capital: Spatial Dynamics of Collective Efficacy for Children." *American Sociological Review* 64(5): 633–60.

Sampson, Robert J., Jeffrey D. Morenoff, and Thomas Gannon-Rowley. Forthcoming. "Assessing 'Neighborhood Effects': Social Processes and New Directions in Research." *Annual Review of* Sociology 28.

Sampson, Robert J., Stephen W. Raudenbush, and Felton Earls. 1997. "Neighborhoods and Violent Crime: A Multilevel Study of Collective Efficacy." *Science* 277 (August): 918–24.

Shaw, Clifford R., and Henry McKay. 1942. *Juvenile Delinquency and Urban Areas.* Chicago: University of Chicago Press.

South, Scott J., and Eric P. Baumer. 2000. "Deciphering Community and Race Effects on Adolescent Premarital Childbearing." *Social Forces* 78: 1379–407.

Sullivan, Mercer L. 1989. *Getting Paid: Youth Crime and Work in the Inner City.* Ithaca, N.Y.: Cornell University Press.

Tempkin, Kenneth, and William Rohe. 1997. "Social Capital and Neighborhood Stability: An Empirical Investigation." Paper presented at Fannie Mae Foundation Annual Housing Conference, Washington, D.C.

Waitzman, Norman J., and Ken R. Smith. 1998. "Phantom of the Area: Poverty-Area Residence and Mortality in the United States." *American Journal of Public Health* 88(6): 973–6.

Weinberg, Bruce. 2000."Black Residential Centralization and the Spatial Mismatch Hypotheses." *Journal of Urban Economics* 48 (July): 110–34.

Weinberg, Bruce A., Patricia B. Reagan, and Jeffrey J. Yankow. 2000. "Do Neighborhoods Affect Work Behavior? Evidence from the NLSY79." Unpublished paper, Department of Economics, Ohio State University.

Wial, Howard. 1991. "Getting a Good Job: Mobility in a Segmented Labor Market." *Industrial Relations* 30(3): 396–416.

Wilson, William Julius. 1987. *The Truly Disadvantaged: The Inner City, the Underclass, and Public Policy.* Chicago: University of Chicago Press.

12

Neighborhood Poverty, Housing Assistance, and Children's Educational Attainment

Sandra Newman
Joseph Harkness
Wei-Jun J. Yeung

A central question drives research on poverty deconcentration—does neighborhood poverty affect children's outcomes? The answer should influence debates about the direction of federal housing policy, metropolitan and regional fair share housing, and the differential effects of welfare reform for those living in distressed versus non-distressed neighborhoods. Currently, almost 40 percent of the nation's public housing units are located in high-poverty census tracts; nearly 20 percent are in tracts where a high proportion of residents receive public assistance(Newman and Schnare 1997).[1] Moreover, about 200,000 (out of 2.1 million) of the households with children under age 19 receiving housing assistance from the U.S. Department of Housing and Urban Development live in high-poverty census tracts (HUD User 1997).

The MTO program offers the best framework to date to address this question. If designed and implemented well, its experimental research design, data collection on dropouts, and tracking of households for 10 years represent the best approach for tackling the core methodological challenge of neighborhood effects research, namely, disentangling the independent effects of neighborhood characteristics from the effects of parental and family characteristics.[2] But as we await the maturation of the demonstration and subsequent research, nonexperimental research may also provide some insight into the role of neighborhood in child outcomes. Such studies may also have the additional benefit of highlighting potentially productive avenues for analysis of the experimental data.

The present chapter was prepared in this spirit. The analysis is unique in at least two ways. First, it considers the neighborhood effects on children who have lived in public housing, or privately owned but publicly subsidized housing, using a novel database. (The analysis excludes Section 8 certificates and vouchers.) The database, constructed by matching all sample addresses in the Panel Study of Income Dynamics (PSID) to assisted housing unit addresses, contains a wealth of information on assisted housing patterns. It allows us to identify PSID sample children that had lived in assisted housing at some point, what type of housing assistance they received, and how long they received housing assistance, information not available previously. The data enable us to disentangle the effects of assisted housing on children from the effects of the surrounding neighborhood.

Second, the analysis considers neighborhood effects at all stages of childhood, including up to age 5 as well as between ages 6 and 15. Most previous studies limited their analysis to older children (e.g., Aaronson 1997).[3]

The analysis finds that housing assistance does not affect educational attainment. Neighborhood poverty experienced between ages 6 and 10 adversely affects educational attainment, but no such effects were found in early or late childhood. Residential moves, especially in early childhood, also have negative effects.

Theories of Neighborhood Effects

Two different models explaining the link between neighborhood characteristics (e.g., poverty rate, receipt of public assistance and unemployment) and individual outcomes (e.g., educational attainment, labor force participation) inform the neighborhood effects literature (Ginther, Haveman, and Wolfe 1993; Jencks and Mayer 1990).[4]

The epidemic model (also called the contagion and collective socialization model) holds that adult role models and peers most influence children's perceptions of appropriate values, norms, and behaviors (Clark 1992; Crane 1991; Wilson 1987). For example, according to this view, children who encounter successful, hardworking adults are likely to think hard work pays off. Similarly, if children interact with peers who behave well in school, they are more likely to behave well too (Aaronson 1997). Thus, by this view, poor children who grow up in decent neighborhoods are more likely to adopt mainstream values and behaviors than poor children who grow up in impoverished, low-employment neighborhoods.

The competition or relative deprivation model contends that children judge themselves against their peers. This relative assessment can result in one of two effects, depending on many factors, including an individual's psychological makeup. This self assessment can cause a child to work harder or it can cause a child to give up. The epidemic, contagion or collective socialization effect suggests that poor children living in more affluent neighborhoods will have better outcomes than other poor children. The competition or relative deprivation effect suggests the opposite. Both views, however, predict significant neighborhood effects.

Findings about the effects of neighborhood quality on outcomes are inconsistent. Wilson (1987) established a convincing theoretical case that the social isolation and concentrated poverty among the ghetto poor hurt residents' aspirations and achievement. This theory is partially supported by empirical studies suggesting that growing up in a more affluent neighborhood positively affects adolescents' educational attainment, criminal behavior, drug abuse, labor force participation, and other outcomes (Aaronson 1997; Brooks-Gunn, Duncan, and Aber 1997; Case and Katz 1991; Clark 1992; Crane 1991; and Datcher 1982). According to these studies, concentrating the poor in discrete geographic regions is the opposite of what is needed to improve poor children's prospects. Some of these researchers also find that the positive effects of middle-income neighbors are more powerful than the detrimental effects of poor neighbors.

Duncan (1994) finds that some low-income children benefited from having neighbors with higher socioeconomic status (measured by percentage of households reporting incomes of $30,000 or more, the percentage of college graduates, the percentage employed in professional or managerial occupations, and other indicators). In particular, white and black low-income girls and white low-income boys saw gains. For black low-income boys, however, such improvements were only significant when the middle-class neighbors were also black. On the other hand, some studies find few, if any, neighborhood effects (Corcoran et al. 1991; Evans, Oates, and Schwab 1992; Ginther et al. 1993; and Plotnick and Hoffman 1993).[5]

Notably, even researchers reporting significant neighborhood effects find that the impacts are more modest compared with the effects of family background. For example, according to the fixed-effects model in Aaronson (1997), a 10 percent increase in the neighborhood poverty rate reduced the likelihood of graduating from high school by 7 percent. By most measures, neighborhoods are not the major force determining how a child fares in life.

Our analysis data lack direct measures of peer influence, role modeling, and a child's self-assessment against his or her peers. Thus, most studies, including this analysis, control for neighborhood poverty as a proxy for an array of neighborhood characteristics.

Conceptions of Assisted Housing Effects

Defining a child's "microenvironment" and "macroenvironment" gives us a rough conceptualization of how living in such housing developments might affect children's opportunities and outcomes. A child's macroenvironment comprises all the units in the development and the neighborhood. The microenvironment is his or her individual housing unit. Each affects the child in a different way.

In this conceptualization, the theories of how neighborhood affects outcomes should apply to how the macroenvironment of assisted housing affects young residents. Public housing, according to recent studies, is disproportionately located in neighborhoods with very low incomes, high unemployment and poverty rates, and poor quality housing in surrounding areas. The neighborhoods surrounding assisted private developments are roughly equivalent to the neighborhoods of welfare households that do not receive housing assistance (Newman and Schnare 1997). Roughly 75 percent of all assisted housing units are located in distressed neighborhoods. Many children living in large public housing developments rarely venture into the neighborhood, and their orbit of activity tends to be restricted to the development (Shlay and Holupka 1991). These developments also have large concentrations of households with very low incomes, high welfare dependency rates, and low educational achievement (Newman and Schnare 1993). If the concentration of disadvantaged neighbors negatively affects child outcomes, then children growing up in public housing may experience worse outcomes than comparably poor children outside these settings.

By contrast, the quality of the child's living conditions—one component of a child's microenvironment—may not necessarily be worse if he or she lives in assisted housing. Assisted housing regulations require all dwelling units to meet housing quality standards. Thus, the condition of these units should be higher than for comparable households that do not receive assistance. This expectation is borne out by Newman and Schnare (1993). Nonetheless, a review of a sample of dwellings passing inspection found that "some properties clearly violated" assisted housing standards (GAO 1994). The quality of furnishings and other material possessions might also be better in public assisted housing units, as residents there generally pay only 30 percent of their income in rent.

Surprisingly, few researchers have systematically tested the effects of housing quality on child outcomes. Mayer (1997) suggests that housing quality has some effect, but this study's measures of physical quality are difficult to evaluate.[6] On balance, then, assisted housing environments may be more physically adequate than other low-income rental properties. Whether this difference matters for child outcomes, however, is not well understood. Because the expected effects of the macroenvironment are negative but those of the microenvironment are positive, it is difficult to predict the overall effect of assisted housing on children's educational attainment.

Another microenvironment component is how the family responds to the housing subsidy. This component could plausibly have both more positive and more negative effects on children (Newman and Harkness 1999). If housing subsidies allow families to purchase necessities that would have otherwise been unaffordable, then children might see positive effects. But to the extent that the housing subsidy discourages parents from engaging in work, or other activities leading to self-sufficiency, children might experience negative effects.

As this overview demonstrates, it is difficult to predict whether—or how—living in assisted housing will affect child outcomes. For example, we do not know whether any exposure to assisted housing affects later outcomes, whether a child needs to have lived continuously in assisted housing for a specific period to see an effect, or whether the stage at which the child lives in assisted housing is critical to later outcomes. Our task is more complex because we are ultimately interested in the interaction of two factors—assisted housing and neighborhood conditions—on children. To simulate the MTO condition, however, the child must experience a move from a high- to a low-poverty neighborhood. This requirement adds a third element to the mix.

Given this conceptual complexity and the limits of our data and sample sizes, we pursue basic, exploratory models. Each uses an alternative approach in conceptualizing the effects of neighborhood poverty, mobility, and assisted housing residence on educational attainment.

Methodology, Measures, and Research Questions

A common research problem when assessing neighborhood effects is that unmeasured family characteristics may affect both children's outcomes and the family's choice of neighborhood. For example, parents who value education highly may choose to live in higher-quality neighborhoods with better schools. In these cases, the unobserved parental characteristics affecting neighborhood choice would also affect child outcomes, which could produce biased estimates.

To minimize this problem, we use a two-pronged approach: an individual-level analysis and a family fixed-effects analysis. Each type of analysis has strengths and weaknesses. The advantage of the family fixed-effects approach is that it eliminates unobserved variable bias—as long as we assume that family characteristics are the same for all children in the same family. Its weakness, however, is that it restricts the sample to individuals with siblings. It is also questionable to assume that parental characteristics affecting neighborhood choice do not vary among siblings, particularly when family structure changes.[7]

Although parenting may change from one child to another, this adjustment may be slight and less significant than other influences (e.g., family economic circumstances, parents' educational background, and the child's ability). Developmental psychologists and sociologists continue to debate whether parents treat siblings differently and how such differences may affect children's outcomes (Baumrind 1993; Hauser and Wong 1989; and Scarr 1992).

One strongly held view is that as long as a child's environment and parenting are "good enough," or within the normal range of reasonable parenting, he or she will develop along the course set by his or her inherited attributes (Scarr 1992). The issue is far from settled, but there appears to be at least as much evidence supporting the family fixed-effects models as against them. Moreover, among the families examined, changes in family structure do not appear to be highly associated with moves to certain neighborhoods. (See "Variation in Family Characteristics between Siblings" section.)

Table 12.1 provides the definitions and univariate statistics of the variables used in the models. The appendix describes the variables, estimations, and statistical features of the models. The analysis sets out to explore four questions that MTO cannot fully answer.

Constructing Models to Address Four Questions

Does Housing Assistance Receipt Affect Children's Educational Attainment?

Although the microenvironment of assisted housing is expected to be associated with more positive outcomes for children, the macroenvironment should work in the opposite direction. It is, therefore, difficult to predict the net effects of assisted housing on educational attainment.

We test for these effects using two specifications of assisted housing, the first capturing the sequence (e.g., assisted to unassisted), and the second the childhood stage in which assistance was received for three years or longer. We define three such stages: early, age 0–5; middle, age 6–10; and late, age 11–15.

Does Neighborhood Poverty Experienced during Childhood Affect Children's Educational Attainment?

MTO addresses this question by comparing outcomes for two experimental groups: the one receiving Section 8 vouchers and the one receiving vouchers plus counseling to move to a low-poverty area. We explore such effects for a nationally representative sample of the low-income population.

We use three methods to capture the relationship between neighborhood poverty and educational attainment. First, we test the linear effect of average neighborhood poverty over all of childhood (age 0–15). Second, to determine whether a nonlinear effect of average neighborhood poverty over all of childhood applies, we use a piecewise linear spline function with breakpoints at 10, 25, and 40 percent. Third, to test whether the timing of childhood neighborhood poverty matters, we test a model with neighborhood poverty specified for each childhood stage.[8]

Does Moving Affect Educational Attainment?

The empirical literature suggests that residential moves negatively affect educational attainment (Haveman, Wolfe, and Spaulding 1991). These

Table 12.1. *Definitions and Univariate Statistics of Variables Used in Models*

Variable	Assisted (N = 222)			Assisted + eligible unassisted (N = 923)		
	Mean	Median	Std. Dev.	Mean	Median	Std. Dev.
Dependent variable						
Years of completed education age 20	11.76	12.00	1.39	11.88	12.00	1.37
Housing assistance variables						
Assisted to unassisted	0.17			0.04		
Unassisted to assisted or always assisted	0.43			0.10		
Limited or not assisted	0.36			0.85		
In assisted housing 3+ years						
Age 0–5	0.34			0.08		
Age 6–10	0.39			0.09		
Age 11–15	0.42			0.10		
Neighborhood poverty rate variable (%)						
Age 0–5	29.28	27.70	14.81	23.90	21.60	14.21
Age 6–10	28.78	26.20	16.01	22.26	20.00	13.69
Age 11–15	27.91	23.70	17.03	21.99	19.40	14.11
Age 0–15	28.65	25.93	14.22	22.72	20.80	12.79

Residential mobility variable (no. of moves)						
Age 0–5	1.87	2.00	1.37	1.68	1.00	1.39
Age 6–10	1.62	1.00	1.36	1.24	1.00	1.27
Age 11–15	1.32	1.00	1.38	0.99	1.00	1.20
Age 0–15	4.82	4.00	3.07	3.92	3.00	2.90
Control variables						
Cohort (year born minus 1967)	4.48	4.00	2.63	4.69	5.00	2.65
Black	0.84			0.59		
Female	0.46			0.49		
Number of siblings	2.76	2.00	2.20	2.49	2.00	2.06
Age of mother when born	20.74	21.00	2.39	20.84	21.00	2.25
Mother's years of education	11.68	12.00	2.30	11.90	12.00	2.28
Years of unemployment of household head	3.67	3.00	2.86	3.28	3.00	2.84
Years county unemployment > 10%, age 11–15	0.59	0.00	0.94	0.62	0.00	1.05
Born into two-parent family	0.46			0.62		
Number of childhood phases with marital change	0.79	1.00	0.83	0.59	0.00	0.78
Number of childhood phases mother worked full-time	1.92	2.00	1.14	1.74	2.00	1.14
Average income < $15,000	0.33			0.23		
Average income $15,000–$25,000	0.34			0.34		

Source: Panel Study of Income Dynamics (PSID) Assisted Housing Database.
Note: Universe includes PSID sample members born between 1968 and 1976 with family data age 0–15 and years of education at age 20.

negative effects of moving on educational outcomes may occur because moving is disruptive and stressful or because a child may have difficulty making close friends or adapting to the new setting. If the literature is correct, then the MTO results on the effects of neighborhood poverty on children may be understated, because the hypothesized positive effects of moving from a high- to a lower-poverty neighborhood will be offset by the negative effects of the move itself.

We first test for linear and nonlinear effects on educational attainment of the number of years of childhood in which a move took place. Next, because the effect of moves may vary depending on when they occur, we test a model with variables measuring the number of years with a move in each of the three stages of childhood.

Does Moving Affect the Impact of Neighborhood Poverty on Educational Attainment?

Children and adults who are familiar with an environment can potentially devise coping mechanisms to contend with its worst features. High-poverty neighborhoods could therefore have worse effects on those who move frequently than on those who remain in the same residence. Accordingly, we test a model interacting average neighborhood poverty and the number of moves over all childhood.

Data

Database

The analysis relies on the PSID-Assisted Housing Database constructed in two stages. First, we collected addresses of housing units receiving subsidies from the federal and/or state government from administrative records and through surveys of housing agencies. These data include all HUD project-based assisted housing programs (both public housing and privately owned units that receive subsidy), units developed under the Low-Income Housing Tax Credit program, units subsidized by the Farmer's Home Administration Section 515 program, and state-subsidized rental units. (A description of the Assisted Housing Database can be found in Newman and Schnare 1997.)

Second, we matched these assisted housing addresses to the residential addresses of all sample members in the PSID during the period 1968–95.

The resulting file indicates whether the PSID's individual sample members had lived in assisted housing in each year and, if so, the housing assistance program they participated in. In the sample, roughly 10 percent of children 0 to 15 years old who lived in assisted housing, or had family income that qualified them for assisted housing at some point during their childhood, had spent time living in public housing. The public housing developments in the PSID-Assisted Housing Database have, on average, almost 100 units; the privately owned, subsidized housing complexes have an average of 33 units. The PSID records are geocoded to either the census tract or ZIP Code area.

Analysis File

The analysis file draws from the 1968–95 waves of the PSID. In each year since 1968, the PSID has interviewed a representative sample of 5,000 families and their "split-offs"—children leaving home and spouses of divorced couples. The result is an unbiased sample of families and a representative sample of children born into these families each year.[9] The original sample included an oversampling of poverty households. Weights have been constructed to adjust for this oversampling and to account for differential attrition.

The analysis uses data for the nine PSID cohorts born between 1967 and 1976. The individuals in this sample were age 0–15 during the years 1968 through 1990. Measures of educational attainment at age 20 begin in 1987 and continue through 1995. Only individuals for whom we had complete data are included in the analysis. The number of grades they completed is measured at age 20.

The analysis sample, our best approximation of the full target group for HUD's assisted housing programs, consists of children who spent at least one year in assisted housing during childhood or who lived in a family that, at some point during their childhood, was eligible for assisted housing programs based on income, according to 1998 eligibility definitions.[10] The individual-level sample contains 923 observations, including 222 observations of children age 0 to 15 who have spent at least one year in assisted housing. The sibling analysis sample contains 552 sibling pairs, the basis for the family fixed-effects analysis from 236 families. Of the 236 families, 175 have two siblings, 51 have three siblings, and 10 have more than three siblings. Given the cohort range, siblings cannot be more than nine years apart in age. Neighborhood poverty rate data come from the

PSID geocode match files and are at the census tract level, where available, and ZIP Code level otherwise.[11]

Description of Sample

Table 12.2 provides descriptive information on educational attainment and the key policy variables of interest: neighborhood poverty, residential mobility, and assisted housing. The full sample and the assisted housing group have similar average educational attainment (slightly less than 12 years).[12] But children who live in assisted housing are more than twice as likely to experience neighborhood poverty rates of 40 percent or more (24 percent versus 11 percent), and their average neighborhood

Table 12.2. *Neighborhood Poverty, Residential Mobility, and Assisted Housing Attributes of the Analysis Sample*

	Assisted (N = 222)	Assisted + eligible unassisted (N = 923)
Average years of completed education age 20	11.76	11.88
Average neighborhood poverty age 0–15		
< 20 percent	32.0	46.6
20–29 percent	25.8	26.8
30–39 percent	18.7	16.0
40 percent or more	23.6	10.6
Total	100.0	100.0
Number of moves		
0	4.0	9.0
1–2	21.8	28.9
3–5	36.0	34.0
6+	38.2	28.1
Total	100.0	100.0
Transitions out of high poverty		
≥ 40 to ≥ 40 percent neighborhood poverty	61.8	50.0
≥ 40 to 30–39 percent	17.7	20.4
≥ 40 to 20–29 percent	10.3	14.2
≥ 40 to 10–19 percent	4.4	13.0
≥ 40 to < 10 percent	5.9	2.5
Total	100.0	100.0

Table 12.2. *(Continued)*

	Assisted (N = 222)	*Assisted + eligible unassisted* (N = 923)
Percentage point change in poverty from early to late childhood		
< −5	36.0	32.9
−5 to 5	36.9	44.6
> 5	27.1	22.5
Total	100.0	100.0
Exposure to assisted housing		
Ever assisted	100.0	24.0
Ever public	60.0	14.4
Ever other	45.3	10.9
Ever both	5.3	1.3
Mean years in assisted housing	5.9	1.4
Public housing (excluding zeros)	7.1	7.1
Other assisted housing (excluding zeros)	3.7	3.7
Assisted housing transitions		
Assisted to unassisted	20.4	4.9
Unassisted to assisted	26.2	6.3
Always assisted	16.9	4.1
Limited assistance	36.4	8.8
Never assisted	0.0	76.0
Total	100.0	100.0

Source: Panel Study of Income Dynamics (PSID) Assisted Housing Database.
Note: Universe includes PSID sample members born between 1968 and 1976 with family data age 0–15 and years of education at age 20.

poverty rate is 25 percent higher than children in the full sample (29 versus 23 percent).

Children who have spent any time in assisted housing are also more likely to have moved. On average, they have at least one additional move compared with children in the full sample (five versus four). Almost 40 percent of the children who have lived in assisted housing made six or more moves during childhood, compared with about 30 percent of the children in the full sample.

Transitions out of high-poverty neighborhoods are rare for children who ever spent time in assisted housing as well as for the full sample.[13] Of those who lived in a high-poverty neighborhood in early or middle child-hood, few moved to neighborhoods with less than 10 percent poverty: less than 3 percent of children in the full sample and 6 percent of children who lived in assisted housing made such moves. Thus, absent a demon-stration project like MTO, moves from high to very low poverty neigh-borhoods generally do not occur.

More frequent, however, are modest improvements in neighborhood. For example, more than a third of children in both samples experienced neighborhood poverty decreases of 5 percentage points or more. On the other hand, roughly a quarter of children saw neighborhood poverty *increase* 5 percentage points or more between early and late childhood.

More assisted-housing children are likely to have lived in public hous-ing (60 percent) than in other forms of assisted housing (45 percent).[14] In the full sample, 76 percent of children in income-eligible families have never lived in assisted housing, reflecting the nonentitlement nature of assisted housing and approximating the national estimate that only about one-fifth to one-quarter of those income-eligible for housing assistance actually receive it. Children who have spent any time in assisted housing tend to live there for a total of about six years (not always consecutively), with longer stays in public housing (7.1 years) than in other types of assisted housing (3.7 years).

Variation in Family Characteristics between Siblings

As noted earlier, the ability of the family fixed-effects approach to address the potential bias from unmeasured characteristics may be problematic if unmeasured family characteristics vary from sibling to sibling. In par-ticular, if changes in family structure are associated with moves into particular types of neighborhoods, unmeasured differences in family conditions could cause sibling differences in neighborhood experience. In our sample, however, differences in neighborhood moves for families that experienced different types of marital transitions appear unrelated to type of neighborhood.

A much higher proportion of movers than stayers experience marital transitions (table 12.3). However, among children experiencing a move and a parent's marital transition, the relationship between the type of marital change and the type of neighborhood change is only modestly significant. Although a higher proportion of children who lost a parent through separation, divorce, or death moved to a higher-poverty neighbor-

NEIGHBORHOOD POVERTY   353

Table 12.3. *Association of Marital Status Changes with Residential Moves to Higher- and Lower-Poverty Neighborhoods*

	A. Differences in marital status change for stayers and movers[a]			B. Differences in neighborhood poverty change for movers with marital status change[b]							
	Stayers	Movers	P^c	n	Higher	Lower	P^c	5 % points higher	P^c	5 % points lower	P^c
Assisted + eligible unassisted											
N	9,810	3,816									
Divorced, separated, or widowed	0.03	0.04	0.00	151	0.43	0.32	0.07	0.13	0.13	0.14	0.86
Married	0.01	0.04	0.00	148	0.36	0.33	0.51	0.12	0.12	0.14	0.71
Assisted											
N	2,169	1,094									
Divorced, separated, or widowed	0.04	0.05	0.29	54	0.43	0.30	0.16	0.13	0.13	0.13	1.00
Married	0.02	0.05	0.00	53	0.36	0.36	1.00	0.08	0.08	0.08	1.00

Source: Panel Study of Income Dynamics (PSID) Assisted Housing Database.
Notes: Table includes PSID sample members born between 1968 and 1976 with family data age 0–15 and years of education at age 20.
a. Unit of observation is the person-year.
b. Unit of observation is the person-year with a move and the denoted marital change.
c. Two-tailed *t*-tests assuming unequal variances.

hood than to a lower-poverty neighborhood (43 versus 32 percent), the changes in neighborhood poverty were slight, with equivalent proportions moving to neighborhoods with poverty rates 5 percentage points higher or lower than their previous neighborhoods. Children who gained a parent through marriage and moved were as likely to move to a higher-poverty neighborhood as to a lower-poverty neighborhood. Thus, family structure and neighborhood change should not skew the analysis.

Table 12.4 shows the fraction of the full sample variance that occurs within families for selected key variables. Overall, the proportion of the total variance that occurs within families is much larger for years of completed education than for the key explanatory variables. However, because the proportion of the variance in neighborhood poverty within families is of roughly the same magnitude as that for other time-varying family characteristics such as income, family changes should not dominate changes in neighborhood poverty.

Model Results: Answering the Four Questions

Does Housing Assistance Receipt Affect Children's Educational Attainment?

The regression results for the key variables of interest are shown in table 12.5. Models 1 and 2 suggest that housing assistance does not have a significant effect on children's educational attainment. Neither specification of the assisted housing indicator even approaches significance.[15]

Does Neighborhood Poverty Experienced during Childhood Affect Children's Educational Attainment?

Models 1 and 2 indicate that average neighborhood poverty experienced from birth to age 15 is associated with reduced educational attainment. The individual-level results for model 2, for example, show that every 10 percentage point decrease in neighborhood poverty is associated with a loss of more than one-tenth of a school grade. The family fixed-effect specification confirms this negative impact: each 10 percentage point increase in neighborhood poverty is associated with a loss of 70 percent of a grade. These results suggest that a decrease in average neighborhood poverty of 30 percent (the MTO condition) would produce a gain in

Table 12.4. *Percentage of Within-Family Variance on Selected Variables*

| | Years of education | Income ($1,000s) | Entire childhood averages | | |
			Neighborhood % poverty	Years in assisted housing	Number of moves
Assisted and eligible unassisted					
Mean	11.9	2.5	22.8	1.4	3.9
Sample standard deviation	1.4	1.2	12.8	3.4	2.9
Within-family standard deviation	1.2	0.3	2.6	0.7	1.0
% of variance within families	72.3	6.7	4.2	4.7	11.1
Assisted					
Mean	11.8	2.1	28.9	6.0	4.8
Sample standard deviation	1.4	1.0	14.2	4.5	3.1
Within-family standard deviation	1.3	0.2	2.6	1.2	1.0
% of variance within families	79.3	5.2	3.3	7.2	10.5

Source: Panel Study of Income Dynamics (PSID) Assisted Housing Database.
Note: Universe includes PSID sample members born between 1968 and 1976 with family data age 0–15 and years of education at age 20.

Table 12.5. *Regression Results for the Effects of Neighborhood Poverty, Residential Moves, and Housing Assistance on Educational Attainment*

	Dependent variable: Years of education × 100			
	Individuals (N = 923)		Family fixed effects (N = 552)	
	Coef.	(SE)	Coef.	(SE)
Model 1: All childhood neighborhood poverty rate and number of moves, housing assistance sequence specification.				
Assisted to unassisted	−0.83	(19.63)	52.26	(54.60)
Unassisted to assisted or always assisted	(excluded)		(excluded)	
Limited or not assisted	−7.10	(14.16)	8.10	(55.22)
Neighborhood % poverty age 0–15	−1.17	(0.48)**	−7.53	(3.36)**
Total number of moves age 0–15	−5.89	(1.90)***	−10.68	(8.44)
Model 2: All childhood neighborhood poverty rate and number of moves, housing assistance by childhood phase.				
In assisted housing 3+ years age 0–5	2.86	(16.08)	24.44	(51.86)
In assisted housing 3+ years age 6–10	2.56	(21.91)	−85.89	(49.51)*
In assisted housing 3+ years age 11–15	−2.47	(20.41)	−33.50	(53.58)
Neighborhood % poverty age 0–15	−1.13	(0.49)**	−7.00	(3.33)**
Total number of moves age 0–15	−5.92	(1.89)***	−11.32	(8.57)

Table 12.5. *(Continued)*

| | Dependent variable: Years of education × 100 | | | |
| | Individuals (N = 923) | | Family fixed effects (N = 552) | |
	Coef.	(SE)	Coef.	(SE)
Model 3: Neighborhood poverty rate and number of moves, by childhood phase.[a]				
Neighborhood % poverty age 0–15	0.71	(0.50)	−1.17	(1.51)
Neighborhood % poverty age 6–10	−2.24	(0.85)***	−5.69	(1.97)***
Neighborhood % poverty age 11–15	0.51	(0.78)	0.16	(1.99)
Number of moves age 0–5	−3.23	(3.32)	−17.92	(9.68)*
Number of moves age 6–10	−7.38	(3.90)*	−6.14	(11.61)
Number of moves age 11–15	−7.58	(4.12)*	5.26	(12.44)
Model 4: Interaction of all childhood neighborhood poverty rate and number of moves[a]				
Neighborhood % poverty age 0–15	−0.83	(0.64)	−8.80	(3.63)**
Total number of moves age 0–15	−3.77	(3.87)	−27.39	(15.46)*
% poverty × number of moves age 0–15	−0.10	(0.14)	0.79	(0.63)

Source: Panel Study of Income Dynamics (PSID) Assisted Housing Database.

Notes: Universe includes PSID sample members born between 1968 and 1976 with family data age 0–15 and years of education at age 20.

All models include the control variables listed in table 12.1.

a. Model includes housing assistance specified as in model 2.

*$p < .10$, **$p < .05$, ***$p < .01$

schooling ranging from about a third of a grade to just over two school grades.[16]

According to model 3, the age a child experiences neighborhood poverty appears important in determining educational outcomes: middle childhood (age 6–10) appears to be the critical phase. The individual model shows that each 10 percentage point increase in average neighborhood poverty during middle childhood reduces completed schooling by nearly one-quarter of a grade. The family fixed-effects model confirms these findings: each 10 percentage point increase in neighborhood poverty during middle childhood reduced completed schooling by more than half a grade. Neighborhood poverty in early or late childhood has no noticeable effect. These results suggest that MTO may more strongly affect children who are living in a lower-poverty neighborhood by age 6. However, as noted next, moving may somewhat offset MTO's positive impact.

Does Moving Affect Educational Attainment?

In the individual-level results of model 1, the effect of residential moves over all of childhood is significant, negative, and small, with each move reducing educational attainment by only 0.06 of a grade. While the coefficient is negative and roughly the same size in the family fixed-effects specification, it is insignificant, suggesting that the individual-level results may partly reflect the unmeasured characteristics of families that move frequently, rather than the sole effects of moving.

These results suggest that the positive effect of changing from a high- to a lower-poverty neighborhood may be slightly offset by the disruptive effect of the move. Net of the positive effect of moving to a lower-poverty neighborhood, each additional move reduces educational attainment by roughly one-tenth of a grade. While not a large effect, it may be worth thinking about mechanisms to smooth the transition children experience when they move, such as counseling to help them adjust to their new surroundings.

There are no significant departures from linearity in the effect of the moves, but the timing of moves appears to modestly affect educational outcomes, according to the results of model 3. The individual-level and the family fixed-effects results differ on when moves are most detrimental. According to the individual analysis, residential moves in middle or late childhood are more harmful to educational achievement. By contrast, the family fixed-effects results show that moves in early childhood have the greatest negative impact.

Does Moving Affect the Impact of Neighborhood Poverty on Educational Attainment?

Most relevant for the MTO demonstration, the nonexperimental results of model 4 suggest that moving does not seriously affect the impact of neighborhood poverty on educational attainment. The interaction of average neighborhood poverty and the number of moves between ages 0 and 15 is not significant and is of opposite signs in the individual and family fixed-effects specifications. Thus, while residential moves appear to have a modest negative effect, this effect should be no different for children in the MTO experimental group who come from a high-poverty neighborhood than for children from lower-poverty neighborhoods.

Conclusions

This analysis uses a unique database to explore whether neighborhood poverty and exposure to assisted housing affect educational attainment. At a descriptive level, the data provide previously unavailable information about children's neighborhood and housing experiences from age 0 to 15. On average, children who lived at any time in assisted housing during the 1968–90 period spent an average of 5.9 years there. Children in public housing lived there for an average of 7.1 years. Children who lived in other project-based assisted housing resided there, on average, for 3.7 years.

Residential moves from high- to very low poverty neighborhoods are rare. Among children living in assisted housing in a high-poverty neighborhood before age 11, less than 10 percent were living in a low-poverty neighborhood between ages 11 and 15. Less than 3 percent of the children in the full sample (children in assisted housing and children living in income-eligible families that never received assistance) experienced such moves. Thus, the MTO demonstration moves—with families relocating from neighborhoods of 40 percent poverty or greater to neighborhoods with lower than 10 percent poverty—rarely occur under normal circumstances.

Five principal findings emerge from the regression analysis. First, housing assistance does not affect children's educational attainment. Second, neighborhood poverty negatively affects children's educational outcomes, but only when it is experienced between ages 6 and 10, not in other stages of childhood. Third, residential moves adversely affect educational attainment, and residential moves experienced before age 6 may have the worst effect. Fourth, neither neighborhood poverty nor residential moves exhibit nonlinear effects. Finally, although residential moves are detrimental to children's educational attainment, the negative repercussions of residential moves are not exacerbated by high neighborhood poverty.

Despite methodological shortcomings, the estimates of the negative effect of neighborhood poverty, especially when it is experienced between ages 6 and 10, seem fairly reliable: the individual and family fixed-effects models produce consistent estimates. However, the estimated size of neighborhood poverty's impact on children's educational attainment varies from model to model. In the individual models, every 10 percentage point increase in neighborhood poverty reduces educational attainment by less than one-quarter of a year, but in the family fixed-effects models, the negative effects of neighborhood poverty are at least twice as large. The difference could arise from the exclusion of single children from the family fixed-effects models, or it may indicate, counterintuitively, that families with unobserved characteristics that lead to greater educational attainment for their children live in higher-poverty neighborhoods than their otherwise comparable peers. The underlying reason for the discrepancy in effect-size estimates is an important topic for future research.

The estimates for the effect of residential moves are less robust. For example, the result that moving in early childhood (before age 6) is most detrimental to educational attainment appears only in the family fixed-effects models, not the individual models. The near colinearity of the number of moves across different childhood stages may contribute to the instability of these effect estimates.

Recent papers by Manski (1993) and Moffitt (2001) demonstrate the methodological challenges in securing reliable estimates of neighborhood and peer effects. Thus, the results presented here, obtained using fairly crude methods, should be treated with some caution. With that caveat, three expectations for the MTO experiment may be hazarded. First, because the effects of housing assistance appear to be negligible, the change from public to tenant-based assisted housing should have little effect. Second, the model results clearly indicate that the benefits derived from reducing neighborhood poverty by 30 percentage points are larger than the detrimental effect of moving. Thus, the MTO experiment should produce positive results. Finally, because neighborhood poverty does not exhibit nonlinear effects, we may see significant differences between the MTO experimental group that moved to a low-poverty neighborhood and the voucher-only group.

NOTES

The research reported in this chapter was supported by the U.S. Department of Housing and Urban Development, Office of Policy Development and Research, the Ford Foundation, and the Rockefeller Foundation. The authors thank Greg Duncan for his keen insights during the development of the analysis plan, David Kantor and Sally Katz for research assistance, and participants at the MTO conference for their comments.

    1. Defined as above 40 percent.

    2. The current MTO design will have difficulty assessing some effects. Because children in the MTO experimental groups will move not only from high- to low-poverty areas, but also from public housing to private rental housing with a Section 8 certificate, it will be difficult to disentangle the effects of the change in neighborhood, the change in housing, and the move itself.

    3. One exception is Brooks-Gunn, Duncan, and Aber (1997).

    4. For simplicity, we have taken the liberty of collapsing five theories presented in the literature into two broad categories.

    5. Studies of the relative deprivation theory focus mainly on the effects of a high school's socioeconomic mix on the college plans of graduating seniors—not the effects of neighborhood socioeconomic mix per se (Jencks and Mayer 1990).

    6. For example, several key items on the index were collected through interviewer observations, which have reliability problems.

    7. An instrumental variable approach instead of an unmeasured variable model is an alternative for dealing with unmeasured variables, but finding plausible instruments for neighborhoods is difficult.

    8. The correlation between neighborhood poverty in different childhood stages may affect standard errors, but coefficients will not be biased.

    9. The PSID does not add new U.S. immigrants.

    10. As the best approximation of the varied income eligibility thresholds in effect over the study period, we use 80 percent of county median income, adjusted for family size per HUD's rules in this analysis. With some exceptions, HUD currently uses a cutoff of 80 percent of metropolitan area median income adjusted for family size.

    11. Values for intercensus years were derived by interpolation using the values from the two bracketing decennial censuses. For census years, and for cases where the data from only one of the bracketing censuses were available, we used values from a single census. (From 1986 forward, the PSID geocode match provided data from the 1990 Census only.) Data from two censuses were used in 81 percent of the cases, one census was used for 17 percent of the cases, and less than 2 percent of the cases were missing census data. Approximately 65 percent of the two-census interpolations were obtained from tract data alone,

12 percent used ZIP Code data alone, and 3 percent used a combination of tract and ZIP Code measures. In the remaining 20 percent of the two-census cases, data at the tract or ZIP Code level were available for only one of the bracketing censuses. For these, we used the value at the tract or ZIP Code level that was available relative to the Minor Civil Division (MCD) value for that census to impute a tract or ZIP value for the missing census based on its MCD value. The MCD corresponds roughly to a township or a quarter of a county. Values for the MCD, or something conceptually similar to it, were available for all years. The interpolation was then performed using the actual and the imputed values. Of the single-census cases, 75 percent used tract-level data, and 25 percent used ZIP Code–level data. Finally, for the 1.6 percent of cases with missing values, we proceeded by determining whether the missing value appeared within a sequence of no-move years with other non-missing values. If so, we averaged over the nonmissing values, or interpolated if possible, and assigned this value to the missing values. Eighty percent of the originally missing observations (1.3 percent of the total) were modified in this way. We dropped the remaining 0.3 percent of missing cases from the sample.

12.   The slight difference between the assisted and eligible unassisted groups is not statistically significant.

13.   Transitions include residential moves and changes occurring in neighborhood poverty without a move.

14.   These numbers add to more than 100 percent because some children lived in both types of assisted housing.

15.   The analyses for this chapter were completed in 1997. In subsequent work that used instrumental variables to account for unmeasured differences between families with and without housing assistance, growing up in public housing was found to have favorable long-term effects on children's economic outcomes (Newman and Harkness 2002).

16.   The sequence of housing assistance (e.g., assisted to unassisted, etc.) produced similar results. The test of neighborhood poverty threshold effects shows no noticeable nonlinearity in the relationship between neighborhood poverty and years of completed schooling.

REFERENCES

Aaronson, Daniel. 1997. "Using Sibling Data to Estimate the Impact of Neighborhoods on Children's Educational Outcomes." In *Neighborhood Poverty. Volume 2: Policy Implications in Studying Neighborhoods,* edited by Jeanne Brooks-Gunn, Greg J. Duncan, and J. Lawrence Aber. New York: Russell Sage Foundation.

Baumrind, Diana. 1993. "The Average Expectable Environment Is Not Good Enough: A Response to Scarr." *Child Development* 64: 1299–317.

Brooks-Gunn, Jeanne, Greg J. Duncan, and J. Lawrence Aber. 1997. *Neighborhood Poverty. Volume 1: Context and Consequences for Children.* New York: Russell Sage Foundation.

Case, Ann, and Lawrence Katz. 1991. "The Company You Keep: The Effects of Family and Neighborhood on Disadvantaged Youth." NBER Working Paper 3705. Cambridge, Mass.: National Bureau of Economic Research.

Clark, Rebecca. 1992. "Neighborhood Effects on Dropping Out of School among Teenage Boys." Population Studies Center Discussion Paper Series. Washington, D.C.: The Urban Institute.

Corcoran, Mary, Roger Gordon, Deborah Laren, and Gary Solon. 1991. "The Association between Men's Economic Status and Their Family and Community Origins." *Journal of Human Resources* 27(4):575–601.

Crane, Jonathan. 1991. "The Epidemic Theory of Ghettos and Neighborhood Effects on Dropping Out and Teenage Childbearing." *American Journal of Sociology* 96(5): 1226–59.

Datcher, Linda. 1982. "Effects of Community and Family Backgrounds on Achievement." *Review of Economics and Statistics* 64:32–41.

Duncan, Greg. 1994. "Families and Neighbors as Sources of Disadvantage in the Schooling Decisions of White and Black Adolescents." Ann Arbor: University of Michigan, Survey Research Center, mimeo.

Evans, William, Wallace Oates, and Robert Schwab. 1992. "Measuring Peer Group Effects: A Study of Teenage Behavior." *Journal of Political Economy* 100(5): 966–91.

GAO. See U.S. General Accounting Office.

Ginther, Donna, Robert Haveman, and Barbara Wolfe. 1993. "Neighborhood Characteristics as Determinants of Children's Outcomes: How Robust Are the Relationships?" Paper presented at the Fifteenth Annual Association for Public Policy Analysis and Management Research Conference, Washington, D.C., Oct. 28–30.

Hauser, Robert, and Raymond Sin-Kwok Wong. 1989. "Sibling Resemblance and Intersibling Effects in Educational Attainment." *Sociology of Education* 62(3): 149–71.

Haveman, Robert, Barbara Wolfe, and James Spaulding. 1991. "Educational Achievement and Childhood Events and Circumstances." *Demography* 28(1): 133.

HUD User. 1997. "A Picture of Subsidized Housing." http://www.huduser.org/datasets/assthsg/statedata97/allst.html.

Jencks, Christopher, and Susan Mayer. 1990. "The Social Consequences of Growing Up in a Poor Neighborhood." In *Inner-City Poverty in the United States,* edited by Laurence Lynn and Michael McGeary (111–86). Washington, D.C.: National Academy Press.

Manski, Charles F. 1993. "Identification of Endogenous Social Effects: The Reflection Problem." *Review of Economic Studies* 60(3): 531–42.

Mayer, Susan. 1997. *What Money Can't Buy.* Cambridge, Mass.: Harvard University Press.

Moffitt, Robert A. 2001. "Policy Interventions, Low-Level Equilibria, and Social Interactions." In *Social Dynamics,* edited by Steven N. Durlauf and H. Peyton Young (45–82). Cambridge, Mass.: MIT Press.

Newman, Sandra J., and Joseph Harkness. 1999. "The Effects of Welfare Reform on Housing: A National Analysis." In *The Home Front: Implications of Welfare Reform for Housing Policy,* edited by Sandra J. Newman (29–80). Washington, D.C.: Urban Institute Press.

———. 2002. "The Long-Term Effects of Public Housing on Self-Sufficiency." *Journal of Public Policy Analysis and Management* 10(1): 21–43.

Newman, Sandra, and Ann Schnare. 1993. "Last in Line: Housing Assistance for House-holds with Children." *Housing Policy Debate* 4(3): 417–55.

———. 1997. " '. . . And a Suitable Living Environment': The Failure of Housing Programs to Deliver on Neighborhood Quality." *Housing Policy Debate* 8(4): 703–41.

Plotnick, Robert, and Saul Hoffman. 1993. "Using Sister Pairs to Estimate How Neighborhoods Affect Young Adult Outcomes." Paper presented at the Fifteenth Annual Association for Public Policy Analysis and Management Research Conference, Washington, D.C., Oct. 28–30.

Scarr, Susan. 1992. "Developmental Theories for the 1990s: Development and Individual Differences." *Child Development* 63:1–19.

Shlay, Anne, and Scott Holupka. 1991. *Steps toward Independence: The Early Effects of the Lafayette Courts Family Development Center.* Baltimore, Md.: Johns Hopkins University Institute for Policy Studies, mimeo.

U.S. General Accounting Office. 1994. *Federally Assisted Housing: Condition of Some Properties Receiving Section 8 Project-Based Assistance Is Below Housing Quality Standards.* GAO/T-RCED-94-273. Washington, D.C.: U.S. General Accounting Office.

Wilson, William J. 1987. *The Truly Disadvantaged.* Chicago: University of Chicago Press.

13

MTO's Impact on Sending and Receiving Neighborhoods

George Galster

Researchers evaluating subsidized housing programs that are designed to geographically deconcentrate low-income households typically ask: How are *MTO participants* affected by conditions in their sending and receiving neighborhoods? This chapter, taking a different approach, asks the reverse: How are *sending and receiving neighborhoods* affected by the migration of MTO participants?

MTO research must measure the impacts on sending and receiving neighborhoods to assess the overall social efficiency of the program. Social efficiency here is defined as the net reduction of socially problematic behaviors aggregated across movers and nonmovers in neighborhoods that send MTO households away as well as in those that receive them. To get at this question, this chapter presents a conceptual model that demonstrates how only modest differences in the functional relationship between neighborhood poverty rates and resultant social cost (dysfunctional behaviors, low achievement, etc.) will radically affect conclusions about the desirability of MTO, in particular, and deconcentrating, subsidized housing programs, in general. A brief review of the scant extant evidence about the effects movers have on neighborhoods suggests a threshold relationship, with dramatic changes occurring in neighborhoods having between 15 and 40 percent poverty rates.

So far, the evidence suggests that MTO and other subsidized housing deconcentration programs in the United States can be justified on the grounds of social efficiency under two conditions: as long as low-income households move to very low poverty neighborhoods and as long as none of the receiving neighborhoods exceeds the threshold after the in-migration. Only future research can confirm this conclusion.

Evaluating Neighborhood Impacts and Net Social Benefits of MTO

The social science literature has widely acknowledged a causal relationship between a neighborhood's socioeconomic profile and individuals' propensities toward socially problematic behaviors.[1] Most empirical studies, in some sense, support the notion that *neighborhood matters* in individuals' decisionmaking, although few agree on why it matters, how it matters, or on which social outcomes reflect which neighborhood factors (Briggs 1997; Leventhal and Brooks-Gunn 2000; Sampson, Morenoff, and Gannon-Rowley 2002; Turner and Ellen 1997). In particular, researchers continue to debate the degree to which conditions associated with the neighborhood's aggregate poverty rate affect individuals' behaviors, independent of socioeconomic status.

Curiously, the literature so far has evaluated MTO in a highly selective fashion. Only the potential impacts on the participating MTO households associated with their moving from a high-poverty to a low-poverty neighborhood have been considered. Yet it is equally valid to consider the effects from another angle: How might MTO, to the extent it changes a particular neighborhood's poverty rate, marginally affect nonmoving residents' lives in both places?

The lack of any consensus on causal explanations for neighborhood effects indicates the need to theoretically analyze a variety of plausible alternatives.[2] Figure 13.1 depicts different possible relationships between the concentration of poverty and social problems in a hypothetical set of metropolitan neighborhoods. For simplicity, the concentration of poverty is measured by the percentage of low-income households in a neighborhood. The degree of social problems may be considered an index of neighborhood conditions that reflects the aggregate levels of crime, nonparticipation in the labor force, long-term welfare dependency, substance abuse, school dropouts, delinquency, and social isolation or alienation. Five distinct situations are shown, each one representing a different possible effect of shifting low-income populations from a high-poverty area to

Figure 13.1. *Possible Relationships between Poverty Rates and Aggregate Incidence of Social Problems in a Neighborhood*

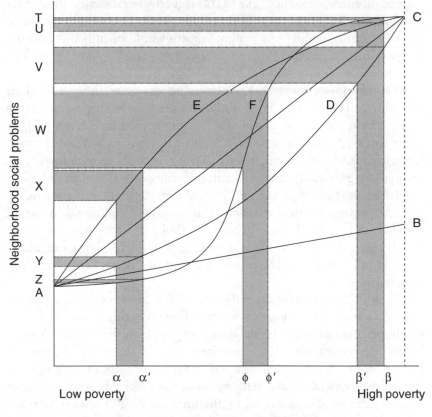

Source: Author's calculations.

a lower-poverty area. Each alternative varies on the degree to which the neighborhood's poverty rate is assumed to independently influence the behavioral choices of individuals in the neighborhood (movers and non-movers alike).

The first proposed relationship assumes that people's likelihood of undertaking socially problematic behaviors is linear and directly related to their personal degree of poverty (line AB). It implies that the aggregate poverty rate of neighbors has no independent effects on behavior. Therefore, social problems are observed to be more common in low-income neighborhoods, but only because more low-income people live there. According to the dynamics of this relationship, a subsidized housing deconcentration policy (like MTO) is ineffective, because the reduction in the incidence of social problems in the sending neighborhood of the deconcentrated low-income households would be fully offset by the increase in social problems in the receiving neighborhood of the deconcentrated low-income households.[3]

The second hypothetical relationship assumes that individual behavior is linearly associated both with families' own poverty status and with the aggregate poverty rate of their neighbors (line AC). In other words, all low-income individuals carry a constant social problem propensity with them (so long as their incomes remain low). This propensity externally influences their neighbors' decision calculus, regardless of the low-income individual's residential environment. As in the first hypothetical example, this proposed relationship would provide no justification for deconcentrated subsidized housing policies, because the increase in social problems in the receiving neighborhood would offset the lessening of social problems in the sending neighborhood.[4]

The third hypothesis assumes that the probability of undertaking problem behaviors is a function of one's own poverty status and that of one's neighbors, but that the marginal impact of the neighbors' poverty is nonlinearly decreasing (line AEC). In other words, in this situation, the first low-income entrants into an otherwise nonpoor neighborhood so greatly disrupt the social fabric that many nonpoor households begin to engage in socially problematic behaviors. By the time the neighborhood becomes solidly low income, however, entry of an additional low-income entrant has a very modest impact on the propensity of any resident to engage in problematic behaviors. Under such circumstances, it would be unwise to begin a subsidized housing deconcentration program, as it would yield a net increase in social problems.[5] The next case also assumes that the probability of engaging in problem behaviors is a function of an individual's poverty status and that of his or her neighbors, but that the marginal impact of the latter factor is nonlinearly increasing (line ADC). That is, the behavioral consequence of one more low-income neighbor is trivial when the overall poverty rate in the neighborhood remains low (perhaps because the dominant neighborhood social milieu persists as "middle class"), but rises progressively as the poverty rate in the area increases. Here, subsidized housing deconcentration would be recommended, because net social problems would decrease (see the difference between gray bands V-Y in figure 13.1).

The final case combines features of the previous two cases and adds a threshold (AFC). Here, areas with a very high or a very low concentration of poverty are similar in one way: shuffling a handful of low-income households into or out of these areas will have little or no impact on the overall social costs in that neighborhood. Under this proposed relationship, areas of very high poverty will not experience any significant benefits from losing a *few* low-income, assisted housing tenants inasmuch as the character of the milieu will not be altered (band T is small in figure 13.1). For similar reasons, the addition of a few low-income households in an otherwise middle-class area will spur few problem behaviors among the middle-class residents there (band Z is small). However, if a program deconcentrates a sufficient number of low-income households in any *particular* high-poverty neighborhood—so that the sending neighborhood's poverty rate falls below the threshold and none of the receiving neighborhoods rises above the poverty threshold—total social costs in the metropolitan area will fall significantly. (For a proof, see the appendix.)

But between these two relatively stable social environments exist neighborhoods (like ϕ in figure 13.1) near the threshold poverty rate. Here, removing a few of the low-income households could have significant positive results for the entire neighborhood. Conversely, adding a few more low-income households would drastically increase the area's social problems. This alternative emphasizes the importance of the conditions used when deconcentrating assisted housing tenants. Relocating tenants into threshold communities that have only marginally lower poverty rates than their previous neighborhood may exact much higher social costs from the recipient neighborhood (such as band W due to changing ϕ to ϕ' in figure 13.1) than would be removed from the sending neighborhood (band T). On the other hand, relocating low-income tenants out of either high-poverty or threshold neighborhoods and into low-poverty areas should benefit the sending neighborhood, without noticeably affecting the receiving community.

In summary, this straightforward graphical exercise demonstrates that simply arguing that neighborhood poverty rates positively affect an individual's propensity to engage in socially problematic behavior cannot sufficiently justify MTO or any other housing deconcentration strategy. On the contrary, the precise mathematical way this neighborhood effect manifests itself will determine whether social problems contained within the community at large will, on net, decline, remain constant, or even rise under a particular sort of deconcentration policy. Does previous evidence tell us anything about the nature of this mathematical relationship?

The Relationship between Neighborhood Poverty Rates and Behavioral Responses

This chapter does not attempt a detailed review of the "neighborhood effects" literature (for a review, see Briggs 1997; Galster and Killen 1995; Haveman and Wolfe 1995; Jencks and Mayer 1990; Leventhal and Brooks-Gunn 2000; Mayer and Jencks 1989; Sampson, Morenoff and Gannon-Rowley 2002; and Turner and Ellen 1997). Rather, the section focuses on the nonlinearities in the marginal relationships between neighborhood poverty rates and social problem behaviors.[6]

Consider limited employment and earnings as a social problem. Researchers have thoroughly investigated the ways in which neighborhood might affect residents' earning capacity, such as through spatial mismatch (Ihlanfeldt and Sjoquist 1998; Kain 1992), job search (Rogers 1997), and social isolation (Wilson 1987; 1996). Of these studies, Wilson (1987) contends that as the middle class (first white and then black families) left the inner city, the low-income blacks left behind eventually became isolated from the role models offered by the middle class, implying a nonlinear relationship. Without such role models, by Wilson's view, low-income individuals cannot see the way people with similar constraints cope with occasional unemployment. Joblessness becomes "a way of life" and takes on a different social meaning for low-income individuals than for higher-income individuals. The concept of threshold is manifest in this phenomenon of social isolation. In Wilson's words, "Poverty concentration effects should result in an exponential increase in . . . forms of social dislocation" (1987, 57).

Only one statistical study, however, tests for nonlinearities in the marginal impacts of neighborhood poverty rates on the incomes of current residents or on the future earnings potential of youths. Vartanian (1999a) uses merged Panel Study of Income Dynamics and 1970 and 1980 census tract data to investigate the childhood neighborhood conditions that may influence indicators of subsequent economic well-being (average labor income, wage rate, hours worked) of those age 25 and over during the 1968–85 period. The study operationalizes the neighborhood poverty rate as categorical variables in the following percentile ranges: 0 to 10 (least poverty); 11 to 33; 34 to 67; 68 to 90; and 91 to 100 (most poverty). Average wages and labor income evince two thresholds or break points, one at the 33rd percentile (a drop of 13 and 21 percent, respectively, compared with lower-poverty neighborhoods) and the other at the 68th percentile (an added drop of 6 and 8 percent, respectively) of neighborhood poverty rates. Average hours worked annually exhibits only one threshold or break point: Compared with those growing up in neighborhoods in the lowest two-thirds of poverty rates, those in higher-poverty neighborhoods have an average of 162 less hours of annual work (figure 13.2).

Neighborhood poverty rate is converted from deciles to the corresponding proportion (33rd and 66th deciles translate to $N \approx 0.15$ and 0.30, respectively) to improve comparability with other figures. Scales of all three dependent variables are made comparable: Each has as its maximum (minimum) value $= A$, its observed value in the lowest- (highest-) poverty neighborhood range (see figure 13.2).

The specification of nonlinear relationships for socially problematic behaviors shown by AFC in figure 13.1 has long-standing theoretical support. Sociologists have demonstrated the importance of local social interaction in shaping an individual's attitudes, values, and behaviors (e.g., Simmel 1971; Weber 1978). More recently, economists have incorporated the role of social norms into neoclassical models of economic behavior (e.g., Akerlof 1980; Galster 1987; Manski 2000). The tenet of this "collective socialization" approach is that a social group can influence others to conform to its customs, norms, and behaviors to the degree that (a) the individual comes in social contact with said group and (b) the group can exert relatively more powerful inducements or threats to conform to its positions than other, competing groups.

These two preconditions imply the existence of a concave-upward relationship, perhaps even a threshold-type relationship. If the individuals who make up the group in question are scattered thinly over an urban area, they are less likely to be able either to convey their positions effectively to others with whom they might come in contact or to exert much pressure to conform. Only when a given group approaches some critical mass over a predefined area is that group likely to become a potentially effective vehicle for shaping others. Past this threshold, as more members are recruited to the group, the power of the group to reward and sanction those outside it likely grows nonlinearly. This relationship is especially likely when the positions of the group become so dominant as to become the norm.

Figure 13.2. *Observed Relationships between Neighborhood Poverty Rate and Selected Economic Outcomes*

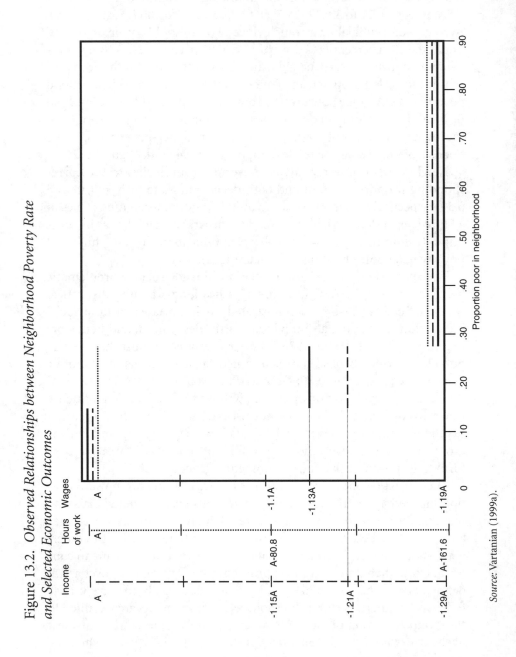

Source: Vartanian (1999a).

To illustrate this dynamic, Murphy, Shleifer, and Vishny (1993) have developed a theoretical model demonstrating how a criminal subgroup can create synergies that encourage a dominant criminal culture in a neighborhood. As the number of criminals in an area grows, three things may happen simultaneously. First, returns from noncriminal activities will be reduced as crime siphons a portion of those returns away. Second, the number of individuals who monitor, report, and/or directly sanction criminal behavior will fall (relatively and perhaps absolutely). Finally, the stigma associated with criminal activity will be eroded as crime becomes the norm. In concert, these three factors likely interact to alter in a nonlinear fashion the relative economic and social payoffs from crime relative to noncriminal activities, and the successful recruitment of criminals will escalate dramatically.

Unfortunately, only scattered empirical work provides insights into the issue of nonlinear effects of neighborhood poverty on male dropout rates, duration of poverty, violent crime, and property crime.[7]

Clark (1992) used 1980 Census tract data linked with PSID data to explore the relationship between neighborhood poverty rate (expressed as spline variables) and the probability of a male dropping out of secondary school. The study finds an essentially linear relationship between the two, with one exception: Only when a neighborhood's poverty rate dropped from 5 percent to 0 percent did male dropout rates decline faster than the prior trend. These results proved robust across race and ethnic groups, though black males appeared to benefit less from living in non-poverty areas than others.

Vartanian (1999b) investigates the relationship between childhood neighborhood poverty rate and average duration of poverty spells as a young adult. The results show the average time below the poverty level has one threshold at the 66th percentile (registering an increase of 16 percent). This threshold point is followed by an essentially linear function that increases at a rate of 1.3 percent per decile change in childhood neighborhood poverty rate.

Unlike all the empirical studies of the social problems associated with neighborhood poverty mentioned so far, which use the individual as the unit of observation, Krivo and Peterson (1996) employ data aggregated to the census tract level as both independent and dependent variables. Although this approach raises the specters of ecological fallacy, self-selection, and aggregation bias (Duncan and Raudenbush 1999), it is nevertheless worthy of review, as it is the only study of potential nonlinear relationships between crime and neighborhood poverty rates. Krivo and Peterson match FBI crime data for both violent and property crimes with 1990 Census tract poverty rates for the Columbus, Ohio, metropolitan area. They categorized tracts as low poverty (less than 20 percent), high poverty (20–39 percent), and extreme poverty (40 percent and higher) rates. In addition, within each category of neighborhood, they estimated a distinct slope coefficient.

Krivo and Peterson's (1996) findings for property crime indicate two distinct nonlinearities suggestive of thresholds. They show no significant difference between high- and extreme-poverty neighborhoods, but find that both have at least 20 percent higher property crime rates than low-poverty neighborhoods, suggesting a threshold around the 20 percent neighborhood poverty rate. In the case of violent crime, a regular step-function across the three neighborhood poverty categories applies. Further experimentation with category-specific slope coefficients allows Krivo and Peterson to ascertain that there is a constant slope between neighborhood poverty rate and violent crime over the low- and high-poverty ranges, but no further association once neighborhood poverty exceeds 40 percent (see figure 13.3, which applies the same conventions as figure 13.2).

What Can Be Made of This Evidence?

It is clear that no firm conclusions about the relationships between neighborhood poverty and individual behaviors can be drawn from the thin evidence thus far provided by social scientists. Nevertheless, the evidence most strongly supports the relationships portrayed in figure 13.4.

Vartanian's evidence (figure 13.2) consistently indicates that the neighborhood poverty–income earning relationship is not characterized by a simple quadratic, but rather by a logit-like function having two horizontal segments and thresholds at neighborhood poverty rates of approximately 15 and 30 percent. This relationship is shown in simplified form in the lower panel of figure 13.4 as line F' – A'.

The evidence is less consistent on the relationship between neighborhood poverty and certain socially problematic behaviors. The majority of the estimated functions in figure 13.3 again resemble a logit, with thresholds at about 20 and 40 percent poverty rates (see simplified function F – A). However, two studies are more suggestive of a quadratic, with concave-downward curvature (not shown here).

Figure 13.3. *Observed Relationships between Neighborhood Poverty Rate and Selected Social Problems*

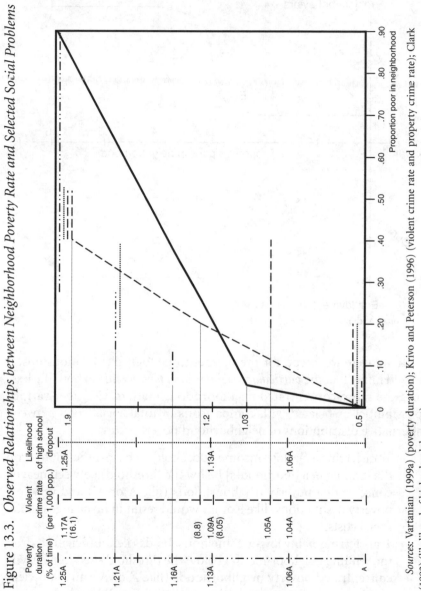

Sources: Vartanian (1999a) (poverty duration); Krivo and Peterson (1996) (violent crime rate and property crime rate); Clark (1992) (likelihood of high school dropout).

Figure 13.4. *Summary of Observed Relationships between Neighborhood Poverty Rates and Socially Problematic Behaviors*

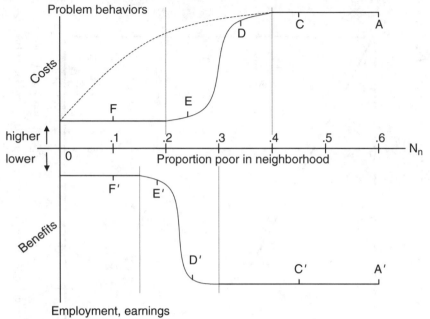

Source: Author's calculations.

If we were to accept, for the moment, the logit-like relationships, it would imply that the *particular neighborhood poverty rate* in both the less- and the more-concentrated neighborhoods matters. Consider various possibilities associated with comparisons of total social costs between alternative distributions of neighborhood poverty rates:

- Transferring a *few* low-income households (i.e., insufficient to drop the sending neighborhood[s] below the threshold) between heavily concentrated poverty neighborhoods (like A or A′) and very low poverty destinations (like F or F′) would result in no change in total social costs.
- Transferring *many* low-income households (i.e., sufficient to drop the sending neighborhood[s] below the threshold) between heavily concentrated poverty neighborhoods (like A or A′) and sufficient numbers of low-poverty destinations (like F or F′) such that none would exceed the threshold (like E or E′) would result in significant reductions in total social costs.

- Transferring a few low-income households (i.e., insufficient to drop the sending neighborhood[s] below the threshold) between heavily concentrated poverty neighborhoods (like A or A') and moderate-poverty destinations (like D, E or D', E') would result in increases in total social costs.
- Transferring any low-income households between moderately concentrated poverty neighborhoods (like D, E or D', E') and sufficient numbers of low-poverty destinations (like F or F') such that none would exceed the threshold would result in reductions in total social costs.

Assuming that the threshold functions in figure 13.4 are scaled correctly, the analysis implies that metropolitan areas would have lower total social costs if neighborhoods with greater than about 15 percent poverty rates were replaced with (an appropriately larger number) of neighborhoods having less than 15 percent poverty rates. However, total social costs would be higher if neighborhoods with greater than about 40 percent poverty rates were replaced with (an appropriately larger number) of neighborhoods having between about 15 to 40 percent poverty rates. These findings imply that MTO restrictions requiring receiving neighborhoods to have no more than 10 percent poverty rates are well founded. Other housing subsidy programs, by implication, should ensure that low-income participants do not use the program to move into neighborhoods with moderate poverty rates (Galster et al. 2003).

Conclusions and Further Directions

Theoretically, it is insufficient to justify the social efficiency of a subsidized housing deconcentration strategy like MTO merely by demonstrating that the socioeconomic status of one's neighbors is inversely related to the probability that an individual will engage in socially problematic behaviors. Rather, deconcentration of low-income households will only lead to a net reduction in problem behaviors if the relationship between the neighborhood poverty rate and individual propensity to engage in problem behaviors is such that neighborhood poverty rate has little impact at low levels but (perhaps past some threshold) becomes progressively more harmful at higher levels.

Given this requirement, little extant empirical work is directly relevant. Multivariate statistical analyses of the cross-sectional relationship between neighborhood poverty rates and socially problematic behaviors abound, but only a handful have attempted to measure potential nonlinearities. Arguably, the weight of the evidence is consistent with the threshold relationship. This relationship implies that subsidized housing programs aimed at deconcentrating low-income households will have the greatest likelihood of reducing the overall incidence of social problems in the metropolis if they (1) substantially reduce the poverty rates (say, below 30–40 percent) in the recipient neighborhoods, or (2) reduce poverty rates in neighborhoods between 15 and 40 percent poverty, AND (3) target low-poverty neighborhoods (say, below 15 percent) as destinations for low-income in-movers, while ensuring that none exceeds a 15 percent poverty rate as a result.

Of course, this conclusion must remain tentative, pending further research on nonlinear neighborhood effects. Such studies, however, represent only a first step toward understanding the question of how low-income relocation programs affect sending and receiving neighborhoods. Note several others:

- To what extent are changes in socially problematic behaviors capitalized into corresponding changes in neighborhood property values and thus indirectly measurable?
- To what extent are changes in neighborhood poverty percentages equivalent in behavioral impact to changes in the percentages of residents who are middle class?
- To what extent are relationships such as that shown in figure 13.4 generalizable across various racial-ethnic, age, and gender groups? Across various sorts of socially problematic behaviors?
- To what extent might subsidized housing programs move out those with the greatest social capital, thereby leading to worse rates of problematic behaviors among those remaining in sending neighborhoods?
- To what extent can social and political forces influence the potential negative impacts on receiving neighborhoods?
- To what extent do subsidized in-movers affect the residential stability of the receiving neighborhoods (i.e., is there a "class tipping point")?

If ever a crucial policy situation called for additional research, surely this is it. Without additional MTO research focused on the question of movers' impacts on sending and receiving neighborhoods, future policy-

makers will confront the unenviable situation of debating a major housing strategy with only the vaguest sense of such a program's effects. They
will need more evidence on a deconcentration program's potential effects
on the aggregate level of social problems such as violence and crime, on
residents' participation in the labor market and earnings, and on students'
propensity to drop out of high school.

A P P E N D I X 13A

Given a simple function for total social costs (TSC), which rise by an
amount Z once the threshold φ has been exceeded:

$$\text{TSC} = \begin{cases} X + \beta N & N \le \varphi \\ X + \beta N + Z & N > \varphi, \end{cases}$$

where N = proportion of low-income households in the given household's neighborhood.

Let N_R = number of nonpoor households, N_P = number of low-income
households.

Then in a situation where low-income households are concentrated in
all-poor neighborhoods: there will be N_R households having costs = X
(because $N = 0$ for them) and N_P households with costs: $X + \beta N + Z$
(because $N = 1$ for them). Thus,

$$\text{TSC} = (N_P + N_R)X + N_P\beta + N_PZ.$$

In an alternative situation where low-income households are evenly distributed across space, all households will have $N^* = N_P / (N_P + N_R)$,
assumed $< \varphi$. Thus, all will have costs = $X + \beta N^*$. Then:

$$\text{TSC} = (N_P + N_R)(X + \beta N^*) = (N_P + N_R)X + N_P\beta.$$

TSC in the poverty concentration scenario therefore exceeds that in the
poverty deconcentration scenario by N_PZ.

NOTES

1. For early examples of such studies, see Coulton and Pandey 1992; Coulton, Korbin, and Su 1995, 1999; Crane 1991; Elliott, Wilson, and Huizinga 1996; Fick and Thomas 1995; Franklin, Smith, and McMiller 1995; Hill and O'Neill 1993; Hill et al. 1996; Jencks and Mayer 1990; Kupersmidt et al. 1995; Massey, Gross, and Eggers 1991; Stern and Smith 1995; Wilson 1987.

2. For a more complete and rigorous analysis, see Galster (2002).

3. Graphically, moving out one low-income household from concentrated poverty neighborhood b so that it becomes b' requires that some receiving neighborhood such as a become a'. Because AB is linear, the reduction in social problems experienced by b is offset by the corresponding upsurge in a, and there is no net change in social problems overall in our hypothetical metropolitan area.

4. Removing low-income households from b (thereby creating b') would reduce the incidence of social problems there to a larger extent compared with AB, because there would not only be fewer low-income households there but their absence would also make the remaining households less likely to engage in problematic behaviors. Because AC is linear, however, the increase in social problems in the receiving neighborhood a (thereby creating a') would be greater than in the case of AB and would exactly offset the reductions in b.

5. Small problem decreases are associated with converting β to β' (the width of the thin, gray band U at the top of figure 13.1), but large increases are associated with converting α to α' (the width of band X).

6. Caveats in interpreting this evidence about neighborhood effects are in order. The robustness of the findings has been challenged on the following grounds: (a) inappropriate geographic scale of the neighborhood; (b) inappropriate measures of the neighborhood as causal agent; (c) inadequate controls for individual family background characteristics; and (d) endogeneity between choice of neighborhood and unmeasured family characteristics (Duncan and Raudenbush 1999; Duncan, Connell, and Klebanov 1997; Plotnick and Hoffman 1999).

7. Crane (1991) was the first to test statistically for nonlinearities in an individual's dropout rate and out-of-wedlock childbearing rate and neighborhood indicators. His work is not used here, however, because the only neighborhood indicator he employs is the fraction of workers employed in professional and technical occupations. There is no defensible way to convert such a measure to the percentage of poor in the neighborhood. Other studies of nonlinear neighborhood impacts are not cited here for the same reason (see Quercia and Galster 2000 for a review).

REFERENCES

Akerlof, George. 1980. "A Theory of Social Custom, of Which Unemployment May Be One Consequence." *Quarterly Journal of Economics* 94 (June): 749–75.

Briggs, Xavier de Souza. 1997. "Moving Up versus Moving Out: Neighborhood Effects in Housing Mobility Programs." *Housing Policy Debate* 8(1): 195–234.

Clark, Rebecca. 1992. *Neighborhood Effects on Dropping Out of School among Teenage Boys.* Washington, D.C.: The Urban Institute. Discussion Paper PSC-DSC-UI-13.

Coulton, Claudia J., and Shanta Pandey. 1992. "Geographic Concentration of Poverty and the Risk to Children in Urban Neighborhoods." *American Behavioral Scientist* 35(3): 238–57.

Coulton, Claudia J., Jill E. Korbin, and Marilyn Su. 1995. "Community-Level Factors and Child Maltreatment Rates." *Child Development* 66 (October): 1262–76.

———. 1999. "Neighborhoods and Child Maltreatment: A Multi-Level Study." *Child Abuse and Neglect* 23 (11): 1019–40.

Crane, Jonathon. 1991. "The Epidemic Theory of Ghettos and Neighborhood Effects on Dropping Out and Teenage Childbearing." *American Journal of Sociology* 96: 1226–59.

Duncan, Greg, and Stephen Raudenbush. 1999. "Assessing the Effects of Context in Studies of Child and Youth Development." *Educational Psychologist* 34(1): 29–41.

Duncan, Greg J., James Connell, and Pamela Klebanov. 1997. "Conceptual and Methodological Issues in Estimating Causal Effects of Neighborhoods and Family Conditions on Individual Development." In *Neighborhood Poverty. Volume 1: Context and Consequences for Children,* edited by Jeanne Brooks-Gunn, Greg J. Duncan, and J. Lawrence Aber (219–50). New York: Russell Sage Foundation.

Elliott, Delbert S., William Julius Wilson, and David Huizinga. 1996. "The Effects of Neighborhood Disadvantage on Adolescent Development." *Journal of Research in Crime and Delinquency* 33 (November): 389–426.

Fick, Ana C., and Sarah M. Thomas. 1995. "Growing Up in a Violent Environment: Relationship to Health-Related Beliefs and Behaviors." *Youth and Society* 27 (December): 136–47.

Franklin, Donna L., Susan E. Smith, and William E. P. McMiller. 1995. "Correlates of Marital Status among African American Mothers in Chicago Neighborhoods of Concentrated Poverty." *Journal of Marriage and the Family* 57 (February): 141–52.

Galster, George. 1987. *Homeowners and Neighborhood Reinvestment.* Durham, N.C.: Duke University Press.

Galster, George. 2002. "An Economic Efficiency Analysis of Deconcentrating Poverty Populations." *Journal of Housing Economics* 11(4): 303–29.

Galster, George, and Sean Killen. 1995. "The Geography of Metropolitan Opportunity: A Reconnaissance and Conceptual Framework." *Housing Policy Debate* 6(1): 7–44.

Galster, George, Peter Tatian, Anna Santiago, Kathryn Pettit, and Robin Smith. 2003. *Why NOT in My Back Yard? Neighborhood Impacts of Assisted Housing.* New Brunswick, N.J.: CUPR Press, Rutgers University.

Haveman, Robert, and Barbara Wolfe. 1995. "The Determinants of Children's Attainments: A Review of Methods and Findings." *Journal of Economic Literature* 33: 1829–78.

Hill, Hope M., Monique Levermore, James Twaite, and Lauren P. Jones. 1996. "Exposure to Community Violence and Social Support as Predictors of Anxiety and Social and Emotional Behavior among African American Children." *Journal of Child and Family Studies* 5 (December): 399–414.

Hill, M. Anne, and June O'Neill. 1993. *Underclass Behaviors in the United States: Measurement and Analysis of Determinants.* New York: Center for the Study of Business and Government, Baruch College/CUNY.

Ihlanfeldt, Keith R., and David L. Sjoquist. 1998. "The Spatial Mismatch Hypothesis: A Review of Recent Studies and Their Implication for Welfare Reform." *Housing Policy Debate* 9: 849–92.

Jencks, Christopher, and Susan Mayer. 1990. "The Social Consequences of Growing Up in a Poor Neighborhood." In *Inner-City Poverty in the United States,* edited by Laurence Lynn and Michael McGeary (111–86). Washington, D.C.: National Academy Press.

Kain, John. 1992. "The Spatial Mismatch Hypothesis: Three Decades Later." *Housing Policy Debate* 3: 371–459.

Krivo, Lauren J., and Ruth D. Peterson. 1996. "Extremely Disadvantaged Neighborhoods and Urban Crime." *Social Forces* 75(2): 619–50.

Kupersmidt, Janis B., Pamela C. Griesler, Melissa DeRosier, Charlotte J. Patterson, and Paul W. Davis. 1995. "Childhood Aggression and Peer Relations in the Context of Family and Neighborhood Factors." *Child Development* 66 (April): 360–75.

Leventhal, Tama, and Jeanne Brooks-Gunn. 2000. "The Neighborhoods They Live In." *Psychological Bulletin* 126(2): 309–37.

Manski, Charles F. 2000. "Economic Analysis of Social Interactions." *Journal of Economic Perspectives* 14(3): 115–36.

Massey, Douglas, Andrew Gross, and Mitchell Eggers. 1991. "Segregation, the Concentration of Poverty, and the Life Chances of Individuals." *Social Science Research* 20 (December): 397–420.

Mayer, Susan E., and Christopher Jencks. 1989. "Growing Up in Poor Neighborhoods: How Much Does It Matter?" *Science* 243 (March): 1441–5.

Murphy, Kevin, Andre Shleifer, and Robert Vishny. 1993. "Why Is Rent-Seeking So Costly to Growth?" *American Economic Review* 83(2): 409–14.

Plotnick, Robert D., and Saul D. Hoffman. 1999. "The Effects of Neighborhood Characteristics on Young Adult Outcomes: Alternative Estimates." *Social Science Quarterly* 80(1): 1–18.

Quercia, Roberto, and George Galster. 2000. "Threshold Effects and Neighborhood Change." *Journal of Planning Education and Research* 20(2): 146–62.

Rogers, C. L. 1997. "Job Search and Unemployment Duration." *Journal of Urban Economics* 43: 109–32.

Sampson, Robert, Jeffrey Morenoff, and Thomas Gannon-Rowley. 2002. "Assessing 'Neighborhood Effects': Social Processes and New Directions in Research." *Annual Review of Sociology* 28: 443–78.

Simmel, George. 1971. *George Simmel on Individuality and Social Forms.* Chicago: University of Chicago Press.

Stern, Susan B., and Carolyn A. Smith. 1995. "Family Processes and Delinquency in an Ecological Context." *Social Service Review* 69 (December): 703–31.

Turner, Margery Austin, and Ingrid Gould Ellen. 1997. "Does Neighborhood Matter? Assessing Recent Evidence." *Housing Policy Debate* 8(4): 833–65.

Vartanian, Thomas P. 1999a. "Adolescent Neighborhood Effects on Labor Market and Economic Outcomes." *Social Service Review* 73(2): 142–67.

———. 1999b. "Childhood Conditions and Adult Welfare Use: Examining Neighborhood and Family Factors." *Journal of Marriage and the Family* 61: 225–37.

Weber, Max. 1978. *Economy and Society.* Volumes 1 and 2. Berkeley: University of California Press.

Wilson, William Julius. 1987. *The Truly Disadvantaged.* Chicago: University of Chicago Press.

———. 1996. *When Work Disappears.* New York: Alfred A. Knopf.

14

Comments on Future Research and Housing Policy

John Goering

I t is possible to draw three conclusions from MTO, including one policy and two research conclusions. First, MTO's operations demonstrate
that it is possible for the U.S. Department of Housing and Urban Development (HUD) and local public housing authorities to successfully operate an economic and racial desegregation program using Section 8 rental
assistance in different metropolitan markets. It has shown that, on a small
scale, such programs can reverse the historical practice of concentrating
poor minority households in poor minority neighborhoods and limiting
their housing choices.

Second, preliminary research on MTO's effects on families demonstrates
that beneficial, statistically significant changes have occurred in families'
lives within two to four years of their participation in MTO. Neighborhood
matters, with significant neighborhood effects occurring most notably in
the lives of children. The first phase of MTO research reveals that households in the treatment, as well as some Section 8 comparison group families, have experienced improvements in multiple measures of well-being
relative to the in-place control group. Improvements in educational performance, reductions in criminal behavior, improvements in adult mental
and physical health, and reductions in welfare dependence have been found
at one or more sites. In the treatment group, family members experienced
declines in depression and asthma following their moves from public housing, and male children were much less likely to have disciplinary problems.

In the area of education, despite the potential difficulties of making the transition out of poor neighborhoods and into new schools, children age 5 to 12 in Baltimore experienced substantial gains in academic achievement, measured by standardized test scores, compared with children in the control group. If subsequent research corroborates these results, the demonstration will have achieved major educational benefits for younger children much earlier than anticipated. There is a third straightforward research conclusion: we do not yet know enough. The unclear effects for older children and adults, as well as the essential requirement to seek cross-site verification of single-site outcomes, compel additional MTO research.

While MTO provides an understanding of how residential mobility programs can operate and identifies the quantifiable effects that this change in neighborhood has already had on the lives of parents and children, there are a number of limitations of what we have learned to date. Most centrally, each of the MTO research studies presented in this collection is based upon unique designs. Sample sizes are consequently small and results usually apply to only one site.

Next, while we have measured important, statistically meaningful experimental differences, we know too little about *why* and *how* these changes took place. Researchers will need to gather more information about which neighborhood processes directly or indirectly affect outcomes. Included in such causal queries will be efforts to measure the actual effects of housing mobility counseling. The services provided by the nonprofit counseling organizations to the treatment group families varied across the five sites (Feins et al. 1997) and such variations need to be better understood to evaluate programmatic outcomes.

Larger samples and a clearer understanding of causality are not, however, sufficient for MTO to be counted among the small number of successful policy experiments. Crane's (1998) criteria for deciding whether a new social program has been successful include "unusually convincing evidence that the program delivers substantial benefits regardless of cost . . . convincing evidence of long-term effects; and new hope of making progress to solve a seemingly intractable social problem" (1–2). He also includes measures of the program's cost-benefit relationships as a central concern.[1] For MTO to be counted a clear policy success, it would need then to demonstrate major long-term effects achieved in a cost-effective manner.

MTO's average counseling costs of roughly $3,000 per family (for those that leased-up a unit) would need to be offset by evidence of reductions in expenditures for health care, unemployment, welfare, crime reductions, or other compensating improvements in educational attainment and labor force engagement.

One of MTO's objectives was to have a roughly decade-long set of analytically linked research investigations that would help address the methodological problems we noted. MTO research does not stop with the results reported in this collection.

Evaluating and Understanding MTO's Effects

MTO was planned with roughly seven more or less chronologically ordered stages, culminating in a final impact evaluation and data release (figure 14.1). The first five stages have either been completed or received funding from HUD, private foundations, and other agencies.

The design and implementation of the demonstration, including random assignment, were completed by 1998. The results from the small grant research projects at each of the five MTO locations are reported within this collection. Two waves of regular canvasses, or surveys, of MTO families to determine their current location have already been conducted.

Figure 14.1. *Key Stages in MTO Research*

1. EXPERIMENTAL DESIGN [Volunteer families randomly assigned to one of three groups]

2. BASELINE SURVEYS [Administered to all heads of household at enrollment]

3. PANEL TRACKING/SURVEYS [Periodic tracking and surveys to verify current address information]

4. SMALL GRANT PILOT RESEARCH [HUD grants for one-site research]

5. INTERIM EVALUATION [five-site, multi-method impact evaluation, under way]

6. FINAL IMPACT ASSESSMENT [Planned]

7. RELEASE OF RESTRICTED ACCESS DATA FILES [Planned select data released by HUD with confidentiality restrictions]

Most recently, a multimillion dollar midterm evaluation has been funded and is currently under way.[2] The only major outstanding portion of the MTO research plan is the final, longer-term impact assessment that can be expected sometime after 2007. Following both the interim and final impact evaluations, HUD expects to make available to researchers restricted-access data files that protect family confidentiality.

In the next section of this chapter, we address in a little more detail what we believe are the salient research questions, based on all we have learned to date. In the final section of this chapter, we address policy questions that emerge from these studies, including the question of what it would mean to replicate MTO as a new HUD program.

Future Research

The first stage in MTO research has shown us that neighborhood effects have occurred. For some, MTO has already been a "home run" in social science research (Katz 2002). Research to date, though, has enough limitations that we need to ask additional questions to be clearer about what happened to families when they moved to suburban-like opportunities. We need to understand how useful the new communities are to families, as well as any social, economic, or psychological costs of their moves. Below we sketch out several specific lines of inquiry intended to answer the as-yet-unanswered puzzle: has MTO brought unique, long-lasting, and cost-effective benefits to participating families? Has MTO done more good than harm?

Are There Comparable, Cross-Site Experimental Outcomes?

The most important accomplishment in the next stage in MTO research will be to make use of comparable methodologies in all five sites to learn what role neighborhood has in affecting the lives of extremely poor families. Using standardized instruments, in contrast to the relatively unique research plans reflected in this collection, will potentially uncover statistically meaningful effects not previously reported and challenge others that may be important in only one city. Larger samples will also enable us to learn which treatment group effects differ from those experienced by either control population.[3]

Cross-site differences may assume increased salience in this next wave of investigation. Understanding how the differences across the participating metropolitan areas may affect outcomes is important since we suspect that not all cities are alike in their capacity to assist the poor, either directly through employment and services or indirectly through the structure and operation of their housing markets (Abu-Lughod 1999; Edin and Lein 1997; Waldinger 1996). The tightness or looseness of a city's housing or labor markets may profoundly affect opportunities for poor adults or teenagers. Differences in the willingness of suburban schools to welcome and help former public housing children could determine subsequent school performance. Whether site differences are more significant than differences between fully suburban and city neighborhoods is another subsidiary question the next wave of inquiry can address. The power, consistency, and sources of variability of neighborhood effects are central to the next stage of research.

Will Changes Last?

The time that has elapsed between the first small studies, reported within, and the next stage of evaluation research is vital. It permits us to understand the extent to which effects may persist, atrophy, or evolve in previously immeasurable developmental pathways. We can learn for the first time about the probable timing of developmental effects for children and adults: not only what happens, but when. Learning when and at what ages effects are most likely to occur is an irreplaceable benefit of future MTO research inquiries.

Once a child or parent has achieved some positive improvement in employment, health, or education, will the changes continue in some predictable path? Will parents' and children's lives be permanently and irreversibly altered by MTO, or will there be some degree of reversal or "backsliding"? Do treatment group children's futures dramatically improve, with students moving on to college and better-paying jobs compared with their control group counterparts? Or will the appeal of low-poverty areas wear thin, leading families to retreat to their former, more familiar communities? Will reversals in the growth rate of the economy shake the hold MTO families have on their new situations?

We also need to be clearer than we are that MTO is not *detrimental* to the well-being of adults or children. Will the appeal and benefits of more-affluent neighborhoods become depleted if parents' isolation and loneliness overwhelm them? Will mothers or grandmothers who moved from their former neighborhoods grow lonely in a community without the friends, religious groups, or other familiar ties they acquired over decades? Will teenagers be subjected to more police scrutiny and risk in areas unused or resistant to their presence? Will landlords in the new communities treat their new Section 8 tenants respectfully? What harm, if any, has been caused to families that moved?

Will MTO Effects Spill Over into Other Areas?

Closely allied with the above is the question of whether early positive changes in certain domains will help leverage change in other aspects of families' lives. It is possible that new research will reveal evolving, positive synergies of effects: a cascading or ripple effect. As noted in several of the chapters, the sense of relief from fear of crime and violence after moving led many mothers to permit their children more time to play outdoors with other children in their new, lower-poverty neighborhoods. What, if any, measurable consequences will greater peer interaction have on sub-sequent peer socialization? Will improvements in physical or mental health alter other choices, such as interest in education or employment? In what ways, and how quickly, can a mother's improved sense of her own potential translate into better, or different, choices about her and her children's need for schooling? Does a child's improved performance at school reduce parents' anxiety and improve their mental health? Does a child's feeling of being safe translate into better school performance if their parents are also adapting well? Moreover, there are questions raised in a number of the research chapters in this collection about whether males and females have different propensities to take advantage of their new communities. Interdependencies or trajectories of change are an intriguing part of MTO's future.

Will Parents' as Well as Children's Lives Change?

The bulk of the research reported in this collection suggests that MTO has more likely benefited children's and teenagers' behavior and health than parents'. While many mothers feel better and appear more positive about their futures, it is still not known whether previously unemployed adults' employment situations and wages will improve. Qualitative research conducted recently with MTO adults (Popkin, Harris, and

Cunningham 2001), as well as research on adults living in public housing who were participating in another HUD demonstration (Martinez 2002), report substantial medical problems, including anxiety and depression, that limit their ability to seek and find employment. The absence of any experimental change in labor market outcomes could change as time goes on. Or perhaps MTO was not the right, or a sufficient, demonstration to improve the employment potential and incomes of very poor mothers. Studies of the labor market and welfare programs suggest that a host of complicated interventions is required before low-income adults from poor communities see major improvements in their job and wage situations (Haveman 1994; O'Regan and Quigley 1999; Scott et al. 2002).

Why Have Changes Occurred?

For many of the statistical and quantitative statements in this collection, our understanding of why they happened is still limited. Quantitative measures of school, health, and criminal outcomes often do not tell us convincingly and clearly the reasons for positive change and personal transformation. Through what social mechanisms and process have positive effects occurred; what is it about their new neighborhoods that has caused these benefits? Why are MTO teenagers in Baltimore committing fewer violent crimes? Why have asthma cases in Boston declined—what was it about the move out of ghetto poverty that caused such statistically meaningful improvements? How and why did younger children in the treatment group achieve improvements on their reading tests? What has caused families' lives to change and to what degree—and through what social processes—have their neighborhoods been the cause?

Qualitative research is one tool that will help to get inside the "black box" of such experimental effects and to learn about the institutions, networks, and processes that have led to change in adults, children, or both.[4] A first round of qualitative research was completed for HUD in 2001 and suggests issues and problems that will need additional research. A number of parents, for example, kept their children in the schools serving their original high-poverty neighborhoods rather than moving them to new schools (Popkin et al. 2001). The extent to which families have moved their homes into low-poverty communities but have not taken advantage of local resources and institutions represents a crucial question for the next stage of MTO research. There are many more comparable questions about why the "black box" of experimental effects may have occurred.

Will Neighborhood Change Affect MTO Families?

Neighborhoods are not static. The form and rate of neighborhood change will likely affect families' perceived and actual opportunities (Berube and Forman 2002; Gephart 1997; Sampson 2000; Sampson, Morenoff, and Gannon-Rowley forthcoming). Furstenberg and Hughes (1997) have noted, "neighborhoods also have developmental trajectories, and the rate and manner in which a particular neighborhood is changing may have important implications for child (and adult) development" (36). Neighborhood change, including any evidence of thresholds of change, needs to be studied to appreciate how 21st century developmental dynamics operate to help or harm poor MTO families.

Neighborhoods also vary in how long local residents may live there and how long it takes for the neighborhood to influence their lives (Crane 1991). Does a family that makes constant moves among low-poverty areas differ from families whose lives are largely spent in a single, better-off area? Do their choices and paths in turn systematically differ from those who move through more heavily poverty-impacted communities?

Will Receiving Neighborhoods and Neighbors Experience Change?

Has MTO had detrimental effects on the communities into which MTO families have moved that can be causally attributed to the demonstration? Can the impact of the tiny scale of the MTO movers, roughly 143 families in each of the five sites, be reasonably detected given the welter of other social, economic, racial, and attitudinal alterations that normally occur in the course of neighborhood life?

Galster (in this collection) considers how MTO families might affect the overall rate of problematic behaviors in both sending and receiving neighborhoods. He speculates that they will not have a major impact, but wonders whether a low-income family's relocation from one neighborhood to another will bring problematic behaviors to the destination neighborhoods. Are changes in socially problematic behaviors "capitalized" into corresponding changes in neighborhood property values, and are these changes thus indirectly measurable? Is there a concentration "threshold" of low-income families after which a neighborhood's rates of problematic behaviors increase (Turner, Popkin, and Cunningham 2000)?

It is essential for future researchers to develop measures of actual or perceived impacts to address this question: How do receiving communities or neighborhoods react to small numbers of low-income, largely minority public housing families? It is possible that we will learn that receiving community neighbors and neighborhood organizations are not all alike (Guhathakurta and Mushkatel 2002). They might have different thresholds of tolerance and acceptance for children and adults of varying racial and ethnic groups, depending on their own racial and ethnic composition, their perceived vulnerability or susceptibility to other changes, and their access to social resources and programs that might be of use to the new families.

Are Effects for Regular Section 8 Families Enough?

Among the policy and research questions that future MTO research will clarify is whether the social, educational, and health benefits from MTO are experienced relatively equally by both groups that moved away from "the projects." If regular Section 8 control group families benefit in ways that are closely comparable to those experienced by the treatment group, there may be support for continuing the use of the regular rental assistance program as the key tool for poverty deconcentration. The research in this collection on New York, for example, suggests that a number of benefits were obtained by both sets of families that moved away from high-poverty areas of the city.

At this point in time, we believe the evidence suggests that there are clear, important, and measurable benefits from allowing families to move to low-poverty communities that outweigh the benefits received by the regular Section 8 participants. We must also recall that the families that volunteered for MTO are different in measurable ways from others remaining within public housing so that their selection of the choice to move out differentiates them in term of both motivation and characteristics from the remaining "average" public housing resident. Moreover, the long history of federal housing policy failures at deconcentration, and the harmful effects of letting public housing authorities (PHAs) continue to do what they have always done, is part of MTO's raison d'être. We feel that any conclusion that Section 8–only effects are sufficient is both premature and unwarranted by the evidence gathered to date.[5]

Do We Understand the Costs and Benefits?

One potential result of future research will be a clearer understanding of the total or net costs of an MTO program, including an appreciation of savings that result from the improved outcomes for treatment group families. How does the cost of MTO counseling compare with the social, economic, and health costs and benefits that families have experienced? Are improved test scores, lower levels of welfare use, and lower violent crime rates common across all sites, and if they are, do they save government agencies money in ways that justify the costs for counseling for treatment group families (Johnson, Ladd, and Ludwig 2002)?

Policy Concerns and Quandaries

Are there any sensible policy observations that can be reached about MTO given the provisional nature of the available research evidence? Is there enough good news to warrant proposing a broader, more permanent program modeled after MTO for use by local housing agencies? One possible response to the positive results reported in this collection might be to adapt the MTO model into a national program linking intensive housing counseling to a geographically limited voucher. The Millennial Housing Commission (2002, 11), for example, finds that MTO research "demonstrates that relocating families to better neighborhoods can improve educational, mental health, and behavioral outcomes."

The political scientist Phillip Thompson (1999), however, is convinced that MTO could not become a general, large-scale program, at least in the New York area. "Given the fierce resistance," he argues, "to even modest public housing development in nearby Yonkers, the notion that significant portions of the NYCHA (the New York City Public Housing Authority) population could be integrated into Long Island and Westchester is fanciful. Political problems aside, HUD's entire $70 million national MTO budget would have only a minor impact on deconcentrating public housing in New York City" (126). Many other skeptics of HUD's capability to softly engineer deconcentration echo Thompson's pessimism.

Others might note the improved level of employment reported in this collection for *all* MTO families and conclude that this reflects the impact that macroeconomic improvements have on the lives of most Americans. This could suggest that economic improvement needs to take priority over narrowly tailored housing programs (Haveman 1994). Still others may find the single-site results reported within this collection unpersuasive and feel that we do not yet know enough to suggest that MTO be considered as a national policy option, whether for economic or housing programs.

Does the positive news of effects on children suggest that MTO should become a national policy option? If so, what might bringing MTO "to scale" be like?

Going "to Scale"?

Perhaps the most frequently asked question when MTO is discussed among social scientists and policy analysts is, What might "bringing MTO to scale" be like? Central to answering this question appears to be the concern that millions of families might be involved in any future MTO clone. This speculation, however, is based upon a misunderstanding of the demographic composition of public housing projects in high-poverty areas; it misunderstands the scale of the problem.

What, then, are the numbers of public housing families that might be implicated in a potential replication of MTO? If we made use of the same authorizing provisions that exist in MTO, going "to scale" would mean providing all families with children, living in high-poverty public or assisted project-based housing, the option of receiving a voucher with counseling assistance to help them move to low-poverty areas. Following MTO's design, this could not *require* families to move since MTO envisions assisting only volunteers.

There are currently approximately 200,000 families with children living in high-poverty project-based housing nationwide that could be given the option to move. We would then estimate, based upon the MTO experience, that approximately 25 percent of those families would volunteer, or "take up," the opportunity to move. Of this number, if lease-up rates remained comparable, roughly half (48 percent) would succeed at moving. Therefore, going to scale for MTO could optimally involve 24,000 families nationwide actually moving from high poverty to low poverty.[6]

Moreover, there would likely be a staggered allocation of vouchers, just as occurred in the Gautreaux program. Allocating the total number needed over 10 years leads to an annual goal of serving 2,400 families. This allocation would, in turn, be apportioned among the relevant PHAs or jurisdictions. Assuming that roughly 60 PHAs would be targeted, this would result in an annual allocation of roughly 40 vouchers for each of these PHAs over a 10-year period.[7] Shortening or lengthening the time period or increasing the number of PHAs involved could reduce the burden on any individual site. At such a modest size, an MTO extension would have only a limited deconcentration effect in any one city and not likely lead to massive deconcentrations of poverty into any one receiving neighborhood or city.

It would, however, be naïve to assume that it would be an easy task for HUD and cooperating PHAs to move from the relocation of roughly 800 treatment group families in MTO to 24,000. Virtually endemic political opposition and the social costs of HUD program innovation are difficult and familiar obstacles to virtually all prior efforts to promote any significant degree of economic or racial mobility (Downs 1973). As Heclo (1994) reminds us, "Dealing in any realistic way with this socioeconomic catastrophe [poverty] is going to be costly and will demand a long-term commitment to people whom many Americans would not want as neighbors. This is the dirty little secret buried in the shelves of social science poverty studies" (422).

Howard Husock (2000), a consistent critic of the Section 8 program, frequently speaks of the fear of such unwanted Americans. He states that, "in the blue-collar and middle-class neighborhoods where voucher holders increasingly live, longtime residents hate the program. It undermines and destabilizes their communities by importing social problems into their midst." Part of his solution is to leave families in conventional public housing projects, fixed so that residents would be both time limited and required to get "instruction in parenting." If this doesn't work, he argues, no system would be better than Section 8 vouchers. At this time, however, such criticism appears to be marginal to mainstream public policy debate about federal housing policy. It is of course impossible to confidently predict that it will remain so.

There are, for example, fairly constant complaints to HUD about undue concentration of voucher recipients in certain neighborhoods. Some observers worry that the Section 8 program, left to its own devices, will create additional submarkets or niches within which Section 8 families will be served and concentrated in the same way as project-based housing residents (Stegman 2000). Quigley (2000) cautions, "research suggests that demand-side subsidies have only modest effects in decentralizing the urban poor" (85). As the Section 8 program continues to grow, it may be subject to increasing criticism for contributing to such concentrations of poverty. The program appears to need a new generation of policy tools to help families that wish to move to communities with lower levels of poverty. HUD has already revised the rules (called SEMAP) to avoid poverty concentration, but it now requires local housing authorities to develop and implement plans for the actual deconcentration of poor families.[8]

Not all policymakers are, however, focused on the issue of Section 8 deconcentration. Many policymakers wish to reduce the failure rate within the regular Section 8 program. The argument is that, with abundant evidence of significant housing need, the failure rate in moving families into private rental apartments is already too high. Any further rules and restrictions will only further reduce the Section 8 program's ability to serve as the only source of federal housing assistance for the needy poor. A few years ago, even the fact that only 80 to 85 percent of families could lease-up under the regular program appeared a cause for concern. Stegman (2000), for example, argued, "Because a voucher can be a ticket out of a ghetto into a middle-class neighborhood, with better schools and services, we should be concerned about the 15 percent of families who cannot use their voucher to find acceptable housing in the private sector" (93). How to promote access to better neighborhoods and to also increase lease-up rates is a major part of the ongoing policy conundrum for which MTO does not provide an answer. It is our belief, though, that the tension between meeting localized housing need and promoting deconcentration desperately needs to be resolved so that while HUD may often be the houser of last resort it need not be known as the nation's largest ghetto landlord.

To accomplish this, Congress must assess the principal policy trade-off between getting needy families into private rental housing quickly at a higher lease-up rate and providing some families access to low-poverty areas at a lower success rate. If, for example, a family with average income and tenant characteristics in a city such as Los Angeles can receive regular Section 8 assistance with no counseling services, their lease-up probability based on MTO evidence is roughly 70 percent. If, however, another MTO family receives the highest intensity counseling services and is required to lease-up in a low-poverty area, its lease-up probability is roughly 50 percent. This 20 percent reduction appears as a considerable cost. Some families will rightfully be unwilling to give up their ability to relocate within higher-poverty areas—unless a location-specific requirement was the difference between receiving and not receiving a Section 8 subsidy.

There is another complicating factor that affects the future ability of the Section 8 program to meet the goal of either assisting the housing needy or promoting deconcentration. Recent evidence indicates that families' ability to make use of their rental vouchers has dropped notably within the past several years (Finkel and Buron 2001). Lease-up rates declined from more than 80 percent in 1993, just as MTO was being planned, to only 69 percent in 2000. The report notes, "PHAs [public housing authorities] generally attribute the decline in success rates between 1993 and 2000 to a tightening of rental markets during the intervening years" (1). The authors note that local agencies that required tenant screening and counseling typically achieved *higher* rates of lease-ups than those who did not. Tighter markets may require counseling just to remain more or less even with average or normal lease-up rates. It is also necessary to recall that many people without any prior subsidy lease in place, so that declining overall lease-up rates suggests that going "to scale" with a new MTO in a tight housing market could have even lower leaseup rates. In tight or loose markets MTO can impose a cost on lease-up probabilities that personally affects families' lives and choices.

One part of resolving whether lower lease-up rates are an acceptable cost of administering an MTO-like extension depends, nontrivially, on the effects lower-poverty neighborhoods have on Section 8 families' lives. If the 2000 Census should reveal that the many regular Section 8 families leased-up in or moved to impoverished and deeply distressed neighborhoods, the option for an MTO-like, expanded program will appear more persuasive. If, however, Section 8 families benefit in ways that are closely similar to the benefits achieved by the MTO treatment group, the case for an MTO program extension will be lessened. The developmental or self-sufficiency benefits from the option to move out appears, even at this early stage in MTO research, a compelling argument for more rather than less flexibility for localities administering housing programs for the poor.

The question of which administrative agencies would be best suited to deliver MTO-like Section 8 assistance over the long run also needs to be considered. Some analysts will argue that the local public housing authorities, an agency system conceived in the 1930s, are outmoded, ineffective mechanisms for responding to housing and employment needs on a regional basis. The traditional 3,000 or more public housing authorities need not manage housing programs such as MTO Section 8. Such initiatives might be better delivered by linking real estate brokerage services to nonprofit counseling agencies, with public housing authorities offering consistent and prompt income verification and housing inspections. Alternatively, some local housing authorities have already recognized the advantages of linking information and services across a wider region and are using their annual and five-year plans to assess how to best offer their clients a regionwide, diverse range of neighborhood choices (Tegler, Hanley, and Liben 1995).

State and regional PHAs could also be offered incentives to make affordable regional housing markets materialize and function at a controlled enough scale so that they, local landlords, and neighborhood associations become comfortable with their role in managing a "fair" share of the city's poor, assisted families (Katz and Turner 2001). Such policy transitions may take a decade or more in communities resistant to the poor and public housing, but may move more quickly if private organizations, nonprofit groups, and PHAs throughout the region combine their skills and resources. HOPE VI redevelopment options would likely also need to be included as part of the mix of choice offered families, so that options do not remain so narrowly zero sum. Housing policies need not be one-size-fits-all, since the past 50 years of standardized programs has often proven ruinously inflexible and inept (Downs 1994, 99; Haveman 1994, 444).[9]

Improving HUD's and local PHAs' reputations for responsibly administering programs that simultaneously benefit the lives of the poor but also respect the concerns and vulnerabilities of receiving communities would be an allied, critical improvement (Downs 1973; Hays 1995). Learning to work patiently with residents and community leaders in the thousands of potential receiving communities for future MTO-like volunteers was not part of MTO's mandate. Gautreaux managers, though, learned to put ceilings, quotas, or caps on the number of families it would allow moving into buildings and neighborhoods, thus limiting impacts. They also offered the opportunity to move fewer than 400 families in any single year, thus stretching out for decades the movement of their target group of roughly 7,000 families (Rubinowitz and Rosenbaum 2000). While the federal government currently has no authority or tools that would permit it to limit the choices of its recipient families, they could be authorized as part of any larger, comprehensive Section 8 deconcentration program that operated across city and suburbs. A larger MTO-like extension would also need to address the concerns of neighbors by increasing the resources aimed at offering counseling and assistance to new landlords and neighbors. Such assistance could not just be aimed at pacifying racial fears, but rather could work to address legitimate concerns over neighborhood stability that are part of the pool of Section 8 eligible areas.[10] If legislators did consider adopting another larger-scale program modeled after MTO, some preliminary policy suggestions would apply. The most important question is, what have we learned that might help guide a successor to MTO being expanded to a somewhat larger scale?

IMPLEMENT THE PROGRAM SLOWLY AND INVOLVE THE PUBLIC

Among the lessons from the opposition to MTO in 1994 is the sense that with better notice to the affected communities, and at a slower pace, opposition might have been lessened if not altogether mollified. The explicit and up-front exclusion of areas that did not have 10 percent or less poverty should have been announced and publicized more clearly, since a nontrivial number of protesters came from areas that were not eligible sites for MTO families to locate.

EXPLAIN THE DESIGN AND IMPLEMENTATION OF THE PROGRAM

The imbroglio in Baltimore County in the first months of MTO's existence suggests that both HUD and local PHAs could do a better job of explaining the potential links between any large-scale public housing demolition programs, such as HOPE VI, and MTO-like housing mobility. Housing mobility options should not become the political patsy for badly administered tenant relocation programs tied to HOPE VI. This may also mean that MTO-like options cannot be implemented concurrently with inner-city demolition programs or until the public throughout the region understands and accepts the role screening and counseling will play in allocating families to their communities.

RECOGNIZE THAT RESTRICTED VOUCHER PROGRAMS WILL NOT WORK FOR EVERYONE

Among the issues affecting any future expansion of MTO is the evidence from this collection that it is not suited for everyone (Popkin and Cunningham 2000). The research reported in the first chapter in this collection points out that those who volunteered for MTO and then found a private-market apartment differed from other poor public housing residents. One of the questions that can be answered by additional research is to appreciate the full extent to which MTO families differ from others. To whom do the positive outcomes found in the research reported in this collection best apply? To what universe of families will future research outcomes best apply and how will that information help shape any future program outreach? While MTO is not a relevant option for all public housing residents, the fact that thousands of families volunteered for

MTO suggests that they are not alone in their fear of crime and desire to move out of "the projects."

It is of course possible that as MTO's results become more clearly established and accepted by public housing tenants, the differences between "volunteers" for any future program and those remaining behind may narrow. Agencies can learn to better explain and motivate families making use of demonstrated benefits. This is of course a fundamental assumption that is at the heart of "normalizing" MTO and is subject to at least three qualifiers:

Crime rates and interest in MTO. Given the critical importance of fear of crime as a root source for families' interest in MTO, will the apparent decline in urban crime rates since the mid-1990s mean that fewer families will be impelled to seek to get out through an MTO-like program (Blumstein 2000; Fountain 2001; Gettleman 2002)? Or will crime rates return to higher levels?[11]

HOPE VI and enrollments. To what extent will inner-city revitalization programs, such as HOPE VI, result in more families wanting to remain back in the old neighborhoods, in newly refurbished housing units? Will the presence of more viable inner-city choices reduce interest in housing mobility options that risk sending families far from their old neighbors?

Community resistance to HUD's program initiatives is poorly understood. It may be that the frequency, timing, and virulence of such opposition can be better measured, anticipated, and managed (Bonastia 2000; Downs 1973; Hirsch 1983; Rieder 1985).

COUNSELING APPEARS TO HELP

Although it is not yet statistically certain whether restricted-use vouchers or counseling had a greater effect in achieving the effects shown to date, housing counseling (see Shroder's chapter; Finkel and Buron 2001) appears to have benefits in promoting lease-ups in low-poverty areas. Further research will clarify whether cross-site differences in the use of counseling had impacts on families. This will enable us to have a clearer look inside the now fairly opaque box of strategies and educational techniques that constitute "housing mobility counseling."[12]

While counseling has clear effects, we also encountered limits to what it can accomplish in attempting to alter patterns of housing search and locality choice by the public housing residents of the five MTO cities. In

New York, for example, virtually no mothers who were selected from Manhattan projects for MTO would discuss the possibility of moving to relatively nearby New Jersey suburbs or consider a move to Staten Island or most parts of Queens. Although the latter boroughs are technically within the limits of New York City, they are seen and felt to be much farther away in effective social distance. They are "strange" places, and no amount of counseling could alter these patterned geographic choice limits. In Los Angeles, while there were some who moved long distances, all too often the lack of efficient mass transit made such choices extremely costly to manage within the daily round of work and family duties. While the cities of Boston and Baltimore and their suburbs are more compact than either New York or Los Angeles, racial and income fragmentation make moves to many low-poverty communities a daunting challenge for low-income families (Farley, Danziger, and Holzer 2000).

Overcoming ingrained, historic patterns for evaluating housing and neighborhood choices—within racially fragmented markets—requires some measure of risk for families and considerable skill for housing counselors. It also requires skills and information currently unavailable within most large PHAs. Unlike many PHAs, such as New York's, that provide "almost no assistance to tenants in the housing search" (Kamber 2000, 6, 30), an extended MTO option would require that poor families receive help in searching widely enough to make dispersed housing choices possible and meaningful to the family.

RECOGNIZE LIMITS AND THE MEANING OF OPPORTUNITY
Galster's comments in this collection offer reason for policymakers to examine the precise percentages of poverty and affluence that might best facilitate the least harmful process for selecting receiving neighborhoods to ensure that there will never be too many Section 8 families allocated into any one vulnerable area. Balancing limits or temporary quotas with the principle that Section 8 families should have the freedom to choose whatever neighborhood they would like will require a new generation of policy thinking within both HUD and Congress, especially as long as the Section 8 program continues to serve as "the only (housing) game in town" (Quigley 2000).[13]

WHAT IS "OPPORTUNITY"?
It is important to ensure that 10 percent poor does not remain the sole definition of what is meant by an area of opportunity. Future expansion of

MTO can include labor market and school characteristics as among the variables that can assist in selecting a set of neighborhoods for MTO-like counseling.

MAKE TIMELY USE OF COST-BENEFIT ANALYSIS

When future research provides a clearer understanding of the total costs and social and economic benefits of MTO, policymakers will find it easier to explain the cost of funding additional MTO-like housing mobility vouchers and counseling. Until that time, improvements in reading scores and reductions in childhood asthma appear to offer adequate justification for allowing PHAs to offer such a choice to families without waiting. If, in a clinical medical experiment, patients were found to benefit from a trial medication in the way that MTO has, there would be adequate justification for permitting other lives to be aided without delay. There remain ample reasons for caution, but the chance that some children's lives can be substantially improved by the mere choice of a different neighborhood suggests families should be offered this choice now and allowed to decide for themselves.

Conclusion

The evidence gathered for the first time in this collection helps answer the question of whether there are clear benefits to a replication of MTO. The answer is that there are measurable, positive benefits and there appear to be circumstances under which a modest-scale replication of MTO could be made to work.

Community residents, elected officials, and researchers now have clear and reasonably persuasive evidence that poor families benefit significantly from their ability to leave slum projects behind. The next stages of MTO research will become critical in refining and robustly answering the question posed by and for MTO: Can families' lives be improved by simply offering them the choice to move? Further research will also enable us to more comprehensively learn whether the benefits for regular Section 8 movers are similar and positive enough when compared with the treatment group to conclude that Section 8 alone is an adequate remedy. Much is at stake in getting the answer to this question right; MTO's life as a critically relevant policy experiment is not over.

MTO is the first multisite experimental study of neighborhood effects by HUD. It is also unique in that it represents a nearly 15-year research commitment to gather experimental evidence on the effects of living in public housing projects compared with the effects of regular Section 8 assistance and of living in low-poverty communities. Over the next decade, it will be possible to better understand what effects occur, for whom, when, and through what mechanisms. If Downs (1999) is correct in his assessment that most efforts to revitalize deeply poor communities through community development have "almost universally failed," then regional housing mobility efforts, such as MTO, are a necessary accompaniment to other policy options (Katz and Turner 2001).

The cancellation of the second wave of MTO families strongly suggests caution in implementing any future MTO expansion, even if only 20,000 more families might benefit. Baltimore is certainly not alone in its fears and sense of outrage at federal program interventions into the fabric of their communities. HUD currently has only minimally persuasive evidence to respond to either Congress or local communities about what the effects would be like of moving public housing families into their communities. Up until MTO and HOPE VI—both authorized by Congress in 1993—the United States had made no attempts as a matter of formal federal policy to conduct simultaneously economic and racial mixing on any scale, as well as the concomitantly necessary research on effects. MTO evidence is still incomplete and research on the effects of HOPE VI in promoting economic and racial mixing is just at its beginning stages. We currently have little evidence about whether—and under what circumstances—additional American communities might welcome somewhat larger numbers of minority public housing families.

Part of the evidence that will be helpful in assessing future options is that none of the families that moved as part of MTO encountered racial hostility or violence; none became the subject of community meetings to evict them. Also encouraging is recent social science research by Ingrid Gould Ellen (2000), Turner et al. (2000), and Farley et al. (2000) that documents improvements over the past decades in the levels of acceptance and tolerance across racial lines. Such gradual transformations seem to bode well for careful, innovative implementation of additional efforts to promote housing mobility. But this research also reveals the persistence of negative stereotypes as a potential political constraint on options for substantial movement of racially and economically diverse populations into nontraditional neighborhoods. There is indeed little in current public discourse that would suggest a substantial change in openness if there were the prospect that thousands of public housing families would be relocated to low-poverty areas (Hochschild 1995).

Some neighborhoods and families will continue to oppose housing relocation programs to protect their communities. Others may argue that any effort to take minorities out of their traditional communities is racially perverse and politically and socially destructive (Downs 1973, 80–83; Leigh and McGhee 1986). In response we can only offer the voices and wishes of mothers and their children. Evidence from MTO families, including the evidence gathered in this collection, is that many mothers and children want and need to leave behind dangerous inner-city projects for a different, better neighborhood. Acquiescing to opposition to MTO would, in my judgment, leave in place public housing as a "federally funded, physically permanent institution for the isolation of black families by race and class" (Massey and Kanaiaupuni 1993). It would leave in place, for a large if uncertain number of families, an end of choices and opportunities. MTO is not the silver bullet for ghetto poverty but it appears to be, at this early stage in its life as a research demonstration, an invaluable aid in better understanding the risks and benefits to families of the choice to move out.

NOTES

1. On the latter Crane (1998) notes: "determining the cost-benefit relationship is easier said than done. Although the costs are usually easy enough to measure, determining the monetary value of the benefits is often difficult" (3). See also Brooks-Gunn et al. (2000).

2. This research has been initiated with a $3.2 million evaluation contract awarded by HUD to Abt Associates. An additional $5 million has been provided by the National Institute of Child Health and Human Development, the Russell Sage Foundation, the Smith Richardson Foundation, the William T. Grant Foundation, the National Science Foundation, the Spencer Foundation, the MacArthur Foundation, and the Robert Wood Johnson Foundation. The reader may find additional information on this evaluation at http://www.mtoresearch.org.

3. MTO research permits a clearer understanding of the social and behavioral consequences of living in HUD's two major forms of assisted housing, conventional public housing developments and regular Section 8 rental units. There has never been prior systematic research investigating the long-term behavioral outcomes from life in project- and tenant-based housing.

4. Edward Glaeser (2000, 127), for example, is curious about "the channels through which [these MTO] peer effects operate."

5. We disagree with Turnham and Khadduri (2002), who argue that the existing tenant-based housing program already provides sufficient neighborhood benefits and that further support for mobility counseling is not cost-effective.

6. This is based on an analysis of HUD's 1998 Picture of Subsidized Housing data, which show that approximately 520,000 units of public housing and Section 8 project-based assisted units are located in census tracts with greater than 40 percent poverty (as of 1990 Census). Of these units, approximately 40 percent are occupied by households with one or more children under the age of 18.

7. Massey and Denton (1993) make use of roughly 60 metropolitan statistical areas in their analysis. Chicago would likely not be included as it is currently engaged in large-scale demolition of public housing projects with concomitant Section 8 relocations, including a "new Gautreaux" program.

8. Pursuant to a statutory requirement to deconcentrate poverty, HUD published a Final Rule (FR-4420-F-10) on deconcentrating poverty in public housing on December 22, 2000, after months of controversy resulting from its Proposed Rule. The Final Rule requires a PHA to identify developments where the average income of residents is above 115 percent or below 85 percent of the PHA-wide average. A PHA must then include in its PHA plan either an explanation of why the income of residents in those developments varies from the PHA-wide average or a plan to deconcentrate those developments. A PHA's plan to deconcentrate identified developments may include providing incentives to families to live in certain developments, establishing preferences for working families in developments with low average incomes, and skipping applicants on the waiting list. The rule provides flexibility to PHAs, leaving the decision of how to deconcentrate up to the PHA.

9. Communities could offer a set of mixed choices in which families are fully informed of options and enabled to realize those choices. The production of new affordable units may be called for to reduce scarce supply. So, too, local jurisdictions should be able to allocate administrative fees to help ensure that their low-poverty communities are "ready" for Section 8 mobility programs.

10. Thirty years ago, Anthony Downs (1973, 141) anticipated the issue of managing neighborhood integration and strongly endorsed the use of "quantified mixture targets" or control devices.

11. Recently conducted research by the Manpower Demonstration Research Corporation on public housing families in five cities, including two MTO sites, reveals that fear of crime remained a pressing concern for roughly half the adults interviewed in 1999 (Martinez 2002).

12. Popkin and Cunningham (2000) have documented important difficulties to enabling public housing residents to make use of the regular Section 8 program in Chicago and have recommend aggressive counseling aimed at deconcentrating families.

13. Some analysts believe that it is currently politically infeasible for HUD to limit Section 8 to low-poverty neighborhoods. The inept implementation of HUD's Regional Opportunity Council program leaves uncertainty about how much difference counseling alone can make relative to the restrictions on where a voucher can be used. Perhaps policymakers could encourage everyone to consider a wider diversity of neighborhoods so that the ultimate choices are more fully informed while adding additional landlords in lower-poverty areas. A careful evaluation of the typical housing search process for Section 8 recipients may well suggest that "voluntary" choices are deeply constrained by prior imprints of racial discrimination, fear, and lack of information. Therefore, restricted-use vouchers are important in certain markets to establish new "norms" for housing search.

REFERENCES

Abu-Lughod, Janet. 1999. *New York, Chicago, Los Angeles: America's Global Cities.* Minneapolis: University of Minnesota.

Berube, Alan, and Benjamin Forman. 2002. "Living on the Edge: Decentralization within Cities in the 1990s." *Center on Urban and Metropolitan Policy* (October). Washington, D.C.: The Brookings Institution.

Blumstein, Alfred. 2000. "Disaggregating the Violence Trends." In *The Crime Drop in America,* edited by Alfred Blumstein and Joel Wallman (13–44). New York: Cambridge University Press.

Bonastia, Chris. 2000. "Why Did Affirmative Action in Housing Fail during the Nixon Administration?" *Social Problems* 47(4): 523–42.

Brooks-Gunn, Jeanne, Lisa Berlin, Tama Leventhal, and Allison Fuligni. 2000. "Depending on the Kindness of Strangers: Current National Data Initiatives and Development Research." *Child Development* 71 (January/February): 257–68.

Crane, Jonathan. 1991. "The Epidemic Theory of Ghettos and Neighborhood Effects on Dropping Out and Teenage Childbearing." *American Journal of Sociology* 5 (March): 1226–59.

———. 1998. "Building on Success." In *Social Programs That Work,* edited by Jonathan Crane (1–42). New York: Russell Sage Foundation.

Downs, Anthony. 1973. *Opening up the Suburbs: An Urban Strategy for America.* New Haven: Yale University Press.

———. 1994. *New Visions for Metropolitan America.* Washington, D.C.: Brookings Institution.

———. 1999. "Some Realities about Sprawl and Urban Decline." *Housing Policy Debate* 10(4): 955–74.

Edin, Kathryn, and Laura Lein. 1997. *Making Ends Meet: How Single Mothers Survive Welfare and Low-Wage Work.* New York: Russell Sage Foundation.

Ellen, Ingrid Gould. 2000. *Sharing America's Neighborhoods: The Prospects for Stable Racial Integration.* Cambridge, Mass.: Harvard University Press.

Farley, Reynolds, Sheldon Danziger, and Harry J. Holzer. 2000. *Detroit Divided.* New York: Russell Sage Foundation.

Feins, Judith D., Debra McInnis, and Susan J. Popkin. 1997. *Counseling in the Moving to Opportunity for Fair Housing Demonstration Program.* Cambridge, Mass.: Abt Associates Inc.

Finkel, Meryl, and Larry Buron. 2001. "Study on Section 8 Voucher Success Rates: Quantitative Study of Success Rates in Metropolitan Areas. (November). Final Report." Washington, D.C.: U.S. Department of Housing and Urban Development, Office of Policy Development and Research.

Fountain, John. 2001. "Violence Is Down, but Some Areas Still Suffer." *The New York Times,* January 11.

Furstenberg, Frank, and Mary Elizabeth Hughes. 1997. "The Influence of Neighborhood on Children's Development: A Theoretical Perspective and a Research Agenda." In *Neighborhood Poverty. Volume 2: Policy Implications in Studying Neighborhoods,* edited by Jeanne Brooks-Gunn, Greg J. Duncan, and J. Lawrence Aber (23–47). New York: Russell Sage Foundation.

Gephart, Martha. 1997. "Neighborhoods and Communities as Contexts for Development." In *Neighborhood Poverty. Volume 1: Contexts and Consequences for Children,* edited by Jeanne Brooks-Gunn, Greg J. Duncan, and J. Lawrence Aber (1–43). New York: Russell Sage Foundation.

Gettleman, Jeffrey. 2002. "Ashes and Tears in Lost Battle of Drug War." *The New York Times,* October 18, A1, A28.

Glaeser, Edward. 2000. "The Future of Urban Research: Nonmarket Interactions." In *Brookings-Wharton Papers on Urban Affairs 2000,* edited by William Gale and Janet Rothenbeg Pack (101–49). Washington, D.C.: Brookings Institution.

Guhathakurta, Subhrajit, and Alvin Mushkatel. 2002. "Race, Ethnicity, and Household Characteristics of Section 8 Clients and Their Impact on Adjacent Housing Quality." *Urban Affairs Review* 37 (March): 521–42.

Haveman, Robert. 1994. "The Nature, Causes, and Cures of Poverty: Accomplishments from Three Decades of Poverty Research and Policy." In *Confronting Poverty: Prescriptions for Change,* edited by Sheldon Danziger, Gary Sandefur, and Daniel Weinberg (438–48). New York: Russell Sage Foundation.

Hays, R. Allen. 1995. *The Federal Government and Urban Housing.* Albany: State University of New York.

Heclo, Hugh. 1994. "Poverty Politics." In *Confronting Poverty: Prescriptions for Change,* edited by Sheldon Danziger, Gary Sandefur, and Daniel Weinberg (396–437). New York: Russell Sage Foundation.

Hirsch, Arnold R. 1983. *Making the Second Ghetto: Race and Housing in Chicago, 1940–1960.* New York: Cambridge University Press.

Hochschild, Jennifer L. 1995. *Facing Up to the American Dream: Race, Class, and the Soul of the Nation.* Princeton, N.J.: Princeton University Press.

Husock, Howard. 2000. "Let's End Housing Vouchers." *City Journal* 10(4): 84–91.

Johnson, Michael, Helen Ladd, and Jens Ludwig. 2002. "The Benefits and Costs of Residential-Mobility Programs for the Poor." *Housing Studies* 17(1): 125–38.

Kamber, Thomas. 2000. "Local Politics and Housing Vouchers." Unpublished Ph.D. Dissertation, Department of Political Science. Graduate Center of the City University of New York, December.

Katz, Bruce. 2002. "Housing in the Context of Community." Remarks at the annual Fannie Mae Housing Conference, *Raising the Nation's Housing Agenda,* Washington, D.C., Oct. 9.

Katz, Bruce, and Margery Turner. 2001. "Who Should Run the Housing Voucher Program? A Reform Proposal." *Housing Policy Debate* 12(2): 239–62.

Leigh, Wilhelmina, and James McGhee. 1986. "A Minority Perspective on Residential Racial Integration." In *Housing Desegregation and Federal Policy,* edited by John M. Goering (31–42). Chapel Hill: University of North Carolina Press.

Martinez, John. 2002. "The Employment Experiences of Public Housing Residents: Findings from the Jobs-Plus Baseline Survey." New York: Manpower Demonstration Research Corporation.

Massey, Douglas S., and Nancy A. Denton. 1993. *American Apartheid: Segregation and the Making of the Urban Underclass.* Cambridge, Mass.: Harvard University Press.

Massey, Douglas, and Shaun Kanaiaupuni. 1993. "Public Housing, the Concentration of Poverty, and the Life Chances of Individuals." *Social Science Research* 20: 397–420.

Millennial Housing Commission. 2002. *Meeting Our Nation's Housing Challenges.* Washington, D.C.: U.S. Government Printing Office.

O'Regan, Katherine, and John Quigley. 1999. "Accessibility and Economic Opportunity." In *Essays in Transportation Economics and Policy,* edited by José A. Gómez-Ibáñez, William B. Tye, and Clifford Winston (437–66). Washington, D.C.: Brookings Institution Press.

Popkin, Susan J., and Mary K. Cunningham. 2000. "Searching for Rental Housing with Section 8 in the Chicago Region." February. Washington, D.C.: The Urban Institute.

Popkin, Susan, Laura Harris, and Mary Cunningham. 2001. "Families in Transition: A Qualitative Analysis of the MTO Experience." Final report submitted to the Office of Policy Development and Research, HUD. Washington, D.C.: The Urban Institute.

Quigley, John. 2000. "A Decent Home: Housing Policy in Perspective." In *Brookings-Wharton Papers on Urban Affairs 2000,* edited by William Gale and Janet Rothenbeg Pack (53–88). Washington, D.C.: Brookings Institution Press.

Rieder, Jonathan. 1985. *Canarsie: The Jews and Italians of Brooklyn against Liberalism.* Cambridge, Mass.: Harvard University Press.

Rubinowitz, Leonard S., and James E. Rosenbaum. 2000. *Crossing the Class and Color Lines: From Public Housing to White Suburbia.* Chicago: University of Chicago Press.

Sampson, Robert. 2000. "The Neighborhood Context of Investing in Children: Facilitating Mechanisms and Undermining Risks." In *Securing the Future: Investing in Children from Birth to College,* edited by Sheldon Danziger and Jane Waldfogel (205–27). New York: Russell Sage Foundation.

Sampson, Robert, Jeffrey Morenoff, and Thomas Gannon-Rowley. Forthcoming. "Assessing Neighborhood Effects: Social Processes and New Directions in Research." *Annual Review of Sociology* 28.

Scott, Ellen, Kathryn Edin, Andrew London, and Rebecca Kissane. 2002. "Welfare Recipients Struggle to Balance Work and Family." *Poverty Research News* 6(4): 12–15.

Stegman, Michael. 2000. "Comments." In *Brookings-Wharton Papers on Urban Affairs 2000,* edited by William Gale and Janet Rothenbeg Pack (89–93). Washington, D.C.: Brookings Institution Press.

Tegler, Philip, Michael Hanley, and Judith Liben. 1995. "Transforming Section 8: Using Federal Housing Subsidies to Promote Individual Choice and Desegregation." *Harvard Civil Rights-Civil Liberties Law Review* 30 (summer): 451–86.

Thompson, Phillip. 1999. "Public Housing in New York City." In *Housing and Community Development in New York City: Facing the Future,* edited by Michael H. Schill (119–42). Albany: State University of New York Press.

Turner, Margery Austin, Susan Popkin, and Mary Cunningham. 2000. *Section 8 Mobility and Neighborhood Health: Emerging Issues and Policy Challenges.* Washington, D.C.: The Urban Institute.

Turnham, Jennifer, and Jill Khadduri. 2002. "Synopsis of Issues and Options for HUD's Tenant-based Housing Assistance Programs." Paper presented at the annual Fannie Mae Housing Conference, *Raising the Nation's Housing Agenda,* Washington, D.C., Oct. 9.

Waldinger, Roger. 1996. *Still the Promised City? African-Americans and New Immigrants in Postindustrial New York.* Cambridge, Mass.: Harvard University Press.

About the Editors

John Goering is a professor at the School of Public Affairs at Baruch College and a member of the doctoral faculty in political science at the Graduate Center of the City University of New York. Before joining CUNY, he helped design and implement MTO as well as prepare the evaluation framework for the demonstration while in the Office of Research at HUD.

Judith D. Feins, a principal associate at Abt Associates, directed the implementation of the MTO demonstration under contract to HUD and is currently directing the interim evaluation of MTO. She conducts research on public housing and housing mobility.

About the Contributors

Jeanne Brooks-Gunn is Virginia and Leonard Marx Professor of Child Development and Education at Teachers College, Columbia University. She is also director of the National Center for Children and Families at Teachers College and codirector of the Institute for Child and Family Policy at Columbia University.

Nancy A. Denton is an associate professor of sociology and director of graduate studies at SUNY Albany, where she is also a research associate at the Center for Social and Demographic Analysis.

Greg J. Duncan is professor of education and social policy and a faculty associate in the Institute for Policy Research at Northwestern University. He is director of the Northwestern University/University of Chicago Joint Center for Poverty Research.

Ingrid Gould Ellen is an assistant professor of public policy and urban planning at the Robert F. Wagner Graduate School of Public Service at New York University.

George Galster is the Clarence Hilberry Professor of Urban Affairs at Wayne State University. Before joining Wayne State, he served as director of housing research at the Urban Institute.

Maria Hanratty is an associate professor of economics and public affairs at the University of Minnesota Hubert Humphrey Institute of Public Affairs. She also served as senior economist at the White House Council of Economic Advisers.

Joseph Harkness is the research statistician for the Housing Research Group of the Institute for Policy Studies of the Johns Hopkins University. His recent work focuses on housing and social welfare policy.

Laura Harris is a research associate in the Metropolitan Housing and Communities Policy Center at the Urban Institute in Washington, D.C.

Lawrence F. Katz is a professor of economics at Harvard University, a research associate of NBER, and editor of the *Quarterly Journal of Economics*. He previously served as chief economist of the U.S. Department of Labor.

Jeffrey R. Kling is assistant professor of economics and public affairs in the Woodrow Wilson School of Public and International Affairs at Princeton University and an NBER faculty research fellow. He previously served as assistant to the chief economist at the World Bank and special assistant to the secretary at the U.S. Department of Labor.

Helen F. Ladd, professor of public policy studies and economics in the Sanford Institute of Duke University, also directs the graduate program in public policy. She is the author or editor of several recent books on educational accountability, school finance, and school choice.

Tama Leventhal is a research scientist at the National Center for Children and Families at Teachers College, Columbia University.

Jeffrey B. Liebman is associate professor of public policy at Harvard's Kennedy School of Government and an NBER faculty research fellow. He recently served in the White House as special assistant to the president for economic policy.

Jens Ludwig is associate professor of public policy at Georgetown University and a member of the National Consortium on Violence Research. He has also been a visiting scholar at the Northwestern University/ University of Chicago Joint Center for Poverty Research and the Brookings Institution.

Sara McLanahan is a professor of sociology and public affairs at Princeton University. She directs the Bendheim-Thoman Center for Research on Child Wellbeing and is an associate of the Office of Population Research.

Sandra Newman is professor of policy studies at Johns Hopkins University and director of the Institute for Policy Studies. She holds joint appointments with the departments of Sociology, Geography, and Environmental Engineering, and Health Policy and Management.

Becky Pettit is an assistant professor of sociology at the University of Washington and an affiliate of the Center for Studies in Demography and Ecology and the Center for Statistics in the Social Sciences. Her research includes studying the effects of residential mobility during childhood and poverty and inequality.

Todd M. Richardson, a social science analyst at HUD, is currently the government manager for the Moving to Opportunity Interim Evaluation.

Emily Rosenbaum is an associate professor of sociology and demography at Fordham University in New York and a research fellow at NYU's Furman Center for Real Estate and Urban Policy.

Mark Shroder, an economist with HUD's Office of Policy Development and Research, has been involved with MTO since its inception.

Margery Austin Turner directs the Center on Metropolitan Housing and Communities at the Urban Institute. From 1993 through 1996 she served as deputy assistant secretary for research at HUD.

Wei-Jun J. Yeung is a research scientist at the Center for Advanced Social Research and associate professor of sociology at New York University (NYU). Before joining NYU, she was at the University of Michigan's Institute for Social Research as a co-principal investigator of the Panel Study of Income Dynamics.

Index